# THE LAST PLANTAGENETS

# BOOKS BY THOMAS B. COSTAIN

THE LAST PLANTAGENETS:
*The Pageant of England*

THE CHORD OF STEEL

THE DARKNESS AND THE DAWN

THE THREE EDWARDS:
*The Pageant of England*

BELOW THE SALT

STORIES TO REMEMBER
*(with John Beecroft)*

MORE STORIES TO REMEMBER
*(with John Beecroft)*

THE TONTINE

THE MISSISSIPPI BUBBLE

THE WHITE AND THE GOLD:
*The French Regime in Canada*

THE SILVER CHALICE

THE MAGNIFICENT CENTURY:
*The Pageant of England*

SON OF A HUNDRED KINGS

THE CONQUERORS:
*The Pageant of England*

HIGH TOWERS

THE MONEYMAN

THE BLACK ROSE

RIDE WITH ME

JOSHUA: A BIOGRAPHY
*(with Rogers MacVeagh)*

FOR MY GREAT FOLLY

THE PAGEANT OF ENGLAND

# THE LAST
# PLANTAGENETS

## THOMAS B. COSTAIN

DOUBLEDAY & COMPANY, INC.
GARDEN CITY, NEW YORK
1962

LIBRARY OF CONGRESS CATALOG CARD NUMBER 62–7616
COPYRIGHT © 1962 BY THOMAS B. COSTAIN
ALL RIGHTS RESERVED
PRINTED IN THE UNITED STATES OF AMERICA

W

# CONTENTS

## PART TWO: THE RED AND THE WHITE

PART ONE

# THE KING WHO LOST A SHOE

CHAPTER I

## A Prince Is Born

1

A PRINCE was born to the royal line of England on January 6, 1367, in the abbey of St. André at Bordeaux and given the name of Richard. His mother, who had been a widow when she dazzled and cajoled the seemingly impervious bachelor, Edward the Black Prince, into marrying her, had no doubts at all that the boy was the most beautiful baby ever born in a royal bed and then laid to sleep in an ermine-lined cradle. Somewhat limp and exhausted after the ordeal of motherhood, for she was thirty-nine years old, she gazed through her window at the highest spire in all France, that of St. Michel, and the thought may have been in her mind that she herself had climbed to an equal height. She had done her duty and now none of the sly councilors of the old king nor the sour dowagers of the court at Westminster could have anything more to say. She would soon be the Queen of England and, after that, she would see a son of hers on the throne.

It should be told that, after her marriage to Prince Edward in the face of parental disapproval, the vivacious Joan (who is called in history the Fair Maid of Kent) and her somewhat taciturn husband had been glad to get away from the frowns and fogs of London to settle down to the government of the Aquitanian possessions in this beautiful city where the sun shone all the year round, or nearly all, and the plane trees sighed in the cool breezes from the sea, and life was very romantic and very gay. Three years earlier a son had been born to them and named Edward, who was the apple of his great father's eye. Now, with the arrival of little Richard, who was to become known as Richard of Bordeaux, the succession was assured.

The father of the new arrival shared this satisfaction, but it was not his custom to unbend and so he had little to say as he towered above the cradle. Lying very still, his face neither wrinkled nor mottled in the way of newly borns but pale and handsomely composed, Richard gave the impression of being delicate enough to be wafted away by any careless whisk of a midwife's arm. His father may have been disappointed in one respect, for what he most admired in male children was the promise of massive thews like his own or the strong frame of his great-uncle Richard (four times removed), who had been called the Lion-hearted. Would this undeniably beautiful boy prove to be of stout heart? Would he have a firm seat in the saddle to ride the shocks of conflict? Such thoughts must have been in the father's mind, for he began at once to make plans for a Spartan upbringing. Richard's lullabies must be the ballads of chivalry, his toys must be swords and bows, his tutors must not be learned priests but the stoutest of warriors.

The court at Bordeaux was acknowledged to be the most brilliant in Europe and, at the moment when the second son arrived, it was crowded with visitors. King James of Majorca had arrived to act as chief sponsor, and Pedro of Castile was there with Constance and Isabella, the two daughters born to him by a mistress. Pedro, who was called "The Cruel," had been removed from the throne by his angry subjects, led by an illegitimate brother, Henry of Trastamara. The purpose of Pedro's visit to Bordeaux was to solicit the aid of the great English warrior in winning back his crown, and the Black Prince had decided to take the adventure in hand, although he was in poor health and seemingly incapable of conducting a vigorous campaign. Edward's reasons for taking this rash step, which would plunge him deep into debt, were typical of this grandly aloof and determined prince. He would fight for a brother knight or undertake the rescue of a degenerate king like Pedro even if it cost the lives of thousands of common men and hopelessly entangled his affairs at home. For the benefit of his councilors, all of whom seemed opposed to the step, he had written: "I do not think it either decent or proper that a bastard should possess a kingdom as an inheritance, nor drive out of his realm his own brother, heir to the throne by lawful marriage; and no king or king's son ought ever to suffer it as being of the greatest prejudice to royalty." He had other reasons, but this was enough to indicate how his mind worked. His plans for the organization of an army to march down through the Valley of Roncesvalles into Spain were already complete and he, Edward, planned to leave for Dax in a matter of days.

The arrival of little Richard of Bordeaux was, therefore, badly timed. Back of the stern façade with which he faced the world, the Black Prince was concerned with problems of equipment and provisions and not with this frail son that his plump, middle-aged wife had added to his other and greater responsibilities. The event, nevertheless, was to create a considerable stir. A hum of excited talk started the instant the prince stalked into his wife's chamber, accompanied by his two royal visitors. It was true that James of Majorca was a mere cantlet of a king (he also had been shoved off his miniature throne and was seeking aid) and Pedro the Cruel was a fugitive from his Spanish dominions. Neither visitor was a wise man and that adjective was not one to be applied loosely to the Black Prince. But there were gifts in the hands of all three; and was it not Twelfth Night? By'r Lady, here was the scene at Bethlehem repeated! Everyone at court, and later throughout the civilized world, knew this meant that the child would become a man of greatness and power and that his deeds would resound throughout Christendom.

The prince acted promptly because he had not more than a few hours left before he started on his costly and injudicious Spanish adventure. He announced that two of his favorite campaign companions, Sir Guichard d'Angle and Sir Simon Burley, would share the tutoring of the little prince as soon as the promises to the ex-King of Castile had been fulfilled. They were both held in high esteem by all men, but the appointment was destined to provide the link in a chain of events that would involve the little prince in disastrous conflicts in the years to follow.

*2*

A ray of light can sometimes be turned on blank periods in history through events which follow after. Little is actually known of the early boyhood of Richard of Bordeaux, but certain conclusions may reasonably be drawn from subsequent developments. During the four years at Bordeaux he was in his mother's care and the bond of affection between them was maintained until the last sad days that the Fair Maid of Kent spent on earth. This needs no documentary proof, for all the men were off to the wars, the Black Prince himself, such of his brothers as were in France, and all of his knights and attendants, including the gallant and gentle Sir John Chandos, who always rode beside him, and the two favored companions already appointed as the boy's tutors. From his brief contacts with his father later, and the things he learned about that unbending parent, Richard absorbed ideas which were prevalent enough in all branches of royalty but were not likely to form a good character foundation for a future king. From the atmosphere of the court he also developed other tastes which, though admirable in themselves, were not likely to fit him for the task of handling the proud but unlettered baronage of England.

Bordeaux was, of course, completely under Gallic influences. Although France was impoverished and exhausted by the English wars and the depredations of the Free Companies, Paris was still a center of the culture born in the Magnificent Century, the thirteenth, and which had been growing and spreading ever since. Richard was a perceptive child and even in his most tender years he acquired a taste for the artistic aspects of life.

When the bones of Richard II were disinterred and examined in 1871, it was found that he had been almost six feet in height. It was apparent from the first, however, that he would not be of powerful build. His limbs, slender and gracefully turned, lacked the knotted muscles of the warrior. His face was round and his features were delicately modeled, making him appear slightly effeminate. At first he was of a gentle disposition.

In the household at Bordeaux were his brother, Edward, three years his senior, and two sons of his mother by her first marriage. Thomas Holland was fifteen and John twelve. Little is known about Edward, who died four years later, but the Holland sons were typical of the age—noisy, swift in temper, addicted to horseplay, and rough in games. Little Richard, who liked music and took pleasure in paintings and the songs of minstrels, was out of his element in this group. His mother looked after her quiet son with true maternal solicitude, protecting him from the wild antics and practical jokes of her earlier brood.

The young prince's spirits were high and from the first he demonstrated that he possessed a full share of the passionate pride of the Plantagenets. His few contacts with his father strengthened in him the feeling that life was shaped to the glory of kings and that the prerogatives of royalty must be free of the meddling of vulgar fingers. The Black Prince returned after winning the Battle of Navarrete, which placed the base Pedro back on his throne for a brief period. It had been a disillusioning experience, for Pedro had dishonored all his promises, and the army, made up of stout Englishmen and loyal Gascons, had been decimated in the fighting and by the spread of unfamiliar diseases. A sick man when he started off, the prince knew beyond all doubt when he returned that the fateful wings had brushed his shoulder. Two years later little Edward died, and this meant that the bright white light had shifted its focus and was beaming now on the little prince with the long golden curls and the thoughtful manners. The boy Richard would be the next King of England.

Richard seems to have had a liking for Sir Simon Burley from the very beginning. When he returned from Spain, his face tanned to a walnut hue from exposure to the Castilian sun, Burley took his small charge in hand for a very brief period. He talked to him about horses and the handling of a sword, and he told him tales which brought an excited glow to the boy's cheeks. Unfortunately for Richard, the French war was resumed almost immediately and Burley was plunged into the thick of it. The small boy saw him leave with a lump in his throat. The absence of the bachelor knight (for Burley never seems to have had the time or the inclination for matrimony) was to prove a long one. Leading a small force in the Lusignan country, he was attacked by superior French forces and made prisoner. He was held in captivity for a year and on his release found that the Black Prince, who was now barely capable of sitting in a saddle, was setting about the siege of Limoges, a military venture destined to leave a stain on the princely reputation for all time. And, of course, Burley rode in his royal master's train.

It was apparent to all that the days of the great warrior were numbered. His eyes were sunk deep between protruding cheek bones, his fine color had deserted him for the tallowy hue of illness, he frequently stumbled as he walked. His physicians advised that he give up all responsibilities and return home at once. Accordingly he prepared reluctantly to leave the softer airs of Bordeaux for what he remembered as the rigors of England. He turned over all his offices to his brother John, now called Lancaster but best known in history as John of Gaunt. This he did in a saddened mood for he knew that now the tide would turn more swiftly in favor of the French. Although a man of parts, and with his share of military capacity, Lancaster had never acquired somehow the habit of success. Edward III had it and so had the Black Prince. Luck had combined with boldness to win battles for them. But Lancaster, an able enough planner and a knight of courage, had acquired nothing but the habit of failure.

Biscay waters in the winter are boisterous and unsafe and so it is certain that the royal party which set out in January 1371 embarked in the largest cogs available. The cog was a type of vessel much used in England because of its stoutness of construction. It was round of prow and stern, which made for a measure of security but accelerated the tendency to pitch and toss when winds were high; safe, but not to be recommended for those of weak stomach. The health of Edward did not improve under these conditions and it may also be taken for granted that his lady wife seldom deserted the comparative comfort of her accommodations below for the flooded decks and the bitter winds whistling through the rigging. Little Richard may not have been a good sailor either, but when he found his sea legs, as any boy will in time, he spent his days almost exclusively in the company of stout Sir Simon.

Burley was a sailor as well as a soldier. He had played his part in the naval battle of Sluys which had started Edward III's string of victories. He walked the decks, even when awash as they almost invariably were, with a rolling gait and a solid planting of heels. When the boy prince ventured up to join him, they splashed along together through the water which rolled from scupper to scupper, little Richard grappling the knight's hand with a desperate tightness. Burley was able, therefore, to begin the tuition of his future king, which he did no doubt by telling what they would find when they reached England.

The knight would unquestionably consider it necessary to inform the boy that he would find his grandfather no longer the brilliant monarch who had dazzled Europe, but an old and ailing man, surrounded by the wrong kind of state officers. No mention of names would be wise but a wink and a sly allusion might plant the supposition that certain royal uncles were not above suspicion. Burley would explain also that English man power had been cut in half by the Black Death and he would hint darkly that the survivors were being misled by base hedge priests into demanding what they called their *rights*, an absurdity in men who had no rights, and one which must be crushed under iron heels. Nor must the prince expect to find in England the courtly airs and bodily comfort of Bordeaux. The English did not even dress the same but were for the most part attired sadly in plain cloth. This might elicit a question, for the boy was much interested in questions of dress. Did they not wear the fine new houppelandes? No, just the old-fashioned tunics and somber cloaks. Never seen were parti-colored hose or doublets and never puffed sleeves. But shoes, surely, with high curling toes? The little prince had none but shoes of the latest style and the toes invariably curled up so high that it was necessary to attach them with silken cords to the calves of his legs. Even at this early age, Richard had some knowledge of such matters, and he must have sighed at the prospect of dressing in such dull ways.

When it became evident that he was giving the prince too poor a picture of the land which would now be his home, the knight would hasten to explain that England was, after all, a country of the stoutest soldiers and the most daring sailors, and that the land was bountiful beyond belief. Enough wool was raised on the backs of fat sheep to supply cloth to most of Europe. No, there was nothing wrong with England that a better knowledge of foreign ways would not correct.

Certainly the boy heard from his mentor about the order of which his father spoke with such loftiness, chivalry. It was not an order in the sense that it had definite form, with a code written down fair in black and white and with acknowledged leaders. Rather it was a state of mind, a passionate belief which had grown out of crusading faith. All men whose station in life permitted could enter of their own free will into this lofty realm of knightly ideals and high emprise and remain as long as they broke none of the unwritten laws. If the point came up in their many talks as to what part common men played in this world of the spirit, Sir Simon brushed it aside. Chivalry was the creed of the *status quo*. Knights swore fealty to their liege lords and were ready to render up their lives for fellow knights; but the existence of men who tilled the soil or worked at benches was of no concern whatever.

The ships carrying the royal entourage dropped anchor at Southampton in mid-January. The Black Prince was to be carried ashore on a litter, and an escort of soldiers stood at attention on the wharf, their noses red and their breath freezing. It was by the side of his knightly companion, therefore, that Richard stood when he had his first glimpse of the land over which he would some day rule, a day which was not far distant. There was a mournful note in the piping of the gulls. The royal banners hung limp, as snow fell straight down from leaden skies. Being so very young, he was tempted, perhaps, to shed a tear for sunny Bordeaux and to look with dread on this inhospitable and lowering land.

CHAPTER II

## The Struggle over the Succession

1

THE Black Death had been followed by black years of failure in England. The once brilliant Edward III was an old man; his sharp mind had dulled, his eyes were rheumy, his long nose was bulbous and purple-veined, his step slow. If he was aware of the thievish tactics of his closest officials, he made no effort to repress them. Lancaster controlled Parliament and seemed to be preparing himself to step into his father's shoes. The French wars had dwindled to a desperate English effort to maintain the entry ports of Calais, Brest, and Bordeaux and to hold back French invaders along their own coast. Royal extravagance had finally brought the country close to bankruptcy.

Perhaps it was the need for a firmer hand that roused the Black Prince to efforts of which he had previously seemed incapable. He accompanied the king in August of the year after his return on an expedition against the French. This proved an abortive move and the armies did not make a landing. It is chiefly of interest because young Prince Richard was appointed regent of the realm in the absence of his father and grandfather. He was not quite six years old.

In 1374 Prince Edward found it necessary to preside at a meeting of the bishops and barons at Westminster to discuss a demand received from Pope Gregory XI for a large subsidy. Gregory had one distinction, that he had left Avignon and returned to Rome, thus ending what had been called the Babylonish Captivity. However, he had found such disorder in Italy that he sought aid to the extent of 800,000 florins in combating the aggressions of Florence. As England was held, more or less theoretically, to be still under papal control by reason of King John's surrender nearly two centuries before, it was made clear in the Pope's letter that the country was expected to pay a large share of this amount.

This had been a fighting issue through all the reigns which followed that of John, but the bishops, meeting first on May 20, 1374, to consider the demand, decided that the Pope was within his rights. This supine attitude may have been due in part to the illness of Archbishop Whittlesey who ordinarily would have directed the decision into safer lines. His wasted form almost swallowed in the elaborate canonicals of his office, the archbishop hesitated so long to declare himself that the temper of the king's son flared into an expostulation.

"My lord bishop," he exclaimed, "you are an ass!"

Whether this had any effect on the decision, the bishops finally reversed themselves and the Pope had to go without his subsidy.

Perhaps the prince regretted his irascibility when it was learned that the archbishop, who once had been tall, impressive, and quite eloquent, had retired to his favorite manor of Otford in the chalk hills near Canterbury in a weakened condition. The primate proved to be mortally ill. After making his will on June 5, leaving most of his estate to his poor relatives, he breathed his last the following day.

Prince Edward, his manners and wits sharpened by the continuous pains and aggravations of his disease, must have felt as unfavorably disposed to the successor selected for the see of Canterbury, but for a different reason. Simon of Sudbury, Bishop of London, was chosen, with the casual approval of the king and the full sanction of the Pope. Sudbury was most unpopular in London for a number of reasons. He had spent many years in the papal service at Avignon and was regarded as French in his views and sympathies; and the people had a fanatical hatred of the French. He was skilled in law, and all the people hated lawyers. He was blunt of speech and did not care whose toes he trampled upon. Finally, he stood shoulder to shoulder with John of Gaunt, and nothing could induce the Londoners to forgive him for that.

A story may be told of his bluntness of speech. In the year preceding the return of the Black Prince occurred the fourth jubilee of St. Thomas the Martyr, and the roads to Canterbury were thronged with pilgrims. It happened that the outspoken Sudbury, riding with his train, encountered a long procession of the seekers after grace, who set up a clamor for his blessing. Now it happened that the bishop did not believe entirely in the honesty of this fervor which induced so many people to drop everything and plod their way to Canterbury with their penitential staffs. He proceeded to tell them of his doubts.

Most of them, he declared, were going to the shrine of the Martyr because they expected to receive absolution of their sins. He was sure also, and said so in no uncertain terms, that they would backslide and take up again their sinful ways as soon as they returned to their homes.

"How much better would it have been," he declared, "had you remained at home and won the indulgence ye crave by renouncing your sins and living decent lives!"

The pilgrims, needless to state, were deeply offended. A soldier in the party, one Thomas of Andover, stepped out of the line and shook his fist at the blunt prelate.

"Why, Lord Bishop," he demanded to know, "do you dare speak thus against St. Thomas? At peril of my life, I declare thou shalt end thy days in violence and ignominy!"

Thomas of Andover might claim on the strength of this the right to be considered a prophet, for Simon of Sudbury was destined to die at the hands of common men who remembered all the reasons they had for disliking him, not excluding this instance of his unorthodox thinking.

2

At no stage in his career did Edward the Black Prince show to such advantage as in the few years allowed him to live after his return to England. He had won such popularity by leading English armies in the French wars that nothing he did, not even his brutal disregard for the lives of common people, was allowed to detract from the love his countrymen had for him. As administrator of the Aquitanian possessions he had been indifferent and slipshod and always wildly extravagant; but all this was easily forgiven him and soon forgotten. But it was a different man who came back to an England in the slough of defeat and want, to find his once great father verging on senility and the supporters of his brother Lancaster controlling Parliament and the administrative offices.

His decisions from that moment to the day of his death were unerringly right. He strove from his sickbed to direct affairs into the right channels. His judgment of men was as sound as his insight into issues. The Black Prince in eclipse was greater than the victorious leader charging down the vine-clad slopes at Poictiers.

The physicians could not put a name to the disease which had gripped him. From the length of time it took him to die (he lived six years after his return) and the violence of the pains from which he suffered, it seems practically certain that it was cancer. Medical practitioners had little knowledge of that disease, calling it *canker*, and were quite helpless in fighting it. The prince, subjected to all manner of absurd dosages and the undignified methods which ignorance conceived, grew slowly but steadily worse. Through it all his spirit remained high, and his intelligence was sharpened, perhaps, by withdrawal from too close contact with the course of events to a point where he saw all things in the clear white light of understanding. He appreciated to the full the possibility that a boy of Richard's tender years might be shoved aside in the matter of the succession.

On the day before his death he took the only step remaining to him. He asked his father and his brother Lancaster to come to him at Kennington. They arrived together and he had Richard and the princess Joan summoned to the room.

"I recommend to you my wife and son," he said. "I love them greatly. Give them your aid."

When a Bible was produced, the doddering king and the ambitious Lancaster swore upon it to maintain the rights of the boy.

After Edward III had bade his son a final farewell and had left the room, certain members of the nobility were admitted. They all swore to support Richard in his rights. At the finish, the dying man indulged in what perhaps was his last smile. He looked about him and said to the assembled barons, "I give you a hundred thanks."

### 3

The people of England have always taken the liveliest interest in the House of Commons, which is natural enough because they were largely responsible for this form of government. The name seems to be of Italian origin and is found in English records in 1246 for the first time, although it had been in usage long before. No phase of English history is more interesting than the parliamentary records, particularly about the men who were summoned to attend or who came in by the elective method; the great men and the villains, the courageous leaders and the toadies, the farsighted and the backward-lookers, the liberals and the conservatives. A national habit of finding names for certain Parliaments began in the earliest days and has provided a method of appraisal. Generally, of course, the labels applied have had a decidedly partisan bias.

There was, for instance, the Mad Parliament in 1258, so called because of the historic quarrel between Henry III and Simon de Montfort. The Weathercock King called his brother-in-law, Montfort, a traitor and the latter retaliated by declaring that, if Henry were not a king, he would make him eat his words: a warm passage certainly between a ruler and a subject.

Then there was the Unlearned in 1404, which gained its name because there was not a single lawyer among the members. The lawyers of the day were responsible, needless to state, for the label.

Among others were the Parliament of Bats, the Merciless, the Diabolical, the Meddlesome, the Addled (which met in 1614 and was dismissed without having passed any kind of measure at all), the Rump, the Barebones (named after a Puritan member, Praise-God Barebones), and the Drunken. The last named was held in Scotland, the first to be summoned after the Stuart Restoration. There had been much drinking of toasts the evening before and the claret bottles had been passed around and around. When the House opened, the Speaker was incapable of remaining seated in his chair and an adjournment was necessary.

It happened that before the Black Prince died the fiftieth Parliament was summoned. The name Good has been applied to it, and with the best of reasons. It convened in 1376 and found itself saddled with the task of cleaning up the administrative mess which the old king had allowed to develop at Westminster and, fully as important, the settlement of the succession. The members selected Peter de la Mare as Speaker, the first time a commoner had acted in that capacity. He was a man of great courage and ability and he made such a vigorous attack on the group about the king that he was asked to lead the discussion when the two branches of Parliament met together. The result was that two members of the nobility were dismissed from office and sent to prison. They cleaned out as well the rascals of lower degree, mostly London merchants who had been active members of the clique. Then an unprecedented step was taken. The old king's mistress, Alice Perrers, was sent packing and informed that if she showed her handsome nose in court again she would be stripped of all her property. The king, who had been in some respects the most haughty of the Plantagenets, accepted this rebuff without a word of protest.

The sentiment of the Good Parliament was strongly anti-Lancaster. Duke John sensed that, for the time at least, he must bend to the wind. He even visited the House and agreed that the Augean stables at Westminster needed cleaning out.

Parliament took a decided stand in the matter of the succession, declaring that Richard should be considered the rightful heir and requesting that the boy appear before them. Lancaster moved unobtrusively about the fringes of the House and spoke cautiously to this member and that, but made no move to block the will of the majority. He strove, nonetheless, to have a measure passed similar to the French Salic Law which excluded women from ruling. His purpose was to bar the possibility of the crown passing to the daughter of his deceased brother Lionel who had come into the world ahead of him. The daughter, who had been named for her grandmother Philippa, and was married to the Earl of March, was next in line of succession after Richard. The members listened, but gave him no measure of support. Let the French have their

Salic Law; the people of England preferred their own way of doing things.

If Duke John had had his way, the history of the country would have been vastly different.

It was on January 25 that Richard made his appearance before the House. Few of the members had ever seen him and there was a stir in the vaulted chamber and a turning of heads when the ten-year-old youth arrived. His mother had been sensible enough to see that he was attired as plainly as the men he would face. His slender limbs were in hose of one color and his shoes lacked the high curl of the French fashion. He was, without a doubt, the handsomest boy they had ever seen and the gift he had for rising to an occasion, which was to be demonstrated at several crucial moments in his life, stood him in good stead. Seating himself in the elaborate chair which had been placed for his use, he faced the members with complete self-possession. When he spoke, his words were well chosen and his voice clear and steady. Here, said the members one to another, was a real king in the making.

The result of the visit was to clear away any possible doubts. He was called "the very heir-apparent" and, after the death of his father, they petitioned that he be created Prince of Wales, Duke of Cornwall, and Earl of Chester, the titles the Black Prince had held. This was done on November 20.

The succession was now a matter of legal record. But the old king was still alive and in his befuddled mind there seemed to be a certain reservation, based on his liking for the most congenial of his sons, the plausible Duke John. Given sufficient time, Lancaster might be able to fan this small spark of uncertainty into a blaze of action. It might even be possible to win from the doddering occupant of the throne the pronouncement of a wish for his oldest surviving son to succeed him.

4

One question must arise in every mind in considering the state of things in England at this point: if Duke John had so many enemies, why did he possess such great power? Could not those who feared and hated him, which included most of the nobility, many of the bishops, and the citizens of London to a man, combine to thwart him in his ambitious schemes? The answer to these questions consisted largely of one word—Wealth. In addition to the possessions which came to him in his own right as a son of the king, he had at the age of nineteen married his cousin Blanche, the second daughter and co-heiress (there being no sons in the family) of Henry, Earl of Lancaster. The Lancastrian holdings of land were almost beyond computation, as the result of royal grants and a genius for acquisitive marriages. His immediate descendants had continued to gather in castles and estates and had become inevitably the richest family in the kingdom. In March 1361, two years after the marriage of John and the multiple-dowered Blanche, his father-in-law died and he became Earl of Lancaster in his wife's right. The next year the elder daughter, Maud, also died. She had married the Duke of Bavaria and had been left a widow with no children. So all her estates came into the hands of the princely mogul, together with the earldoms of Derby, Lincoln, and Leicester, the older daughter's share. One year later Edward III created his favored son the first Duke of Lancaster.

Blanche died of the plague while John was campaigning in Castile and soon thereafter he married Constance, an illegitimate daughter of Pedro the Cruel. This matrimonial alliance would later involve him in abortive efforts to seize the Spanish throne and, in the fullness of time, to a divorce.

At the time of the death of the Black Prince, Duke John was easily the richest man in England. He owned Kenilworth, the most famous of English castles, and had gone to great effort and expense to turn it into a home of beauty as well as an almost impregnable fortress. To this end, he had erected a new suite of buildings, including a banqueting hall of rare architectural merit. What he accomplished at Kenilworth was a proof of something often overlooked, that he was a man of sophisticated taste and discernment. In the north he owned the almost equally famous castle of Pontefract. He had scores of other possessions, largely in the northern counties, and owned the castles of Leicester, Lancaster, Pevensey, and Monmouth, to name only the better known.

On the bank of the Thames, west of the city, was the palace called the Savoy, which the Lancastrian duke used as his London home. It was packed with the beautiful things the discerning eye of its owner had acquired on the continent. As far as the arts were concerned, John was the best-versed man in England. He could drop into a conversation such names as Niccola Pisano and Guido Cavalcanti. If the Londoners had found nothing in him to dislike or criticize, they would have hated him for the Savoy alone. The richness and wonder of the place was so great a contrast to the poverty and suffering in the city; and John did not hesitate to display his learning and his sense of superiority.

To name the titles he held was like calling a muster roll with the blowing of trumpets and the rat-tat of kettledrums: John, Duke of Lancaster, Earl of Derby, Lincoln and Leicester, Lord of Beaufort and of Bergerac, Roche-sur-Yon, Noyen; seneschal of England, constable of Chester, and, sometimes, King of Castile. And always there were the names that people had coined for him, Great Lancaster and Lord of the North.

The possession of large estates always carried with it overlordships and many retainers. It was in Duke John's power to summon to his banner at any moment thousands of men from all corners of the kingdom, wearing the silver and azure bands on their sleeves or fluttering from their lances. There were other members of the baronage who had wide possessions, such as Edmund Mortimer, Earl of March, but even the greatest of them were of small account when compared with the colossus of the north.

And so, with the victor of Poictiers dead and laid away in his magnificent tomb in Canterbury Cathedral, Lancaster lost no time in asserting his power. The Good Parliament was dismissed and everything it had done proclaimed illegal. Peter de la Mare was placed under arrest and brought before the King's Court. He was declared guilty on several counts short of treason and sentenced to imprisonment.

He was still in confinement when a new Parliament, which should be called the Bad, assembled at Westminster. It had been most carefully hand-picked under the sharp scrutiny of Duke John. One Sir Thomas Hungerford, a Lancastrian adherent, was elected Speaker, which was to be a regular parliamentary post from that time on. Although most of the members were strongly Lancastrian in sentiment, a stout minority fought for the release of Peter de la Mare. They failed in this purpose. De la Mare, who deserves a place in the list of courageous parliamentary leaders over the centuries to follow—Peter Wentworth, Sir Edward Coke, Sir John Eliot, John Pym, and John Hampden—was kept in confinement in Nottingham Castle. Alice Perrers, who was swishing her velvet skirts about the court again and holding the king's favor in her plump hands, had acquired a bitter hatred for de la Mare and vehemently demanded his execution for treason. Being sensible of the enormity of any such action, the duke had to use all his influence over his father to prevent it from being done.

Becoming involved in the dissensions arising out of the teachings of John Wycliffe, the Bad Parliament (a label which was most clearly earned) stirred up a hornet's nest by summoning Wycliffe to appear for a hearing in St. Paul's Cathedral. Nothing came of it except a widespread belief that Duke John was supporting the Lollards, a name applied to the followers of that great teacher. If this were so, it meant that he saw some political advantage to be gained. Certainly he was incapable of a deep enough concern in spiritual matters to take any such position.

In the spring it became necessary for a deputation from the city to wait upon the king at Shene. Having heard stories of his physical disintegration, they were surprised to find him strong enough to sit up straight in his chair and to take part in the discussions not only with clearness of understanding but even a hint of amiability. It was one of the poor old monarch's good days, apparently, but the urbanity of his bearing did not lead him into the making of any concessions. The members of the deputation left the royal residence in a state of concern. The Edward III they had faced was quite capable, it seemed, of continuing to rule for some time longer, long enough, perhaps, to lend his support to the machinations of the duke.

5

The enthusiasm which young Richard had aroused among the members of the Good Parliament was now shared by the country at large. Everything about him seemed worthy of praise. He was the son of the once great hero, the Black Prince. He showed signs of attaining the kinglike stature of the Plantagenets, his face had the beauty of his winsome mother, he carried himself well, he spoke with an intelligence rare in one of his years. If anything happened to him, the people of England, like the Cornish boys of a later century (in what proved to be a better cause), would know the reason why.

The unanimity of city and town, of hamlet and thorp, of castle and inn and toft, in favor of the young prince, was due in some degree to the indifference which other members of the royal family induced in the public mind. No one had any desire to see a woman on the throne, save perhaps Edmund Mortimer who was the husband of Princess Philippa and the most hearty and outspoken hater of Duke John. Edmund of Langley, the son born next after John, was an amiable and ruddy fellow who, to do him justice, had no scrap of dangerous ambition in him at all. He liked soldiering and had taken his part in many campaigns in France. He had done rather well, but not nearly well enough to gain any recognition in the face of the spectacular exploits of the great first son. The last son, Thomas of Woodstock, was at this time in his early twenties and was already showing signs of the arrogance, bad temper, and mulish insensitivity which would cause so much trouble later on. Not of the stuff which makes for popularity, this Thomas.

This being the situation, all England sat in anxiety while the old king clung to life, and Duke John conspired, and the boy Richard was kept under careful watch; for no one had forgotten the sad fate of another royal nephew, the unfortunate Arthur of Brittany. So completely had the people forgotten the victor of Crécy, the golden spendthrift King Edward

III, that his death on June 21, 1377, alone and untended, went almost unnoticed in the enthusiasm with which the boy Richard, with Sir Simon Burley carrying the royal sword before him, was received when he came to London unopposed to claim the throne.

CHAPTER III

# The King Who Lost a Shoe

*1*

THERE is a faintly remembered legend in England about a king of Mercia, in the days when the country was split into four small kingdoms, who died and left his throne to his saintly eight-year-old son, Kenelm. There happened to be a much older daughter named Quendryth who had other ideas. She wanted to do the ruling herself. Accordingly she conspired with accomplices who obligingly murdered the boy king and buried his body in a pass in the Cotswolds; and she then gave it out that anyone who as much as whispered the name of Kenelm would be put to death. Under these circumstances the incident might soon have been forgotten.

But a milk-white dove circled over Rome and finally deposited a piece of parchment, which it had carried in its bill, on the altar in St. Peter's. The papal scribes could not read the message because it was written in an alien language. An Englishman in Rome deciphered the contents, however, which told about the murder and explained where the body would be found in the Clent Hills. A search was made, the body was discovered, and something unpleasant happened, we trust, to Quendryth. The ruins of a chapel, which was built to mark the spot, stand to this day.

It was customary to hold coronations in England on Sundays, but as the eve of the feast of Saint Kenelm fell on Thursday, July 16, it was thought appropriate to crown this new boy king on that date. The idea may have originated with his mother, who had taken the arrangements into her own hands. At any rate, it was so planned and carried out in a blaze of extravagance.

Perhaps it was remembered also that on October 28, 1216, a nine-year-old boy had been crowned king in the cathedral at Gloucester. The barons who filled the nave on that occasion must have felt the same deep-seated unease which permeated the common people in the streets, because the rather handsome prince, who would reign for fifty-six years as Henry III, was son of the incredible John. What kind of a man would he grow up to be and what manner of monarch would he make? The ceremony was on the frugal order, for the Crown jewels had been lost in the Wash and a plain gold circlet was used as a crown. The treasury was empty and the dauphin of France had landed an army and taken possession of London and most of the eastern counties. Even the coronation dinner had to be a plain and hasty one.

A somewhat similar situation existed in 1377. The national finances were verging on bankruptcy and French fleets were ravaging the southern coasts of England. No one seemed to feel, however, that the same reservations felt over the accession of Henry, son of John, need be extended to Richard, son of Edward the Black Prince—except perhaps the closest adherents of the Duke of Lancaster. Had not this boy already given proof of the finest qualities? Let the conduits run with wine and count not the cost of the precious jewels which made the coronation robes as stiff as the lighter forms of armor! The ceremony was carried out, in fact, in an excess of enthusiasm and a wild emptying of pockets, in which the usually cool-headed citizens of London led the way.

Richard left for London, arrayed in a robe of white satin and seated on a handsomely accoutered charger. As has already been stated, Sir Simon Burley stood in front with bared sword. The city had gone to unusual lengths to convert its habitual griminess into a semblance of fairyland. There was a huge floral castle with four towers, each containing a beautiful girl. As the youth rode by, they showered him with what seemed to be small leaves of gold, a bad omen for a king who might so easily develop the extravagant ways of the Plantagenets.

At noon on the next day the ceremony began with what seems to have been the first formal appearance of a king's champion. One Sir John Dymoke, who could trace his descent back to the barons of Fontenay-de-Marmion, hereditary champions of the Dukes of Normandy, rode on his horse into the abbey and in a loud voice issued a challenge to mortal combat to anyone disputing the rights of the new king. There was a dramatic dashing to the ground of a gauntlet and then the proffer of a drink in a golden cup to the candidate for the crown. The champion became the owner of the cup, the charger he had ridden, and the armor he had worn.

The Bishop of Rochester preached the sermon, exhorting all present to support the young king and leaving the impression that Richard was the choice of God and that the new king would be responsible only to the deity for his actions. It had seemed to most of the spectators that by this time the young king was getting too weary to pay much attention to this ecclesiastical bolstering of his own father's beliefs; and yet subsequent events seem to suggest that the sense of it became lodged in his mind.

The archbishop conducted the ceremonies, removing the boy's upper garments, while a cloth of gold was held around him to hide him from the eyes of the curious. Even the royal shirt had been cut in two pieces and was held together by silver links. He was then anointed with chrism, a consecrated oil mixed with balm. There followed the usual coronation ritual, the taking of oaths, the intoning of prayers and hymns, the placing of the crown on his head and in his hands the scepter, orb, and sword, then the stole, the spurs, and over all the jewel-encrusted pallium. After more prayers and hymns and the offertory, in the course of which Richard laid a heavy purse of gold on the altar, there came the Mass and communion, then more chants.

It was plain to see then that the boy was very weary. His cheeks were white and he was finding it hard to hold up his head. Sir Simon Burley, who had a great affection for his young charge, took it on himself at this point to introduce a distinct innovation into the proceedings. Picking the boy up in his arms, he carried him out to a litter on which he was to be taken back to the palace and over which four wardens of the Cinque Ports held a canopy of blue silk.

One of the boy's slippers fell off as he was carried out and the mob in the street fought furiously for possession of it.

2

The day after the coronation a council was chosen to take control during the term of the boy's minority. The selection of members was a total defeat for Duke John. He was not included nor were either of his brothers, Edmund of Cambridge or Thomas of Woodstock, an act of discrimination which raised hackles in the royal family. The list included two bishops, Courtenay of London and Erghum of Salisbury, two barons, Edmund of March and Richard of Arundel, two baronets, and four knights bachelor. That the Archbishop of Canterbury was left out was not only a slap in the face for the primate, Simon of Sudbury, but a further indication of the ground lost by Lancaster, who counted Sudbury among his adherents.

It was recognized that the king would be under his mother's care and that she would be considered his guardian. Despite the belief that she leaned to the teachings of John Wycliffe, she had kept her hold on the sympathies of most men, who remembered her as the beautiful and vivacious Maid of Kent. She was, in truth, growing too stout to be considered beautiful any longer. But she had a shrewd approach to the necessities of the times, except when personal considerations entered in. Her conduct during the period that she acted as head of the royal court did not involve her in any outspoken criticism.

The Parliament which met on October 13 was as anti-Lancastrian as the Good Parliament. Its first act was to choose Peter de la Mare as Speaker. It remodeled the council by the addition of eight members and decreed that the selection of personal attendants for the young king should rest in the Commons. A more vital step was to make impossible the annulment or repeal of measures passed in Parliament except with the consent of the House. This, of course, was aimed at the duke who, after the dissolution of the Good Parliament, had summarily ruled illegal everything which had been enacted.

The House busied itself with the problems of the day and made liberal grants for administration and the defense of the realm, with the stipulation that two treasurers, agreeable to the Commons, should be appointed at once to superintend the collection. The king accepted the condition and named two London merchants, William Walworth and John Philipot, a most direct indication of the extent of the duke's loss of influence.

On December 22, Alice Perrers was brought before the Lords, and the sentence passed against her in the Good Parliament was confirmed. However, this was not the last heard from this persistent lady of most doubtful virtue. A year later her husband (the old king had maintained a fiction that she was not married), whose name was Sir William de Windsor, brought action to have this order revoked. For reasons hard to understand or swallow, revoked it was. She seems to have been as pertinacious as a gadfly and was in and out of the courts on one pretext or another for the next twenty years.

## CHAPTER IV

## Passed Over, Tolerated, Winked At!

1

 T HEY have been passed over, tolerated, winked at!"

The writer was Pope Gregory XI, who had left Avignon and sailed back to Rome, where he was beset by troubles. He was addressing himself to Archbishop Simon of Sudbury and to Bishop Courtenay of London, concerning the reception his previous epistles had met. "Yes, you and the other prelates of the church of England, you who ought to be the pillars of the church, defenders of the faith, you have winked at them! You ought to be covered with shame and blushing, you ought to be conscience stricken, for thus passing over these iniquities!"

The unhappy and perplexed Pope, soon to die, had been trying to drive the heads of the church into positive action against John Wycliffe and his teachings. The papal demands had been passed over, it was true, and even this new attack roused no spirit of suppression in the upper hierarchy. The feeling in England was such that the rise of a leader of dissent from the heavy hand of the papacy had been almost inevitable. Wycliffe, a lecturer at Oxford and a man of great eloquence, had been the one to voice openly this discontent. There was a wide, though perhaps silent acceptance of his views in all classes of society and, when he preached in London, the people of that turbulent and realistic town turned out in multitudes to listen.

This was a form of attack which an organization as strongly entrenched as the church of Rome could not tolerate. And so when Wycliffe grew bolder and began to preach on points of creed and dogma, the Pope had moved quickly against him. Wycliffe had laid himself open to charges of heresy. The letters, which had received so little attention, had been papal demands for action against this daring propagandist.

The final bulls from St. Peter's, boiling with exasperation, went on to make specific demands. The archbishop and Courtenay of London were to proceed, first, to inform themselves of the truth, then they were to arrest Wycliffe in the Pope's name, to extract confessions from him, and finally to send on a report to Rome. The situation was one which could no longer be winked at.

This was a difficult problem to face, with an eleven-year-old boy on the throne, and not only the most powerful man in the country but the queen mother herself more or less openly in support of the Oxford reformer. The two bishops brought divided views to the task which had been set them. The archbishop was a man of liberal tendencies, as he had demonstrated in his protest against the Canterbury pilgrimages and he was, moreover, an adherent in some degree of Duke John. On the other hand, Courtenay (who would succeed Simon as archbishop within a few years) was a son of the Earl of Devonshire and of royal descent, in direct line from Edward I. He was an aristocrat, arrogant, pugnacious, and set in his views. Not being either learned or studious, he was never a seeker after theological truths but was essentially a man of action. In his opinion there should be no room in a world where privilege was so comfortably ensconced for a man like Wycliffe, a commoner, to assert such dangerous thoughts. Courtenay hated the Duke of Lancaster and had nothing but contempt for the kindly and complaisant Simon.

Nevertheless, this ill-assorted pair, with the problem tossed into their laps, proceeded to take action. Wycliffe was cited to appear in the archbishop's palace at Lambeth. Despite the opposition of the queen mother, who sent a message demanding that no action be taken against him, and the action of irate citizens of London in attacking the palace and shouting maledictions against the accusers, there was a long examination of the fifty articles of accusation sent from Rome. Despite the Pope's edict that Wycliffe must be arrested, he did not appear as a prisoner. He was questioned exhaustively but was permitted to state his position and his beliefs without peremptory interruptions.

John Wycliffe was not a fiery reformer, not one to hurl his accusations in the teeth of established authority. He was an orderly thinker who had seen clearly what Christendom was coming to and knew what the inevitable result would be. He made no effort to turn the chapel at Lambeth into a sounding board for daring attacks on Rome. Instead he sat down and reasoned out the meaning of the words he had written or said, being willing even to have an orthodox explanation read into some of them. He was dismissed with an admonition. Never again was he to utter such dangerous and controversial views, neither from the pulpit nor in the schools where he taught, "on account of the scandal which they excited among the laity."

This, in lieu of the vigorous action the Pope had demanded, was a

tame conclusion, for which the complaisant Simon had to bear much of
the blame. Wycliffe retired to his living at Lutterworth in Lincolnshire
where he spent the few years remaining to him in the translation of the
Vulgate, the Latin Bible, into the English tongue and in the promulgation
of still more radical views rising out of the storm following the death of
Gregory.

## 2

It is difficult today to appreciate how close the relationship had become between the Popes of medieval days and the countries acknowledg-
ing their sway. The pontiffs exercised a degree of temporal power which
became greater or less, according to circumstances, but was always considerable. They not only had much to do with the filling of thrones and
the external problems of kings but they were consulted on appointments
and they injected themselves into the private lives of the monarchs.
John of unfragrant memory counted the day fortunate when no chiding
epistle reached him from Innocent III, dealing often with his conduct as
a man. Popes were consulted about marriages and separations. Their
hand was felt in matters pertaining to wills and property.

What was happening at Rome was, on that account, of very great
interest to Englishmen. The course that events took at this particular
moment was watched with the deepest concern.

The Babylonish Captivity had continued for seventy years, during
which time the halls at Avignon had become palaces of luxury and
magnificence. The Popes had all been Frenchmen and it followed that
French appointees packed the ranks of the cardinalate. In the meantime
the empty church buildings in Rome had fallen into disrepair and even
ruin. England had come to expect an adverse bias in all papal action.

Gregory XI, although a Frenchman by birth, had been converted to
the wisdom of returning to Rome, largely by the eloquence of St.
Catherine of Sienna. He died, however, within a year of the change, after
issuing a bull conferring on the cardinals the power to choose the time
and place for the election of his successor. This could be construed
as a measure to make possible the choice of Avignon and, inevitably, the
selection of a French Pope and a return of administration to the French
city. At the time of his death there were sixteen cardinals in Rome, and
eleven of them were French. The chamberlain, who held authority during
vacancies between Popes, was a Frenchman, the Archbishop of Arles.
The people of Rome, and of Italy for the most part, wanted the glory
and prosperity of the Vatican restored. They saw no hope of action
favorable to their cause if the Conclave were held elsewhere.

The nine days of mourning which must be allowed after the death of a Pope were days of deep suspense. St. Peter's found itself in a state of siege. The people of Rome, armed and belligerent, surrounded the Hall of Conclave, where the cardinals had gathered, and loudly demanded that none leave until an election had been held. Even nature took a hand. Black clouds filled the sky and the roll of thunder was heard from the north and west. A bolt of lightning struck the hall where the cardinals were gathered. Not daring to venture out, the occupants of the room huddled together in a body while a fire destroyed the furnishings of the chamber. In spite of the heavy downpour, in fact encouraged by it as a sign of divine will, the mobs continued to fill the streets, chanting interminably, "A Roman Pope! A Roman Pope!"

As soon as the fire subsided, the people rushed into the building to satisfy themselves that the spiritual heads of the church were still there. They examined every foot of space with an insolent disregard for officials, tapping the walls and floors, searching behind hangings, exploring the kitchens, to make sure that there were no secret means of escape.

Finally an ultimatum was delivered to the cardinals. The Conclave must be held in Rome, and without delay. A Roman Pope must be elected. If this were not done, it would be impossible to restrain the rage of the people. A massacre might be the result.

The answer given to the emissaries of the people, who had conveyed the demands, was courageous and dignified. "Tomorrow," said the cardinals, "we celebrate the Mass of the Descent of the Holy Ghost. As the Holy Ghost directs, so shall we do."

There was no secret means of exit from the Hall of Conclave and so the cardinals had only two courses of action from which to choose. They could risk sitting out the storm or they could proceed at once with the election of a new Pope.

The choice of a new pontiff was not as simple as it seemed in the face of the French majority. Most of the cardinals came from the diocese of Limoges and there had been for a long time a rancor over this injudicious preference. Three of the Frenchmen were as determined as the four Italians and the one Spaniard, who completed the body, that the voice of the Limousin should not dictate another selection.

The first votes showed the Conclave to be deadlocked. Out of this situation came the inevitable solution, a compromise election. One of the four Italians was Bartolomeo Prignani, Archbishop of Bari. He was a subject of Queen Joanna of Naples, who also held the title of Countess of Provence. To that extent he had French affiliations to offset his Italian birth. When his name was proposed, the Conclave voted for him unanimously, glad of any solution.

But the tumultuous mobs, who in the meantime had broken into the

Pope's cellars and had fortified themselves with his rich malvoisie wine, were suspicious and dissatisfied. When five of the cardinals who had wanted a French Pope tried to get away, they were quickly detected and forced to scramble back to shelter.

It became apparent at once that the new pontiff, who had assumed the name of Urban VI, was going to be a sore trial to his one-time fellows. He was of common birth and had reached high rank by reason of his piety and austerity. He wore a hair shirt next his skin and did not believe the princes of the church should live in luxury. He was against any display of wealth and was determined to put an end to the packing of offices with the greedy relatives of the church leaders. He announced immediately that no more than one dish should be served at any meal.

Views of this kind generally went with genuine piety and understanding. Urban VI was harsh and domineering. He scowled blackly as he laid down the law. "I am the Good Shepherd!" he cried. He announced at once his intention to remain in Rome and to direct the church from St. Peter's. He would be impartial in all disputes between England and France. The Babylonish Captivity was ended. "Hold your tongues!" he cried, when any voices were raised in protest. The good cardinals, to employ a modern phrase, had indeed caught a tartar.

As soon as they were allowed to leave, the French members assembled in the small city of Anagni, which stands on a hill in the valley of Tresis. It had sometimes been used as a summer home by the Popes and it was here that England's one pontiff, Adrian IV, had died. The bitterly dissatisfied cardinals gave it out that the election of Urban had been forced on them by threats of death. The new incumbent was declared to be a tyrant and unfit to rule, and it was demanded of him that he step down at once and permit a new election, free of undue pressure.

Urban struck back fiercely and a state of war followed. The Archbishop of Arles, the chamberlain of the late Pope, stole out of Rome at night and carried to Anagni the crown and all the jewels of the papacy. Even the Queen of Naples, who had been delighted at first by the selection of Urban, turned against him. Her husband, Otto of Brunswick, had visited the new Pope to discuss the rights of succession and had been treated with indifference and even scorn. On the other hand there was a sentiment throughout Christendom against the men who had permitted fear of bodily harm to influence their votes.

The dissenting cardinals moved to Fondi and here they selected a new Pope in the person of Cardinal Robert of Geneva. He took the title of Clement VII and returned at once to Avignon, thus beginning a division of the church which was to continue for thirty-eight years. He was recognized by France, Scotland, and Savoy and finally by Spain and Portugal. Italy remained loyal to Urban, as did also the Holy Roman

Emperor Charles IV, England, Hungary, Poland, and the Scandinavian countries. Political considerations played a part in this division of the nations. England must stand against France, Scotland against England.

The events which followed this schism in the church were of such a violent nature that they are hard to believe. Urban appointed twenty-six new cardinals, which threw Avignon into a decided minority. He is said to have had Joanna of Naples smothered to death under a mattress and to have thrown six of his cardinals (who were charged with a conspiracy to depose him) into a damp cistern at the castle of Nocera which they shared with snakes. One of them was the sole Englishman wearing the red hat, Adam of Easton. Later the Pope took them with him to Genoa, had them sewn up in sacks and cast into the sea. The English cardinal was spared through the intervention of the young king.

In the meantime, Clement VII, the first of the anti-Popes, as the French pontiffs were to be designated, found himself with no revenue to maintain the magnificence of Avignon. He outdid his opponent by appointing thirty-six cardinals and proceeded to drain the French church by every form of exaction.

Partisan malice, no doubt, has lent exaggeration to this account of what followed the split in the church; but certainly they were black and bitter days for all concerned.

With the rival pontiffs waging as harsh a warfare as was possible with a spur of the Alps and the Ligurian Sea between them, it is not surprising that little attention was paid to echoes from England of the complaisance of the church heads to a growing acceptance of the teachings of a gentle scholar named Wycliffe.

## 3

There were other reasons why the thinking of Wycliffe was allowed to sway the minds of many Englishmen and spread to the continent, there to produce a Jan Huss and to lay the first stones in the foundation of the Reformation. Wycliffe's attacks, in the beginning, were directed at financial aspects. The church, he pointed out, was growing too rich. It was acquiring too much of the land. It was despotic in the assertion of its rights and privileges. In England this was a very sore point, for even in the highest clerical ranks there was rancor over the granting of English benefices to Italians who continued to reside in Rome and were recompensed in this way for their services to the papacy. The principle was bitter in the mouth and it was considered, moreover, that the hand of the Vatican was particularly heavy on England.

For this reason Wycliffe had a ready and favorable audience. The

Lollards, who preached his doctrines, were not for the most part the aggressive type of reformers who raised passions to a fiery pitch. There was a gentle rationality back of what they said to the people. It was not until the leader began to delve more deeply and to attack the church on points of creed that the heads of the church leveled against him the charge of heresy.

There were other reasons to account for the lack of inquisitorial action. As has already been explained, Rome was too busy. The death grapple which followed the open breach between Rome and Avignon left little time for anything else. Wycliffe died before the attack reached anything like the grim and bloodthirsty fanaticism which had wiped out the Albigenses in southern France. It was forty-four years after his death before his grave was opened and his remains burned.

The lack of will to wipe out Lollardy, root and branch, may have been due to the characteristics of the two men in whose hands the decision lay. Things might have been different if the positions of Simon of Sudbury and Courtenay had been reversed, in other words if Courtenay had been Archbishop of Canterbury when the Pope delivered his attack on the apathy of the English church. Courtenay had no spiritual or social sympathy with those who espoused Wycliffean ideas. He was the first to punish spiritual derelictions with corporal penalties. No one was burned at the stake in his time, but he had opened the door to this diabolical method of stamping out heresy.

Another reason for the tolerance which wrapped Wycliffe in the folds of immunity was that he had support in high places. Duke John blew hot and cold, but it was always believed he would back the reformer if the need grew urgent. And he had highhanded ways of dealing with matters if anything went against his will.

There was, for instance, a case in which he allowed adherents of his to violate the church law of sanctuary. From primitive days there had been a belief that anyone, even a criminal with blood on his hands, attained some degree of holiness if he passed the inner portals, and this had been embodied in Roman practices to the extent of establishing certain churches in all countries as sanctuaries. There were crosses placed on all roads leading to such churches at a distance of a mile and marked *Sanctarium*. Although the theory accepted in the first place had been that immunity was established in any part of the edifice, it was only while seated in the frithstool, a stone chair beside the altar, that a criminal was legally safe.

The course to be pursued had been developed in considerable detail. The fugitive must present himself at the front entrance and ring the galilee bell which was reserved for that purpose. When the tolling of the bell brought a response, the desperate applicant had to pay an admission fee, make a full statement of the crime, and, before being admitted, don a black robe with St. Cuthbert's cross on the left shoulder, a strange device in view of the dying statement of the Celtic saint that he did not want the presence of his bones to assist evil men in claiming sanctuary.

In the year 1377, Duke John, who was still actively asserting his claim to the throne of Castile because his second wife, Constance, was the elder daughter of Pedro the Cruel (thus disregarding her illegitimacy), wanted to retain in his custody the son of the Count of Denia who was related to the Castilian royal family. The boy had been left as a hostage by his father in the care of two squires named Schakel and Haule until he could raise the ransom demanded for him. The duke agreed to pay the ransom if the boy were left in his charge but, as this proposal was contrary to the established laws of chivalry, the offer was refused. The duke then used his influence to have Schakel and Haule committed to the Tower of London until they turned the boy over. They escaped from the Tower and made their way to Westminster where they claimed sanctuary. They had been followed by Lancastrian men-at-arms who secured Schakel and took him back to his cell in the Tower. Haule was less fortunate. Returning to the Abbey, the armed men found that High Mass was being celebrated and that Haule was beside the choir. They surrounded him and proceeded to drag him out. Haule drew his sword in defense and circled the altar twice before a blow from one of his assailants shattered his skull.

The incident created much bitterness and the perpetrators of the murder were excommunicated. Duke John, however, was declared exempt. Later he made the claim that Haule had sought sanctuary as a debtor and that the laws limited that right to men charged with crimes of violence, an interpretation to which the bishops servilely assented.

## CHAPTER V

# The First English Bible

## 1

THE market town of Lutterworth in Leicestershire stood on an eminence around which flowed the river Swift. It has often been pointed out that its location should be considered symbolic: for the Swift joined the Avon and the Avon joined the Severn and then they all joined the sea, while on the other side a brooklet rising near the town flowed into the Soar, the Soar flowed into the Trent, the Trent into the Humber, and all of them finally were lost in the German Ocean. Was it not significant that this quiet medieval backwater, from which a prophetic voice would send its message to all parts of the world, should thus feed the waters of both east and west?

John Wycliffe did not retire to his living at Lutterworth because of ecclesiastical pressure. He knew how little time remained to him and that he must use every hour in the completion of his great task, the translation of the Latin Bible into English. He had left followers behind him to carry on his work at Oxford, men who were sometimes more radical and outspoken than he had been. Even Dr. Rygge, the chancellor, belonged to this group. Throughout the country the Lollards, who preached his message, were being heard at village crossroads and in forest glades.

News of this reached the ears of the venerable leader, toiling in his quiet home on the glebe at the church of St. Mary's; but the drone of the outside world came to him faintly and had, perhaps, lost some of its sense of urgency. He may have smiled approvingly when he learned that his Oxford adherents, even Dr. Rygge, had adopted a particular manner of dress, going barefoot and wearing coarse russet gowns which reached to the ankles, because he believed in simplicity and avoided for himself the use of quatrefoil decoration on his alb or the manciple he wore when serving at the altar. It was, nonetheless, a contentious day in matters of clerical apparel. At the time that Wycliffe went into retreat at Lutterworth, the amiable Archbishop Simon of Sudbury was struggling to adjudicate a dispute in St. Paul's, finally approving the right of minor canons to sit in the choir in white surplices with almuces of black, lined with the skins of animals, and black open capes. They were all most tenacious of their little rights, these little men. The same canons had demanded, and had been awarded, seven white loaves and three trencher loaves of black bread each week, to say nothing of twelve weekly bowls of the best ale, called welkyn.

All that can be told of the life at Lutterworth is that the dedicated group who worked with him lived very simply. Wycliffe begrudged himself the morsels of food he took, counting it as so much less for the needy poor; bread, vegetables, cheese in great moderation, and a very occasional egg; that was all. There were no complaints, for their thoughts were too deeply immersed in the task at which they labored.

Little is known of Wycliffe's appearance. Some chroniclers say he carried himself at a good height; others speak of him as small and wasted of frame. There are some portraits in existence, all of which were painted after his grave had been rifled and his ashes thrown into the Swift, and so are based on nothing more than faint echoes of traditional description. They agree in depicting him as the possessor of an eye burning with zeal, with a Messianic arch to his nose and a flowing white beard.

In order to realize the enormity of the task that John Wycliffe had taken on himself a glance forward may be in order to consider what happened more than two hundred years later, from 1604 to 1617, to be exact. King James of Scotland had succeeded Elizabeth on the English throne and, being something of a pedant, had eagerly grasped at a suggestion that a better English version of the Bible was needed. Forty-seven men were summoned to aid in the project, theologians, scholars, professors of Hebrew and Greek, nearly all of them from the universities. They were divided into six groups and sections of the Scriptures were assigned to each. The size of the groups was determined by a consideration as set forth later, when the translation had been completed, "not too many, lest one should trouble another, and yet many lest many things haply might escape them." Each of these learned expounders of the Law and the Prophets prepared his own version of the books and chapters assigned to his group and a final version was decided on between them. Two groups met at Westminster, two at Oxford, and two at Cambridge. They took no particular account of the Latin version but went back to the original sources, Hebrew for the Old Testament, Greek for the New.

This mighty undertaking was placed under the supervision of Dr. Miles Smith, an orientalist who could speak Chaldaic, Syriac, and Arabic, a stout and worthy scholar who had come up the long and hard way, born the son of a butcher in Hereford. His views tended to the puritanical. His personal participation was with the group to whom the prophetic books had been assigned, but later he was active in preparing a final version of the Old Testament. He prepared also a long and learned introduction, addressed to the Readers. For the competence of his work, he was later made Bishop of Gloucester.

His chief aide was Thomas Bilson, Bishop of Winchester, who was descended, it was said, from a Duke of Bavaria. Bilson was quite definitely on the traditional side of the fence, having served in the previous reign as a Crown pamphleteer. His selection undoubtedly was to establish a balance between high church and puritanical viewpoints.

More time was spent in the preliminary steps than in the actual work of revision. It was more than three years later that the forty-seven rolled up their learned sleeves and set to work. After two years and nine months of continuous effort, a final version was arrived at. Nine additional months were needed to prepare the text for the presses.

It was indeed extraordinary that out of so much conflict of opinion there emerged the noble and much loved King James version which has been almost universally accepted in English-speaking countries, even to the present day.

What a contrast is presented by the little group which gathered about John Wycliffe, beginning probably in 1381! They were not scholars in the same sense as the learned architects of the King James version and they had to work exclusively from the Vulgate, the Latin Bible, having no means of drawing on Hebrew and Greek sources. There were as many as five of them, but probably not more, and they lived in the house on the glebe, assembling around one table. The pens of these earnest and dedicated men scratched in tireless industry; their voices were muted in the constant discussion of controversial points. They could not have allowed themselves much leisure, because the pressure of time was heavy upon them. One can picture them as going out together in the cool of evening when the last rays of the sun were falling on the high spire of the church and warming the stained glass to new beauty, walking perhaps two and two, their heads nodding in discussion.

So little is known about this historic labor that the number five, already given, is a guess based on the fact that the manuscript of the final text of the Old Testament carries the imprint of five contributors, differing in handwriting and even in dialect, one possibly Wycliffe himself. The chief aide was Nicholas de Hereford, a subtle and forceful reasoner, who had been with Wycliffe at Oxford. He was such a determined propagandist that he was later excommunicated and went to Rome to plead his case before the Pope, being found guilty of heresy for his pains and committed to prison. After making his escape, he returned to England and became recognized as the leader of the Lollards. Toward the end of the century, when the hue and cry of heresy were on, he was seized and put to the torture. Weakening then, he recanted publicly at St. Paul's Cross and, strangely enough, became a vigorous opponent of his former associates.

Two men who served as curates under Wycliffe at Lutterworth, John Purvey and John Horn, were also engaged in the work, the former being given credit for the much improved *Later Version* brought out in 1388.

Little is known about the Lutterworth undertaking, but it seems reasonably certain that the *Early Version* was completed before the death of Wycliffe. He had not devoted himself exclusively to the work for he had felt it incumbent on him to perform at least part of the parochial work. In addition he had put into pamphlet form some severe strictures on Pope Urban VI which so irked that far from gentle pontiff that the writer was ordered to Rome to explain himself. This peremptory invitation had to be declined by the feeble old man at Lutterworth.

John Wycliffe lived long enough to see the *Early Version* completed. Then, as if nature had purposely abstained until the last words had been scratched on the manuscript, he suffered a stroke. A partial recovery made it possible for him to proceed about some of his duties but he never again officiated in the church. On December 28, 1384, he was hearing Mass when the attack was repeated. His wasted form seemed to shrink into the plain gray robe he had chosen to wear and his heavy breathing was the only sign that he still lived. He was carried out through the high and noble west arch of the church for the last time.

Gathered around his couch, his devoted followers watched intently for three days, knowing that he would never recover full consciousness again. It became apparent that he would not survive to see the new year and, in the last moments, the curate began to read from the manuscript of their Bible.

> *In the hous of my fadir*
> *ben many dwellinges——*
> *And if I go to make ready for you a place*
> *eftsoone I schal come*
> *And I schal take you to myself——*

*Jhesu seith to him,*
*I am weye, treuthe and lyf:*
*No man cometh to the fadir,*
*No but by me.*

The Wycliffe Bible, copied in large quantities by the hands of willing "poor priests," was widely received. So widely, in fact, that it continued to circulate throughout England for nearly two centuries, by which time better translations were available. The reverence with which the book was accepted is evident in the fact that 150 perfect copies are still in existence. Clearly the copyists had made them in the thousands.

## CHAPTER VI

## *When the Bell Was Rungen*

*1*

FOUR years had passed since the little king lost his shoe. He was growing into a handsome and confident boy, and measures were being taken already to find him a princess for a wife. The council governed the kingdom, and the queen mother (who was now a heavy load for any palfrey) governed the council. If the war against France was going on at all, it was going on badly. The treasury, as was always the case with Plantagenet kings, yawned with emptiness. And at this moment, in June 1381 to be exact, there came about one of the most dramatic, significant, and dreadful events in English history—the rebellion of the peasants.

Historians have found many words to apply to this upflaring of class discontent, including "mysterious." It is true that it had many elements of mystery, particularly the suddenness with which it began and its almost instantaneous spread across the southern and eastern counties like a stubble field afire. Had the seeds of rebellion been carefully planted in advance? Had it been possible to do this with such secrecy that villeins by the tens of thousands were ready and waiting while their masters had no inkling of impending trouble?

The discontent was due to the land laws which held a large proportion of the peasants in a state bordering on peonage. They were called villeins and were allowed to cultivate some acres of land belonging to the lord of the manor, paying in lieu of rent by giving a portion of their time to the land reserved for the lord himself. This was called the *corvée* and it would not have been entirely unfair except for the "boons," the right of the owner to call on them for extra work without remuneration at any time he saw fit, particularly if rain were expected and he wanted his crops harvested in time. The boon in that event might mean that the poor villein's own crops would be beaten down by the autumnal storms and go unharvested. There were other class restrictions under which the peasant labored. He was bound to the land and could never leave without his lord's consent. His children were bound also. Nor were they allowed to marry save with seignorial approval.

The grim harvest of the Black Death had intensified these conditions. The villeins died in such numbers that it was no longer possible to cultivate all the land. At first this benefited the workmen because they could demand better terms for their labor but it did not take the law long to step in. It was stipulated that a man could not seek new employers and demand what he wished. He must remain on the demesne where he was born and work for his own lord *on the terms which had prevailed before the coming of the plague.* This was the worst kind of injustice because the shortage of crops had sent up the cost of living.

It also rankled in the minds of the yeomen that it was the longbow (even the least expert of them might have shot the plume off a French helmet at a hundred yards) which had won the great victories in France, not the armed knight on horseback. Had they not proven their worth? Should the sons of men who had drawn a stout bow at Crécy be subjected to such unfair laws?

Finally, because of the cost of the abortive struggle against the French, there had come the poll tax. Parliament had decided that a certain number of groats, which the common people called "thickpennies," should be paid by everyone, the lowest rate being three groats for all over fifteen years of age. The peasants found this an intolerable burden on top of the penny on every hearth which had to be paid for the Romescot (Peter's Pence). Already on the verge of starvation, they refused to be taxed further.

It should not be assumed that the peasants were involved in a solidly knit and secret organization. It was more certainly a deep-seated conviction they held in common, a bitterness of desire for full freedom, which led to the sudden outburst. Any discussion of what happened when this discontent reached the breaking point must begin with the story of a hedge priest named John Ball.

Jean Froissart, the French historian who had held office once at the English court and who wrote of English affairs, dubbed Ball the Mad Monk of Kent. Ball did not come from Kent but from Yorkshire, nor was he mad. Nevertheless, the label has stuck to him for nearly six hundred years. The validity of the causes for which he preached has been confirmed, the rights he sought for Peterkin the Ploughman and Jack Trewman and John the Miller have been granted and the march of social progress has gone so far beyond them that they seem almost quaint in their modesty. But still in most writing on the period he is depicted as an incendiary, a fomenter of trouble, in short, a mad monk. A note of sympathy for the manner of his death is seldom expressed.

There is no source from which a picture of the man might be drawn and so, in lieu of the contemptuous term tossed off by a toady who knew no more of England than he could gather on the tilting grounds and on the edges of a gay court, it may be in order to quote from a work of pure imagination, the beautifully conceived fantasy by William Morris, *A Dream of John Ball*. The poet in Morris was convinced that there existed a great sense of beauty among the common men of those faraway days, that they dressed plainly but in the good taste of simple colors, that their voices were musical, that they lived in small homes of their own devising and building, which might have wattled doors and roofs of thatch but still had a certain beauty of their own; and that their husbandry was of such high order that the furrows they plowed were as straight as the road to heaven. And for John Ball, Morris saw him as one who shared with all great minds a dream of the equality of man.

It has been charged that Ball preached a form of communism and versions of what he said are given in some of the chronicles. None of them agree and all seem garbled and clumsy. Those who think of the years he spent on the road and the memories which remained in the minds of those who heard him, and moreover of certain later evidences of the honesty of his intent, may find it more enlightening to hear the phrases which Morris puts into the mouth of the inspired hedge priest.

What else shall ye lack when ye lack masters? Ye shall not lack for the fields ye have tilled, nor the houses ye have built, nor the cloth ye have woven; all these shall be yours, and whatso ye will of all that the earth beareth; then shall no man mow the deep grass for another, while his own kine lack cow-meat; and he that soweth shall reap, and the reaper shall eat in fellowship the harvest that in fellowship he hath won; and he that buildeth a house shall dwell in it with those he biddeth of his free will; and the tithe barn shall garner the wheat for all men to eat of when the seasons are untoward, and the raindrift hideth the sheaves in August; and all shall be without money and without price. Faithfully and merrily then shall all men keep the holidays of the church in peace of body and joy of heart. And man shall help man, and the saints in heaven shall be glad, because men no more fear each other; and the churl shall be ashamed, and shall hide his churlishness till it be gone and he no more a churl; and fellowship shall be established in heaven and on earth.

*2*

To say that John Ball was a hedge priest meant that he had no church and no charge, nor any post which linked him to the established order. Neither had he house nor table under which he could place his feet to partake of the loaf, the joint, and the jug of wine to which, surely, every good priest was entitled. It was equally true that he had no bed in which to sleep, no cell in monastery, no snug corner in a deanery. As his feet carried him hither and yon according to what he deemed to be the Lord's will, he slept for the most part under hedges. Sometimes he preached boldly at village crosses but more often cautiously in thick woods by moonlight.

For twenty years he wandered over the face of England. Three times he was confined in the prison of the archbishop and finally he was put under a ban of excommunication. This made no difference, for he never ceased to preach what he believed, and what he believed sent his hearers into transports of wonderment and anticipation. His feet deserted early the relatively solid ground of Lollardy and carried him up high into a spiritual world where all men were equal. He always left hope behind him in the minds of those who had hung on his words. They must bide their time and be in readiness. When the right moment came, he, John Ball, would sound the bell.

This was heady stuff and some word of the gospel of unrest that he was spreading inevitably reached the ears of authority, hence his imprisonments. It is said that only the most courageous among the brawny tillers of the soil committed themselves to taking a part and that they found it wise to maintain strict conspiratorial silence. When one man who was pledged met another, whose sympathies were unknown, he would not resort to any of the usual artifices, a certain gesture, a low catchword, or perhaps a special manner of handshake. Instead he would whisper,

*John the Miller grinds small, small, small.*

The other, if he also believed in the message of John Ball would answer,

*The King's son of heaven shall pay for all.*

This may sound clumsy and even nonsensical but it must be borne in mind that this was an age of deep faiths and that men had a hunger for the poetic and the mystical which made such phrases sound warmly in their ears. There is nothing in the records to indicate that the use of these words ever led to any break in the seal of silence which had been imposed.

It is generally assumed that the messages in rhyme, which were distributed throughout the country, and were clearly the work of the bold hedge priest, did not get into circulation until the rising began. It seems more likely, however, that some of them at least had been used to strengthen the faith of the unhappy villeins through the years when the yoke rested heaviest on their shoulders and the day of reckoning seemed to get no closer. Otherwise the uprising would have lacked the spontaneity which brought the peasants out in tens of thousands in a matter almost of hours.

When the missives were written, and how they were distributed, must remain part of the mystery. All that can be set down as certain is that they came from the pen of John Ball and that they struck straight to the hearts of the common people.

> "Help truth and truth will help you," he wrote.
> "Now reigneth pride in price,
> And covetise is counted wise,
> And lechery withouten shame,
> And gluttony withouten blame."

A more direct appeal could be found in some of them, particularly the verses signed by such names as John the Miller, Jack Carter, and Jack Trewman. In these missives, or tracts as they soon came to be called, occurred such phrases as "make a good end of that ye have begun" and "now is the time," which made it clear that these at least were issued after the insurrection had started.

The rebellion flared up first in green and richly fertile Kent, where villeinage had never been introduced. The scene was the village of Dartford, which lay seventeen miles southeast of London. It was a busy place and served as first stop on the famous pilgrimage road between the capital and Canterbury. Here a tegheler, or tyler named Wat was so incensed at the indecency of a poll-tax collector who insisted that the man's daughter was old enough to pay the tax, and had proceeded to strip off her clothes to prove it, that he seized a hammer and knocked the collector's brains out. Whether this indignant father was Wat the Tyler who later became leader of the march on London seems uncertain. There were two men of that name, one of them from Maidstone, and some historians claimed it was the latter who assumed command of the peasant army. To this day, however, the site of Wat the Tyler's house in Dartford is pointed out to visitors.

The incident threw the little Kentish town into an uproar. By night-fall hundreds of men had gathered, some with bows over their shoulders, some carrying pikes or oak quarterstaves, some armed only with flails and bill hooks or the crude handles of plows. Many had come from all the villages thereabouts and a contingent of hundreds had heard of what had happened and marched in from the Channel shore.

The next morning they marched south instead of north and came to Maidstone on the Medwige (Medway) River, a distance of more than twenty miles. The reason for this long detour was plain to all of them. John Ball was being held in the archbishop's prison in Maidstone and, as he was the spiritual leader of the forces of discontent, he must be released before anything more could be done.

There was an archbishop's palace of considerable size and beauty in Maidstone, which was said to have been built and presented to the episcopal see during the term of Stephen Langton of immortal memory. It was a graceful building of the native ragstone, with two Norman towers and a cluster of steeply angled roofs. It stood between the square-pillared church of St. Mary's and the squat and gloomy prison where offenders against clerical law were held.

It is stated in one chronicle that when John Ball was last sentenced in the archbishop's court he had cried out, "I can summon twenty thousand friends to win me free!" and that the somewhat sour-faced officials had paid no heed. There is nothing in the record of John Ball, who had wandered for so many years over flinty roads and rough forest paths to carry comfort to the common people of the land, to lend any substance to a charge of boastfulness. In addition to the improbability of such open bravado, it must be taken into account that he would not thus betray the strength of the movement, which had been kept under cover so carefully and for so long.

If he had been guilty of such an utterance, however, he would have found proof on this day that his friends were indeed rallying in sudden and almost unbelievable strength. There was no exercise ground for the inmates and the prison looked down directly on the street. Nevertheless, it would take a tall man to see through the small high windows. William Morris pictures the itinerant priest as "tall and big-boned, a ring of dark hair surrounding his priest's tonsure," so perhaps he could look out on the main road of Maidstone, which was the widest in all of England, and see the peasants pouring in, their improvised weapons over their shoul-ders; thousands of them, shouting, cheering, and calling for John Ball; many of them bare of torso and of leg, for who would risk damage to a jerkin at such a time? From this he would have realized that circumstances had forced his hand, that this uprising of the embattled sons of the soil would precipitate the inevitable conflict. Secrecy was no longer possible or necessary.

When the prison gates had been broken open and he had come out, a free man again, he consulted with those who had assumed leadership of the brawny peasants and they proceeded at once to arouse the villeins everywhere. Messengers were sent out over the whole arc of west, north, and east, as far away as Cornwall and the Humber in the north. They were sent to all parts of Kent and Sussex, to Essex, Suffolk, Norfolk, and Cambridge, to Hertford, Hants, and Somerset, to York, Lancashire, Lincoln, and Durham. The message was the same to all:

*John Ball hath rungen thy bell.*

## CHAPTER VII

## The Blaze Spreads

*1*

IN ALL accounts of this amazing outbreak the emphasis is laid on the men of Kent under Wat Tyler and John Ball. But there had been trouble earlier in Essex. Before Whitsuntide, which fell that year on June 2, the men of three communities, Fobbing, Corringham and Brentwood, had been haled into court because they refused to pay the poll tax. Violent scenes resulted and the angry people had rallied under the leadership of a common priest who took the name of Jack Straw. A number of the court officials and the jury had been killed and their heads carried on the ends of pikes in wild scenes of mob hysteria.

Here again taxation had been the main issue. A specific demand had been made to allow the villeins the use of land at a rent of fourpence an acre and to have the *corvée* abolished.

It was quite a different situation in Suffolk and all of East Anglia where the men of the towns as well as the tillers of the soil had been at war with the abbey of St. Edmundsbury for nearly a century. The abbots had been granted charters which gave them a despotic hold on the countryside. They held the gates of Bury St. Edmunds, they owned a large part of the land, they were hard masters of the *corvée*. They had even been given the wardships of all orphans in the district and had not hesitated to collect good fees from the estates. To add the final touch of dissension, the abbey had gone into the lending of money and the archives were stuffed with bills against all the substantial citizens. When the stern overlordship of the monks was called into question, the abbot of the moment could always go back to his papers and produce charters which supported his pretensions.

The archives of St. Edmundsbury had become synonymous with sinister power. Whenever the victims of the monastic maw got together they would whisper bitterly that "the abbot's papers have a sharper edge than the headsman's ax."

And so in 1327 the abbey had been burned by an infuriated mob. The charters and bills had been seized and torn into shreds, to be tossed about jubilantly like stage snow. Troops had been sent, of course, to put down the uprising and twenty of the rioters had been hanged. The charters had been replaced and the old tyranny had begun again. Hate and discontent had continued to smolder. And so when the word reached Suffolk of the ringing of the bell, the people were ready to respond.

It happened that the post of abbot was vacant and that Prior John of Cambridge was temporarily in charge. This Prior John was a precise and thin-lipped man with the shrewd head of a lawyer on his narrow shoulders. He fluttered his white and well-tended hands most effectively during services, but the townspeople muttered darkly that his thumbs were callused from the tightness with which he applied the screws to all debtors. The sweetness of voice with which he chanted the prayers changed to the habitual whine of the usurer when matters of money were at stake. Prior John was cordially hated.

He happened to be in his manor house at Mildenham. Suddenly an infuriated clamor broke out and the gardens were filled with a mob which had come to settle scores with him.

Prior John tried to escape but it is said that his household servants had small reason to love him and that they betrayed him to the angry people. A mock trial was held and without a whisper of dissent he was sentenced to die. They took him out to the gardens where his head was cut off. His naked body was tossed on a dunghill.

Returning to town, the mob broke open the abbey gates and demanded again that all charters and bonds be turned over to them. The frightened monks produced everything they could find and there was another scene of exuberant demolition.

The madness was now spreading like a forest fire. The townspeople of Cambridge burned the charters of the university. In Norfolk a man named Geoffrey the Litster, or Dyer (the revival of dyeing was a recent development in England) emerged from the reek of his copperas vats and set himself up as leader of the people. He proceeded to introduce some elements of comedy into the tragic scene. Believing himself inspired to command the movement, he selected for himself the title of "King of the Commons." Riding a horse, and with bay leaves sewn into his greasy hat, he led the hastily assembled mob to the work of destruction. However, he insisted that none of the nobility who fell into his hands were to be killed. Instead he forced them to serve him at meals;

on their knees, no less. One of the barons had to act as official food taster for this self-made master.

Geoffrey the Litster was one of the maddest of the worthless rogues who inevitably rise to the top under such circumstances. More will be told about him later.

At St. Albans, also, the uprising was directed against the abbey. One of the prime grievances of the people was that no one was allowed to grind his own corn or even to take the grain to a miller. The abbey held a monopoly and with an eye perhaps to security had set up the millstones within the sheltering shadow of the cloisters. Breaking their way in, the townspeople smashed the stones into such small pieces that each one was able to carry away a fragment as a memento of the day.

The men of East Kent rose early and laid siege to the tall castle which looked out over the walls of Rochester to the mouth of the Medway. The besiegers had been reinforced by levies from Essex and in some chronicles it is said that they numbered 30,000 men. What happened at Rochester would be duplicated centuries later when the *sansculottes* of Paris attacked the Bastille; sheer mass strength would triumph over high stone walls. The peasants used the trunks of trees to break in the doors and then smothered the garrison in hand-to-hand fighting. The governor capitulated when he found himself and what was left of his men penned in the upper reaches of the Keep.

And so it went in every part of southern and eastern England. Hatreds of long standing caused instantaneous explosions, in the course of which the common people struck, furiously and blindly, at institutions and people associated in their minds with oppression and injustice.

2

In the meantime the Road of the Pilgrims, running from London to Canterbury, was black with marching men. The doughty Wat, who was showing an unexpected skill in the handling of men, was hurrying with a picked band to the cathedral city to settle a long-standing score with Archbishop Simon. The sons of the soil had three counts against the primate. To vacate the post of chancellor for him, a fine soldier and friend of the people named Richard le Scrope had been removed from office. Simon had always worked hand in glove with John of Gaunt. And, finally, they had never forgiven him that slighting reference to pilgrimages. It was a race against time and only the youngest recruits were included in the fast-stepping band.

When the tatterdemalion horde (only 500 strong by one report) finished the twenty-five mile tramp, they were hungrier than ever and their beards had grown ragged and long. To their surprise, the gates were thrown open for them. The mayor of Canterbury welcomed them and the townspeople gave every indication of sympathy. And there was food for them, food a-plenty, served in the town square. They visited the cathedral, but Simon was not there. They searched his palace from top to bottom, burning masses of parchment and piles of illuminated books. The head of the church was not there either and they concluded he must be in London where the head officials of the king had gathered in the Tower. They turned immediately and began to retrace their steps.

A clamor for action was rising from the ranks. Nothing could prevent them from destroying a few manor houses on the way, without any consideration as to ownership, and burning all documents they could find. They killed all the Black Robes they encountered, a term applied to lawyers who always traveled in austere black gowns with inkhorns in their belts. They blamed all their misfortunes in the past on the connivance of men of the law.

Their numbers continued to swell. Thirty thousand from the success at Rochester fell into line, according to one chronicle. Word reached them hourly of the nation-wide scope of the uprising. Their confidence climbed and their cries of "By the Bowstring!" now carried a note of triumph. They demanded of everyone they passed adherence to the oath they had coined: "With King Richard and the true Commons."

Nearing Blackheath they overtook a member of the royal family hurrying to reach shelter after a visit to the shrine of St. Thomas at Canterbury, none other than the queen mother. She had always been popular with the people and was still called the Fair Maid, and so she had no reason to fear the ragged yeomen who suddenly swarmed about her. She was making the journey in a carriage, having become too stout to ride a palfrey. It was quite a remarkable contraption for that day and may very well have been invented and built for her special use. Certainly it was more elaborate than the whirlicote, a giglike conveyance which was used rarely, very rarely indeed, by the ladies of the nobility. One historian describes it as a wagon twenty feet long, red and gilt, with a high white hood on which the royal insignia of the white hart was painted. It would seem that in it the queen mother might enjoy comfort as well as security. But the condition of the roads had to be taken into consideration. When the marching peasantry overtook the carriage, the wheels were sunk deep in Kentish mud. Men-at-arms stood on guard while the royal servants struggled and sweated to make the mired wheels turn.

There are two versions of what followed. One is that the peasants helped to extract the wagon and that the queen mother showed her gratitude, and her desire to win their support, by allowing several of the more bold to kiss her and rub their bristling whiskers against her white cheeks.

The other story is that the marchers cheerfully put their shoulders to the wheel and hauled the coach out of the mud. This much accomplished, they expressed a desire to see the queen mother. One of the soldiers raised a corner of the curtain over the entrance to the hood and conveyed this desire to the royal lady within. Perhaps she had already peered out through some convenient peephole and had been both astonished and frightened by the numbers and the desperate appearance of the rebels. Perhaps with the hauteur of her position she felt it incumbent on her to refuse the request. At any rate the soldier reported that she had said no.

"Her Grace has no wish to speak with you," he said. Then he added, "For our part, gramercy for your help."

The story of the friendly bussing of the queen mother is the version most often told and believed; and it must be said that it has about it the colorful quality which wins a permanent acceptance for historical episodes. But there is a ring of authenticity about the second version. It can be more readily believed that the queen mother would maintain an aloof attitude, even though it might involve her in unpleasant consequences.

One way or the other, the royal lady was allowed to drive down the Pilgrimage Road in her creaking, swaying vehicle without any interference and with loud shouts of "For King Richard and the true Commons" to speed her on her way.

## CHAPTER VIII

# The Voice of John Ball

## 1

HISTORY has been disposed to accept the estimates of the number of peasants in revolt that were fixed in the chronicles of the period. Some place the total as high as 100,000; the more conservative say 30,000.

In reaching anything in the nature of an accurate figure it is necessary to call up a picture of the roads of the period. They were narrow and rough and inclined to follow the lines of least resistance, skirting hills and avoiding grades and creeping through forests like an adder's trail. Summer suns baked them to the consistency of hard clay and after a heavy rain they were almost impassable. Conceive, then, of fifty thousand men, say, marching down one of them, sun-browned and dusty of heel, stopping frequently for rests, delaying incessantly to forage for food, sleeping by the wayside, halting to talk excitedly with new recruits and to arrive at agreements on policy. A modern logistics expert could easily arrive at a reasonable solution; and the answer would be in days and weeks and not in hours. Take into consideration also that the country through which they marched had been decimated by the Black Death and that food was scarce enough even for the regular inhabitants. Unless each peasant had slung a bundle over his shoulder before starting out, filling it with the plain food on which he usually subsisted—bread crusts soaked in oil, dried beans and leeks, a few "curds and an oaten cake," and perhaps a parcel of his favorite dish, the *froise*, a form of pancake filled with bacon—there would have to be continuous halts to beg along the way, to raid orchards for unripe fruit and strip berry patches. That they carried much food is doubtful because of the dramatic suddenness with which it all began and the frenzy which had gripped them.

The truth, surely, is much closer to the minimum figure, and it is probable that the peasant body which finally took possession of London did not much exceed ten thousand. London, it should be recalled, was a crowded little town behind its low walls, depending on the supplies of food which came down on the river barges and from the country thereabouts. An invasion of lusty and empty-bellied tillers of the soil would soon strip bare the cupboard of London.

In point of time it is possible to be completely accurate. The revolt of the peasants, from the day when the groat collector yanked the kirtle from the shoulders of Wat the Tyler's daughter to the time when the last of them turned their backs on the capital city and began the homeward march, lasted a little over fourteen days, certainly the most grim and fateful fortnight in the history of England.

2

Allowing for such limitations, it was still a mighty throng which reached Blackheath and settled down there as a preliminary step to the occupation of London. It was said they came from both sides of the river but this seems impossible unless the bands from East Anglia commandeered boats to ferry them across the Thames; and again the law of logistics sets a limit to the number that could be accommodated in this way. Most of the expectant multitude which filled to overflowing the broad and bare strip of commons known as Blackheath came, therefore, from Kent and Sussex.

In those days Blackheath was a chalky stretch of empty land which adjoined the southern edge of the gardens around the royal demesne of Greenwich. In later centuries it would serve a variety of purposes. It would become a popular dueling ground. Highwaymen would lurk among the few scrub trees and hide in the yellow gorse and bracken. John Wesley would preach there to crowds which sometimes exceeded ten thousand. Gradually the tide of expansion would submerge it, first with lordly houses but later with the close-packed homes of poorer citizens. But in the days of the revolt Blackheath was no more than a place of rendezvous, a halting point for trade caravans and a playground for venturesome boys.

Here the marching peasants halted while their leaders strove to establish contact with the national officers who were known to have gathered about the young king in the Tower of London. As the unshaved and bone-weary men drew in their belts and stretched themselves out to sleep in such comfort as the heather provided, the word passed from mouth to mouth that on the next day John Ball would preach to them.

They were noisy when they rose in the morning. In anticipation of success they called to one another, waving their bills and staves above their heads, their eyes gleaming with excitement. Banners had been erected in all parts of the huge field and there was enough breeze to set them rustling. It has been said that John Ball stationed himself on a convenient stump, but no trees of any size had ever grown on this dreary stretch of rock and chalky soil. More likely he chose the highest hummock he could find. Whether stump or hummock, an altar was erected around it with cross and candles, and on each side the tallest of the banners were planted. While the men of Kent went down on their knees, a Mass was celebrated.

Then John Ball came forward and gazed about him in silence at the sea of upturned earnest faces, his own eyes filled with the love he felt for these brave fellows massed in front of him and waiting for his message. It is clear that his main purpose in speaking to them at this point was to strengthen their morale for the serious days ahead of them. In addition he saw the need to stiffen their backs so they would approach the men who ruled this land, where the laws of caste were so tightly and cruelly drawn, not as serfs creeping to the feet of their masters, but as men created in the image of God, with the courage to demand their rights. It is possible that he wanted to instill in them the will to behave with sobriety, to set aside their hates and their prejudices, to think only of the honest objectives which had brought them here.

He seems, at any rate, to have passed by the immediate problem of the groat tax, plunging at once into the broader questions of the laws and rules under which they lived.

"Good people," he began, his voice reaching to the farthest corner of the commons, "things will never be well in England as long as goods are not held in common. And as long as there are villeins and gentlemen."

A cheer was raised at this bold utterance, but the arm of the hedge priest cut it short by gesturing for silence.

"Why," he demanded, "do they hold us in serfage?" Another uncontrollable cheer and again the demanding sweep of the arm. "They go clothed in velvet and warm in their furs and their ermines while we are covered with rags. They have wine and spices and fine bread; and we have oat cake and straw and water to drink. They have leisure and fine houses; and we have pain and labor, the rain and the wind in the fields." How well he knew what it meant to lack a roof over his head and a bed, this pilgrim of twenty years! "And yet," he added, "it is of us and of our toil that these men hold their state."

The crowd kept their feelings in check while he enlarged on the injustices under which they suffered, and under which their children and their children's children would live if they themselves did not now stand out for change. Sometimes a cry would be wrung from an emotional listener, but for the most part the peasants listened in silence. Much of what he said they had heard before, when he had preached at a village cross or declared himself boldly in the comparative safety of a forest glade. But now for the first time a voice was proclaiming their beliefs so openly that all England would come to hear.

Finally the eloquent priest reached a pause before delivering his concluding passage. His eyes swept over the closely packed audience, taking in the roads and the low roofs of the suburb to the west, and reaching as far as the gray stone of the royal walls. The morning sun was climbing back of him and flooding the field with light, as though to cast all possible illumination on this memorable moment in history. Raising his voice to its highest pitch, as John Wesley would do centuries later in speaking to the sober thousands who gathered about him, John Ball expressed his concluding thought in a couplet which has come down the ages and will never be forgotten.

> *When Adam delved and Eve span,*
> *Who was then the gentleman?*

For a moment there was silence and then his listeners realized that he had reached an end, and a mighty shout went up which could be heard far beyond the privileged gardens of Greenwich. They cried out with one voice that no one else would they accept as head of the church in England but John Ball, and that none else should sit in Westminster in the courts of the chancellery to administer the laws.

### 3

John Ball does not appear much in the records after this, not at least until the tragic concluding scenes. He is mentioned once as being seen in London when the rioting and the burning and the slaying began. There is no mention of him in the highly dramatic contacts between court and mob, and this is strange because his presence and his voice, after the speech at Blackheath, would seem inevitable and essential. If all had been going well he would have stood beside Wat the Tyler when the young king rode out to face the peasants.

It seems possible that he had realized the sorry truth that leaders of popular causes have to face sooner or later; that an issue, based on idealistic reasoning, cannot hold men together for any great length of time. Few are capable of holding to a faith without any concern for personal satisfaction or gain. A certain proportion of every mass recruited to demand a change or to further a cause will seize the opportunity offered for looting and thievery. Still more will let their emotions involve them in uncontrollable excesses, in the destruction of property and the massacre of those who stand in their way. It was too much to expect that all of these many thousands of angry peasants could be held for long on a tight rein or under any form of discipline. John Ball, being a zealot and a dreamer of dreams, had not realized how quickly the men who had rallied to the ringing of the bell would get out of hand. An effort was made to enforce discipline, as will be evident later in the story of what happened at the Savoy, and it is not unreasonable to believe that this was the work of John Ball. It proved, unfortunately, as futile a gesture as Canute's airy demand to the tides to turn back and leave the sands dry for the soles of his royal feet.

It is certain that the eloquent priest was disillusioned and saddened by the madness of the forces he had unleashed. With the prescience of a true leader, he must have seen what the ending would be.

It is quite probable, however, that he did nothing to prevent the first large-scale riot which resulted in the burning of Southwark. Clustering thickly on the southern banks of the Thames, Southwark was at this time the home of the very poor and the unfortunate, living in misery and in close proximity to the evil and the criminal. It was natural perhaps that many prisons had been established here—the Marshalsea, the King's Bench, the Compter, and the Clink. The name "clink" may have come from the sound of the turning of a key. At any rate, it seemed so appropriate that it was used later for prisons elsewhere, generally for ones which were small and mean. The district contained as well the Stews, which included the Street of the Women. The peasants overran Southwark, broke open the prisons, released the prisoners, and burned the Street of the Women to the ground.

Across the river the citizens of London watched the sack of Southwark with a rising sense of fear. Would the city itself meet the same fate at the hands of the savage peasantry? Among the watchers was William Walworth, the mayor of London, who had the best of reasons for anger and dismay. He leased the land on which the Stews stood from the Bishop of Winchester and undoubtedly the revenue he derived from it was large. A shrewd man of business, he was said to have filled the houses with young women from Flanders, who were plump and blonde and attracted a good clientele. Was not the largest of the houses called the Sign of the Cardinal's Hat?

Walworth saw his investment south of the river go up in a blaze much redder than any form of clerical headgear, and his feeling against the rioting countrymen ran deep and strong. Turn again, Walworth (to borrow from an incident in the century following), lord mayor of London;

and observe the end which often comes to ventures of this kind.

William Walworth is an enigma, even in this period when men's motives were likely to be mixed. He was shrewd and bold in a crisis and he had no fear in him. He was free-handed in civic matters. Knighted for his part throughout this forbidding fortnight, there still clings to his name the halo of historical praise. Portraits of him were hung in prominent places, such as the Fishmongers Hall, and he was often represented in pageants and civic ritual. But in assessing the man it is impossible to overlook his control of the Stews.

## CHAPTER IX

# Not a Blow Struck, Not a Head Broken

**1**

THE queen mother came creaking in her red and gilt carriage across London Bridge and into the Tower well ahead of the peasants. The report she gave was a terrifying one: the countryside inundated with invaders, men without hats, with glaring eyes, with heavy beards, men who talked a strange lingo and who laughed and sang strange songs. They had followed close on her heels and would soon be pounding on London's gates for admittance. The young king and his advisers heard her story with pale, set faces. The danger was more imminent than they had supposed. What was to be done?

It is hard to understand why the group about the king had neglected to take any vigorous steps to meet this crisis. And yet perhaps not; they were, it must be said, a weak lot. The royal uncles were all away: John of Gaunt in Scotland, Edmund of Cambridge with the fleet on a mission to Portugal (which proved a futile one), and Thomas of Woodstock on some business or other in the Marcher country. Not that they were missed particularly; none had the judgment and force of character to control this situation with a firm hand. The group also included Simon of Sudbury in his dual capacity as archbishop and chancellor, and Hales, the treasurer, who was blamed for the poll tax. Richard's half brothers on the Holland side were there, neither of whom had the right kind of heart or mind, a proud, quarrelsome, swaggering pair. The king's cousin, Henry of Bolingbroke, was in the group. He was to play a leading part in the tragedy of Richard's life; but at this stage he was a fast-growing stripling of fifteen years. Three members of the baronage completed the number: the youthful Earl of Oxford and two veteran earls of the French campaigns, Warwick and Salisbury. All of them heard the queen mother's story without volunteering any opinion.

The aging archbishop was the first to make a move. He placed the Great Seal of England on the table and begged to be allowed to retire at once from public office. It was not from fear that he acted but because he did not feel himself capable of coping with the situation. The others stared at him with stony eyes, but did not move. Ordinarily there was not a man in England who would not have welcomed the chance to take the seals of office, but under the circumstances not a soul in the room wanted to assume the responsibility.

There were two men in London with enough vigor and decision to break through this inertia in official circles. One was Mayor William Walworth, who did not want to see the city fall into destructive hands. The other was Sir Robert Knowles, who had been counted in the French wars as second only to that amazing soldier Old John Hawkwood as a leader of the *condottiere*. Knowles had a mansion in London large enough to house the garrison of 120 trained soldiers he still kept about him. If the royal council, that inept and fumbling lot, had seen fit to transfer all authority to the old soldier, he would have handled the situation with vigor and decision.

Walworth had already taken one step. As soon as the queen mother's conveyance had crossed London Bridge, he had raised the drawbridge between two of the central piers and so made it impossible for the rebels to take the only easy way into London. When summoned to appear before the palefaced group about the king, he declared he could arm and throw into action a force of 6000 men. The members of the council looked at him with doubt in their eyes. Was he certain the Trained Bands would follow him? Walworth, the type of man who was always sure, said yes, they could be depended on to serve under him. He had a high opinion of the importance of his office, this Mayor Walworth. Once the Sergeants of the Coif had tried to seat ahead of him at a public dinner a member of the nobility below the rank of earl, which was against the recognized rules of procedure. His eyes blazing above his forked beard, Walworth had stamped out of the hall. But he failed to convince this solemn and almost impotent group. They were very doubtful of London's loyalty.

With the best of reasons, it may be said. The criminal population of the city would support the rebels, from the Upright Man at the top to the lowest sack-law cuffin. The apprentices were lively and pugnacious and opposed to all authority. When the storm broke, there would be cries of "Clubs! Up, Clubs!" and the apprentices would swarm out of shops and warehouses, every man jack of them armed and panting for action. But it would not be to help enforce the feeble edicts of the royal circle but to take sides with the men from Kent. Among the solid citizens, the owners of property and of guild memberships, there was a definite feeling of discontent. It was even whispered, and with good reason, that some of the aldermen were infected with the same fever for change which had aroused the peasantry to active rebellion.

One step was decided upon, a feeble measure. A committe of aldermen would be sent to Blackheath for the purpose of issuing a warning to the rebels. Three were chosen: Adam Carlisle, John Fresch, and John Horne. The first two followed out their instructions, even going a step further and warning the army of disorder to return to their homes at once. Horne had other ideas. During the trials which followed the revolt, it was stated that, while Carlisle and Fresch harangued the mobs who crowded about them, Horne took Wat Tyler and several of the other leaders aside.

"Pay no heed to these who came with me," he whispered. "They speak with crooked tongues. Listen to me and believe. You have your cause won, for the whole of London is ready to rise. Cause a tumult around the gates and at the Bridge and you'll find the city ready for you. I speak for those who know their minds and don't change sides twice a day."

Accordingly, three of Tyler's most trusty men accompanied the alderman back to the city and were present at a secret meeting of disaffected citizens in the house of one Thomas Farringdon. They all favored forced entry the following morning. Plans of the city were poured over and the black forefinger of a rebel traced the line of the river to a spot on the north shore, somewhere between Ludgate and Westminster, where there apparently stood a place of considerable importance.

"And this?" he asked.

He was told it was the Savoy, the great palace packed with untold treasures, from the cellars to the tops of the crenelated walls, which belonged to the wealthy, discriminating, and thoroughly hated John of Gaunt.

No comment was made beyond perhaps an "ah!" from the men who had come to spy out the land.

It later came out at the trials that Horne went to Mayor Walworth immediately after and assured him the mission of the aldermen had been successful. They had found the rebels honestly anxious for a peaceful settlement.

"I'll wager my head," he is reported to have said, "that they won't do any damage if they're allowed inside the walls."

Horne, very clearly, was confident that the court faction was going to be overturned.

2

The next step was taken by the royal council on the urgent insistence of the young king himself. Sir John Newton, who had commanded the garrison of Rochester Castle and had been held as a hostage, came to the Tower with a message from the rebels. He first assured the official group that he was acting under duress and under oath, moreover, to convey the wishes of the peasants exactly as they had been expressed to him.

"They profess loyalty to the king," he declared. "They want a chance to lay before him the grievances they hold against his councilors and his ministers of state. Even against other members of the royal family. All these, they hold, have been mismanaging the land."

Richard, no doubt, had never forgotten the impression he made when he was taken to the House of Commons before the old king died. He recalled that the members had been so impressed that they had demanded he be declared heir to the throne at once and that he be allowed the titles his father had held. This triumph had sunk deep into his juvenile mind. Would not these ill-born and unlettered hordes be equally impressed if they had a chance to see him? Was he not four years older now? Every day during those four years he had listened to his praises being sounded.

Whether or not this had any part in his decision, he announced to his reluctant councilors that he intended to meet the rebels. After it had been decided to act on his wish, Newton was sent back to tell the peasants the king would come down the river the next morning as far as Greenwich and would listen to what they had to say.

Early the following day the state barge started out, with most of the royal councilors grouped anxiously about the royal minor. Four other barges followed. The weather was warm and fine and the sun was climbing in a cloudless sky. What better augury could there be for the success of this daring move?

The river banks about Greenwich were black with the peasant hordes, and to the nervous eyes on the barges it was only too clear that this was a mob completely lacking in order and discipline. Some cheers were raised for the gaily dressed king standing on the prow, but most of the voices were clamoring loudly for the heads of his unpopular ministers. Froissart says they were brandishing their weapons and "shrieking like men possessed." It was an awesome spectacle, without a doubt. Not waiting for orders, the men in charge of the barges brought them to a standstill a considerable distance from the shore.

Still confident of his power to control the situation, the boy king stepped close to the rail of the royal barge.

"Sirs," he cried, in a voice which adolescence made shrill and high, "I have come to listen. What want ye?"

The rebels did not leave it to their leaders to answer. They began to cry out that they could not talk with him unless he came ashore. The noise was so great that Richard had no chance to make himself heard again.

It is not on record that the king made any further efforts, but the men about him would not have permitted him to go ashore. It would be the height of folly, so ran their minds, to deliver him thus into their hands to be held as a hostage. The Earl of Salisbury called out that an audience was impossible under these circumstances. It is even said he protested that the noisy petitioners were not suitably dressed to face the king, but this, surely, is beyond belief.

They swung the barges about and began the return trip. The oars dipped and swayed and the backs of the rowers strained at the task, while the men about the youthful king watched the crowded shores with apprehensive eyes. They knew that a single discharge of arrows from the longbows that many of the peasants carried over their shoulders would sweep the barges like a lethal hail.

But not a bow was bent nor a single bolt launched against the cloudless sky. It was clear that the peasants were sincere in their devotion to the youthful king.

3

The effort to confer with Richard having failed, the men from Kent began to march in angry haste toward London Bridge. Another disaffected alderman comes into the story at this point, Walter Sibley, whose district was Billingsgate. He was posted on the bridge with a small company of men, and his instructions were to prevent the lowering of the drawbridge. Whether from fear or because he was in accord with the plans drawn up the previous night, he took one look at the multitudes assembling at the southern end and threw up his hands.

"We can't hold out," he said to his supporters.

Signaling to drop the bridge, he turned and led his company from behind in an exit from the great stone bridge.

If a pause is permissible at this stage, something should be said about London Bridge. This miracle in stone (for in the eyes of all men it was nothing short of miraculous) had been started in 1176 by Peter of Colechurch, a charity priest. It had been built to stand for all time. Starting at the foot of Fish Street by the church of St. Magnus the Martyr, it stretched to the far shore. It was carried by twenty stone piers about which the daily tides and freshets of Father Thames roiled and protested in vain. It was no less than forty feet wide, and the citizens of London Town had quickly availed themselves of the possibilities of this broad highway, building shops and houses and even chapels on both sides. Life on the bridge had many advantages. A man in trade was afforded the chance to attract the eye of a visitor before he reached the city, and in no part of town were the apprentices more vociferous in their chorus of "What lack ye?" "Come, sir, a bolt of the best cloth?" "A pair of shoes?" "A gaud for your lady?" The mere householder enjoyed a vista of ever changing excitement: the wool barges coming down the river, the heavily weighted tin boats, the foreign ships sailing as far up the estuary as their tonnage allowed, the arrival and departure of notables. By dropping a bucket on a rope they could scoop in a quick supply of fresh water or a piece of ice in the spring.

They probably did not count it a disadvantage that over their homes on elevated pikes were the heads of men who had died at the block, staring up the river with empty sockets (for the crows found the human eye a delectable morsel), the flesh rotting and falling off in reeking strips. It needed the elevation of a new head to win the attention of the bridge dwellers.

Close by the central arch, which formed the drawbridge, was a chapel in which lay the bones of Peter of Colechurch. It is conceivable that he turned in his grave on this warm June morning, for never before had his great bridge witnessed anything like the passing of the peasants. Without so much as a pause at the toll booths, they came in perfect order. The leaders rode on horseback, followed by three swaying banners of the insurrection (with slogans coined, no doubt, by John Ball), and after them an endless parade of ragged and determined men, gathered into companies according to the county or town from which they came, on their now ragged tunics the medals of pilgrimage which they had purchased for themselves in Canterbury. They marched four abreast, the tramp of their feet sounding without any cessation hour after hour.

John Horne's promises were borne out. The peasant army met with no opposition. The apprentices were out to welcome them, waving their clubs and screeching loudly. The brothers of the salamon (a term much in use in the cant of the crooks) had slunk out from their cellars and the dark corners of deserted mews, ready to bear a hand in breaking open the prisons and in pillaging the houses of wealthy citizens. The substantial burghers, anxious to make the best of it, offered food to these hungry seekers of justice. The peasants partook of their hospitality with voracious appetites, and it is said that a few of them paid for their meals!

An extraordinary occasion, indeed, a day long to be remembered: June 13, when the embattled tillers of the soil took over the city of London without opposition of any kind. Not a blow struck, not a head broken.

### 4

With well-filled stomachs, the invaders turned to the pleasing prospect of revenge. They knew that John of Gaunt was away, but down the Thames stood his great palace. "To the Savoy!" was the almost unanimous cry.

The leaders were still in control and strict orders were issued that there must be no thievery and no killing. Any man who tried to benefit from the loot of this royal structure must suffer as Achan did; Achan, the son of Israel who secreted gold and silver after the walls of Jericho fell and who was taken out on Joshua's orders and stoned to death.

At first these strict injunctions were obeyed. The household at the palace was permitted to leave, even Gaunt's beautiful mistress and future wife, Katharine Swynford, who had been left there in possession with her children. The walls of the Great Hall were stripped of priceless tapestries and silver sconces, the prayer rugs from the East and the rare weapons and relics. The State Chambers were ransacked, and the Privy Suite where the duke's red velvet bed stood. In the Avalon Chamber was the marble mantel which had taken two years to carve, the most beautiful possession of all. The mantel was hacked to pieces with furious picks. The bancas of oriental woods (a special form of bench) were carried out to the courtyard and thrown into the bonfires already blazing high. The gold and silver plate was hacked into small pieces, so small that each bit could be carried off under a belt as a souvenir of the day. One man disregarded the stern orders which had been issued. He secreted a silver goblet of rare design under his jerkin. Still conscious of the need for sobriety and honesty, and remembering the fate meted out to Achan, the rioters took this miscreant and drowned him in the river.

Others were more successful. A group of men from Rochester got their hands on the duke's strongbox which contained a veritable fortune, £1000 no less. They managed to smuggle it out of the grounds and vanished across the river in the direction of Southwark.

During the looting, a ceremonial cloak belonging to Duke John was found in the Privy Suite, a handsome thing of Lancastrian blue with pearls sewn in the sleeve embroideries. This was stretched around the trunk of a tree and those who had their bows with them proceeded to fill it with arrows. No other incident was as significant of the depth of personal hatred the common people had conceived for this glossy son of the old king.

As soon as the hatred of the mob had been thus vented in the destruction of the execrated duke's treasures, they exploded some barrels of gunpowder and sent the building up in flames. By nightfall nothing was left of the magnificence which the duke had gathered about him. The fire trapped some members of the mob who had broken into the cellars and ensconced themselves before the pipes of rare wines. Their cries were not heard until the fire was out of control, and they were burned alive.

It should be made clear that the loot of the Savoy was not the work exclusively of the peasants. Many of the lower orders of the citizenry joined in the work of destruction and were much less scrupulous in their handling of the costly contents. Many a cutpurse had rings and precious stones hidden away in secret pockets under belts. Many apprentices thereafter flaunted belts of Spanish leather and purses of velvet.

Having thus cast discretion and sobriety to the winds, the men who had marched to London to demand justice and had turned to license proceeded to burn the Temple to the ground. They turned out the archives and threw all the state and legal papers into the bonfires. The lawyers, the Black Robes, had departed long before, being shrewd enough to know that the mobs could not be held in check, and thereby had saved their skins.

The alien residents were less fortunate. A lust for blood had risen with the flames. Many aliens from Flanders, merchants and dealers in wool and cloth, had fled to sanctuary, but the mob paid no heed to the rules of the church. They dragged these unfortunate and innocent men out from the church shadows where they cowered and butchered them in the streets.

The prisons of the Fleet and Newgate were then broken open, and the exultant brothers of the salamon welcomed their fellows who had been lying there in irons, some with limbs limp from the rack and with the mark of the white-hot branding iron on cheeks and forehead. It was a wild and desperate night in London. The citizens put up their shutters, bolted them tight, and huddled behind them, trembling for the safety of their families, while bands of drunken rioters paraded the streets, carrying the dripping heads of victims on the ends of pikes.

The final stage was to march on the Tower and to encamp in a tight circle about it. Here, they knew, were the men whom they sought, in particular, Simon of Sudbury and treasurer Hales, who was called Hobbe the Robber in the rhyming letters of John Ball. No one inside the great Norman keep must be allowed to escape.

And so the peasants slept in the fields about the Tower, while their sentries kept close watch outside the walls. The frightened group about the king, who had not yet decided on any sound course of action, kept vigil on the battlements, watching the fires of the Savoy and the Temple slowly die down, hearing the drunken uproar in the streets, and wondering what the morning would bring.

## CHAPTER X

## The Boy King Takes Hold

### 1

THE boy Richard took matters into his youthful hands after a long discussion with his circle of advisers which lasted through several hours of that eventful night. The two men of action, Walworth and Knowles, were present. The former was strongly for an armed sortie, although the number of men-at-arms in the Tower did not exceed 600 in number. With his usual bluff confidence, he visioned the loyal citizens rallying to their support. Salisbury was too conservative to agree with this.

"If we begin what we can't carry through," he declared with a sober shake of head, "it will be all over with us. And with our heirs. And England will be a desert."

If Sir Robert Knowles declared himself (one always recalls the couplet about him in the French campaigns—*Sir Robert Knowles all France Controls*), it must have been on the side of caution. He was too sound a soldier to discount the longbows he had seen on so many rebel shoulders. English yeomen with that deadly weapon could sweep the narrow streets clean of royal supporters.

Richard must have missed the friendly pressure of one hand on his shoulder during these perilous days. Sir Simon Burley, who had become the mainstay and affectionate mentor of the young monarch, was not in London. He was in Bohemia, negotiating a match for Richard with a princess of the Hungarian royal family. Lacking the guiding whisper of this friend, and finding his advisers at odds, Richard finally pronounced himself in favor of opening negotiations with the peasant leaders.

The council would consent at first to half measures only. Two knights were sent out to run the gamut of the sentry lines and get to the heads of the insurrection with an offer from the king to consider all grievances which were submitted to him in writing. The knights got as far as St. Catherine's Wharf on the river but their announcement, made under the light of torches, drew laughter and hoots of derision.

"Trifles and mockery!" cried the rebels. "Think you we are Anthony pigs to come snuffling and begging of ye?" An Anthony pig was an animal too diseased to be used by the butchers and which, after having its ears slit for identification, was turned loose to survive or die in the streets of London.

"Get ye back!" was the final word given the messengers, "and bring us a fair offer. The king must talk to his loyal commons face to face."

Richard decided then to do as the peasants demanded and won the reluctant consent of his council. Word was sent back that he would ride next morning to Mile End and meet the leaders there. Mile End was an open stretch of ground outside the walls near Aldgate. Here Londoners went on holidays and Sundays to promenade and fill their lungs with fresh air. It was said later that the council consented because it might be possible to leave the Tower and even close all the city gates if the peasants marched en masse beyond the walls.

No surprise need be felt when it is recorded that Richard and a small chosen company rode out from the Tower at seven o'clock next morning. Men were early risers because the medieval myth still held that whereas the day belonged to God the night was the devil's own. It was the custom for men to bolt the shutters and go to bed, concealing their heads under blankets, as soon as the sun went down and to be up with the first light of dawn. Kings were no different from ordinary men on this point. It is certain that Richard had taken a bath (he was regular in attention to the rules of cleanliness, an example which most of the nobility and even some of the Plantagenets refused to follow), dressed with meticulous care, and had partaken of a solid breakfast before getting to horse.

There was an immediate disappointment for those who had entertained the hope that Wat Tyler would lead all his men to the meeting place. The lines about the Tower opened to let the royal party ride through and then closed tightly. Guards were maintained on all the gates of London. The leaders were not to be taken in as easily as that.

It was so uncomfortably warm that the pennons with the White Hart hung limply on the spears of the outriders, and the white plume in the small hat of the boy king, which had to be buttoned under his chin, lay perfectly flat. The peasants swarmed about the horsemen, attempting to seize the king's stirrups and reins and bawling loudly their demands for changes in the laws and the punishment of the head ministers. For a long time the horses had to be kept at a walk, and if the unwashed and unshaven peasants felt any degree of loyalty it did not show. The ride through the city, in fact, was like a nightmare, one which might end in violence at any moment.

When they passed Aldgate, however, the horsemen had more freedom. The king's two half brothers took advantage of this to drop out of line and then wheel their horses on to the north road, disappearing quickly from sight. These admirable young noblemen had no stomach for more of this kind of adventure.

The rebel leaders had heard much of the beauty (no other word seems to fit the case) of this king of fourteen years and, of course, they had caught fleeting glimpses of him on the royal barge. Now, for the first time, they met him face to face.

He was of good height for his years but he lacked the virility which had always been characteristic of the Plantagenets. There was almost a transparency about his slightly olive skin, and his features had a delicacy in contrast to the sharp, bold regularity of his immediate ancestors. He was elaborately attired in a coat of blue and silver, cut on the order of a tabard; and this was not wise. A better impression would have been made if he had come in plainer garb. As it was, Wat Tyler and his rough fellows must have gaped at this resplendent vision, a figure straight out of folklore.

The boy king had ridden to Mile End in a mood to conciliate the insurgents. Without taking a foot from the silver stirrups and, in spite of the heat, keeping his slender white hands in jeweled gloves, he listened to the demands of the unkempt multitudes as propounded by their leaders, Wat Tyler, Jack Straw, and others—but not John Ball. As no mention was made of the eloquent priest, it must be assumed that he was not there.

Richard listened with the ease of manner of a veteran. He asked questions, discussed the knottiest of the points raised, even smiled, a rare thing for one of his haughty lineage when confronted with men of such low degree. He nodded in confirmation of five important points.

1. Villeinage was to be abolished.

2. The *corvée* was to be abolished (the obligation to work for the lord of the manor on demand).

3. The peasants would have the status of tenants and pay four pence an acre per year to the owner.

4. Restrictions on buying and selling would be removed.

5. A general amnesty would be extended to all participants in the uprising.

An effort was made by the peasants to include in the agreement a promise that the ministers of the Crown who were obnoxious to the Commons would be punished. On this point the young king, who seems to have conducted himself with dignity and firmness, refused to give in.

"There shall be due punishments," he declared, "for those who can be proven traitors by due process of law." Further than that he would not go.

For many hours thereafter a corps of tabellions from Westminster, thirty in all, labored at writing charters containing these agreements. A copy was to be provided for each district represented in the ranks of the seekers after freedom. A banner would accompany each charter, to be carried home as an earnest of agreement.

A feeling of confidence now permeated the rebel ranks. Their demands had been met.

2

But while the youthful king conferred with the rebel leaders, and everything seemed to be moving with the speed of Mercury toward the desired ends, the city was thrown into scenes as violent as on the previous day. This may have been planned by the leaders, but the more reasonable explanation was that the rank and file were now completely out of hand and that their feelings flared into murder and rapine as soon as all restraints were removed. It is affirmed that Wat Tyler returned to the city in time to lead the new riots. This is highly improbable. There was no reason at that point to doubt the honesty of the concessions made by the king. No leader with any judgment (and Tyler had displayed plenty of that quality) would risk what they had gained by an outburst of class hatred.

Young Richard was badly served through this crisis. The officers at the Tower, whether through carelessness or sympathy with the uprising, neglected to raise the drawbridge after the king and his party rode off to Mile End. No defense was attempted when the peasants who had been left on watch swarmed in under the portcullis, still suspended high over the gate.

"Where are the traitors?" was the cry raised, making it clear that the archbishop and the treasurer were the chief targets of their enmity. "Where are those who plunder the people?"

They searched the rooms of the king, even peering behind the velvet curtains and under the royal bed. Next they visited the queen mother and pried with their weapons under the bed on which she was reclining. The poor lady had already seen too much of these rough men from the fields and forests and she fainted dead away. As soon as they could, her maids dressed her and she was taken, in a state of shock, to one of the barges and rowed up the river to the Wardrobe.

It should be explained, in passing, that although London was spoken of as small and crowded, it was in reality a city of many great palaces. The large landowners, who had acquired wealth through the wool trade, had all set up establishments in the city. The de Veres, who held the earldom of Oxford, were at St. Mary Axe, the Earls of Essex on Throgmorton Street. Between Amen Corner and Ludgate Street the high tower of the Earls of Richmond stood up against the skyline. Oddly enough the great barons seemed to prefer the center of the city, in fact, the very heart of commerce. The FitzAlans lived on Botolph Lane, which was narrow and mean and much too close to the fish market. The FitzWalters were in the Poultry and the Stafford family, the Earls of Buckingham, were on Milk Street.

One writer claims that London contained more fine palaces than the Italian cities of Venice, Florence, Verona, and Genoa combined. Few of them, it must be said, had any pretensions to beauty (except the ill-fated Savoy), consisting of tall grim walls jutting up above the level of the parish churches and the two-storied huddles of lath and plaster where the townspeople lived. But they gave security, something which the Wardrobe lacked. That the queen mother chose it is strange because it shared the shadow of St. Paul's Cross with Baynard's Castle, which had come into the possession of the royal family and was an imposing structure. Perhaps it was felt that the insignificance of the Wardrobe would offer more protection than stone walls and tall ramparts.

Early in the morning, when the first rays of the sun apprised the unhappy city that God's sway was starting again, Archbishop Simon went, on the king's urgent advice, to the Little Water-gate where a boat was ready to take him away to safety. But an old beldam saw what was happening and raised an outcry. Realizing he could not escape from the inevitable pursuit, the prelate returned to the Tower, no doubt looking up at the sun with saddened eyes and thinking this would be his last glimpse of it.

The archbishop was saying Mass in the Tower chapel when the eruption occurred. He knew that his end was near, but his voice did not falter as he chanted the Seven Penitential Psalms and the Litany. When the door burst open and the drunken rioters (they had been drinking all night, quite clearly) filled the chapel with their shouts of "Where is the traitor?" the old man stepped forward to meet them.

"Behold the archbishop whom ye seek," he said in a calm voice. "No traitor, no plunderer of the Commons, he."

While he was speaking, his arms were pinioned from behind. He was then led up to the battlements where he could be seen by the cheering crowds now filling the courtyards, and even by those who stood without the walls.

For the death sentence which the infuriated people were determined to see carried out on Tower Hill there was neither block nor executioner. A substitute for a block was found and finally one man, who came from Essex and was named John Starling, volunteered to wield the ax. The arms of the victim were unbound and he was given a few minutes to pray and to deliver any last message.

"Take heed," he said, raising his voice, "my beloved children in the Lord, what thing ye now do. For what offense is it that ye doom to death your pastor, your prelate? Oh, take heed lest for the act of this day all England be laid under the curse of the interdict."

His captors were beyond any fear of interdict or Pope. The old man was ordered to lay his head on the improvised block. This he did with no signs of fear.

The nervous hand of the volunteer headsman was so lacking in precision that the first bow did no more than inflict a deep wound in the prelate's neck. The aged man could not repress a cry of anguish.

"Ah! Ah! *Manus domini est!*"

Instinctively he raised a hand to the wound, and the ax, falling for the second time, amputated some of his fingers. The victim gave no further signs of his terrible suffering, even though it took eight blows in all to sever his head.

Later the man Starling stalked about London, with the ax suspended around his neck, boasting loudly that his had been the hand which killed the archbishop. When, inevitably, he was brought to the gallows, he continued to exult in the part he had played.

Blood ran freely all through the hours of this terrible day. Treasurer Hales, a Franciscan friar named William Apuldore, who served as the king's confessor, and John Legge, collector-in-chief of the poll tax, died on Tower Hill after the venerable churchman. One hundred and fifty Flemish residents were dragged from their homes or from the churches where they had sought sanctuary and killed without mercy or delay. Many lawyers shared their fate. Houses were looted and burned.

This was not the work exclusively of the peasants. The city had fallen into an anarchy in which people paid off grudges by killing those who had offended them or by bringing false witness against them. Some debtors killed their creditors, thinking their culpability would go undetected in these mad and bloody hours. The undisciplined apprentices took revenge in the killing of their masters. The criminals of the city were everywhere, taking the major share of the rewards from the rape of London.

It was stated in the *Anonimalle* Chronicle that everything had been planned and that the peasant leaders urged the intoxicated mobs to slay and burn; and this has been solemnly affirmed by many historians. But it is inconceivable that it was part of a concerted plan. Most of the peasants asked for nothing better than the chance to get their wrongs righted in an orderly way and then march home to their families and their work in the fields as quickly as possible. It was the dregs who remained, the men who had lost sight of the issues, who led the revolt.

It seems certain, nonetheless, that much of the madness and the destruction can be traced to the megalomania of Wat the Tyler. He and his group of leaders seem to have conducted their part of the talks at Mile End in a reasonably rational way. Perhaps he was surprised by the wide scope of the king's concessions. Perhaps, on returning to the city, he drank with the rank and file in an exuberance of triumph. Whatever the reason, the power he wielded went to the head of the leader. Visions of personal grandeur filled his mind as he hobnobbed with his followers, these once humble men who had been roused to assert their rights and who now saw themselves as masters of the realm.

On this fateful Friday night, after the meeting with the king, Wat the Tyler behaved like a new-made dictator. Although the large party of the peasantry, the better part, had taken their charters and their banners and were tramping with weary feet the long road home, he continued to lord it in town among the baser elements and the more subservient of his followers.

"I will go wherever I please," he announced, gesturing in a grand manner. "There are twenty thousand of my stout fellows to go with me and help enforce my will. As for those who would oppose me, I shall shave their beards for them!"

The boast won loud plaudits, for what he meant was that he would cut off the heads of those who stood in his way.

"There will be no laws in England," he ranted, "saving those I declare. With my own mouth shall I declare them!"

The following day was marked by a diminishing of violence and a tendency to make excursions into territory close to the city in search of loot and victims. London still cringed, nevertheless, under the reign of terror. The shutters of all shops and homes remained bolted.

During the afternoon an unexpected message was received by Wat from the royal council, in which it was suggested that, inasmuch as the insurgents were not sufficiently content to accept the promises of the king by departing for their homes, a further conference be held. They were invited to meet the king before nightfall.

What sudden weakening on the part of the king's councilors had led to this pusillanimous attitude can be no more than a matter of conjecture. It may have been due to the conditions they encountered on returning from Mile End and the fears they felt as they sat in the turrets of the Tower and looked down on the seething streets and the fires which burned in all directions. It might be their heads which would roll in the dust the following day unless the fury of the mobs could be appeased.

And so one king had spoken to another; the delicate and dandified boy had found it necessary to approach the powerful head of the peasantry of England. He, Wat the Tyler, would go to this meeting and be much more demanding. In the meantime he spluttered and declaimed his greatness to those about him.

No other explanation can be given for the strange turn events took on that day.

## CHAPTER XI

# "I Will Be Your Chief and Captain"

1

UNDER the wall near Aldgate stood the hospital of St. Bartholomew and a short distance farther into the open fields was the priory. The hospital was a venerable institution which had been founded by Rahere, the court jester of Henry I. The pay of royal buffoons was small enough, but they generally had the ear of the king and so had opportunities to make fortunes for themselves. Rahere had applied his perquisites to a noble purpose. Beyond these buildings that he had raised stretched the plains of Smithfield, famous for its fairs and markets. Every Friday there was a cattle sale which drew large crowds.

This historic suburb served another purpose which drew even greater crowds. It was the place of execution. Tyburn would take that distinction from it in the following reign, but Smithfield had already witnessed many of the saddest events in English history. The end of the road for so many men, and women, was in the Elms which lay between a horse pool and Tunmill Brook. The first champion of the rights of the common people during the Norman period had died here, William FitzOsbert, popularly known as Longbeard. Most distressing of all had been the bitter day when Scotland's peerless leader, William Wallace, was taken from the Tower and dragged at the heels of horses to Smithfield, to be hanged, drawn, and quartered, the inhuman method of execution first used in the reign of Edward I, by which the disemboweling was done while the victim still lived.

It was reserved for Smithfield to bear the notoriety of the religious burnings, first in the reign of Henry VIII and, then, in that of his neurotic daughter, Mary. Here died an unsung martyr named John Badby, who was chained in a tun lined with tar, which burned much more fiercely than wooden faggots; here also the end came for one of the most beautiful and brave of women, gentle Anne Askew. Here the stout bishops were brought to be chained to the stake and burned for the constancy of their faith.

The most grueling exhibition occurred in the time of that kindly ruler, Burly King Harry, when two people convicted as poisoners were boiled alive while thousands watched in fascinated horror.

It was Smithfield that Richard had selected for his final parley with the insurgents.

2

The appointed time was the hour of vespers. Before taking to horse, the young king spent some time with a confessor and received absolution. Those who were to go with him filed through the Shrine of the Confessor for the same consolations. Then the party, 200 strong, wearing armor concealed under their cloaks and tabards, rode eastward through the city. None had any confidence they would come through this ordeal alive.

The knights took their stations on the east side of the wide plain in front of the walls of St. Bartholomew, a venerable pile, discolored by time and lack of care. On the other side, some distance away, were such of the peasants as still remained, many thousands nonetheless. They were drawn up in some pretense of military order.

An unwonted silence settled over the field, quite different from the usual noisiness of the place, the lowing of cattle, the loud hum of commerce, or, on tragic occasions, the agonized cries which came from the flaming stakes. The king's men were too apprehensive to indulge in talk and far across the fields the peasants were strangely mute, waiting, no doubt, for direction from their leaders. Finally two figures on horseback detached themselves from the dull green of the rebel ranks, one riding a small hackney. This was, of course, Wat Tyler, and behind him a banner bearer. Arriving within speaking distance of the king, the leader dismounted and bowed. Then he took a liberty which caused much boiling of irate blood in the baronial ranks. He seized the royal hand and shook it vigorously.

"Sir king," he said, "within a fortnight you shall enjoy the thanks and loyalty of all true Commons."

Richard made no protest but contented himself with demanding why the peasants had not returned to their homes. "All that you have asked has been conceded," he added.

The leader of the insurgents answered that there were many points still to be discussed. There is much difference of opinion among contemporary historians as to the nature of the demands made during this unprecedented discussion between king and artisan, but the best authorities agree as to the sweeping nature of Tyler's proposals. He raised a point of the relationship between lords and Commons which seems vague in the light of later examination. No one, he contended, should hold the privilege of lordship except *civilly*. Then he went far afield and raised issues which were later made the basis of charges against the Lollard priests, who were believed to have instilled such thoughts in the minds of the common people. The lands held by the church should be confiscated and returned to lay ownership. There should be one bishop only in the land, presumably the archbishop. One report has it that a demand was made for the abolition of the forest laws. In the end they came back to Ball's appeal that there should be no distinction in rank and privilege among men, "save the king alone."

It must have been clear to the leaders of the peasantry that they were demanding the impossible, unless they had taken literally the bluster and boasting of Wat Tyler and believed themselves in a position of national mastery. It is probable the demands were made for the purpose of marking time. To disband now and go home would be to surrender the upper hand. There must be a pretext for remaining under arms and keeping control of London.

The king replied briefly that such changes would require much thought and earnest discussion, adding that he would grant all that he had the right to concede, "saving the regalities of my crown," a phrase which would be used on many historic occasions later when the people of England were at odds with their rulers.

A silence fell at this point. Tyler had spoken at considerable length and so he waited for something further from the king. When the silence became difficult, he called for a drink of ale. One of his men obliged by carrying a flagon across the open space and the leader tossed it off in thirsty gulps. Then he stared truculently around the set and angry faces of the king's men and sprang into the saddle. His intention was to return to the far side of the plain where his followers stood in long lines, so far out of earshot that they had no means of knowing how things were progressing. The conference might very well have ended there, and what the final outcome would have been can only be surmised. But, as so often happens, a minor actor in the drama chose this moment to intrude himself.

A voice from the ranks behind the king spoke up.

"I recognize this fellow. He's a notorious highwayman and robber."

This stung the inflamed pride of Wat the Tyler. He swung his horse around and gave the lie to his accuser. The latter repeated the charge.

Wat kicked the flank of his mount and rode head on into the ranks about the king. Walworth acted with equal dispatch, planting his horse in the rebel's path and crying that he was under arrest. The dagger in Wat's hand cut a deep rent in the mayor's tabard but slipped harmlessly off the armor plate beneath. Walworth's sword was surer, wounding the peasant leader in the head and neck and forcing him to try blindly to escape. The hackney had galloped only a short distance into the open space when he fell out of the saddle.

The peasants were too far away to hear, but they saw what had happened. Their ranks broke and they began to race across the fields, many of them fitting feathered bolts into the notch as they ran. "Kill! Kill!" was the shout they raised. A moment's delay in facing the situation would have resulted in a flight of arrows and the annihilation of the king's party.

Richard rose to the occasion with true Plantagenet courage. Not waiting for the support of his followers, he touched the flank of his horse and rode out to face the angry mob charging across the plains. Never again in the course of his stormy career would the boy king show to such advantage.

"What need ye, my masters?" he cried. "Ye seek a leader? I am your captain and your king. Follow me!"

The angry men of Kent and Essex came to a halt. Hands were withdrawn from taut bows. They stared in wonder at this youth who faced them alone. For the moment they forgot that the body of their leader, pierced with many sword wounds, lay motionless on the ground while his riderless horse galloped off the field.

Then these men from the soil, who had started out honestly to claim the right to be free, demonstrated it had been a sincere loyalty which inspired the oath, "For Richard and the True Commons." They returned to the positions they had held before, the king riding with them. They began to ask him questions. Would he grant them the reforms they believed necessary to make life bearable? Could they return to their homes in full confidence that the promises would be carried out?

In the meantime a small group had gathered about the body of Wat the Tyler. Although he was not dead, it seemed certain he had been mortally wounded. They carried him to the hospital. Later in the evening, when darkness had fallen and the peasantry had left the plains, Mayor Walworth returned to find that their leader had died. He had the head severed from the body to replace that of Archbishop Simon above London Bridge.

Thus died Wat the Tyler who had proven himself a man of considerable parts. He had been a king for three days.

## 3

The shades of approaching night made it difficult to see clearly across the plain. The relatively few knights grouped about the recumbent form of Wat the Tyler could tell that the king had been engulfed in a mass of excited peasants and led away to the far side. Should they launch an attack to rescue him? But to begin open warfare might result in the death of Richard. Rightly or not, they made no move.

Walworth, always the man of action, rode back to the city at top speed and sent criers about the streets to let the citizens know that the king had fallen into the hands of the rebels. The response was instantaneous. From all sections the solid citizens issued out with weapons in their hands and rushed with mounting excitement in the direction of the Aldgate. The number who responded was later computed at a figure in excess of 5000.

The control of this hastily improvised army was put in the hands of Sir Robert Knowles, and that soldier of wide experience succeeded in establishing some degree of order. With his own trained men in the van, stout Sir Robert, recognizable in the shadows by his heavy frown and split upper lip, led the way out to the plain. The peasants had begun to disperse, but many still stood about the king, arguing excitedly about their demands. They made off with great dispatch, apparently, when they perceived that the open space was filling rapidly with armed men. During the hours of the night which followed they melted away. Most of them drifted back into the city and crossed over London Bridge to the southern shore. By morning the occupation of London had come to an end.

The attitude of the king was what might be expected of a boy of fourteen who knew that he had met a crisis with amazing coolness and courage. He assured his rescuers that he had been in no real danger. The peasants had not blamed him for the killing of Wat Tyler and had treated him with the respect due his rank. Knowing that his mother had left the Tower, he proceeded at once to see her at the Wardrobe.

The queen mother was almost hysterical in her relief at finding him free and unharmed. Her eyes filling with tears, she cried: "My son, my son! I have been so fearful for you!"

The boy was understandably boastful in his response.

"Rejoice and praise God," he said. "For I have recovered this day my heritage, which was lost, and the realm of England!"

## CHAPTER XII

# The Days of Retribution

## 1

SANGUINARY as the revolt had been, the measures which followed were infinitely more terrible. The uprisings in scattered counties burst like balloons when word came of the finish at London. The Bishop of Norwich, with sword in hand like the palatine churchmen of Norman days, fell on the undisciplined mob which followed Litster, the King of the Commons, and scattered it like chaff, thus relieving the highborn hostages who had been serving him as scullions; and Master Litster returned no more to his vats.

At Bury St. Edmunds the monks took heart and returned to their cloisters. In Yorkshire the disturbances subsided. At St. Albans those who had led the attack on the abbey were tried and convicted. William Grindecobbe, who had been in London and had returned jubilantly with a charter and a banner, was promised his life if he would persuade the people to return the charters they had taken. His answer was given in words which should never be forgotten. "If I die," he said, addressing those about him who also stood in peril of their lives, "I shall die for the cause of the freedom we have won, counting myself happy to end my life by such a martyrdom."

The chronicles of the period were so bitterly opposed to the cause of the peasants, that it is difficult to arrive at any conclusion on the part Richard played after the last of the marchers had returned home and the echo of the last cheer had died away. It is a matter of record that on June 22 Sir Robert Tresilian was made chief justice and proceeded to exact the full rigors of the law. During July, Richard annulled the charters he had issued. But when Parliament met in November he brought in a report of the course he had followed. He had issued the charters under restraint, he pointed out, knowing them to be contrary to the law, but seeing no other course open to him. "If," the statement went on, "you desire to enfranchise and set at liberty the said serfs by your common assent, as the king has been informed some of you desire, he will consent to your prayer." There is more than a hint here that he would have liked to see his charters validated. The House decided that it was proper to revoke the rights he had granted. They asked, however, for some measures of reform and deplored the severe measures taken to stamp out the rebellion.

It is perhaps reasonable to grant Richard the benefit of the doubt and assume that he allowed himself to be dictated to by the royal uncles and the great landowners who had seen their wealth and privileges threatened. Those who write of him as a hypocrite and a perjurer should picture what undoubtedly happened after the uncles and the baronage came riding in, full of bluster and fury and with plenty of armed men at their backs. Conceive of a boy of fourteen beset by the combined strength of the powerful men of the kingdom, all of them raging at him for giving away *their* rights of villeinage, *their* advantages from *corvée, their serfs,* filling the chancellery with their threats and demands and then, red-faced and angry, gathering in their various palaces to settle upon a course of action. They had not been on hand to face the music of insurrection with him; in fact, they did not seem to have exerted themselves to come to his assistance. If his juvenile intentions had been of the purest, he would be unable to ride out a storm as bitter as this.

It is quite possible, of course, that the boy felt himself a victim of the violence of these uncouth men from the fields and was easily persuaded to acts of repression. Certainly he is reported to have said, in a message directed to the peasantry: "Villeins you were and villeins you are. In bondage you shall abide."

The blackest mark against him is found in one report where clearly there has been gross exaggeration. It is said that in early autumn he marched through the eastern counties with an army of 40,000 men, ravaging the land with fire and sword. The first exaggeration is in the size of the army. It would have been an impossibility to raise such a force and absurdly fantastic (reverting again to the laws of logistics) to think of moving such numbers. To recruit an army many times in excess of the forces which won the historic victories in France would be tantamount to invoking a whirlwind to extinguish a candle. The country had settled down by that time and the men who had marched courageously to London had now sought the shelter of their poor wattled homes and were trembling at the blast of retribution blowing through the land. A few thousand men would have been ample and it may be assumed that such was the force which took the hangman's trail and followed the young king to St. Albans.

Sir Robert Tresilian, with the complete disregard for justice which would in a later century characterize the Bloody Assizes and brand with infamy the name of Judge Jeffreys, sat first at Chelmsford and then proceeded to St. Albans. When a first jury refused to find against the peasant leaders, he selected a second and then a third. The jurors served under threat of death if they failed to act according to the will of the black and beetling judge. Tresilian made it clear that every man who came before him would be found guilty and punished by the severest penalties of the law. The trees began to sprout the grimmest fruit, the bodies of men swinging in the breezes. The cleavers of the executioners were never idle.

King Richard sat on the bench beside Tresilian and watched the trial of John Ball. The hedge priest, who had been responsible more than any other for the outburst, had fled into the Midlands when he perceived that the cause was lost. He was captured at Coventry, hiding in a ruin, according to Froissart, and was brought in chains to St. Albans.

Even those who see him as no better than a mad rabble rouser concede that he conducted himself with calmness and dignity. Permitted to speak, a privilege not accorded to others, he again expressed his belief that the equality of man was what God had planned and that all feudal laws must some day be abolished. He was condemned to be hanged, drawn, and quartered.

This was a sorry end for the man who for more than twenty years had preached against the evil of the existing customs and laws, who had wandered over the country, footsore and weary, facing pain and labor, the rain and the wind in the fields. But it was inevitable.

It was Tresilian's way to send the prisoners straight from his presence to block or gallows, but John Ball was granted two days' respite. It is said that the stay was at the demand of Courtenay, who had succeeded Simon of Sudbury as Archbishop of Canterbury and had later been persuaded to act as chancellor also. Now Courtenay was not one to stand in the way of the most rigid exercise of the law. He was a cousin, several times removed, of the Black Prince, and the eye with which he regarded the uprising had nothing of understanding in it. Perhaps, however, in this moment he was overtaken by a sense of history and saw in John Ball a man of vision and courage. Perhaps also he had been asked to exercise the authority of his office on behalf of the courageous priest, a request from someone higher than himself. This, of course, is pure conjecture. And yet no other explanation seems as reasonable.

After the forty-eight hours expired, the sentence was carried out and

John Ball experienced death in its most horrible form. The desire of
vicious authority to make a victim suffer excruciatingly to the last moment of consciousness had never been served more effectively than in
the method of death devised for traitors. One story has been told of an
executioner pausing, after having removed the stomach and intestines
of a condemned man, to ask if he desired a cup of wine. The victim still
had enough life left in him to whisper No. There was no place left, he
said, to put it.

Yes, they killed John Ball by this inhuman method. And, according to
some computations, they hanged 6999 others.

2

It seemed at first that the revolt of the peasantry had done nothing but
intensify the will of the landowners to hold them in the chains of
feudalism. There was no mistaking the furious intent of the baronage.
The king, they declared, could not take their goods from them but by
their own consent. "And this consent," they affirmed in Parliament, "we
have never given and never will give, were we all to die." They proceeded to pass legislation of the most severe nature. No child born on
the land was to be allowed to be apprenticed in a town nor were any
to be sent to school "because this would give them the opportunity of
advancement in the world by going into the church." Never before had
there been such a grinding of the tusks of authority.

But the effect of these savage restrictions was not to be felt for long.
The peasants had shown their strength, and the fear of another such
demonstration was never lifted. The high stone walls of feudal castles
were no longer an adequate defense. Drawbridges were seldom lowered.
The new laws could not be rigidly enforced and in course of time, although they remained on the statute books, they were forgotten.

A century after Judge Tresilian sat in black majesty on the bench
and sentenced the yeomen of England to ignoble deaths, there was
practically no trace of villeinage left in the land. The tenant farmer and
the small landowner had replaced the serf. The baronage, as stubbornly
opposed as they had always been to social advance, could not hold
back the tide. The men of 1381 had suffered for their courageous efforts,
but they had planted the seed of a rich harvest.

John Ball and Wat the Tyler and William Grindecobbe, and the hundreds and thousands of unnamed men, had not died in vain.

CHAPTER XIII

## *The Gay Court of the Young King*

*1*

RICHARD resembled his grandfather most particularly in two respects. He was madly extravagant and he loved the royal castle of Shene where Edward III had lived out his last years and where he had died in neglect. Perhaps Shene reminded the young king of his early boyhood in Bordeaux where the royal palace was spacious and wide open to the sun and the warm breezes. When he married, as will be told later, his charming little wife, Anne of Bohemia, shared his liking for Shene, and so they made it their summer residence. Here they seem to have held high revel, for it is stated that they sometimes entertained as many as 10,000 guests in a single day. This figure, of course, is one of the worst exaggerations of an age which dealt in superlatives and hyperbole. Still, the royal household was an extravagant one and to this can be attributed the early criticism of the young king. It will be recalled that even the poor peasants had included the luxuries of the court in their bill of grievances.

Edward I, who was a model king in so many respects, kept careful accounts of all court expenditures and so made it possible to reach reasonably accurate estimates of the money raised and the money spent. Edward III was the exact opposite. That great warrior king not only spent everything he could get his hands on, either through the usual revenues (customs, escheats, profits on coinage, levies from clergy and laity) or by dipping lavishly into the national wool profits. Never having enough money, he borrowed right and left, raising huge loans from Lombardy bankers as well as from his own subjects, and seldom paying back. As he used the money to win victories and bolster the national ego, he was forgiven.

But the sins of profligate warrior kings are always visited on their successors, who must keep the peace through sheer lack of funds and the war weariness of their subjects. In the early years of Richard's reign the royal revenue was lavished on a huge household and not on armies to fight the French. The people complained and the popularity of the youthful monarch, which began on such a high level, sank lower and lower.

It has been estimated, largely from the details supplied in the time of Edward I, that Richard's normal revenue was about £65,000 a year. When an army was raised to fight in Scotland or France, the grand annual expenditure would soar as high as £155,000. Normal expenditures included much giving of alms. A furious rate of expenditure was maintained for horses, the necessary masters, knights, and grooms, as well as stud costs and the upkeep of the great royal stables. Whenever men got together over mugs of London ale (the greatest luxury of the lower classes), they spoke in awed tones of young Richard's favorite steed, Barbary, the choice grains on which he was fed and the number of precious stones set in the silver of his equipment. The cost of the pampered Barbary, it was apparent, would have relieved much of the poverty of a London parish.

The most open dissatisfaction was felt over the lazy and dissolute nobility who held posts at court. That one young dandy could swagger in satins and have a household of his own in order to conduct the superintendence of, say, the royal soup spoon raised the hackles of hardworking merchants and bent-backed yeomen. Annual court salaries ran in the neighborhood of £9000 and this at a time when a gallon of the finest ale could be purchased for a groat, and a smart doublet, slashed with cloth of gold, cost half a mark!

Then there was the victualing of the royal castles, a staggering total of over £18,000. And finally the maintenance of the Wardrobe, which cost the nation £15,000. The term Wardrobe was somewhat misleading, for this was not purely a matter of regalia and personal attire, although in this popinjay period the sums expended on royal and noble backs were quite stupendous. Household expenses were included: the kitchens, the sculleries, the spiceries, and the pittances paid to hundreds of cooks, grooms, maids, and varlets in general. Even some military costs, including the upkeep of naval bases, were entered in this category.

All in all the handsome boy king was an expensive luxury for the realm of England.

**2**

Because the looters of the Savoy had found it packed with beautiful things from France and the East did not mean that the palaces of all noblemen were furnished on the same scale. Some of the grimness of Norman days was being eliminated, but there had been no radical departures yet in architecture. The Great Hall was still the focal point of the house, which extended up to the very roofs where no light penetrated, and the ghostly rustling of pennons could be heard in the drafts and the fluttering of bats and birds which had found their way in and could not get out. Here the whole household gathered for meals around trestle tables. Sleeping chambers had been airless holes scooped out of the thick masonry, but in the preceding two generations there had been a change to more luxurious accommodations. For a lord or lady of high rank there would be tiled floors and the windows might even be filled with colored glass. There probably would be cupboards or presses of handsome wood, richly decorated and secured by steel locks from the East. And the beds! Here is where the highborn of the late Plantagenet period displayed their magnificence. They were large and high, with canopies of colored silks, satins, or velvet. With a king of the artistic tastes of young Richard, there would be gold decorations on the headboard above the royal pillow. The pillow, naturally, would be of the finest linen and would carry heraldic embroideries.

In spite of these advances, the possession of a feather bed still meant that someone in the family had been to the wars in France. Tapestries and rugs were prizes from the Crusades.

A chamber on the first floor called the Solar had begun to take the place of the Great Hall in smaller manor houses and in the town residences of affluent citizens. The Solar seems to have served either one of two purposes. With the nobility it could be used as a reception room, but in the smaller houses it was a community bedchamber. This was a step in the direction of comfort and would lead in time to revolutionary changes.

The last full meal of the day began at four o'clock, but none of the trappings of the ceremonial dinner, served at 10 to 11 A.M., were missing. There would be the procession first from the kitchens, led by the manciple or perhaps the sergeant of the ewery, followed by pipers blasting away on their instruments and then by the cooks and scullions proudly holding up the main dishes of the repast. As soon as the last gravy-soaked trencher of bread had been scraped off the board and the final bone had been tossed among the rushes, to be scrambled for by the dogs, there would be cries of "A hall! A hall!," the signal to clear the floor. This would bring a rush of servants from all directions to dismantle the trestles and pile them up along the walls, thus making room for the jugglers, tumblers, and wrestlers who provided most of the entertainment, although an occasional goliard might be given the floor to send the company into belly-shaking laughter with bawdy songs about strumpets and cuckolds. Sometimes there was dancing, particularly the sword dance which had survived from Anglo-Saxon days, or balancing on a tightrope to the mad rattle of kettledrums.

This had been the usual thing, even in the glamorous days of the conqueror Edward, but changes were coming in with Richard and his mother. The food was much more varied and appetizing. There was every conceivable spice and herb. Roses and violets were stewed and served as vegetables. An herb called Robert was actually a garden geranium. There was something very special called an alexander, or horse parsley which was eaten in sticks like celery. A sharp French concoction called verjuice was used in place of lemon juice and there were, perhaps needless to state, a great many new French sauces. No longer did the host try to deceive his guests by putting powdered darnel or passerose into the white wine to turn it red; the most costly of red wines from the South were always served: malvoisie, malmsey, cypress, and muscadel. Even the water used for hand-washing after any course had to be boiled with sage, camomile, and lemon peel.

Perhaps the innovation which suited English palates the least was in the dishes called entremets, the sweets. They were very artistic and gay, piled high in a dish with a base for the most part of jellies or fresh fruits in season, and served with light sweet wines. Now the English people liked pastry, served in the form of pies and tarts. They liked it so much that in Great Eastchepe, where the bakers clustered, every second shop seemed to be given over to the baking of pies. First there were the deep-dish kinds: pork, beef, kidney, cony (rabbit), venison, chicken, goose, fish, eels, made in the shape of *coffyns* with crust done to a rich, juicy brown. These contained the merest hint of vegetables—these luscious, crumbling pies—perhaps a carrot or two or a slice of young turnip. And, ah, the great spoonfuls of gravy, with just a bit of suet! In season, of course, there would be open-faced tarts, called flans—cherry, plum, costard apple. These were so rich that the apprentices had only to hold up a fresh tray to bring trade on the run. Beggars, too poor to buy, clustered in Eastchepe to content themselves with snuffling the rich odors.

In other words, Englishmen liked pastry which "stuck to the ribs" and considered the fancy French concoctions as no more satisfying than a soft south wind blowing down the throat.

Most of the conversation was conducted in French and the entertainment offered after the meal was largely music, conducted by Richard's head minstrel, one John Camuys, a native of Bordeaux. There would be singing, of course, mostly love ballads and rondels. The young king was passionately addicted to music and had already composed a few things of his own which the people of the court professed to find inspired. Sir Simon Burley had encouraged Richard to read and he had become avidly attached to French romances. At Shene there were scores of them, and the zealous Froissart kept sending over more. The conversation, in consequence, was lively and good, led by the young king and his mother with the unlettered nobility trailing silently and glumly far in the rear.

There was at this time an institution called the Board of the Green Cloth, consisting of the Lord Steward and his staff. This Board had control of the household purse and was responsible for the purchase of all supplies. It had full authority over the household staff, with the exception of the masters of the horse and the king's own particular squires, of whom there were no fewer than forty. The innovations made by the young king kept the Board of the Green Cloth very busy indeed.

### 3

Fear of the end of the world hung heavy over the people of medieval days. It was coming to pass soon. Its imminence was preached from every pulpit and all the expected signs were being detected in earth and sky and in the course of human events. Would it come today? Tomorrow? At haying time? When the black mulberries turned? Or would it wait until the next year when the freshness of spring wrapped the earth in beautiful colors?

The Black Death had been the first sure sign, for was it not the Lord's punishment for the wicked among men before the establishment of His domain? The clergy railed at men and women for vanity in dress when it was so clear that the Hand of divine retribution lay on the land.

And yet a period of extreme extravagance and absurdity in styles began with the ending of the Black Death. The chaperon with its sensible combination of cape and cap went out. The cote-hardie with its rather plain horizontal stripes ceased to be popular. Ladies' skirts became very full, almost bouffant, with deep fur bands and facing hems of different materials and colors. The feminine neck was often exposed, but to make up for this the sleeves covered the hands and fancy capes protruded from shoulders like the wings of angels. The plastron, used in male armor, was adapted in sideless surcoats of sufficiently stout material

to permit of as many as a dozen golden buttons down the front, sometimes with precious stones mounted in them. Fair ladies wore their
hair long, but kept it coiled up under something resembling a caul
and which was called a dorelet. The dorelet was not as absurd as the
high hennin which came in early in the following century, but it
permitted all manner of tall hairdressing and trailing bands. It robbed
the poor women, trying so hard to keep up with their foppish husbands,
of much of their natural beauty and charm.

What lovely woman did to herself was nothing compared to the
eccentricities of male attire. Consider one of the illustrated manuscripts
still in existence which gives a picture of the young king. His robe is of
blue, lined with ermine, and his legs are encased with a trimness which
led at this time to the coining of the word "tights." Richard's tights were
parti-colored in a diamond-shaped pattern of maroon and pink. His shoes
were so long and pointed that the toes curled up and had to be banded
to his knees. To climb a stair he had two courses open; he could remove
his shoes or go up backward. It was necessary to keep his arms folded
in order to save his sleeves from trailing on the ground. A very odd-
looking figure he cuts, without a doubt; quite as absurd as the Tudor
courtier of a later century with his neck ruff like the cart wheel of a fairy
coach and his sleeves puffed up like colored clouds.

Richard was a victim of his times. He felt a compulsion to follow the
French styles and it was not his fault that the designers at the French
court happened to be so completely deficient in good taste as to verge
on the idiotic. He had some good ideas of his own. He invented the
handkerchief, certainly a most useful article in a climate so conducive to
colds in the head. If it had not gone through several stages in naming,
beginning with hankercher, and had been called simply a richard, he
would have been much surer of his place in human remembrance than
by grace of his part in history.

When his first wife arrived in England, she brought a number of
innovations, including the sidesaddle for ladies, but this will be dealt
with at greater length later.

Everything was loaded lavishly with jewels. Once Richard raised the
sum of £5000 in the city of London and gave some of his personal
belongings as security. Among the items listed were hoods embroidered
with diamonds, sapphires, rubies, and balasses (a variety of ruby spinel);
beaver hats literally shining with pearls; a coat of cloth of gold, encrusted
with golden balls; a doublet of tarse silk with every inch of its five-foot
spread of sleeve like a jib boom heavily encrusted with pearls; rings
with every kind of precious stone, some even inscribed with the magic
names of The Three Kings, a protection from sudden death. It was
whispered about that he had paid as much as 30,000 marks for one robe

so heavily bedizened that it weighed almost as much as "white armor," the term used for steel.

This extravagance was not confined to the nobility. The rich merchants of London liked to swank in handsome attire. The wives of wealthy kempsters, lavenders, ganters, plumers, and stockfish (for modern terms, read wool combers, laundrymen, glovemakers, feather merchants, and dealers in dried fish) were not permitted by law to ape their betters but they did not hesitate to line their cloaks with ermine or vare. Their plump bodies were seldom subjected to the touch of anything but the finest linens or silks. A fig for the sumptuary laws! Styles in the provinces might be fifty years behind the times but in proud and prosperous London they seldom lagged as much as a season. They did not criticize Richard in London for his eccentricities of dress; they strove to keep up with him.

The size of the royal household did rouse the ire of the citizens who paid the taxes. Should the king have so many guests that hundreds of cooks were needed in the royal kitchens? Was it necessary for him, a mere boy, to have councilors, constables, stewards, chaplains, almoners, pursuivants, scriveners, trumpeters, mimics, prothonotaries, pages, yeomen of this and that, grooms of many varieties and duties? Should carvers who served only one kind of dish be considered artists and paid as such? Did he need forty squires about him at all times, to wait on him hand and foot? And must each squire have two horses and two servants of his own?

The citizens of lusty London and the haughty landed gentry were not pleased to know about the bathing habits of the young king. Must he (good St. Francis forfend!) wash himself every day? The ritual followed caused much grumbling among men who believed in a piece of soap in a firm hand. First the king would be stripped to his fair white skin and seated on sponges in front of a fire. Then he would be enclosed in a narrow space about which clean sheets had been draped and hot water would be poured over him which had been boiled first in all manner of herbs. At the finish the young king would be sprinkled with rose water and popped into his bed by two squires of the bedchamber.

These were French ways. And had not the English beaten the French in every battle they had fought?

The men and women that a king gathers about him (and most often it is the women rather than the men) do much to create the opinions that his subjects form of him. Richard had not been fortunate in this respect. Parliament had appointed a council to govern the realm while the king remained a minor, but certain changes had come about rather quickly. The queen mother had been a predominant influence and the boy had early proven himself the possessor of a will of his own. Some changes in the personnel of the council had resulted and a small inner circle had become the advisers on whom the adolescent ruler relied.

First there was Sir Simon Burley, for whom Richard had conceived a strong affection from the very first. Burley had proven himself stout of heart in the French wars and had been a special favorite of the Black Prince. He was a gentle knight and a man of some culture, but willing, and even eager, to improve his social and financial position. A younger son in a Herefordshire family, he had no estates and the slimmest of prospects generally. In fact, when he was first introduced at court by an uncle, his income was said to have been no more than twenty marks a year! When Richard became king he moved quickly to save his genial and sympathetic tutor from such penury. Burley was appointed governor of Windsor Castle and master of the king's falcons, as well as constable of Guildford and Wigmore. The duties which thus devolved on Burley kept him continuously in and out of court. He saw more of the king certainly than any of the council, even the chancellor and the archbishop. Richard gave him generous grants of land and a house in London on Thames Street, which was close to the royal residence of Baynard's Castle. As a result, from a meager inheritance his income grew to one of 30,000 marks.

He does not seem to have injected himself into the problems of the chancellery, but anything having to do with the royal falcons would always engage the royal attention in preference to problems of state. The king seems to have listened to Burley on points of foreign policy, as witness the fact that the personal side of the negotiations for the king's marriage had been entrusted to him. They had been so well handled that Burley remained a member of the closest triumvirate at court, made up of the king, the queen, and himself.

There must have been a haughtiness about his manner which those less close to the king resented. An open feud developed between him and the Earl of Arundel. The latter was admiral of the fleet in the west and he had, in the years between 1377 and 1386, achieved nothing but defeat and loss. The year 1378 had been a particularly bad one for the proud Arundel. First he attacked the French port of Harfleur and was driven off. In joint command with the Earl of Salisbury he was beaten in a naval battle with the Spanish. Arundel became the target of popular abuse and Burley seems to have been particularly outspoken in his criticism of the sluggish handling of the naval operations. The proud and overbearing Arundel was to become one of the leading figures in the tragic circumstances of Richard's reign, and so will be dealt with at considerable length later. It is not necessary at this point to say more than one thing further about him. He never forgave Burley.

The difficulties which Richard encountered early were largely due to his friendship for a young member of the upper baronage. Robert de Vere, Earl of Oxford, was hereditary great chamberlain of England. The de Veres, or Veers as it was sometimes spelled, traced their history back to the Conquest and to Aubrey de Vere, who had been given all the estates of a great Saxon thane named Wulfwine. Coming down in such steady succession, the de Veres had added to their holdings by strategic marriages, notably the union of the third earl with the heiress of the Bolebec family, which brought into their hands huge stretches of land in Buckinghamshire. Accordingly young Robert, ninth in a line which ultimately extended itself to twenty (no wonder the term Vere de Vere was coined to signify the very ultimate in blue-bloodedness), was not only born with a gold spoon in his mouth but, figuratively speaking, a heap of honors and titles piled up around his pillow.

Richard, eight years his junior, seems to have conceived a close liking for him from the beginning. Efforts to prove a relationship between them on the order of Edward II's infatuation for Piers Gaveston progressed no further than an unsupported rumor, and it may surely be dismissed on the strength of Richard's subsequent conduct. It was more likely the affection that a boy can have for one a few years his senior, although it is hard to understand why he decided to make the young Earl of Oxford his friend and model. Robert de Vere was not handsome, talented, or brave. Later he was to prove himself of weak and unreliable character. Nevertheless, Richard liked him enough to heap honors on him. It may have been that at this early age, de Vere had an open eye for the main chance. He had been married when sixteen years old to Philippa, daughter of Princess Isabella and Enguerrand de Coucy and was therefore a cousin-in-law of the king. He proceeded to ingratiate himself with Sir Simon Burley, realizing in all probability that Burley held the largest share of Richard's affection. He conveyed one of his manors in Herefordshire to the still impecunious knight. Much of the enmity that Burley drew down on himself was due to a general belief that he was pulling strings behind the scenes in favor of de Vere.

This may have been true, but the facts seem to indicate that de Vere had no need of his help. Richard had doubled the yearly allowance paid from the estates to the young earl (who was a ward of the Crown) as soon as he became king. He then proceeded to shower honors on him. The custody of the town and castle of Colchester was handed to him, the castle and lordship of Queenborough, and the wardships of several rich estates. A ward acting as a guardian must have been something new in the annals of favoritism. Quite as unusual, and even more aggravating to the older barons, was the selection of this brash and grasping youth as a member of the privy council and of the Order of the Garter.

De Vere was with Richard in the Tower when the peasants took possession of London, but he does not seem to have distinguished himself in any way, except that he did not run away as the half brothers of the king had done.

It is hard to understand why a third member of the king's immediate entourage, Michael de la Pole, was also selected for popular disfavor. Pole was the son of Sir William de la Pole, the shrewd wool merchant of Hull who became the first great English merchant prince. The father had been so rich, in fact, that at various times he made loans amounting in all to a total of £76,180 to that most unsatisfactory of debtors, Edward III. The victorious Edward had dined once in the Great Hall of Pole's house on the High Street of Hull and had listened with absorbed interest to the talk of that able man of business. In the end, of course, Pole had been sent to prison for no legally tenable offense, but he had left a sufficient estate to start his son William off on a firm financial footing.

The first years of Pole's official career were spent with the armies abroad. He fought under the Black Prince at Limoges and was afterwards with John of Gaunt on several expeditions. That he had acquitted himself well was evidenced in his selection as captain of Calais, the spearhead of English operations in France, and later as admiral of the fleet north of the Thames.

Pole was a logical choice for a place among the king's councilors. He had practical commercial experience, which all of the others lacked. It had not taken him long to justify the wisdom of his selection and he had been made governor of the king's person as well as one of the two councilors in constant attendance on the king.

Pole had always been an adherent of John of Gaunt and he now began to show himself as a born king's man. At any rate he was quickly drafted into the inner circle of court intimacy and, in spite of the sound common sense he displayed in his official transactions, the ever watchful and belligerent barons began to regard him with suspicion.

There were others who were counted as members of the king's coterie: Alexander Neville, the Archbishop of York, Sir Robert Tresilian, whose hands were still red with the blood of common men but who was holding the post of chief justice, and Sir Nicholas Brembre, a grocer of London and a "worthie and puissant man." Only two of these men of proven capacity deserved the storm of criticism which would descend on all of them—de Vere and Tresilian.

## CHAPTER XIV

# Good Queen Anne

*1*

THROUGH Bohemia passed much of the trade from the East. Here also the shock of the Mongolian invasion had been shared with Poland and Hungary more than a century before. The English understood the importance of this country, so beautiful and fertile that it was sometimes called the Golden Road. But the Bohemians had no real knowledge of England. An island, small and fogbound, was their impression of the country where the conquering Plantagenets had reigned so long, but from which, strangely enough, there had emerged at intervals small armies capable of cutting the French forces to pieces, largely because of a death-dealing weapon known as the longbow. A king of Bohemia named John, who was blind, had been with the French at Crécy and had ridden into battle with his horse chained to the steeds of knights on each side. The bodies of all six, the three men and the three horses, had been found on the field later by the victorious English. A son of John's named Wenceslaus (but not the Good King Wenceslaus of the Christmas carol) had succeeded. Changing his name to Charles, he became the Holy Roman Emperor and remained a firm friend of France. He was a shrewd and cautious man, preferring to gain his ends by conspiratorial methods; in appearance sallow, black-a-vised, and huddled of shoulder. He had been married four times and by the last of his wives had a daughter named Anne.

The little princess, who was only twelve when he died, does not seem to have taken after her Machiavellian father. She was fair of complexion and in figure rather tall, straight, and trim. She had a gift for winning affection.

Charles of Bohemia died in 1378 and his successor, much to his mortification, found it impossible to maintain the alliance with the French. The Christian world had been broken into two camps by the schism over the papacy. France, Spain and Scotland stood with Clement VII, who was called the anti-Pope, while England, Flanders, most of Italy, and all of Germany were ranged behind Urban VI. Even when Charles of France asked for Anne as a wife for his son, it had been necessary for Bohemia to refuse.

Early in 1379, before it was known that the French match had been broken off, the English council began to look over the field. Sir Simon Burley was in Milan to negotiate a marriage between Richard and Catherine, daughter of Bernabò Visconti. This move was not successful. Bernabò and other members of his family were at odds, with the result that his nephew Gian Galeazzo succeeded in poisoning him. Burley had warned Westminster that the proposed alliance would be a mistake and he is next reported at Prague where his mission was to foster a match between King Richard and the princess Anne.

He found the princess Anne gentle, bright, even intelligently educated. If not beautiful, she was clearly of "goodly person" and pleasing address. It seems certain that even at this initial stage the little princess and the courtly Englishman found themselves on good terms. He must have painted for her an enticing picture of the handsome boy king, for on his return to London he brought assurances of her personal willingness.

The next step seems to have been the arrival in England of Duke Primislaus of Saxony, an uncle of the princess. He had been sent by Anne's mother, who still held the title of empress, to spy out the land, so to speak, and in particular to see if favorable financial terms could be arranged. Apparently the duke was well impressed, for he produced a letter from the empress which read in part: "I, Elizabeth, Roman empress, always Augusta, likewise queen of Bohemia, empower Duke Primislaus to treat with Richard king of England concerning the wedlock of that excellent virgin, the damsel Anne, born of us; and in our name to order and dispose and, as if our own soul were pledged, to swear to the fulfillment of every engagement."

Things were now reaching solid ground. An English party, headed by the Earl of Kent and including "two others," later identified as Michael de la Pole and Sir Simon Burley, set out for Bohemia. It did not require any further efforts on the part of Burley or his fellow ambassadors to obtain the consent of the daughter of the Caesars. Anne, in fact, wrote a letter to the council of England, saying she would become the wife of their king "with full and free will."

The shrewd Bohemians, however, succeeded in driving a stiff bargain with the Englishmen, one which later created much dissatisfaction at home. There was to be no dowry and it was further stipulated that England should pay to Anne's brother Wenceslaus, the new emperor, the sum of 10,000 marks. All expenses of her journey were to be borne by the country of the prospective bridegroom. It must have been that Richard's advisers saw great advantages in an alliance which would help to cement relations with the great cities of Flanders and prevent the French king from driving a wedge between England and her profitable markets on the continent. Otherwise they would not have agreed to such conditions.

2

The Peasants' Revolt made it necessary to postpone the wedding. The English ambassadors remained in Prague and so missed the opportunity of playing a part in that dramatic page in English history. Belated reports reached them and it may be taken for granted that Sir Simon Burley missed no chance to let the anxious princess know of the remarkable role her intended husband had played. The delay had one advantage. It gave the little Anne a chance to achieve her fifteenth birthday, the earliest age at which her family would part with her.

It was a large and picturesque party which set out. The Duke of Saxony and his duchess were in charge and there was a long train of Czech knights and ladies in waiting, as well as a very large number of servants, for the practical Bohemians were not yet convinced that the country to which their princess was being taken was quite civilized enough to provide properly for her comfort and well-being. They left under another, and greater, cloud of apprehension. The agents they maintained in France (espionage was as fine an art then as it is today, even perhaps a shade more subtle) had discovered that Charles V of France was in no mood to let Anne reach England. He was planning to patrol the waters of the Channel with a fleet of battleships, under stern orders to secure possession of the person of the princess and send her to his court.

The French king, as already explained, had wanted Anne as a wife for his eldest son, a boy of eleven years. Even though that plan had fallen through, he was bitterly determined that she was *not* to become the bride of Richard of England. Such a match would completely upset his plans to weaken the relationship between the island kingdom and the wealthy cities of Flanders. By the time the nuptial party reached Brussels, where the bride was to visit her uncle and aunt of Brabant, the French fleet, stripped for action and in fighting mood, was plying up and down the coast and preventing any ships from crossing the Channel. No steps had been taken to clear the path, for there was not an English sail on the horizon.

Under the circumstances, Anne's uncle Wenceslaus sent two envoys to Paris, the lords of Rousselaus and Bousquetion, to protest the French action. King Charles, it developed, was quite ill when they arrived. He had been an able ruler and had been responsible for the recovery of much French territory in the preceding ten years. But, with death staring him in the face, the need to continue rigid diplomatic measures grew less and less urgent. He listened to the Flemish ambassadors without making much effort to combat their views. Finally he gave vent to a deep sigh.

"So be it," he said. "I shall order my vessels back to port. I do this out of love for my cousin Anne. Not," he added, with a resurgence of his old fire, "out of regard or consideration for the King of England."

He died on September 16 while the bridal party still lingered at Brussels.

As soon as word arrived that the coast was clear, the final stages of the journey were begun. Escorted by a large company of her own countrymen, including one hundred men-at-arms, they traveled down toward the waters which separated the Low Countries from England. There was a short delay at Bruges because the Earl of Flanders had arranged entertainments which lasted three days. At Gravelines an English escort awaited them, made up of 500 spears and an equal number of those most dreaded of battle troops, the English archers. They progressed to Calais where, at last, an English fleet awaited them. The order of things on the Strait of Dover had been reversed. The French flag no longer flew on any craft within sight, but the leopards of England were everywhere.

They had to wait for favorable winds but finally, on the morning of Wednesday, December 18, the daughter of the Caesars was escorted up a gangplank covered with velvet and ankle deep with English roses. The convoy reached Dover the same day.

A most strange and tragic occurrence followed the safe landing of the princess. She had no sooner set foot on English soil than the waters of the Strait were so violently agitated that all the ships were tossed about in the wildest confusion. Some collided and were so badly damaged that they sank, including the one on which she had sailed. The frightened princess saw it go down under the rush of waters.

This unusual convulsion of nature did not lend itself to any reasonable explanation. There had been little wind, not enough certainly to create such havoc. The angry waves soon subsided, although the flow of waters between Dover and Calais continued to carry all traffic before it. Mariners had no explanation to give. Never had they seen the like before. Scientists thought of many possible reasons but none of them was in any sense acceptable. It was even believed by the populace that a huge sea serpent had made its way through the Strait and had agitated the waters with the lash of a mighty tail.

All agreed on one point, that it was an omen. But was it an omen of good fortune or of bad?

### 3

Despite the enthusiasm with which the young princess was received in England and the warm liking for her which developed at once, there has been a general tendency to deny her a share of beauty. This has been due, apparently, to the lack of any mention of personal pulchritude in the exchange of official letters prior to the final settlement. Richard, it was therein stated, was requesting her hand because of her nobility of birth and her gentleness of character. There is also the evidence of the only likeness of her in existence, the monument in Westminster Abbey. It should be pointed out that the art of the portrait painter was not successfully practiced in England through the Middle Ages. So pedestrian were the efforts of those who chiseled out of stone the figures on the tombs of monarchs of the day and their wives that it is unfair to draw any conclusions from them. The tools of the sculptors seemed to fall into a groove and the poor ladies have come down to posterity in one familiar guise: eyes reasonably far apart, noses long and thin, mouths tiny and compressed, chins rounded. Isabella, the French princess whose voluptuous charms created so much havoc, is depicted as of strong character but with no hint of her fatal beauty. Edward I's beloved Eleanor of Castile looks sly. Isabella of Angoulême, wife of the infamous John and widely acclaimed the most lovely woman in Europe, is given a bumpkin fullness of face. Even Adelicia of Louvain, the snow-white princess who became Henry I's second wife, appears pudgy and spinsterish. On the other hand, poor Berengaria, neglected wife of the mighty Richard *Coeur de Lion*, who was never considered a beauty, is made to appear bright and vivacious and decidedly pretty in a dark-eyed way.

To criticize the young king's fifteen-year-old bride on such grounds seems unfair. Richard conceived an immediate liking for her, one which grew with the years and became an infatuation. Even if Anne could not be called beautiful in a classic sense, she possessed a charm and grace which more than compensated.

After three days of rest at Dover, the bridal party took horse for Canterbury. This provided the first opportunity for the display of an innovation which would be accepted by all the ladies of England and would remain in common usage for a matter of six centuries. The princess rode sidesaddle.

Up to this time, ladies had ridden astride. No efforts seem to have been made to lend any grace or comfort to this means of travel. The ladies tucked their skirts up behind them and encased their legs and feet in detached garments somewhat on the order of shawls, invariably arriving at their destination in a rumpled and exhausted condition. There was immediate curiosity when it was seen that the princess sat sideways on an entirely new kind of equipment. A rest was suspended from the right of the saddle, which was large enough to accommodate both feet of the rider. Anne allowed only her right foot to touch the rest, and that lightly, while her left knee was raised gracefully above the level of the saddle. English ladies accepted this new and very feminine idea almost immediately and for long centuries continued to ride and hunt and hawk in this less secure but more ladylike position, until in the fullness of time they attained the emancipation of riding trousers.

Another innovation was noticed as soon as the princess was escorted decorously into Canterbury. She was wearing the great horned headgear that was in general use on the continent. Nothing good could be said of this absurdity except that the style had been conceived in France and accepted everywhere. It stood two feet in height and had a corresponding width, the material being suspended on wires. It made the wearers look like birds of prey, but again the ladies of England, determined not to appear old-fashioned, fell into line. Later they accepted the even more exaggerated hennin.

John of Gaunt had been forced to reconcile himself to a new perspective by what happened during the Peasants' Revolt. The hatred for him which had been displayed by the yeomen in arms had been an eye opener. He had been aware before that he lacked the good will of the Londoners and had brushed it aside with lofty pride, but the rage and thoroughness with which Wat the Tyler's men had destroyed his beautiful and most prized possession, the Savoy, had made him realize, perhaps for the first time, that his unpopularity was deep and widespread. He had remained in Scotland after the rebellion subsided in the hope of quelling the tension there and he had even found it advisable to ask Richard for a safe conduct to use in returning to London.

Under ordinary circumstances he would have acted as the king's deputy in welcoming the princess when her train arrived at Canterbury. His concern over the hostility of the public was such that he decided not to go, and the youngest of the royal uncles, Thomas of Woodstock, went to the cathedral city in his stead.

Thomas of Woodstock had shown no trace of liking for Richard from the first. He was a man of furious pride and a degree of self-esteem which made him resent the occupation of the throne by a boy who seemed to him weak and effeminate. However, he carried out his duties as the representative of the royal family by receiving the princess with the customary warmth and courtesy. This attitude was not maintained long, however, for he was soon back to his more familiar role as personal faultfinder.

London had not had time to recover from the terrors of the occupation. The face of the city still wore, like pockmarks, the blackened gaps opened by the fires. Never before had there been so many rotting heads raised above London Bridge. Perhaps it was a natural reaction from so much fear that the citizens now showed great warmth and ostentation in welcoming the girl queen. They met the escorting train at Blackheath, which had been cleared of all traces of the peasant occupation and would never again seem to echo with the voice of John Ball. The worthy burghers were out in great numbers and were giving a display of wealth which must have reassured the attendants of Anne who had more than half expected to find England barbarous and lacking in culture. The men of the guilds rode spirited steeds, their beards were oiled and curled, their cloaks were of velvet and cloth of gold, their hats were heavy with bobbing plumes. The goldsmiths alone were out to the number of seven score, and the other wealthy companies were equally well represented.

The streets of London blazed with flags, there were decorated booths at all crossings, and fountains ran with wine. Beautiful girls showered bouquets on the young couple and danced in front of their horses, strewing the path with yellow flowers like florins.

The cheeks of the little princess were pink with excitement as she rode beside the handsome king and she must have been thinking that all her dreams were coming true. It would be easy to love her royal husband and to respect and like the people among whom she would spend the balance of her life.

The wedding took place on January 14 at St. Stephen's Chapel in Westminster and her coronation followed in eight days, both events being conducted with great pomp and circumstance. In the meantime, Anne's Bohemian escort had returned to the continent, leaving only her immediate attendants and her personal servants, still a considerable train.

The little queen was made a member of the Order of the Garter, wearing a robe of violet and a hood lined with scarlet silk. Even in such fine raiment she was dimmed by the grandeur of Richard who wore his famous coat sparkling with jewels, which was reputed to have cost 30,000 marks. The king did not seem at all perturbed that to pay the costs of the ceremonies it had been necessary to pawn the jewels of Aquitaine, which had belonged to the Crown since Eleanor of that rich duchy had married Henry II, the first of the English Plantagenets. He was completely his grandfather in this respect. The revenues of the Crown were to be spent as lavishly as he might desire.

Anne was too happy to feel any regrets that her royal spouse outshone her. Was it not, after all, a law of nature that the male bird had the richest colors and the most spectacular plumes? From the very beginning Anne was a perfect wife. She wanted Richard to be happy and her attitude was always one of complaisance and agreement.

As she understood three languages, as well as a smattering of English, she was undoubtedly the most learned member to join the Order of the Garter.

### 4

The new queen seems to have reached a quick and cordial understanding with the queen mother. The latter had as good reason for jealousy as any mother-in-law, for up to this point she had been holding Richard in leading strings and her influence had been manifest in everything. Not only did she face the certainty of slipping back to second place but a third of the income from the princedom of Wales, which had been set aside for her maintenance when the Black Prince died, had to be diverted to the holdings of the new queen. Not that Joan would feel the loss to any extent. She had been a very wealthy widow when she married Richard's father and her estates had steadily increased. In addition to the royal castle of Wallingford, which had been assigned to her, she owned manors in twenty-six counties and so, whenever she went on her travels, she could sleep every night in a home of her own.

One emerges from a study of the part the once Fair Maid played in the history of the period with a feeling that she has been underrated. When she was left a widow by the death of her first husband, she decided that the admiration which the Black Prince had felt for her when she was as pretty and vivacious as a butterfly in the royal court could be fanned into a flame now that he was world famous and had reached his middle years without allowing himself to be married for state reasons. Her campaign was masterly. She had to catch him off balance (to use a modern phrase) in order to wring a proposal from him. History does not offer a more romantic comedy than the way she led him step by step to a declaration. Once that aloof and self-centered idol of the people had found himself in the bonds of matrimony, she proceeded to make him a good wife. He was kept reasonably contented during his last difficult years.

She has been described as *une dame de gran pris, qe belle fuist, pleasante et sage.* Certainly she was pleasant and wise in the most difficult situation she and her son Richard faced, the relationship with John of Gaunt. She realized from the first that it behooved them to keep the peace with that wealthy and powerful member of the royal family. During a turbulent period immediately before Edward III died, the citizens of London had tried to capture John and he had sought sanctuary in the royal palace of Kennington. The lady Joan concealed him from the angry mobs and sent out three knights to make peace with them, one of them being Sir Simon Burley. After Richard was raised to the throne, she made many trips to Pontefract, John's great fortress in the north, to patch up family differences. This entailed endless journeying in that lumbering, jolting coach which has already been described. It has been assumed that one of her reasons for doing this was that John of Gaunt was generally believed to be using his immense influence to save John Wycliffe from clerical reprisal. It has never been decided how far the queen mother inclined to agreement with Lollard teachings but there was enough smoke to hint at hidden fire. To hold deep convictions on religious questions was a most unusual thing for a woman of high rank. If it were true that she accepted the views of the man of Lutterworth, it would indeed be proof that she had depths of character seldom suspected.

It may also have been that this constituted an undivulged bond between the two women. Anne's father had been an enlightened ruler and among the many steps he had taken to raise Prague to a prominent place among European capitals had been the establishment of a university there. This institution had been liberal from the first. When Anne was growing up, she could not have failed to come under the influence of the leaven of religious unrest in Bohemia. It is stated that some of the queen's entourage carried back with them an acquaintance with Wycliffe's teachings. Certainly Jan Huss, the great Bohemian leader, acknowledged openly that he had followed the lead of Wycliffe. The young queen never expressed any such leanings, however.

Anne's compassion had been aroused by the fury with which the peasants were being made to pay for their effort to shake off the bonds of villeinage. It was due to her intercession that an amnesty was granted, soon after her coronation, to such prisoners as still remained in the toils of the law.

It was because of this that the people began to call her Good Queen Anne.

## CHAPTER XV

## The Bully of Woodstock

### 1

THROUGH the whole course of his reign Richard was fiercely at odds with his uncle Thomas of Woodstock. This youngest son of Edward III was so proud and quarrelsome that he had no enduring affection for any members of the royal family and was particularly antagonistic to John of Gaunt. For Richard he had nothing but contempt, resenting the accident of birth by which this boy had succeeded to the throne in his father's stead while he, Thomas, had to bow the knee of fealty.

The bad feeling which developed between this outspoken critic and his older brother, John of Gaunt, began before the death of Edward III. John, being the favorite son of the old king, had no difficulty in getting his own very young son Henry (afterward Henry IV) admitted to the Order of the Garter. Thomas, who was twelve years older than the new member, was not chosen. In fact he had to wait until 1380, when he was twenty-five years old, for that honor to be paid him. He never forgave his brother for what he considered a deliberate slight.

A more serious breach came about in 1380 when Thomas commanded an army in northern France. But he could not induce the French army to give battle and so took his forces into Brittany where he laid siege to Nantes. There word reached him that his brother John had agreed to a truce with the new French king. This threw Thomas into a savage mood for he feared the people of England would consider the campaign a failure and lay the blame on his shoulders. He did not return immediately.

It has been pointed out in an earlier volume that there were plenty of heiresses during medieval days, due partly to so many sons of the great families being killed in tournaments and in the incessant wars. There were no richer sisters in England at this time than Eleanor and Mary de Bohun. Their father had been Humphrey, the tenth Earl of Hereford, who held in addition the earldoms of Essex and Northampton and owned broad acres and many tall castles, including Pleshy in Essex, Monmouth, Leicester, and a great, dark, drafty house called Cole Harbor in the Dowgate ward of London. On his death the division of his properties gave to the elder sister the earldom of Essex, the strong fortress of Pleshy, and a claim to transfer the post of constable of England to her husband. The earldoms of Hereford and Leicester went to the younger, with the castle of Monmouth and the tomblike house in London.

Now the elder sister had married Thomas of Woodstock and they had made up their minds between them that it would be more to their liking if they had the whole inheritance instead of half. They coolly made Cole Harbor their London home. Little Mary, who was very pretty (the elder sister lacked the Bohun beauty) and a grave and gentle child, was taken to live in the castle of Pleshy, in close proximity to a convent of the Poor Clares. It would be a proper arrangement all around, they believed, if Mary would take the vows and devote her life to the church, for, in that event, all the properties would come to them.

The Poor Clares (a popular version of the order founded by St. Clara) were the feminine branch of the Franciscans. They had bravely and sternly persevered in the strict discipline and the vows of poverty laid down for his followers by St. Francis of Assisi. They slept on boards and their lives were a perpetual fast. The members could speak to one another only on permission from the prioress. They dressed in loose-fitting gray gowns with linen cord ropes, tied with four knots to represent their four vows. They worked long hours in taking care of the poor and the sick, a thoroughly fine and self-sacrificing order.

John of Gaunt had been appointed guardian of the attractive, dark-haired Mary and he did not approve of the plan of the elder sister and her husband, unless it came about with the full consent of the younger sister. Nature, as it happened, took the decision in hand. Mary met John's son Henry, who later became Henry IV, and the young people fell deeply in love. A match was arranged between them, although the elder sister, in the absence of her husband, opposed it bitterly.

Thomas of Woodstock returned from France still filled with umbrage over the truce his brother had negotiated. When he learned that his plans for the younger sister had been upset by her marriage, he became even more enraged, contending that he should have been consulted first. This was a proper enough objection, except that everyone knew his real concern was that Mary's share of the fat Bohun acres and the well-filled family coffers would not now come into his hands.

The marriage proved to be a most happy one. Although Mary died before her husband became King of England, she had presented him with seven children, including four sons. She was only twenty-three when she died in childbirth with the last of the children, a girl. The four sons took after her in having the dark eyes and brown hair of the Bohuns, but each of the three girls had the brilliant and handsome fairness of the Plantagenets.

The young mother's place in history was assured because her oldest son was the great Prince Hal of legend and song, who became Henry V of England and won the fabulous Battle of Agincourt against the French.

Thomas of Woodstock seems to have spent the first years of Richard's reign in a state of ferment. He was incensed at not being included in the first council to direct the affairs of the kingdom during the boy's minority, although none of the royal uncles had been selected. As a sop, he was made Earl of Buckingham and constable of England at the coronation. Just when it was that he began to assert himself in state matters cannot be determined, but it happened before he was ensconced in a position of authority by Parliament. He seems to have taken advantage almost from the first of the prerogatives of his birth to dip his fingers into the administrative pie. Certainly he was from the very beginning Richard's most unsparing critic.

He showed little or no respect for the young ruler, brushing in and out of the royal presence without asking consent. He even addressed the boy as a stern uncle to an adolescent nephew, without waiting for permission. On occasion he would brusquely interrupt Richard's own remarks and contradict him openly when he disagreed, as he nearly always did. It is even said that he opened the king's letters and then turned them over, not with suggestions but with instructions as to what should be done about them.

Richard's chief concern in these early days of his reign was to escape from under the insensitive thumb of the Bully of Woodstock.

2

Richard, now happily married, should have been in a position to take the reins of government into his own hands. But Parliament was almost unanimous in its opposition. Things were going badly in England. Every naval and military move that was initiated resulted either in disaster or stalemate. The financial position of the country was weak and trade was falling off as a result of the difficulties under which the Flemish cities labored. It was no time for a boy to take control of the nation.

Parliament refused to see that the country was staggering under the costs of a war which could not be won and which should be terminated. The people, still boasting of the victories won over the French, longed for the days when Edward the warrior king and the Black Prince had led the English armies. No national leader, it seemed, had the courage to come out boldly and propose that a peace be made. Instead they devoted themselves to feeble attempts at financial reform. The only spot on which the parliamentary finger of censure could be laid was the extravagance of the king's court. Through lack of courage to face the real issue, the House selected two men who were to act jointly as councilors and be in constant attendance on the king. One was Michael de la Pole, who already belonged to the inner circle about the king, and the other was Richard FitzAlan, the Earl of Arundel.

The king went a step further and made Michael de la Pole chancellor. In that capacity Pole appeared before Parliament and stated in unequivocal terms that a final peace must be made with France unless the nation was prepared to exert all its might in pushing the war to a successful conclusion.

The members listened in glum agreement. Someone had dared at last to put into words what they all knew inwardly to be the truth. It developed at once, however, that they were not prepared for the first alternative and only half ready to accept the second course. Richard came to the House and proposed that he lead an army into France at once. He was beginning to fill out and the first downy traces of what would grow into the handsome yellow beard he wore through all of his adult life were showing on his cheeks. But although he was the son of the Black Prince and might possess the same genius for war, he was still a boy and without any military experience. The members, who were controlled by the nobility, could not agree to his proposal.

Finally the House compromised by deciding to grant supplies for a force to be lead by the warlike Bishop of Norwich in a crusade against the supporters of the French anti-Pope. It will be remembered that the bishop had won a quick victory over the clownish peasant leader, Litster, who had called himself "King of the Commons." But he was soon to discover that facing a large and well-equipped French army was vastly different from scattering a ragtag band without any training and without proper arms. The bishop was so soundly beaten that nothing much was left of the army he had led across the Channel.

The news of this disaster reached Richard at Daventry, which he had reached in the course of a state processional through the Midlands. He was at table and he sprang to his feet, his face livid, crying out that he must return to London at once. The ladies and gentlemen about the board looked at one another with surprise and dismay. What had made the young king behave in this way? Could it be that the peasants had risen again?

With a few of his closest advisers about him, de Vere, Pole, and Burley, without a doubt, Richard took to horse and galloped the rest of the day and all through the night, stopping frequently for remounts but never for food or rest. A seventy-mile ride in one stage was cause for amazement, particularly in view of the bad roads, but some of the driving force of his father was beginning to come out in Richard. When he arrived in London, dusty and haggard and so bone-weary that he had to be helped from the saddle, he went into conference at once with his uncle of Lancaster who had remained there to nurse his disappointment over Parliament's refusal to supply him with an army for the invasion of Spain. The boy declared that the bishop must be impeached as soon as he returned to England. John of Gaunt agreed that the too ambitious prelate should be punished. Later they found support for this step in the House, and when my Lord of Norwich returned he was ordered to turn all his temporalities over to the Crown to be applied against a fine, to be levied "at the king's pleasure."

Richard had been badly shaken by this further evidence of English inability to wage successful war on the continent. He retired within himself and began to make plans for a new kind of warfare by which the balance might be righted. An effort was made to keep this secret, but rumors nevertheless began to circulate. It was whispered that he was concerned with "urgent and secret affairs." Warlike machines of fearful and wonderful design were being constructed in the Tower to equip a new royal army which Richard himself would lead; no more royal uncles, no more headstrong bishops; the son of the Black Prince would no longer consent to such makeshift leadership. The word "gunpowder" was bandied about and there was also talk of "crakys," a term which had been applied to some form of gun or cannon to discharge the destructive force which Roger Bacon had discovered more than a century before. It was announced that one Thomas Norbury had received orders to buy up all available supplies of sulphur and saltpeter. Clearly the secret weapon the young king hoped to use in reviving the war efforts of the nation had to do with gunnery. It was, of course, the kind of thing a boy of his years would turn to and it hardly needs stating that nothing came of it. The mechanical and military genius needed to change the face of warfare was lacking.

Parliament was now desirous of peace but still would not assume any responsibility for dropping the Plantagenet claim to the throne of France. The French would not consider any terms of permanent peace which did not begin with that relinquishment. This stalemate was due to the lack of leadership from which England was suffering. With the possible exception of Michael de la Pole, who was shrewd and able, none of the men about the king or in Parliament, including the great nobles and the upper hierarchy of the church, had the courage and the wisdom to lead the nation out of this dilemma.

3

In earlier days it had been the custom to have Parliament meet at any place which suited the king. Edward I, the originator of so many common-sense regulations, decided this was wrong and that Westminster should be made the permanent parliamentary home. There were the best of reasons for this. A great nobleman never traveled without a long train of knights, men-at-arms, and servants, sometimes running into the hundreds. This was equally true of bishops, who felt the need of advisers, deans, almoners, and clerks of all degree; so many, in fact, that an ecclesiastical party would sometimes be a half mile long, some riding in litters, some on donkeys, some plodding along painfully on foot. Everyone shared the discomfort of a parliamentary meeting in the provinces, particularly the landholders of the neighborhood, who were expected to entertain distinguished visitors. Even the townspeople suffered, for the great lords would billet their retainers with them and then neglect to pay the bills.

It is not on record that the bishops and barons received any payment as members of the House, but the compensation set for mere knights was four shillings a day and for plain citizens two shillings. This was not enough to pay the expenses incurred. Through five successive reigns the sheriffs of Lancashire petitioned to be exempt from sending members because there were no cities or boroughs which could afford the cost. One Sir John Strange, who sat for Dunwich, asked that he be given a cade and a half barrel of herrings instead of money, figuring he would be ahead on that basis.

This being the situation, it is hard to find a reason for calling a meeting of Parliament in Salisbury in April 1384. Salisbury was an established town of consequence, with its own beautiful cathedral and the right to be represented by two members, but it was sheer pandemonium when my lords the bishops and my lords the barons and all their horses and all their men descended upon it.

It was in this bedlam that a dramatic episode occurred. A Carthusian friar, unknown to anyone although it was reported that he came from Ireland, publicly charged the Duke of Lancaster with plotting the deposition and death of the king. Just when or where he made this statement, or the details of the conspiracy, history does not say. It was not made before the House, for certainly he would not have been allowed to enter there. Probably the mad friar (for he must have known that a painful death would be his sole reward) managed to worm his way into the headquarters of the king to divulge his information. The story came to Richard's ears, but his uncle had no difficulty in convincing him that the charge was baseless.

The solid market town of Salisbury, which had been converted into a veritable madhouse by this time, became the scene of noisy demonstrations. The popular dislike of the great Duke of Lancaster had been subsiding, but even the accusation of an unidentified friar was enough to set everyone against him again.

The friar was not sent to prison. Perhaps the gaols had been thrown open to accommodate visitors, for every building in town which boasted a roof was crowded from cellar to garret. Instead he was put into the charge of Sir John Holland, the king's half brother, who would later be made the Duke of Exeter. It was said that this was done on John of Gaunt's suggestion. A worse choice could not have been made, for this son of the queen mother by her first marriage was proud, cruel, and treacherous. The upshot was that on the night before the date fixed for the enquiry Holland coolly reported that the accuser had been killed. It developed that the order for the murder had come from Holland himself.

The crowded streets of the old town seethed with excitement and conjecture. Had the Duke of Lancaster connived with Holland to get rid of the witness against him? Or had the king and his party arranged the killing so that the duke would have no chance to refute the charge and thus be left under a cloud?

Thomas of Woodstock, as might have been expected, took the latter view. Although he and his brother John had continued on bad terms, he came storming into the king's chamber and declared that the whole thing was a conspiracy. The king, he cried, had abetted it.

"I will kill anyone," he declaimed with many oaths, his face black with rage, "who brings such charges against my brother. I will kill anyone. *No matter whom!*"

This could only be construed as a direct threat to the king, and as such was treason. But Richard, whose temper was sharp in most circumstances, and who was surrounded by advisers who confirmed him in an unshakable belief in kingly infallibility, had not yet been able to outgrow a fear of this browbeating uncle. The threat of violence to the royal person went unpunished.

John of Gaunt had, in the meantime, departed for his stronghold in Yorkshire, the castle of Pontefract. In some chronicles his exit is laid to a fear that his nephew would charge him with conspiracy but more likely he had sensed the rebirth of popular hatred and thought it wise to allow time for the storm to blow over. It is hard to believe him guilty. The only hint of complicity on his part is found in his preference for friars as his spiritual advisers. But that some at least of these wandering adherents to the faiths of St. Francis remained true to the strictest Franciscan rules was a proper reason for the duke's leaning to them. In any event could he be weak enough to conceive of a treasonable design which an obscure friar would be in a position to reveal?

The situation remained tense, for Thomas of Woodstock continued to voice threats against the king and those about him. The Commons, after a month of deliberation at Salisbury, made grants which were inadequate for the waging of determined war, contending that no more was needed in view of the truce with France which had still a year to run. The policy of the members could be perfectly defined by a phrase which would come into popular use nearly seven centuries later—too little and too late.

The ailing queen mother, who had reached the stage where she wanted nothing so much as the chance to coddle her aching bones in the comfort of her regal apartments, decided she must do something to aid her son in his difficulties. The first move, clearly, was to cure the differences, if any existed, between the young king and his uncle of Lancaster. Scarcely capable of placing a foot to the ground, she set out for Pontefract, using in all probability the cumbersome and jolting vehicle in which she had encountered those rough fellows, the men of Wat the Tyler. The mighty and forbidding castle (pronounced Pumfret), which covered eight acres of ground and had the same number of tall towers, lay roughly 180 miles north of London. It would take probably three weeks for the invalid to cover that much ground in her lumbering wagon but she accepted the ordeal cheerfully and willingly. In due course she arrived and proceeded to use her best endeavors to divine what was in John of Gaunt's mind and to bring him to a mood of complete reconciliation. In this she succeeded. The proud duke, who all his life had felt a consuming desire to sit on a throne and wear a crown of gold but had lacked the grim will to bring it about, was now accepting the inevitable. Even if the youthful king were removed, the choice would not fall on him. The English people would be willing to fight for the legal succession of the heirs of Lionel, the amiable and handsome six-foot-seven second son of Edward III or, failing that, they would prefer the belligerent Thomas to the suspect John. The only chance left was his nebulous claim to the throne of Castile. Constance, his Spanish second wife, who was living in a degree of confinement which suggested some impairment of her reason, was his sole excuse for this design. She had only one more year to live and nothing would come of his Castilian pretensions, but Richard's mother encouraged him, no doubt, by promises of support.

From that time on, although there were continuous whispers of plotting, the great duke seems to have stood on Richard's side, appreciating the difficulties under which that proud, not too gifted, and somewhat neurotic young ruler labored. But the same was not true of the younger uncle. This blustering member of the family, to whom the appellation of the Bully of Woodstock may fairly be ascribed, grew more and more antagonistic to Richard and even more willing to put difficulties in his path and to voice loud and sweeping criticism of everything he did.

## 4

This seems a good point to pause and propound questions with reference to the once great Plantagenets. Why did they all seem so impotent at this crisis in national affairs? Why was there so much opposition to Richard, who was still a boy and hardly likely to possess yet the force and character to be a strong king?

Perhaps the second proposition should be considered first. The fault with Richard, the chief fault as his kinsmen saw him, was his love of peace. He never acknowledged it openly but there is no mistaking the fact that he shrank from the whole issue of conflict. Possessing the pride, the passion, the revengeful traits of his forebears, he was still at this time a rather gentle and indolent boy who preferred to listen to his minstrels and to dip into those suspect instruments of weakness called books than to fight in tournaments and lead armies against the French. To one of his uncles, at least, he was a highly undesirable graft on the once vigorous and brilliantly leafed family tree. How could the war prosper and men be in a position to enjoy their real purpose in life, which was to leap into a saddle and exchange blows with everyone in sight, while the control of the nation lay in such slight and ineffective hands? Thomas of Woodstock, for one, saw only one solution to this problem. Get rid of him!

And now for the first query. It must seem to observers of the scene that the brilliant family had for the space of one generation, at least, fallen into a decline. The men were still tall and handsome and the women were winsome and lovable in the fair-haired Plantagenet way, but where was the spark, the will to accomplish, the gift of success? No longer was there a real trace of the conquering, firm governing instinct of Henry II. The desire to lead armies to war and to fight furiously with sword and mace on foreign strands and on burning deserts, which animated Richard of the Lion Heart: what had happened to that inheritance, questionable though it seems? Where was the splendid spirit of another warrior king, Edward I, who saw the need to establish decent order in law and procedure in the semi-feudal country he was called upon to rule? Where was the lavish and tinsel greatness of the successful Edward III?

The deterioration (which had broken out with several previous members of the family: the cruel John, the weak gadfly Henry III, and the sad oaf Edward II) had set in with the numerous brood that Queen Philippa brought into the world. Edward the Black Prince was the only one to measure up to the highest Plantagenet standards and yet there was as much to deplore as to admire in that hero of fixed ideas, who vitiated English strength in France to fight for a cruel, degenerate king of Castile in defense of the most rigid conception of monarchial rule, but who, because of the magnificent courage of his death, has remained a shining figure in English history. He lacked, certainly, the wisdom to make a strong and admirable king of England. Then there was John of Gaunt, suave, handsome, cultured, with great ambition, but lacking in the resolution that was the first of the great Plantagenet traits and thus is condemned to a rather shabby role in history. Two of the other sons, the amiable giant Lionel, who died early, and the mediocre Edmund of Langley, had little share of the family fineness. Finally, there was the insensitive, overbearing Thomas of Woodstock, who always appears on the pages of history in moments of black rage, in loud declamation, in selfish maneuvers.

In none of them is it possible to detect the kingly qualities of the family. Not a single spark of genius for government or war could have been struck from the Plantagenets of this generation.

Richard, who would have been happy in warm Bordeaux where he was born, was sadly miscast as King of England. His role, unfortunately for him, was to be that of target for this mediocre group who stormed and conspired around him and were as incapable as he of preserving the imperial heritage which had come down to them.

The Plantagenets would have a resurgence of greatness later—in Henry V, in that handsome and capable soldier Edward IV (until he became fat and unkempt and more interested in his amours than in the toil of kingship), and finally in the traces of grandeur which can be found in the much maligned Richard III.

## CHAPTER XVI

## The Daring Grocer

DURING this summer which saw the reconciliation between the king and John of Gaunt, and very little else to the credit of anyone in particular, there died a man who deserves more attention in the annals of the day than he is usually accorded. First as an alderman and then as lord mayor of London, John Philipot had played a prominent and courageous part in public affairs. Unlike William Walworth, who also played a courageous part, there are no circumstances to be glossed over in his career.

When the Grocers Company of London was formed in 1345 by the union of the spicerers and pepperers, Philipot was a charter member. He soon became wealthy and was returned by London as a member of Parliament. In that capacity he stood out against the efforts of the Lancastrian party to gain control and he was spokesman for the deputation which waited on the very old and ill Edward III to explain the riots in London against Duke John and his followers.

His first great exploit was in 1377, shortly after the accession of Richard to the throne. The initiative in the Hundred Years War had been taken over by the enemy across the Channel. The French ships of war were ravaging the English coast. A party of men-at-arms landed and captured the Isle of Wight. Things came to a serious juncture when a Scot named Mercer, in command of a fleet of French, Scottish, and Spanish ships, sailed boldly into Scarborough and captured all the English vessels there.

Philipot waited for the heads of the nation to act. Nothing was done. A strange apathy seemed to have settled on the nation. When it became certain that there would be no official action, John Philipot decided to take things into his own hands. At his personal expense he assembled some English ships of war with the necessary supplies and equipment, recruited a thousand men, and set out in pursuit of the marauding squadron.

He was spectacularly successful, overtaking Mercer and giving him a sound drubbing. As a result, he recovered all the English ships and captured fifteen Spanish vessels as well. This was the kind of boldness and enterprise which had marked the earlier stages of the war with France and had won so many great victories. The nation responded with wild enthusiasm to the exploit of the bold grocer.

But this enthusiasm was not felt in the higher reaches of the social structure. Most of the barons said openly that Philipot, a commoner and a civilian, had no right to act thus on his own responsibility. The Earl of Stafford took it on himself to confront the amateur admiral and complain of his conduct.

"My lord earl," answered the alderman, "if the nobles of England had not left the country open to invasion, it would not have been necessary for me to interfere."

King Richard had been delighted with Philipot's success and so had to bear a share of the disapproval of the baronage. He was openly referred to as the "King of London."

The city responded by electing Philipot lord mayor for the years 1378 and 1379. In that important office he proceeded to break precedent by many progressive steps. The stench of London streets was proverbial and Philipot had them thoroughly cleaned. Levying a special tax of five pence on each house, he raised enough to dredge and cleanse the city ditch which had always been the recipient of household filth. Another measure he undertook was the erection of two high stone towers on opposite banks of the Thames below London Bridge, which enabled the city to suspend a chain across the river when there was danger of invasion. The patriotic Philipot paid the cost of one tower out of his own pocket.

He was with the king during the Peasants' Revolt and was one of four citizens knighted at Clerkenwell Fields after the killing of Wat Tyler. Granted the right of coat armor, he was given a pension of forty pounds a year for his loyalty and zeal. There were still plenty of dissentients, however. When John of Northampton became mayor he deposed Philipot from his place as an alderman. It was supposed that this action was part of a campaign to lessen the influence of the trade guilds but it seems more likely the result of personal animus.

And now this highly admirable citizen came to the end of his days in his house in Langbourne Ward. His will, which was a generous one, left some lands in the city to be held in perpetual trust for the relief of any thirteen poor people to be designated by the board. London gave the name of Philpot Lane to the street on which his house had stood.

It seems unfortunate that no balladeer saw fit to immortalize him in a legend as unforgettable as that in which a poor apprentice named Dick Whittington, running away from his master, heard in the sound of Bow bells the words,

> *Turn again, Whittington,*
> *Lord Mayor of London.*

The real Richard Whittington, who was a mercer and acquired great wealth, was a young member of the aldermanic board in the days of Sir John Philipot.

## CHAPTER XVII

## The King's Favorite

*1*

ROBERT de Vere, Earl of Oxford, was fifteen years old when Richard became king. He was not a Piers Gaveston, a Robert Carr, nor a George Villiers, to mention a few of the young men who won royal favor by their charm. He seems to have been lacking in that quality, a rather plain stripling, without any particular degree of talent, ambitious without the qualities or the energy to warrant his pretensions, selfish, unreliable, and grasping. But the ten-year-old Richard seems to have picked him as a friend from the beginning.

It is said that Sir Simon Burley had a hand in the role that de Vere assumed, having been generously treated by the youthful earl in the matter of a Hereford manor. But a preference on Burley's part would not suffice to explain the favor that the king proceeded to display. De Vere was given the custody of royal castles and the profitable wardship of heirs. He was given properties and hereditary offices and was made a member of the privy council against parliamentary advice. He became a member of the Garter, ahead of scores of candidates with much better claims.

The critics through the period of the minority were strongly against many of the advisers selected by the king. They granted the knightly qualities of Sir Simon Burley but resented his rapid rise from shabby gentility to affluence. They could not deny the ability of Michael de la Pole, but he was a commoner and they could not stomach his advancement in the royal confidence. But for Robert de Vere there was nothing good to be said. He was of impeccable descent but he lacked all the qualities which men who stand behind a king should possess.

Two years after the charges were brought against John of Gaunt at

Salisbury, the French king landed an army in Scotland. An army of defense was hastily organized and Richard took command himself, with all his uncles around him to lend advice, and Robert de Vere for good measure.

The Scots followed their usual defensive tactics. When Richard crossed the border on August 6, 1385, the Scots fell back, leaving the road to Edinburgh open. While the English took possession of that city, the Scots made counterraids into Westmoreland and Cumberland and ravaged the country thoroughly and savagely. The young king did not know how to come to grips with this elusive foe. John of Gaunt urged him to advance beyond the Firth of Forth and compel the Scottish forces to drop back for defensive purposes. .This was sound advice but the king listened instead to the indolent and untrained de Vere. That young gentleman pointed out that the Scots were behind the royal army and that the English position was becoming untenable. Get back before it was too late, advised the timorous de Vere. To the chagrin of the uncles and of every experienced soldier in the army, this course was adopted. Soured by this adolescent decision, the army retreated back across the border, leaving Edinburgh in flames and finding in the northern counties the smoking ruins that the Scots had left behind them. As usual the campaign had been a complete and sorry failure.

Another member of the inner circle of favorites had ridden in the royal train to Scotland, John Holland, the half brother who had taken it on himself to murder the Carthusian friar at Salisbury. On the march north he became the central figure in a still more violent episode. One of his squires was attacked by an archer in the train of Hugh, the son of the Earl of Stafford. In an army made up of forces brought into the field by members of the nobility, such quarrels were common. Holland did not wait for any explanation, however. He started out that night for the Stafford camp in a surly temper. It happened that Ralph, a Stafford son, decided at the same time to wait on Holland in an effort to make amends. Their paths crossed in the darkness.

"Who rides abroad at this late hour?" demanded Holland, reining in his horse.

"Ralph of Stafford," was the answer, the youth not having recognized the voice of the king's half brother.

Without waiting for another word, the surly Holland drew his sword and lunged out into the darkness. The blade pierced the young knight's side and he fell from his saddle, mortally wounded. Without waiting to take any steps about the body, the killer turned and rode back to his own camp. He did not seem to have any compunction about what he had done. The brother of a king could do no wrong.

But Richard took a different view. Fond as he was of these hotheaded older sons of his mother, he realized that he could not condone unprovoked murder. The Earl of Stafford demanded that the vicious Holland be made to pay for his murderous attack and it was clear that the nobility were back of him. Suddenly realizing that being half brother to a king was not a warrant for wanton murder, Holland fled into sanctuary in the church of St. John of Beverley. The king's first hostile move was an order for the confiscation of all Holland's properties.

Word of what had happened reached the ears of the murderer's mother. Finding that Richard was not prepared to throw the cloak of royal immunity over his guilty half brother, she sent frantic messages north, begging for mercy. Richard remained adamant. The queen mother's condition had been growing worse and this blow was more than she could stand. She died in August of that year while her royal son was leading his army across the Scottish border and before receiving any definite word of her other son's fate.

The punishment finally imposed on Holland was light. He was ordered to provide chantries where Masses could be said in perpetuity for the soul of Ralph of Stafford, two to be stationed at the spot where the murder was committed and the third at his grave. In a very short space of time the confiscated properties were returned to him. He was permitted to marry Elizabeth, a daughter of John of Gaunt, and years later was made Duke of Exeter. The reason for the young king's leniency is, of course, a matter of conjecture. He undoubtedly was influenced by the affection he had always felt for his older and lordly half brother and it seems equally clear that his belief in the infallibility of kings convinced him that Holland was above punishment. It is quite possible also that his grief for his mother swayed him to a belated attitude of mercy. One thing is certain: the family of the slain knight never forgave John Holland and became savagely critical of the king.

In the hope no doubt of placating his troublesome family, Richard made his uncle Edmund the Duke of York and Thomas the Duke of Gloucester. To avoid any confusion of identities in the minds of readers it will be advisable to continue use of the name Woodstock in connection with Thomas, particularly as he will continue to play a prominent part in the annals of this stormy and unhappy reign.

2

Richard realized that he had not covered himself with glory in Scotland, but the failure of his efforts in the field did not persuade him to take a common-sense view of the need for reform in the administrative machinery he had set up. When the faults of Robert de Vere were dinned into his ears, his only response was to pile new honors on his favorite. Unfortunately he thought of Ireland as a suitable field for his friend.

Conditions in that country were growing increasingly bad. The English had become little more than settlers, confining themselves to a section of the country which continued to shrink. There was a belt of land about Dublin, comprising the counties of Dublin, Meath, Kildare, and Louth, which was called the Pale. For some time the English had been staying exclusively within the Pale, even though its limits were growing narrower all the time. The Irish people, living beyond the Pale, continued to do as they pleased and paid no attention to English laws. The line between Irish and English was not as great as it would become later (particularly in the reign of Henry VI when the English were compelled by law to shave their upper lips to mark the distinction), but it was tightly drawn. The feeling had become so high that it was no longer a felony for an Englishman to kill one of the natives. All he had to do was to claim that the victim was a thief. It was not surprising that the English settlers had been steadily dropping back to the comparative safety of the city of Dublin. "The little place" was the term they now used for the Pale.

Around the limits of the Pale the Irish leaders kept close watch and ward. The most active of them was one Art MacMurrough and, when he died in 1377, his son who was also called Art took up the work. Art the Second, twenty years of age, who rode without saddle or bridle and whose voice was a high-pitched and vibrant summons to battle, proved more belligerent than his father. He married an Anglo-Irish wife named Eliza de Veele, a lady of property, but this alliance did not lead to better relations with the English. The viceroy of the moment in Dublin decided that the fair Eliza had violated the law in marrying the handsome MacMurrough. When her lands in Norragh were confiscated, Art declared open war.

From all parts of Ireland came assistance. The O'Briens, the O'Tooles, the O'Dempseys came marching to Art's assistance and it began to look as though the Pale would shrink to the vanishing point.

In London it was realized that a strong hand was needed in Ireland. The solution that Richard found was the appointment of de Vere, with powers that were almost royal in their scope. The selection was reported to a surprised Parliament as being made "in consideration of his noble blood, strenuous probity, eminent wisdom and great achievements." It was stipulated that the conquest and unification of the sister island must be completed in two years and that the annual deficit must be corrected in the same period of time. These conditions made the position an onerous one to assume and there was a sly tendency to look favorably on the appointment as a means of demonstrating the incompetence of the young man in a most unmistakable way.

But the young king went a step further. He named de Vere the Marquis of Dublin, borrowing the title from the French table of nobility, or, conceivably, adapting it from the German *markgraf*. Now the title of duke was reserved for the sons of kings, so that an earldom was the highest honor that a member of the baronage could obtain. The new title was wedged in beneath that of duke, which meant that the holder, this thoroughly unpopular young man, could dangle it in the jealous eyes of all the earls in England. The barons could wink at an appointment which placed unbearable burdens on the shoulders of the favorite but to have him strutting proudly above them was more than they could stand.

De Vere made matters worse by showing no inclination to take up his new and difficult duties. Instead of setting out immediately for Ireland, where there was fighting around the edges of the Pale and the English hold seemed to be weakening, he remained at court and enjoyed to the fullest the honors which went with the new title. The situation grew steadily worse in Ireland, but the marquis went on hunting and hawking and dining fastidiously at court where he was entitled to a prominent seat, close enough to royalty, in fact, to talk directly with the king and queen on matters which had to do with music, art, and books, matters which were well over the heads of the rest of the company who could throw their gnawed bones accurately over their shoulders but had never heard of the French Romances.

De Vere then proceeded to stir the general feeling about him into a positive fury. He fell in love with a Bohemian girl who had come over in the train of Queen Anne and set about getting a divorce.

It is necessary at this point to cast back some years. Edward III had been such a fond father that he dreaded marrying his beautiful daughters, presented to him at regular intervals by Queen Philippa, because it meant they would have to leave England and, perhaps, never come back. He seems to have been especially fond of his oldest daughter, the blonde and lovely Princess Isabella. Although many matches were discussed for her, she remained unmarried until she was thirty-one years old (decidedly middle-aged in those days), when a proud French noble-man named Enquerrand de Coucy was sent to England as one of the hostages demanded in negotiations about the captive King John of France. This French lord was only twenty-four years old and was as proud as Lucifer (*King, duke, prince nor earl am I*, read the motto on his crest, *I am the Lord of Coucy*), but he fell in love with the still rather dazzling Isabella. As it was a love match and as arrangements, moreover, could be made for the princess to spend much of her time in England, Edward had consented to the marriage. The happy pair brought two daughters into the world, the younger being named after her grandmother, Philippa. The princess, whose husband had been given wide estates and the English title of Earl of Bedford, was still one of the beauties of the court and rode to the hunt on saddles of red velvet embroidered with violets of gold; the uneven marriage was a most happy one, in spite of the fact that it broke up later because the proud lord of Coucy felt impelled to fight again on the French side. She was most generous and liked to be a fairy godmother, throwing money about with mad abandon. Naturally she was very much liked and her two little fair-haired girls were symbols of loyalty to the Crown.

And this brings us to the year 1371 when the child Philippa was betrothed to Robert de Vere, who had inherited one of the finest ancestral estates in England. The marriage took place seven years later, on June 30, 1378. While her husband was being made the recipient of these many honors, the lady Philippa had grown into a handsome and well-esteemed lady. The roving eye of young Robert de Vere, however, was caught by the Bohemian girl who had come to England. His far from stable affections seemed to have been suddenly and disastrously unsettled.

In some reports the girl is called a landgravine, and the *Foedera* changes this title to *landgravissa,* an obscure honor which can not be proved to have existed. Some English authorities declare that she was of low birth, the daughter of a Flemish saddler but, inasmuch as she was officially a lady in waiting on the queen, this statement can be dis-missed. There is no more substance to the claim that she was dark and ugly. Dark she probably was, but the gay favorite could hardly have fallen in love with anyone lacking in physical attraction. It is clear, moreover, that she had been sent to England as custodian of the jewels and valuables bestowed on Anne by the empress and that she remained to act as a lady of the bedchamber. Her name was Launcecrona and she was undoubtedly chic and lively, with a foreign kind of prettiness. De Vere would have plenty of opportunities to observe her as she tripped about her duties at court, to note her trimness of figure, her gaiety and volatility of mood.

There are two versions given of the course which events took. One is that Queen Anne was against the determination of de Vere to divorce his highborn wife and marry the vivacious Launcecrona. The other is that Anne, through fondness for her lady in waiting and perhaps under pressure from the king and his favorite, wrote to the Pope, urging that the divorce be granted. In the eyes of the little Anne the king could do no wrong and it is quite possible that she strove to carry out his wishes, even though she may have foreseen troubles ahead. The latter explanation was believed for a time and resulted in some loss of the popularity she enjoyed. The divorce was granted, on false evidence, during the year which de Vere wasted after his appointment to the overlordship of Ireland. The discarded wife being a full cousin of Richard and a niece of Thomas of Woodstock, it did not need the loud and angry protests of the latter to set tongues to wagging throughout the land.

It must have been at this time that the king decided to ride the storm blowing about him because of his support of this unworthy friend by applying a touch of the royal spur. When Parliament met in October of the same year and demanded the resignations of some of the king's advisers, he went to the opposite extreme and raised de Vere from the title invented for him to that of Duke of Dublin, thus putting him on a par with the royal uncles. The administrative position of the new Irish viceroy had in the meantime been clearly defined. De Vere was to have an almost absolute hand, even the right of coinage. The royal rights to homage alone were denied. The ransom of a French prisoner of war, John of Blois, which had been fixed at 30,000 marks, was allocated for the use of the new duke, who was to take with him to Ireland 500 men-of-war and a thousand archers. The right was granted him to quarter with his own arms the three golden crowns on a field azure which had belonged to the early kings of England.

To demonstrate his belief that great things could be expected when this new overlord began his operations in Erin, the king accompanied him to Wales with great state and hurrah. The opposition breathed sighs of relief. They confidently expected developments which would please them when the overdressed, overconfident courtier found himself opposed to Art MacMurrough and the rest of the wild Irish.

But the journey to Wales was a blind. De Vere was not going to Ireland yet.

### 3

Since John of Gaunt had in his later years turned mild and even idealistic in his attitude to the throne, a new party of opposition had been forming in England. As leader, in place of the now quiescent head of the family of Lancaster, was the younger brother, Thomas of Woodstock, a more militant and proud figure than John had ever been. At the right hand of this dark and grasping uncle stood Gaunt's son, Henry of Derby. Despite the fact that it was Henry of Derby who had married Mary de Bohun and so alienated from Thomas half of the fair lands and rich inheritances of the Bohun family, the two were working together now with singleness of purpose. Derby had all the dynastic ambition of his father but combined with this a stubbornness of will and a readiness to gamble which John of Gaunt had lacked.

A waning in Richard's personal popularity in London had led to the elevation of Derby in his stead. The Londoners, tough and assertive in most things, had a weakness for show and had always found it easy to cheer for the Plantagenets and the wives they brought over from the continent. Derby had the same princely appearance as Richard, the Plantagenet reddish golden glow and the straight strong figure, and the citizens and their apprentices were ready enough to transfer their affections. Richard had been so loudly acclaimed at the beginning that he did not fall completely out of favor until toward the end, but his stock could fall as sharply as it rose. It went into a decline when this savagely antagonistic group came together.

This made a dangerous combination, the stormy Thomas and the coldly aspiring Henry of Derby. They could not be expected to stand together long, but for the moment they saw eye to eye and were prepared to work in unison.

Back of the two leaders was the aggressive figure of Richard, Earl of Arundel, who was as bitterly against the king as Thomas of Woodstock and perhaps of a more revengeful nature. In support of this trio came more baronial magnates. Thomas de Beauchamp, Earl of Warwick, was the most prominent, a withdrawn type of man without any pretensions but lacking in the courage for political conflict, as would be discovered later. Next came Thomas de Mowbray, Earl of Nottingham, who was about Richard's age and had been on friendly terms with the young king. He was not prominent in the early stages of the struggle but later would emerge in a contradictory role, most of the time with the king but always an uncertain adherent.

Finally there was Courtenay, who was now Archbishop of Canterbury and so wielded much influence. He had been outspoken in his criticism of the king, in public as well as in private talks with Richard, and had earned the active dislike of the young ruler.

The opposition scored heavily in the Parliament which sat in October 1386. They demanded that the king dismiss his chancellor and treasurer. His immediate answer was an expression of the pride of place and belief in kingly prerogative he had inherited from his father.

"I would not dismiss the meanest varlet in my kitchen at their bidding!"
he declared.

He refused to go before the House to discuss the demands and posted
off instead to the royal residence at Eltham. His uncle of Woodstock went
there to have it out with him, accompanied by the Bishop of Ely, who
was a brother of the Earl of Arundel. Woodstock did not mince words.
If Richard did not return at once, as his oath of office demanded, he
might share the fate of Edward II. On no other occasion in English
history had a threat of deposition been voiced so openly and so sharply
and, it must be said, with so little justification. It was inevitable that a
boy of such immature years would make mistakes, and thus far Richard's weaknesses had not been serious enough to jeopardize the welfare
of the realm. In the matter of the war, his role had been no more dilatory
than that of the House. It still could be anticipated that with sympathetic
guidance he could be taught to play his role. If anyone else had been
wearing the crown, Woodstock would have been bundled off to the
Tower to face charges of treason. He seems to have had no fear whatever, knowing that the adolescent ruler was in no position to play a
strong hand.

Richard's weakness was that he had not built a strong enough party
about him to face the demands of the magnates. In addition he had
placed in their hands a rod for his own back by his persistent favoring
of Robert de Vere. About the king and his adoring queen at Eltham
there was a small group of supporters, but he had no force he could
rally at once to his aid. On the other hand, Thomas of Woodstock could
bring ample strength into action against him. Realizing his impotence,
Richard returned to London and faced the determined House.

The result was that Pole, who now had the title of Earl of Suffolk,
was superseded as chancellor. This able minister was impeached and
sentenced to a term of imprisonment as well as a heavy fine. That
Parliament was content to make him the scapegoat and leave de Vere
alone is hard to understand, unless the members thought that, being a
commoner, he was more vulnerable than the high-placed Duke of Dublin.

Richard was compelled, moreover, to acquiesce in the appointment of a
commission of eleven members to exercise for a year the power of control
in the royal household.

## CHAPTER XVIII

## England Faces Invasion

### 1

WITH troubles enough at home, the nation now found itself threatened by French aggression on a huge scale. The French king, Charles V, called in history Charles the Wise, had died, leaving a situation very similar to that in England. His heir and successor was a year younger than Richard, and the late king had fixed his majority at fourteen years. But, as in England, there was a group of royal uncles who struggled among themselves for authority during the years of his minority and beyond, the Dukes of Anjou, Berry, Burgundy, and Bourbon. They were a troublesome lot, intent on fattening their own pockets and stirring up rebellions in various parts of the country by their illegal exactions. The boy king of France, however, was of a different stamp from Richard. He gained the victory of Roosebeke over Philip van Artevelde in his fourteenth year (with the help, of course, of his marshals) and in quick order seated himself firmly in the saddle. He had one burning desire in his youthful head—to wipe out the stain of the defeats inflicted by the English on his grandfather and great-grandfather in the first half of the Hundred Years War. A mere victory was not going to satisfy him. He wanted to destroy the English as a nation by killing every man and burning the cities and towns to the ground. Like Joshua when he set about the conquest of Canaan, young King Charles wanted no trace left of this hated breed. This seemed mere youthful bravado at first. The English met his threats with confident smiles. But when he began to assemble great armies and fleets along the Channel, things took on a different complexion.

This bellicose young man had been married in 1385 and the story of his romance is so unusual that it seems excusable to pause long enough here to tell about it. Charles was so brimming with confidence that he wanted the best of everything. The wife he would choose must be the most beautiful girl in the world and he paid little attention at first to reports brought him of a Bavarian princess named Isabeau. Finally the girl's father, most reluctantly, agreed to send his daughter to France *on approval*. If the French king did not want her, she would turn about at once and go home. Had such a thing ever happened before? The feeling in Bavaria, however, was one of complete confidence. The princess was a voluptuous and radiant beauty. Her mother had been an Italian princess and so Isabeau combined the clear and rosy complexion of her father's people with the lustrous dark hair and dusky, long-lashed eyes of her mother. Could anyone resist her?

Not Charles of France. He needed no more than one glance to make up his mind. They were married at once.

The ports of northern France were not large enough to hold the fleet they assembled on the king's orders. Not content with scores of cogs and caracks and taricks which were built for war, they collected every other kind of vessel which could be used for naval purposes: balingers, crayers, doggers, lodeships, two-masted fluves, galiots, hockboats, and keels to carry supplies, and the fast liques to serve for communications between the fighting ships and to carry messages ashore.

The ships of war were built stoutly and carried crews of sixty-five men for each hundred tons, as well as archers and men-at-arms. The sails, or "triefs" as they were called in those days, were crimson or yellow. By the time the contractors had collected everything needed in the way of hevedropes, backstays, skalters, uptyes, leechdropes, and ribondes, the ports of France had room for nothing else.

The one great mistake in the calculations of this berserk youth was that he demanded too much of everything. Not content with commandeering ships that could operate under sail, thereby packing the northern ports like poultry crates going to market, he proceeded to assemble large armies, so large that the troops encamping along the French side of the Channel consumed all the food available and drove the inhabitants into such a frame of mind that they did not care about defeating the English as long as the attack was made at once.

"Go to England!" cried the harried and despoiled people. "And may never a soul of you come back!"

The measures taken in England to meet this threat were not thorough enough to reassure the people. Efforts were made at once to have the naval strength of the nation organized but, as usual, there was a great deal of slackness about it. The main ships of war were considered superior to the French, but Spain was now in alliance with France and the Spaniards had ships of extraordinary height. They stood so high in the water, in fact, that it would be impossible to board them. The Earl of Arundel, whose tardiness in action had cost the country heavy losses in earlier years, was put in command of all naval operations. One of the reasons given for his appointment was that "no one can chastise or rule them unless he be a great man," referring undoubtedly to the need of severe discipline—not a sufficient reason, certainly, in itself.

As long as the French fleet remained cooped up in the ports, bound together and with chains across the harbor entrances, there was no need for major measures. But fortunately the example of that bold grocer, Sir John Philipot, was still a vivid memory in English minds. A vigorous campaign of attrition was kept up by private owners and by all vessels not being held in idle reserve. A handful of daring buccaneers sailed up the Seine and captured a number of French ships, including a handsome and costly cog on which Olivier de Clisson, the constable of France, intended to cross the Channel. A French fleet attempting to pass Calais was attacked by the garrison and eighteen ships were captured or sunk.

Not discouraged by the loss of his favorite cog, the constable set out from Trequier for Sluys, which had been designated the main point of French concentration, with seventy-two large ships of war. Young Charles arrayed himself in armor every day, intending to launch the great offensive as soon as the junction had been effected. On one of the cogs were parts of a wooden house to be assembled in England so that Clisson "and the lords could be housed in comfort" after the landing. A great man for useless detail, this bold Clisson. His reason in this case was not that they thought so ill of English architecture. They intended to destroy everything made of sticks and stones or bricks and wattles, so that no roof would be left standing in all of the hated realm. But the weather began to take a hand, as it so often did around this unruly stretch of water. When the proud constable and his armada arrived off Margate there was such a blowing of hostile winds that the ships were dispersed. Three of the largest were captured, including the one which contained the parts for that luxurious wooden house.

It must be acknowledged that a state of alarm prevailed in England while the belligerent boy king of France made these gigantic preparations. There were a few timorous souls who took to the woods with the intention of saving their skins by staying there. The trained band captains of London kept a patrol on the city walls, although the danger of invasion was still remote.

In the main, however, the people were stout of heart. "Let them come!" was heard all over the land. "They'll find us ready for them!"

In the alehouses the boast was still voiced which had grown out of the victories of Crécy and Poictiers: that one Englishman was better than any given number of Frenchmen.

After two years of futile starts and embarrassing stops, of miscalculations and mishaps, the French believed themselves ready. With the oriflamme carried before him, in his shining mail, with a great plume in his helmet and the fleur-de-lis in solid gold on his velvet cloak, young King Charles arrived at Notre Dame for a Solemn Mass. Leaving the cathedral, he saluted his sultry young queen.

"Fairest lady, I go to lead my armies," he said. "I make this my purpose and my vow that not until I have destroyed England shall I return to Paris."

He was more explicit to those who took horse with him. Not only were all Englishmen to be put to death but the women and children were to be carried back to slavery in France.

2

And then something in the way of a miracle happened.

A final assemblage of ships had been ordered, and a great fleet made up of Spanish vessels as well as French set sail from Rochelle for Sluys under the command of Sir Jean de Bucq, a Flemish admiral. Nothing to equal this fleet in strength would be seen again in the Channel until the memorable days when the Spanish Armada would sail in awesome grandeur past the watchers at Plymouth Hoe.

The Earl of Arundel, once so dilatory and lacking in resource, acted with admirable coolness. He waited until an astonished voice from the lookout reported that the whole horizon was suddenly filled with the crimson sails of the enemy. Arundel proceeded to put about in retreat, his purpose being to lure the enemy concentration into pursuit. The French would have none of that. They paid no attention to the English maneuvers, but sailed majestically on to keep their rendezvous.

Because of this aloofness of the enemy, Arundel resorted to another plan of attack. He drew off and waited for the wind to change. When the gods who directed the tides and the weather obliged with a shift in wind which favored the English, Arundel gave the order to attack.

Froissart's detailed description of the battle says that English galleys, filled with eager and expert archers, led the attack. The French sailed on through the hail of arrows which blackened the sky without damaging losses. The larger English vessels then went into action. They "rushed at the French like sparrow-hawks pouncing on small birds." Although some of the French ships had crude cannon which "vomed" (a word preferred at the time to "vomit") heavy stones at the persistent English, the battle quickly shifted in favor of the islanders. It lasted through three turns of the tide, and in the end the English scored a complete victory, capturing as many as eighty of the enemy ships.

Arundel, turned into a veritable demon of aggression by this taste of the heady wine of success, followed the scattered remnants of the great fleet to Sluys where he hoped to destroy the naval strength assembled there. He not only mounted a heavy attack on the French ships but landed troops on both sides of the river and burned all the towns and villages. After ten days he returned and sailed up the Thames in triumph, bringing with him an estimated 200,000 francs' worth of property, in addition to 19,000 tuns of fine wine which had been taken from ships captured during the naval engagement. No form of loot could satisfy more fully the lusty citizens who shared in the welcome.

Hungry for victory after so many years of reverses, the people of England greeted the successful earl with great joy. Arundel found himself a national hero.

This defeat so shook young King Charles that he decided to give up his ambition to invade the stubborn island. With convenient forgetfulness of his vows he sullenly rode back to Paris. He did not at once order his ships back into peace-time activities, but the obnoxious armies were withdrawn from the Channel towns. Olivier de Clisson constructed no more houses from which to direct the conquest of England.

The threat of invasion would arise many times again in the centuries to follow but with no more success.

Charles of France and Queen Isabeau, and the daughters born to them, were destined to play further parts in the history of England. All four of the princesses were charming and intelligent as well as attractive, although none of them equaled their mother for beauty. Two of them were to become queens of England.

It becomes necessary at this point to explain that, soon after the defeat of his plans to overrun England, life went sadly awry for Charles of France. He suffered a fit of madness in 1392 while leading an army to attack Brittany. He was riding in the van and suddenly spurred his horse out into the lead, crying aloud that he was surrounded by enemies who sought his life. Reaching a dusty plain, he rode madly back and forth under a broiling sun until it was seen necessary to take him forcibly in hand. He fought furiously with his guards.

When the queen was brought to see him, he did not recognize her. "Who is this woman?" he cried. "Take her away! Take her away!"

The attack passed, but there were recurrences over a period of several years and finally he became incurably insane.

The voluptuous Isabeau behaved very badly afterward. She had many lovers and figured in bitter feuds and was even believed to have been guilty of planning an assassination. She won for herself an enduring reputation as one of the worst women in French history. But her daughters were lucky enough to inherit none of her worst qualities.

## CHAPTER XIX

## The Merciless Parliament

*1*

THE naval losses suffered by the French did not entirely remove the danger of invasion which had been hanging over the island. But Arundel's victory gave the English renewed confidence and assured them of time to prepare for any further aggression that the youthful king of France, now considerably chastened, might attempt.

The recalcitrant barons, feeling themselves strengthened by Arundel's success and the popularity it had won for him, continued to control the administration at Westminster with firm hands. Thomas of Woodstock and Arundel's brother, the Bishop of Ely, took the Great Seal into their keeping and used it with no regard for the wishes of the unhappy king. Richard's temper was more combustible than the guns he had been experimenting with in the Tower, but he held it in control, having a power of dissimulation upon which he called at many critical stages during his reign. At first he swallowed his pride and accepted the humiliating conditions forced upon him.

Michael de la Pole had been sentenced to imprisonment "at the king's pleasure." Thomas of Woodstock was confident that Richard would never succeed in wriggling free of his firm thumb and believed he could keep Pole in perpetual imprisonment. Richard, quietly, had different ideas.

The ex-chancellor was not kept at the Tower but was sent to Windsor where Sir Simon Burley acted as constable. Burley and Pole were the closest of friends and the former saw to it that his new prisoner had comfortable quarters in the Norman tower which communicated with the king's house by a short interior passage. It was thus possible for Richard to keep in touch with the man he still considered his most dependable adviser. As soon as the cloud of impending danger from

France was dispersed, the king exercised his option and set Pole at liberty.

When word of this reached London, the barons were furiously angry. The Earl of Arundel invaded the king's bedroom while Richard was having a bath and stormed at him for what he had done.

"Burley," he declared, "deserves death of this!"

Always a bad judge of political timing, Richard selected this moment for his excursion into Wales to see his friend de Vere off for Ireland, to which reference has already been made. They were accompanied by Pole, the Archbishop of York, and chief justice Tresilian. All were in agreement that Parliament had acted beyond its rights in forcing such concessions from the young king, and a meeting was arranged with the board of justices at Nottingham to discuss the fundamental issues at stake. Five of the justices gave it as their opinion, first, that the House had infringed on the royal prerogatives; second, that the power of adjournment rested with the king; and, finally, that the Commons had no right to impeach a Crown officer unless acting with the consent of the king. Later the five declared thay had acted under pressure in giving these opinions, but at the time Richard had no doubt that he had won his case.

He returned to London and was warmly welcomed by the citizens. But when he heard that his uncle of Woodstock and the Earl of Warwick had taken up arms and were marching on the city, he appealed in vain to the burghers to arm in his behalf. Even the members of the baronage who had not yet joined the dissentients were lukewarm.

"I have no wish, my lord king," declared one of them, the Earl of Northumberland, "to have my head broken for the Duke of Dublin."

That was the rub. The country could not stomach the continual preference for that proud young man of such indifferent parts. But Richard proceeded to act with the impetuosity and poor judgment of youth. He should have waited for the more moderate of the barons to reach the conclusion that the pressure exerted on him was unfair, a view they would undoubtedly have taken when the highhandedness of the "pressure group" became clear. He sent de Vere to Chester to raise an armed force in the north and thus played into the hands of his opponents.

If there had been any strain of leadership in the still adolescent Earl of Oxford, the king's move would have been effective. Chester was one of the royal earldoms and it lay close to the borders of North Wales where Richard still held the affections of the people. But the lack of dispatch that de Vere displayed enabled the three opposing leaders to take the initiative. Woodstock, Warwick, and Arundel met at Hunting-

don, which straddled Ermine Street, the great Roman highroad running
north and south. It was a sound selection for strategic reasons, lying more
than a hundred miles closer to London than Chester and thus enabling
the barons to close off any attempt on de Vere's part to join forces with
the king in the capital. It is said the trio were determined that the boy
king would have to be deposed and that all the lesser barons who had
joined them were in agreement.

De Vere finally succeeded in raising a force estimated at 5000 men
and started his southward march. Riding proudly in the van with the
folds of the royal standard coiling in the breezes above his head, the
new duke seemed confident of overawing all opposition. He was due for
an unpleasant surprise. The dissentients had already raised a stronger
army than his. They had moreover acted with military acumen in
advancing to Northampton, where they blocked his route to London.
De Vere, who lacked that quality completely, made the mistake of
circling to the westward in the hope of getting around the enemy.
They countered by throwing part of their forces behind him, thus
cutting off any possible retreat to Chester.

De Vere proceeded to display a sorry lack of capacity for command.
In fact, he seems to have fallen into a panic. Approaching the crossing
of the Thames at Radcot Bridge, with his badly organized command
straggling along behind him, he suddenly found himself facing the vanguard of the baronial army under the Earl of Arundel. This was a bad
plight for a military tyro, to face a strong force drawn up in battle
array with his hastily organized and poorly armed rabble. He had a
feeble store of personal courage to begin with and there was no one at
his side to bolster his inexperience. Arundel rode out in advance, demanding a parley. De Vere's columns, lacking order and having already
lost confidence in their leader, opened their ears to the deep voice of
Arundel when he declared de Vere a traitor and advised them to disband while they had the chance. De Vere made ineffectual efforts to
rally his men but they had no willingness to fight and began an immediate retreat. Observing that the main forces of the barons were beginning to arrive, de Vere took to horse and rode through the gathering
gloom of evening for Radcot Bridge. This structure had been closed off
for repair and enemy troops occupied one end of it. De Vere discarded
his armor and plunged his horse into the stream, being lucky enough to
get across and find the road clear.

Arriving in London disguised as a groom, he succeeded in reaching
the king, who was both shocked and chagrined at the report he gave
of his defeat. Richard took steps at once to get him out of the way.
Passage was arranged for him on a vessel sailing from Queenborough and

he arrived in due course at Bruges where he had previously deposited funds for his support with a firm of Lombard bankers—the only trace of foresight he had shown in this whole sorry episode.

He never came back. The safety of the Low Countries seemed to him more desirable than any further part in the struggle at home. Deserted thus by the friend he had supported through thick and thin, the young king found himself called upon to face alone a victorious coalition. Most of his intimates had taken flight. Tresilian had played a prominent part in getting from the justices at Nottingham a verdict in the king's favor. He had, moreover, sealed the opinions and kept them under his hand, thereby making himself a target for the ire of the dissenting barons. Before news was received of the fiasco at Radcot Bridge, Tresilian had sensed what was coming and had gone into hiding. Among the prominent men who would have to face the enmity of the triumphant barons, that stout soldier and man of honor, Sir Simon Burley, had the courage to remain at the king's side.

The uncompromising trio, Woodstock, Arundel, and Warwick, met at Huntingdon and decided they would depose the king. It took much effort and extended argument on the part of two other leading barons, who joined the party later, the Earls of Derby and Nottingham, to persuade them against this radical step. The victorious magnates joined forces then and marched on London, arriving there the day after Christmas. It had not been a pleasant Christmas for Richard and his queen, because reports had reached them every hour of the approach of forces against which they would have no defense. It was almost literally true that the sound of carols and the sweet chimes of the church bells had been blotted out by the clank of steel-clad feet; for in London, too, trouble was stirring and the streets were filled with men of hostile intent.

No resistance was offered when the baronial forces reached the city gates. The following day the creaking doorway of the Tower of London swung open.

The scene which followed was one of extreme tension as well as historical novelty. Five of the leaders, the demanding trio and the two younger earls, linked arms in the anteroom and marched abreast into the royal presence. Richard had been prepared for a bitter encounter, but he must have been taken aback by this ocular proof of their unity of purpose as well as their disregard of court etiquette. Each of the five had donned his own color and so they were a study in contrasts; dark maroon, green, a tawny brown, the antelopes of Lancaster on blue and silver, the crimson of Norfolk inlaid with mulberry leaves. They had all studiously avoided the fashionable excesses of the court. Their muscular legs were encased in hose of one shade instead of the current preference for the parti-colored, their sleeves did not fall below their fingertips, and their cloaks were rather plain.

Richard, who as usual was arrayed in some degree of magnificence, studied this ominous group with eyes which disclosed a sudden sense of real alarm. When they produced letters recovered from the effects of Robert de Vere after his flight from Radcot Bridge, which carried the king's own instructions to that ineffective instrument of his royal will, he realized perhaps the full extent of the danger facing him. To increase his unease his uncle drew him to a window and showed him that the open space on Tower Hill below was black with armed men under the command of the barons.

"Ten times as many more," declared the bombastic uncle, "are ready to join us in our demands!"

De Vere's forces were scattered over the countryside through which that ineffective young man had led them. The citizens were, at best, in an aloof mood and showing no signs of supporting their lawful king. Richard realized that he had no force to support him against the determined baronage. He sought, therefore, to temporize. He would meet them the next day at Westminster to discuss the situation. In the meantime would they stay the night in the Tower and join him in a supper? The three older barons said No, in most decided terms. The two younger hesitated and finally agreed to remain as his guests.

After a night spent in reflection, Richard went to the meeting next day with the intention of standing firm. He was the king, he informed them, and would not accept dictation from anyone. He shared the belief of his strong-willed father that he was answerable only to God.

His uncle of Woodstock and the Earl of Arundel, the latter bolstered by his sudden and dazzling popularity, tried to tear Richard's resolution to shreds with a harsh rejoinder. He was answerable to God, yes, but also to them, the leading representatives of the hereditary baronage. He would do what they wanted or they would depose him. This was not an idle threat: they meant it and, in fact, they seemed only too eager to set the wheels of deposition turning at once.

Richard, white of face, struggled against this iron resolution. He was old enough and sufficiently experienced now to read in the dark and hostile eyes of his chief opponents a purpose from which they could not be swayed. If he refused to give in, they would move at once to take the Crown from him. If he gave in, he was condemning his close friends to a token trial before Parliament. This could have one result only—their condemnation and death on the gallows or at the block.

Could he abandon these men who had been so close to him: Pole the sage adviser and administrator, the Archbishop of York who had never ruffled his feelings as Courtenay of Canterbury had done, Robert de Vere his personal friend, Brembre the stout if rashly combative alderman?

But could he sacrifice his exalted post (which he would always believe had been conferred on him by divine right) in order to prolong a struggle which already seemed lost? Seldom in history has a young man of twenty (a stubborn one, it is true, and unsuited to the kind of rulership he seemed determined to exercise) faced such a bitter choice.

It would have been easier for the king if the issue had been a constitutional one only. But it was clear to everyone that personal considerations as well animated the leaders of the baronage. There was an avid gleam in the eyes of the unshakable pair, Woodstock and Arundel, a determination to vent personal dislikes, an eagerness for revenge. If they had been willing to lay aside their grudges and be content with a thorough housecleaning, the issue would undoubtedly have been resolved without difficulty. But Richard knew quite well that they would demand, literally, their pound of flesh.

The result was inevitable. Richard consented finally to the arrest of his leading advisers: Archbishop Neville of York, Michael de la Pole, Robert de Vere, Tresilian, and Sir Nicholas Brembre, as well as several knights who were his closest friends. They would all be tried, no matter how small their share of complicity might be, at the forthcoming session of Parliament. The matter of their punishment (no one doubted what the verdict would be, even at this preliminary stage) would also be in the hands of that body. Four of the defendants had already fled: Vere, Pole, Tresilian, and Brembre.

Realizing that the king's consent had been wrung from him with the utmost difficulty, the leading barons assembled in conference later. Woodstock and Arundel battled long and bitterly for an immediate abdication. It would come to this in the end, they declared. They even went to the length of having the state papers relating to the deposition of Edward II brought out from the state files for study. To them it was clear that the cases were parallel and that there was every reason for ridding themselves at once of this unstable youth. Again the two younger earls, Derby and Nottingham, stood against it. Richard had met their demands. From this point onward they could keep the control of things in their own hands. In the end the more moderate viewpoint prevailed. Richard could remain on the throne but only if he agreed to a thorough housecleaning without any attempt at interference.

Richard signed the order for the arrests with a heavy heart. He had an affectionate regard for most of the men he was thus condemning to trial for treason. Among the lesser figures whose names had been added to the list was one over which he hesitated with a contraction of the heart and with the deepest apprehension—Sir Simon Burley.

**2**

Parliament met on February 3, 1388, and proceeded at once with the treason trials. The leading hereditary barons appeared to press the charges. They met with no opposition. All of the defendants were found guilty, four *in absentia*. All were sentenced to death, with the exception of the Archbishop of York. One of them, Sir Nicholas Brembre, had run away to Wales, but he was overtaken there and brought back to London to face trial. Soon thereafter Tresilian was captured by a curious coincidence.

That unrelenting judge of the peasants, for whom it is impossible to feel any sympathy, had apparently been drawn back to London by curiosity when Parliament opened. He had grown a beard in the meantime and he came in the guise of a country yokel, believing himself safe from detection. According to one version, he stayed in a common alehouse in the city. Another has it that he took a room over an apothecary's shop near the palace at Westminster. A servant of Thomas of Woodstock saw him and, in spite of the beard, recognized him at once. Prompt action followed and the fugitive was carried in to face the House. The trial of Brembre was under way, but it was adjourned to deal with the new prisoner. Tresilian was asked to show reason why the sentence of death already pronounced on him in his absence should not be carried out.

Tresilian, who does not seem to have been a close confidant of the king and had been retained in office because of his complaisance, had been vehement and harsh of tongue when files of unfortunate peasants had faced him. He had refused them any mercy and had not even permitted them a chance to plead. Now he stood at the bar as they had done, with the same penalty hanging over him, and his tongue clove to the roof of his mouth. He could not speak a word.

The death he suffered was as cruel as the fate he had meted out to the hundreds of peasants to whom he had refused justice. That afternoon he was taken from the Tower and dragged at the feet of horses to Tyburn through the streets of London. There he was hanged, drawn, and quartered.

Shortly afterward Brembre was declared guilty, although he had defended himself with vigor, and suffered the same fate. Archbishop

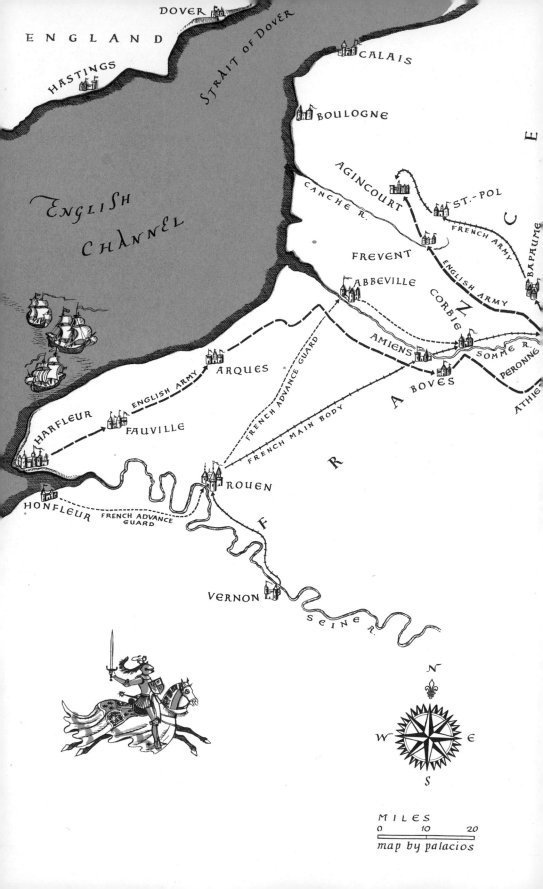

ENGLAND

DOVER

HASTINGS

Strait of Dover

CALAIS

BOULOGNE

English Channel

AGINCOURT

CANCHE R.

ST.-POL

FRENCH ARMY

BAPAUME

E

C

FREVENT

ENGLISH ARMY

ABBEVILLE

CORBIE

Z

AMIENS

SOMME R.

PERONNE

ARQUES

FRENCH ADVANCE GUARD

BOVES

A

R

ATHIE

ENGLISH ARMY

HARFLEUR

FAUVILLE

FRENCH MAIN BODY

ROUEN

F

HONFLEUR

FRENCH ADVANCE GUARD

VERNON

SEINE R.

N

W E

S

MILES

0          10          20

map by palacios

# The Battle of
# AGINCOURT

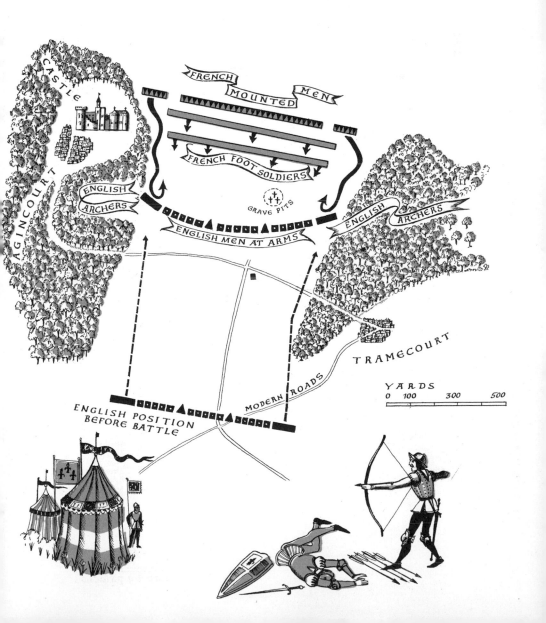

CASTLE

AGINCOURT

FRENCH MOUNTED MEN

FRENCH FOOT SOLDIERS

GRAVE PITS

ENGLISH ARCHERS

ENGLISH ARCHERS

ENGLISH MEN AT ARMS

TRAMECOURT

ENGLISH POSITION BEFORE BATTLE

MODERN ROADS

YARDS
0   100      300      500

Neville was left to such punishment as canonical law might fix for him. When his case was laid before Urban VI, the Pope degraded Neville from his see and translated him to the see of St. Andrew's. As Scotland did not acknowledge Urban and stood instead for the Pope at Avignon, this decision had no weight. Neville accordingly followed his fellows in misfortune by exiling himself to Flanders, where he died soon after.

The judges who had entered a verdict for the king at Nottingham were then brought to the bar of the House and sentenced to death. It was only when the bishops united in a body to support the queen in begging for the remission of this sentence that the judges were condemned instead to perpetual exile in Ireland.

On the twelfth of March four knights of Richard's train were brought before the House. They were Sir John Beauchamp of Holt, Sir John Salisbury, Sir James Berners—and Sir Simon Burley. The last act was now to be played out.

### 3

May 5, 1388. The Merciless Parliament, after a recess for Easter, had completed its part that morning by finding the four knights guilty. It was on one count only that a case had been made against Burley. This was the eighth, which charged him with encouraging the king to gather a corrupt court about him. The four were sentenced to be hanged, drawn, and quartered.

The state of mind of King Richard and his young queen can easily be conceived. Burley had been like a foster father to them both. He had taken the boy's education in hand from the earliest years on the instructions of the Black Prince. He had broken the rules of the coronation by picking him up when he looked too tired to complete the ceremony and had carried him out in his arms, at which time the shoe had fallen from the young king's foot. He had taught him the pleasure and profit of reading and had supplied him with the books which would never have been found otherwise at court. When Richard rode into London, it was his desire always that Sir Simon Burley should carry the state sword before him.

It was this courtly knight who had gone first to Bohemia to open negotiations for the hand of the princess Anne and who had won her assent to the match. Later he had been sent with English troops to escort the bride to England. Anne had become as deeply attached to him as the king.

The course of history often hinges on matters of seeming unimportance.

Burley was not one of the king's chief ministers. It would have cost the relentless barons nothing if they had agreed to commute the death sentence on this very great friend of both king and queen. It is conceivable that Richard would not in that case have carried in his heart the dark design of vengeance which led to such bitterness later.

But there was a reason why they would not yield. Arundel hated Burley. He had never forgiven the latter for his open criticism of naval strategy during the earlier years when the tardy admiral had seemed unable to do anything right. Even after his great victory, which might have brought him to a magnanimous state of mind, Arundel was determined to make the knight pay for what he considered insolence.

It was the king's harsh uncle and the revengeful admiral who shared equally the responsibility for the cruel decisions of Parliament, but instinctively the king and his consort knew that it was Arundel who was pressing for the death of Burley. It was to him they went to plead his case.

Arundel was brusque, discourteous, even brutal, to them. He brushed aside every reason they advanced for remitting the death penalty with acerbic responses. Burley had been given a fair trial and had been found guilty. The sentence must stand. They could see in his dark and passionate eye, in the frown which never left his brow, the real reason which he did not put into words. Burley must now pay for the things he had said in the past.

Queen Anne, growing desperate in her desire to save an old friend, actually went down on her knees to this fiercely unrelenting subject. She pleaded, she wept, she wrung her hands. She was no longer a queen with position and authority to wield, she was a woman willing to lay aside all dignity and all power in this sorry crisis.

Arundel did not stir from his stand. Nothing she could say had any effect on him. He pulled at his beard and glowered about him, anxious to end the scene but not daring to carry disrespect to the point of turning his back on her and leaving the room. It is said that she remained on her knees for three hours, all to no avail.

One statement only from the adamant earl is given in the chronicles of the day.

"Let the request alone, Madame Queen," he is reported to have said. Then, permitting his words to convey in full measure the threat being held over the royal pair, he added: "Pray for yourself and your husband. That is the best thing you can do."

Completely spent and unable to say more, the queen was led finally from the room by her women. There was nothing more she could do.

It may have been that Woodstock was in the room part of the time during which the young queen thus sacrificed her dignity in the effort to save the unfortunate knight. It is certain that he agreed with Arundel. At some stage of this tragic morning he said to Richard: "If you wish to be king, Burley must suffer!"

What would have happened if the weak young king had stood out? If he had refused to sign the warrant, would the other barons have joined hands to prevent the two leaders from carrying out their openly stated purpose of deposition? The Earl of Derby was also against the death sentence and expressed his dissent to Woodstock and Arundel, even though he would have been a probable choice to succeed Richard.

This poses a vital speculation. Looking backward, it seems reasonable to assume that Richard, with Derby's backing, could have succeeded in his one honest and earnest effort and saved Burley. Had he done so, he would still have been held in leash long enough to perceive the error of his autocratic opinions and it would not have been necessary for him to follow a course of dissimulation and to keep always one angry thought in the front of his mind: "Let me have time and I shall make them pay!"

The only concession that he won for his old friend was that the sentence be changed to beheading.

At an early hour of that same afternoon, the fifty-two-year-old knight, who had fought bravely through the wars close to the side of the Black Prince, was subjected to a final indignity. With his hands bound behind his back and his white hair uncovered, he was led through the streets of London for the people to gaze upon. Nothing is told as to the way the staring citizens reacted, but it is to be hoped they did not jeer. Finally he was led back, the ax still carried before him, to Tower Hill where the sentence was to be carried out.

Nor does history tell how the king and queen bore themselves during the last stage of the tragedy. Knowing how close they were to each other and how deeply their feelings were involved, it is certain that they sat together with clasped hands and bowed heads, waiting for the roll of drums to cease, which would tell them that the ax had fallen.

CHAPTER XX

## *The King Raises a Hand*

1

A RESTRAINED and rather silent king, who had learned a
bitter lesson through cruel experience, sat with his hostile council at
Westminster and listened to them direct the affairs of the kingdom.
This continued for a full year. He made no protest when Thomas
Arundel, the Bishop of Ely, was appointed chancellor and later made
Archbishop of York. He did not raise his voice to procure pardons for
any of his friends in exile. He had nothing to say when the confident
barons put through Parliament a grant of £20,000, to be distributed
amongst themselves, presumably to recompense them for the cost of their
forcible seizure of power.

It became clear during this relatively calm year, however, that the
type of man who makes his mark as a critic in opposition does not
always show to advantage when he assumes the responsibilities and
burdens of office. Woodstock and Arundel proved themselves vulnerable
as ministers of the Crown. They did not succeed in putting into effect
any of the reforms they had demanded so vehemently of the young
king. They were as lavish in spending as their predecessors had been.

During this year the silent young king had been giving much thought
to the situation which existed and had made up his mind to act. When
the time seemed ripe, he moved with a celerity which caught his
opponents unprepared.

On May 3, 1389, a meeting of the council was being held. The king
was in attendance but had been silent as usual. Then in a moment when
there was a pause he raised his hand.

"My lords," he asked, "what is the number of my years?"

The question had been directed at his uncle of Woodstock who sat beside him. The latter hesitated briefly and then said, "Your Highness is in your twenty-second year."

"Then," declared Richard, "I am old enough to manage my own affairs."

A silence settled over the room as the members exchanged uneasy side glances. What answer could they give which would express their opposition and yet fall short of open treason?

"I have been longer under guardianship," went on the king, "than any ward in my realm." He reached out his hand. "The Great Seal is to be returned into my custody."

Bishop Arundel, to whom this demand had been addressed, had no course open but to obey. He placed the Great Seal in Richard's hand.

"My lords," said the king, "I thank you for your past services."

His move, so unexpected, so swift, so skillfully made, left the usually clamorous opposition with nothing to say. It was true that the king was long out of his minority. Woodstock and Arundel made no move to protest the royal decision. The silence which settled over the room was deep and long.

The triumph scored by the armed forces of the baronage had been reversed by these few cool sentences.

There followed a brief period of official upheaval. Bishop Arundel was removed as chancellor and the place given to that sage old clerical war horse, William of Wykeham. Bishop Gilbert of Hereford was dismissed from his post at the treasury. The new judges were all relieved of office, although the earlier incumbents were not summoned back from exile. If not actually in disgrace, the baronial leaders found themselves out of control.

On May 8, Richard issued a proclamation to the nation at large. He acknowledged that there had been abuses during the years of his minority but these he promised to redress. There would be "a better peace and better justice" in the land. It was not his purpose, he declared, to exact punishment for the force used in taking his rightful powers from him and none of his earlier advisers would be recalled to office.

If the opposition leaders had expected a popular clamor to be raised in their behalf, they were disappointed. Apparently a realization had been spreading that these lordly critics had been as ineffective in office as those they had so relentlessly expelled.

The king, with his new men about him, proceeded at once to sign a three-year truce with France and her allies, Scotland and Spain. This move the country approved heartily. The people were tired of the costly and cruel war which seemed to drag on endlessly. Taxes would now be lighter. In tavern and alehouse there was a sly tendency to wink at the past and say that "the young one" knew what he was about. Woodstock and Arundel could fume and growl in retirement, but for the time being no attention was paid them.

Later in the year the now aging John of Gaunt returned from Spain, convinced at last that he could not attain his great dream, the crown of that kingdom. He seems to have approved of Richard's bold move but, having a sincere desire to see peace in the family, he persuaded the king to summon back to the royal council the three leading appellants, Woodstock, Arundel, and Warwick. Richard accepted the suggestion unwillingly. He told John of Gaunt that his gorge rose at once more having those three set and grim faces at his council board.

2

For eight years Richard governed the country with wisdom and a full respect for the constitution. The peace with France was maintained by renewals of the truce. Freed from the heavy burden of war taxes, the country became prosperous. Many sound laws were passed, some of them with a distinctly liberal basis. The desire of the king to consider the well-being of his subjects was made apparent when he refused to entertain a statute prohibiting education to the children of villeins and his assent to the checking of "livery of company," the custom in the baronage of maintaining a last phase of feudalism by keeping large armed retinues.

During these years of peace and bounty no effort was made by the king to pardon his early advisers who had gone into exile. Michael de la Pole died abroad. Robert de Vere, existing on the bounty of relatives, left the Low Countries and lived for some time in Paris. In 1392 he went boar hunting and received a wound from one of the tuskers which caused his death. If Richard grieved for his friend, he showed no outward evidence of it. It was not until three years later that he gave permission for de Vere's body to be brought back to England and buried with his ancestors in Earls Colne priory. The king was present at the services and allowed the official mask he had been wearing for so long to drop at the last moment. Requesting that the coffin be opened, he gazed in silence at the embalmed body of his one-time friend. Then with moist eyes he leaned over and lightly touched the hand of the dead man.

During these good years the king's old enemies continued to sit in the council. Later events were to prove he had not forgiven them, that whenever he found it necessary to face them directly he felt a stirring of deep animosity, remembering no doubt the fatal morning when the queen went down on her knees to beg in vain for the life of Sir Simon Burley. The Earl of Arundel seems to have been the one who bore the brunt of the king's dislike. Although he sat on the council, Arundel was never again employed in any administrative capacity.

This did not apply to Arundel's younger brother, Thomas, the churchman. The character of the latter has been a subject of much dispute. He was a handsome and able man who could win friends easily and who undoubtedly was of an amiable bent. The part he was to play later makes it clear, however, that he never lost sight of the main chance and that he allowed himself to consider above everything the ambitious path he had elected to tread. The part he would play during the first years of the reign of Henry IV in the matter of the first burnings for heresy brought to a close a contradictory career. Historians who favored him point out that he tried to be generous and forgiving to the Lollards, but the fact remains that the flames of bigotry were first kindled during his term as Archbishop of Canterbury (for, of course, he attained that highest of posts) and that he watched while William Sawtree and John Badby, the first to die for religous beliefs, were burned at the stake.

As he belonged to one of the greatest families in England, Thomas Arundel's rise in the church was spectacular and rapid. At the age of twenty-one he was made Archdeacon of Taunton and a year later he became the Bishop of Ely. Being of a generous turn, and having the wealth to gratify it, he was always profuse in his almsgiving. Having a liking for show, he celebrated his elevation to the bishopric of Ely by changing the rather modest episcopal house at Holborn into a stately mansion, with a stone wall enclosing twenty acres of beautiful gardens. He presented to his cathedral, among other costly gifts, a gold tablet which had been in the royal family. It was encrusted with pearls, rubies, and sapphires and contained relics of the saints. He liked those who walked in his train to dress in accordance with his own sense of dignity, and so he saw to it that their albs of red velvet were embroidered in gold with figures of griffins.

When Archbishop Neville was dismissed from his see at York, the post was given almost automatically to Thomas Arundel. Richard used him as chancellor later, finding him always amiable and diplomatic. In 1396 Archbishop Courtenay of Canterbury died and, for reasons which will be explained later, the king had Arundel transferred from York to Canterbury, the first time this had occurred in the history of the church in England.

In thus outlining briefly the chain of events which brought Thomas of
Arundel to the highest peak, it becomes necessary to speak of another
figure whose career became curiously tangled with his. Roger Walden,
a man of humble birth, had risen in the world rapidly because he had
many of the same qualities as had Arundel. He was an agreeable and
handsome man, with a gift for getting things done, and with an ease of
manner which made friends for him. Sent to the Isle of Jersey from the
church of Kirkby Overblow in Yorkshire, he rose rapidly from one post
to another, until he was bailiff of Guisnes and treasurer of Calais.
Richard heard reports of this pliable and capable man and had him
brought back to England to act as his personal secretary. Walden polished up the handle of the big front door so industriously that his rise
was nothing short of spectacular. He succeeded the Bishop of Salisbury
as treasurer of England, thus remaining close to the king and having
ready access to the royal ear.

The story of the intertwining of the careers of these two birds of a
feather will have to be left, to be told in some detail later.

3

There has been little tendency on the part of history to allow credit to
Richard for enduring contributions of any kind. This attitude can be
traced to impatience with his unstable character and the delusions which
led to his downfall. The eight years during which he played creditably
the role of a constitutional monarch offer, surely, some evidence of
accomplishment. But it is in an almost forgotten demonstration of fairness
that a more just claim can be allowed him.

Geoffrey Chaucer, born close to the year 1340 and married to Philippa
de Roet, a sister of Katharine Swynford, the beautiful third wife of John
of Gaunt, had been in high favor during the last years of the reign of
Edward III. His poetry had attracted wide attention and he was given
pensions and annuities and many remunerative posts, such as comptroller
of the customs, and a subsidy on wools, hides, and woodfalls. Among his
honors was the rather vague title of king's laureate (the first poet laureate
in the full modern sense was Ben Jonson), which carried with it the gift
of a pitcher of wine every day, a gift to be collected from the king's
butler. Feeling very secure, he had taken a lease for life on a substantial
house at Aldgate.

It was a bad day for Chaucer when Richard fell foul of the appellant
barons and had to submit to their authority. Poetry meant nothing to men
of the stamp of Thomas of Woodstock and the Earl of Arundel. They

were completely materialistic and, moreover, contemptuous of anyone of low degree. One can imagine them looking over the list of annuities and asking, Who is this fellow, this baseborn scribbler of verses, that he should have a pension of ten pounds a year? Why should he hold positions for which he is in no way fitted—and which, moreover, we could give to others to much better advantage? The name of Chaucer, at any rate, was struck from the bounty lists and his comptrollerships were taken from him. His wife had died and so her annuity also was lost. The middle-aged bard, the first to write rich and enduring verse in the English tongue, fell upon evil days.

When Richard, with a lift of the hand and a few terse statements, took back his royal authority and made himself free from the heavy thumbs of the appellants, he proceeded at once to reinstate Geoffrey Chaucer in the service of the Crown. Being a reader, he was familiar with the work of this vigorous bard who had been raised in London, in the Vintry. A congenial post was found for him, that of clerk of the works at most of the royal palaces, including the Tower of London, Shene, Eltham, Kennington, and many others of lesser importance. This carried a yearly stipend of £31, which meant that Chaucer could again live in comfort and with some degree of decent dignity. Soon after he was made commissioner of maintenance of the river Thames between Woolwich and Greenwich, with permission to assign the work to a deputy. Finally, and this was the post which pleased Chaucer the most, he was assigned on July 12, 1390, to take charge of much needed repairs at St. George's Chapel in Windsor.

Geoffrey Chaucer was neither an architect nor builder but he had been at Windsor a great deal, particularly when his wife was serving there as an attendant of the queen. He knew every foot of the ground, every turret, every groin point, every twist and turn of stairway, every stone conceit or fancy of the great builders who had contributed to the rise of that stately pile. He had for Windsor, and particularly for St. George's Chapel, the admiration that an artist in words can conceive for artistry in stone. He approached his task there with enthusiasm and, no doubt, with a sense of relief that his days of want were at an end.

St. George's Chapel was sadly in need of repair. Although it had been standing no more than thirty-four years, it had already fallen into a ruinous condition. This was due in some degree to the fact that Windsor, once much used by the royal family, had been visited very little since Edward III had fallen into senility, and because his young successor had no family to send there. In some degree it had also come about through the precarious nature of the ledge of chalk on which it had been built. The roof was falling in, the walls were cracking, the floors were in dire need of repair. In fact, this beautiful chapel which Edward III had designed as the meeting place for a chivalrous order of knights of a new round table, was in such condition that great haste was demanded of the new custodian.

The chapel inside was still beautiful, with its oaken ceilings plated with gold and its four elaborately designed altars, which carried the names of the Cross, the Thorn, St. Edward's, and St. George's. The interior decorations had, of course, suffered some, but the part to which legend clung most, the altar of the Cross, was still lovely to the eye. It was generally called the Negt because it contained a piece of the cross of Calvary, a fragment of Syrian wood which a Welshman of that name had found on a pilgrimage to the Holy Land. Edward I had carried it with him on all his travels and it was natural that his grandson had planned an altar for it at Windsor.

When he came to Windsor on this urgent errand, Chaucer was a plump man of fresh complexion with thinning white hair and a small pointed beard, still exercising a curious puckish charm. He had been given the power to hire such help as he needed, at a fixed wage, and to assemble his materials wherever he could find them. No craftsman could refuse the summons to help in the work of restoration and no contractor could withhold supplies demanded of him. The injunction placed on Chaucer's own shoulders was even more pressing. He must make haste, haste, more haste, lest the great conception of the old king subside into rubble.

Taking up his quarters in Winchester Tower, and having it pretty much to himself, Chaucer set to work with greater industry than he had ever displayed in the various governmental posts he had held or, even, in the finding of rhymes, in the seeking of chiseled phrase, the perfect simile which went into his immortal verse. He remained at Windsor for a year and a half and in that time he succeeded in checking the disintegration. He must be given at least a share of the credit for saving the chapel.

While he was thus industriously engaged on the king's business, Chaucer had little time for writing, but it is generally believed that while he labored at Windsor or surveyed the work being done on the banks of the Thames, he was gathering material for his great masterpiece, the *Canterbury Tales*. The pilgrims from the west came down the river paths near Windsor and it was there perhaps that he saw the curious individuals who later were brought to life in his rich and resounding verse: the Squire, the Prioress, the Wife of Bath, the Pardoner, the Friar, and the Oxford Clerk. His ears were filled with the accents of the native tongue and the colloquialisms which he later used to such realistic effect.

King Richard had no part in making the *Canterbury Tales* possible beyond this, but certainly, if the poet had not been taken again under the wing of royal patronage, he might have found it impossible to give further rein to his robust imagination.

**CHAPTER XXI**

## The Death of Good Queen Anne

*1*

AN EVENT which occurred on June 7, 1394, can be accepted as the forerunner of a second period of strife. On that day Queen Anne died suddenly.

The love between the king and his consort had been deep and free of any connubial stress. Anne had always been at his side and her influence had been for peace and order. It is not likely that she held any brief for the lords who had been responsible for the deaths of their friends, but she undoubtedly encouraged Richard to be forgiving, on the surface at least. The urge to revenge himself was always at the back of his mind and it seems almost certain that he would have taken steps against the appellants earlier if she had not been there to counsel moderation.

It was due to her, certainly, that during the previous year Richard had taken steps to heal the breach between himself and the city of London. He had asked the city for a loan of £1000 and had been refused. For some reason the citizens resented it bitterly when a Lombardy banker had offered to accommodate the king. He was dragged from his counting-house and torn to pieces in the streets. In a rage Richard removed the courts of law from London to York and announced his intention of making the latter city the seat of Parliament. London soon felt the pinch of these measures and begged the queen to intercede on their behalf. Anne promised to do so and was able finally to persuade the king to grant the city his pardon.

It was decided to make a great event of the reconciliation. The royal couple rode together through the city, the queen wearing her crown and a gown studded with precious stones. The king was presented with a pair of white horses, accoutered with cloth of gold and hung with silver bells, the queen with a handsome white palfrey. As they passed under Temple Bar, the king was sufficiently moved to declare: "Peace to this city! For the sake of Christ, his mother and my patron St. John, I forgive every offense." During the great state banquet at Westminster which followed, the lord mayor was assured of the king's forgiveness. "Take back the keys and sword," said Richard. "Keep my peace in your city, rule its inhabitants as formerly, and be among them my representative."

Little is known of the circumstances of Queen Anne's death. She became suddenly ill and succumbed in two days. There was no great sweep of the plague at this particular moment but the country was never entirely free of it. The germ could be picked up at any time, particularly in London and during the summer months. The symptoms, and the suddenness of her death, seem to indicate that she was one of the victims.

The king was with her when she died and his grief was so great that he gave orders to raze the palace at Shene to the ground. These instructions were not followed, although the state apartments were dismantled later. The king never set foot in Shene after the state funeral. Characteristically he decided that she was to be buried with a pomp suited to "a daughter of the Caesars."

Although one story has it that she was called upon to repudiate on her deathbed the holding of heretical views, there is no evidence to support the statement. It was true there had been whispers that she leaned that way but it would not have been strange if she did. The new teachings were having such wide acceptance in England that it was said two out of three people were Lollards.

The Psalter of the queen was written in Latin, German, and Bohemian and she had read the four gospels in English, which indicates that she had possessed a Wycliffe Bible. Before reading the gospels, however, she had submitted them to Thomas of Arundel that she might have his opinion as to their orthodoxy—a curious choice of mentor for he was not known particularly as a man either of piety or learning. Thomas had assured her that there would be no wrong in studying the version of the man of Lutterworth, although he later declared himself against any distribution of the Wycliffe Bible among the English people. The queen may have felt an interest in the new teachings but not a deep or abiding one. Certainly she could not have been indiscreet enough to declare such an opinion, knowing that her husband, as might have been expected, was as strongly against any hint of change in religious belief or observance as he was against any infringement of royal prerogative.

**2**

It is no exaggeration to say that Richard was brokenhearted over the death of the young queen. After the first wild explosion of grief, when he ordered the demolition of Shene Palace, he could think of no way to display his love save to give Anne the most elaborate funeral that the country had ever seen. It is said that the preparations for this demonstration of royal sorrow took two months, during which time the body was kept at Shene. It was found that there was not enough fine wax in the country to make all the candles that Richard deemed necessary and a large quantity had to be imported from Flanders to supply the flambeaux and torches. This accounted for much of the delay.

Above all else he wanted in attendance every peer of the realm and his wife. To this end he wrote a form letter which was sent to all of them.

*Very dear and faithful cousin:*

Inasmuch as our beloved companion, the queen (whom God has hence commanded), will be buried at Westminster the third of August next, we earnestly entreat that you (setting aside all excuses) will repair to our city of London the Wednesday previous to the same day, bringing with you our very dear kinswoman, your consort, at the same time.

We desire that you will, the preceding day, accompany the corpse of our dear consort from our manor of Shene to Westminster; and for this we trust we may rely on you, as you desire our honour, and that of our kingdom.

Given under our privy seal at Westminster, the 10th day of June, 1394.

This, it will be seen, was a command. In view of the urgency of the notice, it is hard to understand something that happened, which will be told later.

It was ordained further that all in attendance should wear black gowns and hoods and that the trappings of the horses should be of sable hue. Along the route from Shene to Westminster the houses displayed black hangings, the alehouses were closed with their signs draped in black, the church bells tolled in slow and muted measure.

It should be noted that, as the final word on the controversy over the deceased queen's religious beliefs, Thomas of Arundel preached the funeral oration, in the course of which he told of Anne's request that he pass on the question of reading the gospels in the vulgar tongue (as

English was invariably called). He made it clear that he had advised her to do so.

To give some idea of what the scope of the funeral arrangements meant to the city of London, it is necessary to glance at some statistics.

It will be hard to believe how small England had become in point of population as a result of the Black Death. There had once been 4,000,000 people in this land of milk and honey (as the invading Normans had called it), this country so full of life and bustle and contention, its ports packed with ships, its rivers congested with wool and tin barges and with the long trains of its barons, and those of bishops and abbots with their tonsured followers a-muleback, and with parties on pilgrimage, and its inns noisy with merchants and minstrels and lower branches of the fellowship of the *pied poudre,* the dusty feet. In the year 1377 there were no more than 2,200,000 people in England and by the year 1400 the total had shrunk further by 100,000. London, that city of wealth and power and arrogance, had a population at which the least of its suburbs today would sniff with scorn—35,000. York, the metropolis of the north, with its minster and its established wealth packed within the circuit of its Roman walls, could boast of no more than 10,900.

Though the terrible plagues had cut the population in two, there had been, peculiarly enough, no material decrease in the baronage. Including all branches of the nobility, the total in Richard's reign is given, roughly, as 150.

Reference has already been made to the size of the trains which the proud barons took with them on their travels. This was due to pride in some degree but mostly to a feeling of insecurity. The magnates did not trust one another and they had an even greater fear of the king, whichever king happened to be on the throne. The demand of Richard that each should bring his wife was a further complication, for the good ladies seemed to need as many people about them as their lords: falconers, grooms, farriers, confessors, almoners, maids, seamstresses, laundresses.

It goes without saying that the commonality from thereabouts would tramp on shank's mare to see the good queen carried to her early grave.

Considering the tone of Richard's invitation, nay command, it may be taken for granted that as many as 15,000 people would converge on London. For several days there would be chaos in that close huddle of small houses.

Richard's grief had not abated in any degree during the two months which had elapsed and he must have been in a daze when the huge cortege was being formed to accompany the queen's body to Westminster.

He was not so sunk in his sorrow, however, to fail of noting one conspicuous absentee when the peers fell into line according to their rank and importance. The Earl of Arundel was not in attendance.

The smoldering coals of the king's hatred for this antagonistic peer were fanned into an active flame. He considered Arundel's action to be deliberate, a gesture to show how little respect he felt for the queen who had owed to him the most bitter moment in her life. It was clear to the king, as he rode his black charger, that Arundel considered himself above any form of obedience. He, the proud victor at sea and the popular hero of the people, could do what he pleased. Nothing that the earl had done in the past seemed on a par with this willful slight, this insult to the memory of the queen.

The sum of Arundel's offending was still not complete. The funeral services were held the following day and he arrived late at Westminster, in fact after the ritual was under way. This was bad enough but he had the temerity to approach the bereaved husband and ask permission to leave early, giving as his reason the pressure of matters of importance.

It seems to have been Richard's lot to disturb the even tenor of moments of the utmost solemnity at Westminster. He had lost a shoe during his coronation, and now, when his beloved consort was being consigned to the grave, he lost his head. His hands trembled with rage as he considered the ease and unconcern on Arundel's face. Without making any response, he took a baton from the hands of an attendant and struck the earl over the head with it. The blow was delivered with such force that Arundel fell to the floor and his blood spread over a large portion of the paving.

"Remove him to the Tower!" was the order that the king gave to those about him.

After the stunned Arundel had been carried out, the floor had to be cleansed of blood before the offices for the dead could be resumed. It was said that every face in the crowded edifice turned white with fear, because it was a general belief that divine vengeance for the killing of Thomas à Becket in Canterbury Cathedral would not be felt until the abbey at Westminster had been polluted with blood. The thought in each bowed head was, What form would the displeasure of the Lord take, now that this condition had been fulfilled?

No action was taken against Arundel at this time, but he was held in the Tower for a week before being released. If people who placed credence in this prophecy waited for the wrath of the deity to manifest itself at once, they were disappointed. Later there were many who thought back to the incident at the abbey and connected it with the tragic events in the last years of Richard's reign.

This was not the only incident where Arundel's pride had involved him in difficulties. A week before, there had been a dispute in Parliament over his inactivity when John of Gaunt had faced a local insurrection in Chester. The duke brought up the point and produced from Arundel an explosion of wrath in the course of which the latter charged the elder uncle with exercising an undue influence over the king. Not stopping there, he criticized the king for making Gaunt the ruler of the Aquitanian possessions. Hot words passed back and forth and finally Richard had taken it on himself to deny a set of four charges which Arundel had exhibited against the duke.

The king brought the episode to a close by declaring he saw no fault in anything his uncle had done and insisting that Arundel must apologize openly for his conduct. This was a wry dose for the proud earl to swallow. Finally he forced himself to stand up and beg pardon in the following cryptic terms:

*Sir:* Sith it seemeth to the king and the lords, and eke that each here hath been so mickle grieved and displeased by my words; it forethinketh, and I beseech you of your grace and lordship to quit me your man-tallant.

Not a frank and outgiving form of apology, certainly. But it seems to have sufficed at the moment.

### 3

Whether the loss of his wife brought about a change in Richard or did no more than remove a restraining influence, it is very clear that his course from that time on showed a firmer but less admirable approach to the problems of kingship.

Other wives of royal rank died in the same year. John of Gaunt's Spanish spouse, Constance, was the first, to be followed soon after by the delicate and lovely Mary, wife of John's eldest son, Henry of Derby. The passing of these ladies had an immediate effect on the political scene. John of Gaunt was now free to wed a third time and he wanted to marry beautiful and talented Katharine Swynford, his mistress for some years who had borne him a family of handsome sons and a daughter. Richard was agreeable to this and so brought down on himself the ire of the Earl of Arundel, not a hard thing to do at any time. It happened that Arundel had married again also, his bride being Philippa, the widow of the Earl of Pembroke. The point of dissent was that Philippa was a daughter of the Earl of March and on that account stood directly in the line of succession. Under the circumstances the consent of Richard should have been obtained, but Arundel had shrugged this aside, his pride preventing him from deferring to the king. To make matters worse, Philippa proceeded to snub Katharine Swynford, calling her openly "the concubine" and at times employing even more insultingly clear Anglo-Saxon terms. Arundel glowered his approval of the stand taken by his new wife.

In this determination to cause trouble in the royal family another lady had joined, the wife of Thomas of Woodstock, the plain and avaricious older sister of Mary, now deceased. It has already been told how Thomas and his wife, who was said to resemble a parrot, had coolly appropriated Cole Harbor, the London home of the Bohun family which had been willed to Derby's wife, Mary. They had given it up most unwillingly. Although Mary was now dead, worn out by childbearing, Derby retained Cole Harbor for his children while he himself, to forget his grief, set off on a series of crusading junkets.

When Richard agreed to his uncle's marriage with the fair Katharine and even consented to the legitimizing of the Swynford children (giving them the family name of Beaufort), the fat was indeed in the fire. Thomas of Woodstock considered himself the logical contender for the throne if Richard did not marry again and bring children into the world. But these newly acknowledged children of John of Gaunt might now be considered to stand ahead of him in the line of succession. Thomas was furious, his wife even more so. Arundel was only too glad to range himself beside them in refusing to acknowledge Katharine Swynford.

And so there they were again, shoulder to shoulder in discontent, the two furiously angry critics of the king, who had dragged Sir Simon Burley to the block. Queen Anne, always the advocate of moderation, was no longer at Richard's side to whisper her wise counsels. The stage was set for the final acts in the tragedy.

Richard displayed some good sense in this difficult situation. He realized he could do nothing to soften the black tempers of Arundel but it might be possible to placate Thomas of Woodstock, who after all carried the real weight in the partnership. The latter could be bribed. The king agreed to find a title for Lord Humphrey, the oldest son of Thomas, and to pay his uncle 50,000 nobles, a quite substantial sum. The earldom of Rochester was created and conferred on Humphrey. Thomas ceased his grumbling, for the time being.

This condition, however, could not be expected to last for any length of time. Thomas had nothing but contempt for Richard and, as leader of the war party (fancying himself as great a fighting man as the Black

Prince, if given the opportunity), he would never acquiesce long in the king's very wise determination to prolong the peace with France.

### 4

Although Richard continued to grieve for his lost wife, the question of a second marriage arose almost at once. It was the first duty of kings to provide a successor to the throne, preferably a son. There was a very strong feeling in the country that the newly made widower should lay aside his grief and find himself another wife.

Thomas of Woodstock was against this. He did not want Richard to produce an heir because that would mean the final extinction of his own pretensions. If, however, the question of a second marriage had to be faced, he, Thomas, had a plan to retrieve some advantage. Why should not the king marry his eldest daughter, Anne?

Anne had been married in 1392 to the Earl of Stafford but he had died the following year. She must have had more of the Bohun beauty than her mother because she accumulated two other husbands later, the second being a brother of her first spouse. Richard refused to consider this suggestion on the sound ground that they were first cousins.

The king soon made it evident that he had ideas of his own. The militant King of France and the beautiful Isabeau (who, it will be recalled, had come to him on approval) had a daughter named Isabella. She was only seven years old, but that would suit the King of England well. It would be many years before she could become his wife in anything but name and it would not be like replacing his beloved Anne. Perhaps by the time the small Isabella had grown up, the memory of Anne might have dimmed sufficiently. A second reason for this match, and this carried equal weight, was that it would serve to cement the peace between England and France. A sincere lover of peace, Richard wanted nothing so much as a permanent end to the long and bloody war.

He realized that he would have to proceed cautiously in the matter. There was a strong war party in the country, headed by that recalcitrant pair, Woodstock and Arundel. They believed themselves capable of winning another Crécy or a second naval victory like that of Sluys. With both of them it was a case of mediocrity failing, or refusing, to recognize its limitations.

## CHAPTER XXII

## The Days of Development

1

RICHARD had learned other lessons. The lack of strength which had tied his hands when the barons surrounded him in the Tower in that bitter period of the Merciless Parliament must be corrected. It is probable that he had seen the need of well-trained royal forces quite early but had been unable to accomplish anything to that end. When Sir Simon Burley had been negotiating for a royal marriage in Italy he went to Florence for the sole purpose of speaking to John Hawkwood. That great English soldier, it will be recalled, had organized the White Company and had gone to Italy to make a good living in the pay of the warring Italian cities and great families. He had been so successful as the leader of the armies of Florence that he was living in retirement on his fine estate, La Rochetta, and was idolized by the population. If Hawkwood, easily the best professional soldier of the day and perhaps the greatest guerrilla fighter in history, had been induced to return to England, he would have kept the royal cause in the ascendancy against such amateur tacticians as the baronial leaders. But he was old at the time and the ache of many wounds was in his bones. He wanted no more soldiering. In fact, he died in the same year as Queen Anne, and the grateful republic not only gave him a magnificent funeral but erected an elaborate marble monument for him.

With an eye to his future security, Richard now began to recruit a troop, made up almost exclusively of trained archers from the loyal county of Chester. This would prove effective later in the differences he would continue to have with opposition parties in the House.

There were some lessons he had failed to learn. The tendency of his grandfather to borrow money wherever he could find it, without regard to his constitutional rights and certainly with little thought of repaying it, appealed to Richard as a proper course to follow. As there was no longer a need for war funds, the money he acquired in this manner was frittered away in extravagant living. The sycophants who gathered about his brilliant court even worked on his pride to the extent of convincing him he might be elected Holy Roman Emperor to succeed Wenceslaus of Bohemia, a brother of Anne's and an incurable drunkard. This entailed the payment of bribes to the electors and the distribution of costly gifts.

Richard was now in his middle twenties and had become a very handsome man, with a slight tendency to portliness. He wore a well-trimmed golden beard and was even more addicted than before to the elaborate fashions favored at the French court. He talked incessantly in a rather high-pitched voice and did not seem interested in any opinions but his own. Such, at least, is the picture to be found in the chronicles of the day, although it should be taken into consideration that most of them were hostile witnesses.

This much may be accepted as certain. Queen Anne had died too soon.

2

For 200 years there had been no vigorous effort to improve the English hold in Ireland. The earlier plan by which Richard turned over the sister island to Robert de Vere had, of course, come to nothing. De Vere accepted the title of Duke of Dublin but did not set foot on Irish soil and so had not been able to apply his "eminent wisdom" to the situation nor to add anything to his "great achievements." The stage had now been reached where definite steps had to be taken and Richard decided to lead an army across the Irish Sea.

With more than 4000 men he sailed from Haverfordwest in September 1394, leaving his uncle Edmund of York as regent and taking Thomas of Woodstock with him as his chief aide. They found themselves opposed by an Irish army of considerable size led by Art MacMurrough. The resourceful Art did not attempt to meet the English in their heavy armor on open fields and so the invaders decided to march to Kilkenny where the Butler family held the great stone castle which had been built by Strongbow and much enlarged and strengthened by William the Marshal. MacMurrough proceeded to harass them in every possible way. The English found themselves falling into ambushes and subjected continuously to night attack. The Irish would swoop down on them at the most unexpected times, keening their wild battle cries, cutting off stragglers and destroying supply trains. Richard knew nothing of warfare, and little more could be said for Woodstock. When the English forces straggled into Kilkenny they had suffered such heavy losses that they were in a mood to discuss conciliation.

Art MacMurrough agreed to meet the king in Dublin to discuss the situation. He arrived there in high spirits, riding a coal-black steed, still without saddle or bridle, and accompanied by many other Irish leaders. A palace was set aside for them at Hoggin Green and they spent Christmas there in feasting and drinking. The negotiations reached the point where the king conferred the honor of knighthood on Art and several of the other leaders.

At this point word was brought to Richard by Archbishop Arundel which made it necessary for him to return at once. The issue of Lollardy had reached an acute stage. Sir Richard Stury and other knights attached to the royal court had set up scrolls on the door of St. Paul's, containing accusations against the church and proclaiming the Lollard Conclusions.

"Unless they recant, I shall hang them all!" cried Richard.

He returned to England at once, leaving his army, or what was left of it, under the command of the young Earl of March, who had been declared successor to the throne. The Irish proceeded to win such battles as were fought and in one of them the young earl lost his life.

### 3

It developed that the Lollard party at court was headed by Sir Richard Stury and another knight named Sir Lewis Clifford, both of whom had been in high favor with the king. Richard was not in a lenient mood, however. Promptly on his return he exacted an oath from Stury to refrain from all further religious activities. Clifford was subjected to the heavy hand of ecclesiastical authority and recanted publicly. Later he was so disturbed by what he considered his lack of spiritual courage that he put in his will the following clause: "I, Lowys Clifford, fals and traytor to my Lord God and to all the blessed company of Hevene, an unworthie to be cleped a christian man, make and ordeyne my testament: my wreched carcass to be buried in the ferthest corner of the churcheyard, that on my stinking carcass be but a black cloth and no stone whereby any man may wit where my stinking carcass lieth."

That the movement was gaining such strength throughout the country was due in some degree to the conditions which had developed out of the schism in the papacy. With half of Christendom paying allegiance to one Pope and professing to believe the other an outcast from grace, and the nations on the second side believing the exact reverse, it was hard for devout men and women to keep a deep veneration for either

Pope. The need to maintain two Popes with equal state and with parallel organizations made it necessary for both Rome and Avignon to exact a heavier toll. The corrupt practices which had stirred Wycliffe to preaching the need for reform within the church grew steadily worse. The University of Oxford, where the gentle Wycliffe had taught, had at first been the heart and soul of the liberal creed. Well to the west, where communications were slow and an hour's flight of the crow meant a complete change of frontiers, it was far enough away from the firm hand of the bishops to maintain an independent stand. It was significant that the students reacted strongly to the new teachings. Poor, subsisting in cold and common lodgings, fired with zeal for knowledge, they mobbed the messengers of the bishops and went to lecture rooms with arms under their cloaks. But the autocratic hand of Archbishop Courtenay was bound sooner or later to impose the weight of ecclesiastical authority on even as venturesome a seat of learning as Oxford and, when Richard was summoned home, the preachers of the Conclusions were being driven out to find security in more obscure parts of the west.

One of the cradles of Lollardy was Leicester, where an eloquent priest named William Swynderby preached openly. One John Aston journeyed through all parts of the realm, denying the truth of transubstantiation, but suddenly dropped out of sight. John Purvey, one of Wycliffe's closest adherents, established a chapel outside Leicester and preached without fear or favor. Itinerant priests were welcomed into the homes of men of wealth and high station in the Midlands, such as Sir Thomas Latimer. When a London apprentice named Colleyn carried the new doctrine to Northampton, he was received in the home of the mayor of the city.

But by this time the heads of the church were fully aroused to the danger. Much as they resented the heavy financial demands of Rome, they could not stand by while the people were led down the thorny road of apostasy. A housecleaning in Oxford drove the new men out of the town and gradually the firm hand of authority made itself felt in all the cities where the head of heresy had been raised. The Lollard priests were forced to take cover in the northwestern reaches where the forests of Monmouth and Hereford offered sanctuary, and even in the Welsh foothills where the voice of Canterbury was heard feebly if at all.

For two years Richard gave lip service, at least, to the efforts of Archbishop Courtenay and his bishops to clean house in the country at large. On July 31, 1396, Courtenay died, and in his approach to the selection of a successor Richard was guided by considerations far removed from zeal for the orthodox.

The king was now determined to effect a permanent peace with

France, even at the cost of taking the seven-year-old Isabella as his second wife. He knew the idea was not popular with the people, who still blindly hoped for a renewal of the victorious early days. As leaders of the war party. Thomas of Woodstock and Arundel were against the match. The former had been partly won over, as already explained, by the creation of an earldom for his son and the offer of a handsome bribe. All that remained was to conciliate Arundel and, much as he disliked any such move, the king realized there was a way this could be done. Thomas of Arundel had been made Archbishop of York when the adherence of Neville to the king's cause had resulted in his eviction. Why not offer him now the higher post made vacant by Courtenay's death, with an understanding that he would lend his support to the French alliance?

This maneuver, which in later years would have been termed Machiavellian, may have originated in the shrewd minds which surrounded the king. But Richard was beginning to display a degree of craftiness which would later become most marked, and it seems quite probable that the plan was his. The younger Arundel brother, who was ambitious enough to accept the primacy with this hidden stipulation, was chosen to succeed Courtenay, the bull of translation being published in January of the following year. The war on Lollardy must wait until this pressing problem of establishing peace with France had been carried out.

## CHAPTER XXIII

## *"I Shall Then Be a Great Lady"*

### 1

THE state of mind into which Charles VI of France fell at frequent and sudden intervals must have had its effect on his attitude toward the continuation of the war. He now wanted peace as much as Richard. There is every reason to believe that the two monarchs were right and that the war parties which existed in both countries, made up largely of ambitious uncles and strutting nephews as well as the noisy customers of alehouses, were wrong. Only the personal interest of these blustering war panders would be served by continuing the costly war.

An unusual olive branch was sent to Richard by the King of France. A pilgrim from the Holy Land known as Robert the Hermit put in an unexpected appearance at Eltham Castle, escorted by seven horsemen of the French king. It was observed at once that there was a strange glint in his eyes, but it was not until he proceeded to tell his story that his full fanaticism became apparent. The vessel in which he returned from Palestine had been caught in a furious gale. For three days the ship had been driven in the teeth of the wind and all on board were convinced they were lost. But to Robert there appeared an apparition in the clouds, a shining figure like an angel.

"Robert," said this strange visitor from above, with uplifted hand and speaking in a tongue which the pilgrim did not recognize though he had no difficulty in understanding the words, "thou shalt escape this danger. Thou and all with thee for thy sake." The voice went on to explain what he must do. He must seek out the King of France and lay an injunction on him to bring about a peace with England. "This war," continued the heavenly visitor, "has raged too long—— Woe unto such as will not hear thee."

As soon as the apparition dissolved from sight, the winds ceased and a gentle breeze took the vessel to Genoa. Robert went to Avignon and saw the Pope, who instructed him to reach the King of France at once. The French royal uncles scoffed at the pilgrim and his story, so Robert had left France and made his way to England. Richard listened attentively to the hermit's tale. He and John of Gaunt seemed ready to accept it as true, but Thomas of Woodstock, echoed by the Earl of Arundel, refused to believe a word of it. The two war leaders called the story the ravings of a madman and demanded that no credence be placed in it.

For once they were right. Robert the Hermit returned to his home in Normandy and was never heard of again. Fortunately for the cause of peace, however, there were better reasons for pursuing a pacific policy than the visions of a half-crazed pilgrim.

Thomas of Woodstock might rage and rail, but his wings were clipped by the fact that the 50,000 nobles promised him had not yet been paid; and he wanted the money very much. As for Arundel, his brother Thomas was soon to receive the pall as primate of all England, and the earl had to be careful lest this great boon be withheld. Richard had carefully laid his plans before the hermit brought his story to the English court.

To those who objected to the tender age of the French princess, Richard had a reply which silenced them. "Every day will help to remedy this deficiency of age. Her youth is one of my reasons for preferring her, because she can be educated here and brought up in the manners and customs of the English. As for myself, I am young enough to wait for her."

2

It so happened that Jean Froissart, the French historian and romanticist, was in England when the issue was being debated. He stayed with the royal household at Eltham and received his information at second hand from Sir Richard Stury, who apparently had been restored to royal favor. Froissart got the impression that the determination of the king to marry the French princess as a means to peace was so strong that nothing would be allowed to stand in the way. It was while he was at Eltham that the decision to send a deputation to Paris was passed in the House of Commons.

Froissart's impression of the king himself was gained at first hand. Because he had been so well regarded by the late Queen Philippa, Richard received him with open favor.

The Frenchman had brought with him a presentation copy of his own writings, beautifully illuminated and bound in crimson velvet with ten silver gilt studs and roses in the middle. The Sunday after the deputation left for France, Froissart received a summons to take the book to the king in person.

Richard was still in bed but his beard had been freshly clipped and trimmed and he appeared handsome and in high spirits. He took the volume into his hands with every evidence of pleasure and started to leaf through it.

"Of what does it treat, Sir Knight?" he asked.

"Of love, Your Majesty," replied the donor. Later he described it as full of "all matters of amours and moralytees."

This stimulated the interest of the king and he began to read aloud from some of the pages. Froissart records that Richard "read and spoke French in perfection." After this tasting of the contents, the king handed the volume to one of the knights who stood at attention in the spacious and sumptuously furnished apartment, Sir Richard Creedon, with instructions to take it to the royal oratory.

Everything about the court, as seen by the French visitor, bore witness to the truth of the stories circulated at the time of the magnificence with which the king lived and the extravagance he displayed in rewarding those about him. As a return for the book, he gave Froissart a chased silver goblet containing one hundred nobles, a most handsome sum for one who lived by his pen.

### 3

The embassy sent to Paris consisted of three members, including the Earl of Nottingham, who was marshal of England. They arrived with 500 mounted attendants and were lodged on the Croix du Tiroir. The King of France was enjoying one of his sane intervals and he received them warmly, making them a grant of 200 crowns a day for their expenses.

Queen Isabeau had not yet begun on the intrigues and amours which would make her notorious and was still considered the most beautiful woman in Europe. She lived with her rapidly increasing family in the Hôtel de St. Pol. She was an extravagant chatelaine and a careless mother, for her two youngest daughters, Michelle and Katherine, were later brought up in the most neglectful way. Nothing was too good for Isabella, however, who seems to have been the favorite of the family. She resembled the queen in having the fresh Bavarian complexion and the black eyes of the Italian side of the house, but, whereas her mother had the smoldering challenge of a courtesan in her dusky eyes, those of the little princess were sweet and warm.

At first the French council refused the English envoys the right to see the princess, thinking no doubt that the terms on which the mother had come to France should not be repeated. "She is but a child of seven," was the reason they gave. The ambassadors insisted and finally were granted permission to pay a visit at the Hôtel de St. Pol.

Their first impression of Isabella was that she seemed small even for her years. When they arrived, she was seated on a low stool, while the queen and her ladies remained watchfully in the background. As the tailors of the day had not yet conceived it possible to design clothes especially for children, Isabella was a petite replica of her mother: a thin gold chaplet about her dark hair, her slender neck showing white and pure above her bell-shaped gown, her sleeves embroidered in the delicate shades of butterfly's wings, her skirts spread out demurely around her.

The three Englishmen stood in silence for a moment, each thinking the same thing, no doubt: "This miniature of a great lady will grow up into a beautiful queen."

The English marshal then dropped on one knee beside her and said, "Madame, if it please God, you will be our lady and queen."

There was a nervous tension among the women grouped about the queen, for this form of greeting had not been anticipated. How would the child conduct herself? But their fears were wholly unnecessary.

The small princess answered promptly: "Sir, if it please God and my lord and king that I be queen of England, I shall be well pleased thereat. For I have been told I shall then be a great lady."

The balance of the audience proceeded, no doubt, along the lines which had been planned. It passed off smoothly and well. The princess asked the marshal to rise and then led him by the hand to pay his respects to the queen. The latter received them graciously. Her desire to charm all men, even members of the hated English breed, was displayed in the brief talk which followed.

The members of the embassy had been quite carried away by the loveliness and intelligence of the child and so no time was lost in arranging the terms of the marriage contract. It was signed on March 9, 1396, and at the same time the truce between the two countries was tentatively extended for twenty-eight years. It was arranged that the marriage would be held at once, with the marshal acting as proxy for Richard.

The English king was to cross to France later when the terms would be ratified finally. He would then take his little bride back to England where she would be educated in a household of her own.

### 4

Richard decided that the ceremonies in France were to be conducted on the most lavish scale. He notified John of Gaunt and Thomas of Woodstock that they were to accompany him, with their wives, and similar instructions went out to the higher-ranking members of the aristocracy. They all crossed over to Calais together, including the wives who had openly declared their intention of refusing to acknowledge the fair Katharine, Gaunt's wife. Apparently the rancorous ladies were brought to realize there must be no open evidences of ill feeling, for the party arrived at Calais and then proceeded as a unit to a place between Guisnes and Ardres, where a century later another King of England would meet another King of France with an absurdity of extravagance at the Field of the Cloth of Gold.

The two courts met on the vigil of the feast of St. Simon and St. Jude, on October 27, 1396. There was an open space between the two camps and this was guarded by 400 knights from each country, on foot and with drawn swords. The royal parties met in a lane formed by the armed knights, the King of France conducted by the Dukes of Lancaster and Gloucester (Gaunt and Woodstock), and Richard walking between two of the French royal uncles, the Dukes of Berry and Burgundy. When the two kings met, "the eight hundred knights," according to Froissart, "fell on their knees and wept for joy." This sounds like one of the typical high-flown exaggerations in which the French historian indulged, and yet it is probable that some of the knights wept. In the Middle Ages men were intensely emotional and tears poured forth on the least provocation. It was true, also, that many of the nobility of both countries were thoroughly weary of the interminable fighting.

The two monarchs then went hand in hand into the pavilion of the French king, where they conversed privately, sipping wine and dipping into comfit boxes. Richard did not see his bride until the next day, however, when dinner was served in the French tent, with the kings seated alone at different ends of the table. The royal uncles waited on them and it was reported later that Thomas of Woodstock cast a rolling eye on the elaborate gold and silver service and whispered to one of the others that "France was still a very rich country, and that peace ought not to be made," a remark which befitted a burglar staring through a window at the table appointments he planned to steal that night.

After the feasting was over, the bride was brought into the tent, attended by a train of French ladies. Her father, who felt so deeply about losing her that the parting brought about a partial return of his mental malady, took one of her hands and placed it in that of Richard. Isabella looked up into the handsome face of the English king and felt as much fluttering of the heart as was possible in one so young. Apparently he impressed her as the prince charming of her dreams, for she never ceased thereafter to speak of him in any terms but of open admiration.

Richard smiled and whispered a compliment. In accordance with the prearranged etiquette, he shook the hand of his father-in-law and withdrew from the tent.

During these various meetings the English king had appeared in a magnificent variety of costumes which no mythical bird from the East could have equaled. King Charles, in contrast, had worn at the start a cloak of white and gold velvet with a single plume in his hat. This had sufficed also for all of the other events.

It was estimated later that the marriage had cost England £200,000, of which £7000 had been spent in presents lavished by the king on the French nobility. By the terms arranged in advance, Richard had renounced all claims to the throne of France in right of Isabella or the children she might bear. The queen came handsomely endowed, however, in the sum of 800,000 francs, which were to be paid in a series of installments.

The seven-year-old Isabella, who was already being called by everyone the Little Queen, was taken in charge by her ladies and escorted outside to the litter in which she was to travel. Richard had insisted that she was to be raised in the best English traditions, and so none of her ladies would accompany the lonely child to the land of her adoption. The only familiar face in her entourage would be that of Philippa, the first wife of Robert de Vere, who had returned to the English court after the death of her husband and was now called officially the Duchess of Dublin. The records do not say whether or not Launcecrona, the second wife, had accompanied de Vere into exile, but the likelihood was that she had returned finally to Bohemia. Philippa was half French, the second daughter of the Lord of Coucy, and as she was a woman of charm and warmth, her choice was a happy one.

Nevertheless, it must have been with a sinking heart that the Little Queen found herself leaving home in the company of foreigners, the people who had always been referred to at the French court in terms of hatred and contempt—the Go-dams, as they were universally called. She had been pleased by the looks of the man she was to marry and she liked the lady Philippa, but she would have been less than human had she not shed a tear when the movement of her golden draped conveyance told her she was on her way. Soon she would be married, she knew, on soil which was legally considered English and none of her family would be present.

In spite of this, the start of the marriage had been auspicious. The guests who had accompanied the king from England had been won over by the beauty and charm of the child bride. There would be no weeping fits on the part of Isabella, no imploring cries to be taken home. She seems to have been determined to accept the conditions she must now face in this land where she was to be "a very great lady."

The official marriage took place at Calais on November 4, with the expected magnificence. There is no record of the gown worn by the queen but among the finest robes listed in her wardrobe was one of red velvet, embroidered in gold, with strange birds perching on boughs made of emeralds and pearls. This may have been the selection for the ceremony. The French dressmakers had gone to excessive pains to save their princess from being outshone by her resplendent bridegroom. No finer wardrobe had ever been assembled and it was estimated that her jewelry was worth 500,000 crowns. According to the custom of the age, she brought her own chamber appointments. Her bed was as dainty as its occupant, having light hangings of white and red satin.

A large part of the dowry, 300,000 crowns, was paid over before the ceremony began.

## 5

It had been decided that Windsor Castle was to be the home of the girl queen and there had been serious efforts to make the King's House clean and attractive, with polished woodwork and new hangings. She was to have the duchess Philippa with her, and the latter's sister, the Countess of St. Pol. Courtenay, a younger brother of the former archbishop, recently chosen constable of the castle, was charged with her safety. Here a pleasant atmosphere was soon established while Isabella began the education which was intended to make her a good English queen.

Richard visited Windsor often and the Little Queen was always delighted to see him. Her affection seemed to grow with each visit. He would ride in after the long jaunt from London, looking as fresh as when he started; his cloak without a wrinkle, his handsome riding boots free of mud, a splendid new plume in his cap. He took a great interest in her education and seemed chiefly concerned about the subjects which pleased her most. It was his invariable custom to preside over her music lessons and to demonstrate his own skill on the strings or the flute. Always he read to her from the Romances which he himself found enthralling. He never talked to her of war and sieges and death, nor of the hurly-burly of the tournament lists and the sharp clash of spearheads. It is probable also that he took an interest in the clothes being made for her and saw to it that the right materials were found to keep her warm when the raw blasts of winter whistled about the turrets of the King's House.

It is also said that the Little Queen conceived a liking for the fair Katharine, John of Gaunt's third wife, above the other royal ladies. This would not be surprising, for Katharine had become a woman of serene beauty, with natural kindliness and tact, whereas the others, particularly the hard-visaged wife of Thomas of Woodstock and the proud Philippa of Arundel, were troublemakers from the beginning.

As the months passed and merged into years, her memories of home and family began to recede and the Little Queen took on much of the coloring of the new land. If nothing had occurred to disturb her development, she would in time have become what the people of England wanted: an English queen in thought and outlook and training.

CHAPTER XXIX

## *The King Strikes*

1

RICHARD and his young father-in-law, Charles of France, had found one thing in common during their private discussions before the marriage. They both had suffered, and they continued to suffer, from the activities of royal uncles. Charles knew about Thomas of Woodstock and is said to have spoken of him as "the worst-tempered man in England." He seems to have told Richard of his own troubles with the French dukes. The result was a mutual engagement to help each other in any difficulties which might arise from avuncular opposition.

Early in the year 1397 the Count of St. Pol came to England to visit his wife at Windsor Castle. He was reported to have whispered in Richard's ear that the English malcontents were moving silently in the background with the purpose of taking the throne away from him. This may have been the first result of the understanding between the two kings, but the situation was not entirely unknown to Richard. He had already received some inkling of what was afoot from the Earl of Nottingham, who was serving as governor of Calais. Nottingham had been one of the original dissenters but had afterward swung around to the king's support.

The story was, briefly, that secret meetings had been held between Thomas of Woodstock, the Earl of Arundel, and the archbishop at Arundel Castle and at St. Albans. The Earl of Derby had been one of the group of five who had activated the Merciless Parliament but, since returning from his crusading jaunts, he had been on friendly terms with the king, and for that reason he had not been invited to the meetings. Nottingham had been kept in the dark also. Thomas de Beauchamp, Earl of Warwick, had joined the group later, but with some unwillingness.

It had been decided that Richard and his two oldest uncles, John of Gaunt and Edmund of York, were to be seized and placed in perpetual imprisonment. Thomas of Woodstock then took a step which he had immediate reasons for regretting. He confided in Roger de Mortimer, who had been selected by Richard as his successor.

Mortimer was a son of Philippa, the only daughter of Prince Lionel, second son of Edward III. His grandmother, Lionel's first wife. wa᷈ Elizabeth, the only child of William de Burgh, Lord of Connaught and Earl of Ulster. The family were considered first among the Anglo-Norman lords of Ireland and it had been a natural thing for the boy Roger to be chosen by Richard as lord-lieutenant of that island. The boy was only seven when the appointment was made and it had been necessary for an uncle to act as his deputy. But now Roger was twenty-two and was planning to go to Ireland and take up his work there seriously. He was a young man of honesty and amiability and had become justly popular with the people of England.

"You need not wait to succeed to the throne," was the message whispered in his ear when Thomas of Woodstock sought him out. An army would be raised, he was told, to fight under his banner against Richard. The persons of the king and his French wife were to be secured and they would then be kept in the most rigid confinement. Mortimer would be declared King of England.

It had never occurred to Thomas that the youth would see anything but his own advantage in such a plan. He was amazed when Mortimer became pale and so agitated that he could hardly speak. Mortimer, it became clear, was too loyal for treasonable activities, even though his own interests might be served. It was evident he was aghast at the disclosure which had been made.

This brought Woodstock to a realization that he had made a serious blunder. He reacted in a way that was natural to him, blustering and threatening and demanding of Mortimer a promise to keep the matter secret. The latter was so seriously disturbed that at first he did not know what to say. He liked Richard and was completely loyal to him but he realized also that it would mean death for the conspirators if he divulged what he knew. Finally, in a state of panic, he agreed to say nothing. Soon afterward he sailed to Ireland.

The young lord-lieutenant took his duties seriously, even to the extent of wearing the native costumes. His responsibilities included, however, the restoration of order in the land and he was plunged at once into hostilities. Two years after his arrival he was killed in a skirmish with the armed men of an Irish clan and was buried in Wigmore Abbey. In the

meantime the family complications from which he had fled had been
carried through to their sanguinary conclusion.

This story of a second conspiracy is based on the chronicles of two
French writers, Froissart and Gaillard, both of whom were favorable to
Richard. English historians have been disposed to regard the evidence
as inadmissible, although they agree there had been many things to fan
the king's anger during the months immediately following his marriage.
Both Woodstock and Arundel had withdrawn from court and had been
openly critical of the placing of the port of Brest in the hands of the
Duke of Brittany. Whispers had been spread that Richard intended to
return Calais to France. This story, for which there was no foundation,
was circulated all over the country and generally believed, being one of
the reasons for the unpopularity of Richard through the final stages of
his reign. On the arrival of the Count of St. Pol, the whispers took
wings and spread fast. It was said he had been sent over to arrange the
transfer.

Did Richard have the justification of acting in self-defense? Or had it
been his intention from the first to repay the dissenting barons in their
own coin when the opportunity presented itself? There is so much evidence on both sides that it is impossible to point to one and say the
truth lies there.

However, there can be no doubt or dispute in considering the measures
that the king took. His methods can neither be explained away nor
condoned.

**2**

July 10, 1397.
St. Pol had returned to France. Roger de Mortimer had sailed for
Ireland. Woodstock and Arundel were remaining away from court, but
rumors were flying thick and fast.

Richard was in London and his troop of Chester archers, estimated
by some as numerous as 2000, were with him and ready for action. Richard Whittington, who had lived to see the promise of Bow Bells come
true by his elevation to the mayoralty of London, was disturbed to find
the streets of the great city filled with so many armed men wearing the
royal livery of the White Hart and was keeping the trained bands
alerted for trouble. Summonses for a meeting of Parliament had been
sent out. It was to be a "packed" session of the House, according to some
authorities.

The king had sent invitations to his uncle of Woodstock, Arundel, and Warwick to meet him at dinner at the residence near Temple Bar of the Bishop of Exeter, who had been appointed chancellor. There was something about the invitation which smacked of trouble. Thomas of Woodstock sensed it at once and returned word that he was ill and could not leave his castle of Pleshy. No word at all was received from the Earl of Arundel, but he promptly shut himself up in his stronghold at Reigate. Only the unsuspecting Warwick put in an appearance. Expecting a larger company, he was disturbed by the empty seats at the board. The king was cordial, however, and nothing was said to cause uneasiness until dinner was over. Richard then rose to his feet and told Warwick he was under arrest. The earl, who was not made of the stern stuff of conspiracy, was so overcome that it was not difficult later to bring him to the point of a confession. He was sent to the Tower and lodged in a section which later was called the Beauchamp Tower.

Richard used guile in enticing Arundel into the web. He went to the archbishop and asked his assistance in persuading his brother to come to London. The archbishop was too old and seasoned a hand in the political winds and currents which prevailed at court not to realize that something dangerous was afoot. Being warmly attached to his older brother, he was unwilling to take any hand in the matter.

"By St. John the Baptist!" said the king, employing the oath which had become his favored expression. "I mean your brother no harm."

As the primate still hesitated and spoke of safe conducts and guarantees, the king swore a solemn oath that no harm would come to the earl. The archbishop then agreed to act and sent word to Reigate, advising his brother to come to Westminster. Arundel, his alarm subsiding, came immediately and was met by the primate's barge, which took him across the river to Lambeth. Here the two brothers spent the night together. In the morning they were rowed over to Westminster, and the earl was summoned into the royal presence. The primate waited for him for many hours. No word of what was happening reached his ears. He begged everyone he could see for information but was met by stony stares. Finally, with a heavy heart, he returned to Lambeth. He never saw his brother again.

When the earl was escorted into the chamber where the king was engaged with several of his officers, he was not accorded any greeting. Richard sat and stared heavily at him.

"My lord Arundel!" exclaimed the king, finally. Perhaps in his mind's eye he was seeing Queen Anne, her eyes wet with tears, kneeling at the feet of this implacable man and begging for the life of Burley. He stood up and turned to Nottingham, who was one of the company. He gestured angrily. "Take my lord Arundel away!" he said.

The earl was taken first to the Tower and then removed to the Isle of Wight where he was held in the closest seclusion, pending the opening of Parliament.

3

The king left London as dusk was falling and with a small party rode all night to Pleshy. It was characteristic of him that, although he would not encounter anything but the blackness of night and was under the necessity of fast riding, he went accoutered as though for a tournament. The chamfron of his horse was of the finest leather and studded with silver, with even the bright eye of a jewel glinting out here and there. The cloth covers were of costly material and decorated also with jeweled insignia. The stirrups were of silver.

They took the high London Road because the king was anxious to finish quickly what he was setting out to do. Also, he wanted to reach Pleshy before his uncle could learn of his coming and get away. A mizzle fell during the early hours, but it was clearing when dawn broke and, with a cheerful suddenness, the sun came out as they passed the villages of High Easter and Good Easter. They were mounting a slow rise in the road and the towers of Pleshy lay ahead. The castle looked black, grim, formidable. For 250 years it had been the headquarters of the constables of England and it had been planned for defense. One contemporary writer speaks of the keep as "stupendous," the moat "amazing," the bridge of one arch over the moat "magnificent." This part of Essex had been in the Roman country, and the party passed bits of wall of the red brick the Romans had made, sometimes a culvert still sturdy and safe, and against the gray sky even the remnants of towers.

Pleshy itself had once been surrounded by fortifications that the Romans had raised, but little of this was left now. The castle was entirely Norman, the keep ponderous, the outer walls thick, the moat deep and already reeking with seasonable filth. It was well for the success of Richard's plot that he had planned a surprise. Behind the tall barbican, the duke could have held out a long time.

This element of surprise makes a logical choice possible from among the many versions told. In some accounts he is said to have arrived just as his uncle had finished his supper. Others say the king came during the night and had the sleeping duke roused from his bed. Still others set the time of arrival at dawn. The latter explanation seems the right one. Richard wanted to conceal the fact that he was riding into the northeastern country and so would not have left London until after night had fallen. Unless he pushed his troops along at a breakneck gallop, it would take six hours to cover the distance over the dark and hazardous roads. That would bring him to the constable's castle as dawn was breaking.

In the still of morning the ring of iron hoofs on the masonry of the one arch threw the castle into sudden activity. A laconic and startled "The king!" caused the guard on the bridge to raise the portcullis at once. Thomas of Woodstock, who was a temperate man and did not drink enough at night to keep him sleeping late, came out at once.

Richard's greeting was one of few words. "Have them saddle five or six of your horses. You must return with me to London."

A breakfast was laid for the unexpected visitor and his little troop, which they consumed hurriedly. The duke stood by and watched, suspicious of this surprise visit and wondering what purpose filled the king's mind.

"By St. John the Baptist!" said Richard, looking up. "Good uncle, what is to be done is for your good. And for my good."

Without pausing for rest, they took to the saddle again and set out, the duke accompanied by seven of his men. Richard conversed glibly all the way (in most accounts it is agreed that in his last years he was seldom silent), but gave no hint of what he proposed to do. Thomas of Woodstock rode beside him, silent and uneasy, perhaps also with a sense of guilt. If there were any truth in the story of the conspiracy and the effort to draw young Mortimer into it, he had every reason to expect the worst.

Before Richard had ridden into Pleshy, he had left the largest part of his troops behind, concealed in a thick wood. When this part was reached on the return trip, they emerged suddenly from the heavy cover and swarmed across the road. The Earl of Nottingham, who was in charge, laid a hand on the duke's bridle.

"Sir Duke, you are under arrest!" he said. "In the king's name!"

There was a heated passage of words between them and Thomas then became aware that the king had ridden on. He was already some distance down the road, bent over his horse. The duke called out to him in an urgent tone. Richard paid no heed. The call was repeated, with the same lack of result. Thomas of Woodstock realized then that he had allowed himself to fall into a trap. Believing in his power and the support he could rally, he was probably not too much alarmed at first. The people of London would be for him, and the rest of the nobility who felt as he did would come to his assistance.

But the first direct question he asked of Nottingham brought a disturbing response. Where were they taking him? To London? Nottingham shook his head. He was being taken to Calais.

The king was soon out of sight. The prisoner, closed in on all sides by the silent horsemen, tried to get more information out of them. All he was told was that they were to ride straight through to Dover, where a ship would be waiting for them. In this they would cross the Channel to Calais.

4

Calais had grown in importance since the English had taken possession of that famous old port. The wool staple had been established there, which meant that most of the exports of that commodity crossed the Channel to Calais for distribution to the textile cities of Flanders and northern France. Richard had contributed a new Staple Hall a few years before to serve as the trade headquarters, a building which combined grandeur with utility and was perhaps the busiest spot under the English flag.

It was to the ancient castle of Calais, however, that Thomas of Woodstock was taken. This was a grim stronghold which had witnessed much history in the making, with its six round towers and its massive keep behind a moat of unusual depth. Here he was placed in an apartment which was neither very large nor very light. He demanded to know the reason for this violence practiced upon him, but got no satisfaction from Nottingham.

Richard's plans had been carefully laid. On September 7 a justice of the Common Pleas named Sir William Rickhill was wakened out of his sleep at his home in Essingham, Kent, by a messenger bearing instructions for him to proceed at once to Calais. This seemed very mysterious, particularly as the order had been issued three weeks earlier. However, he obeyed his instructions and two days later presented himself at the drawbridge of Calais Castle. There was further cause for mystification when Nottingham told him he was to have an interview with the duke, who was being held a prisoner in the castle. This was indeed astonishing, for a story had spread over all of England a short time before Rickhill's instructions were delivered to the effect that Thomas of Woodstock was already dead. According to the rumor, he had been smothered to death.

"The duke is alive," the governor told the judge, disposing of that story.

Rickhill took a most prudent stand. He insisted on the presence of two witnesses of acknowledged probity. Nottingham thought this over and finally agreed. The witnesses were on hand, accordingly, when the judge was admitted to the chamber where Thomas of Woodstock was being held.

The duke presented no evidence of ill treatment nor did he seem in seriously bad health. He was, however, a changed man. His overbearing temper had deserted him and he seemed even humble and certainly he was deeply apprehensive. When the judge explained the mission on which he had come, Thomas agreed to prepare a statement. Rickhill, in a desire to protect himself as well as the duke, suggested that he keep a copy of what he wrote.

He returned later in the evening, with the same witnesses in attendance. The duke read a long statement of nine articles in which he made many admissions. He confessed to holding the king in restraint in 1386 and to threatening to depose him in 1388. A damaging admission was made of the discussions he had held with others as to the advisability of giving up their homage to Richard. There were references also to his, the duke's, unfortunate habits in dealing with the boy king: of opening his mail, of treating him without respect, of dictating to him what he must do. With this frank statement of what had happened went a denial that he had been guilty since of any form of treason. Most humbly he begged the king's mercy and grace.

Before Rickhill and his witnesses left, the duke suggested that they return the next day in case there were any additions to be made to the statement. The judge came back the following morning and to his great surprise was refused admission. The guards at the drawbridge explained that they were acting on orders from the governor.

Rickhill took the statement back to England and supplied a full report of what had happened at Calais.

## CHAPTER XXV

## "Vengeance Is Mine, I Will Repay"

### 1

THE king had seen fit to provide quite special accommodations for the meeting of Parliament summoned to convene on September 17, 1397. Between the entrance to Westminster Hall and the clock tower there was an open space known as Palace Yard. Here a temporary structure of timber had been erected, with little concession to comfort and none to appearance. Tiles provided a roof against autumn rain, but neither end had been closed. This arrangement gave ample room for the full attendance expected but left the members open to interruption and pressure. In fact, when the meetings began, the open spaces were lined with troops wearing the White Hart livery. The members, had they desired to obstruct the royal will, would have found their personal safety menaced by the scowling archers posted all about them.

London had not been so packed with humanity since the turbulent days when the peasants had marched across the Bridge under the belligerent Wat Tyler and the eloquent John Ball. All the barons and the men of lower degree who came (there were few absentees) had brought larger trains of armed servitors than ever before. The city could not accommodate them all. They spread out from London over a radius of ten miles. Not only were the villages packed but there were clumps of tents on all open ground.

It was significant that the clerical branch of the House was to be represented in the voting by a lay member, a judge, one Sir Thomas de Percy. This was the sharpest of practices, for the clergy could not pass on points involving the letting of blood. That stipulation would not bind a lay representative. Richard had removed the one obstacle to the carrying out of his revengeful design.

It was not until the third day that the weight of the iron glove was felt. There had been intimations, of course, of what was coming. The provisions passed in the session of 1388 (the Merciless Parliament) had been annulled. The pardons granted to the opposition lords, including, of course, Woodstock and Arundel, had been repealed. No dissenting voice had been raised. Perhaps the members were too conscious of taut fingers on the bowstrings about them.

Archbishop Arundel, who knew nothing of his brother's plight save that he was still alive, sat on the right hand of the king, with the Archbishop of York on the left. The Commons, headed by Bushy, their Speaker, marched in with ceremonial step.

They announced their intention to make enquiry into the conduct of various persons of high rank and, if necessary, to impeach them. Then the Speaker began to read in solemn tones from a document he was carrying.

In the name of the Commons of England I accuse and impeach Thomas, Archbishop of Canterbury, of high treason, for that he, being the chief officer of the king, his chancellor, when he was Bishop of Ely, was traitorously aiding, procuring and advising in making a commission, directed to Thomas of Gloucester, Richard Earl of Arundel, and others, in the tenth year of his Majesty's reign; and made and procured himself, as chief officer, to be put into it, to have power with the other commissioners to see it put into execution; which commission was made in prejudice to the king, and openly against his royalty, crown and dignity; and that the said Thomas actually put the said commission in execution.

Also that the said Archbishop, in the eleventh year of the king, procured and advised the Duke of Gloucester with the Earls of Warwick and Arundel, to take upon them royal power, and to arrest the king's liege subjects, viz., Simon Burley and James Berners, and adjudge them to death, contrary to the king's will and without his consent.

The reading was completed in a dead silence. Startled and dismayed beyond measure, the primate was still anxious to speak in his own defense but the king rose promptly and proceeded to address the House. He declared himself anxious to seek advice before proceeding with charges of such gravity against one of such high rank in the realm. The archbishop was compelled to withdraw and for the balance of the term he was kept under close watch in his palace at Lambeth. In his absence he was found guilty and banished from the kingdom. It was subsequently decreed that he must leave in six weeks for France, proceeding by way of Dover and Calais, never to return. All his personal property was confiscated by the Crown.

Richard was in a fortunate position to get his way in the replacing of the archbishop. Pope Boniface IX at Rome was still sharing the Christian world with the appointee at Avignon and he could not afford to offend or obstruct any of the kings who remained loyal to him. The bitter determination of each incumbent to continue in office almost passed belief. The death of Clement at Avignon seemed to open the way to some form of arbitration and, acting on pressure from the University of Paris, the French king sent a letter to the cardinals at Avignon, protesting against the selection of a successor. The cardinals, knowing what the letter contained, did not open it until they had completed their balloting and had elected a successor in the person of Benedict XIII!

Boniface at Rome, therefore, did not consider it expedient to do other than accede to Richard's representations. He declared the see of Canterbury vacant and agreed to act upon the king's suggestion that his able secretary, Roger Walden, be appointed to the primacy. Arundel was translated to the see of St. Andrew's. As Scotland acknowledged Benedict and not Boniface, the transfer meant that Arundel was relegated to outer darkness.

But while Boniface agreed to the election of Walden, he had mental reservations. Certainly he was quick later to reverse the decision and remove the complaisant Walden from office.

In the meantime the ex-archbishop went to Florence where he lived in ease and comfort.

The first step in the program of retribution had been taken. It is easy to imagine Richard, when he regained the solitude of his royal apartments (with perhaps no more than a dozen lords and servants in attendance), seating himself at ease and indulging in triumphant thought. He was certain to reflect on the death of the queen and to address himself to her in his musings on the events of the day. "Ah, my little Anne, were you but here to share this moment with me!"

But if Anne had been there, it is doubtful that there would have been any savoring of triumph to share. Her gentle persuasion might have succeeded in swerving him from this course.

2

When the Earl of Arundel came to trial before the House, he conducted himself with courage and at times with dignity, although tempers ran high and heated words were exchanged. He entered through the ranks of the Chester archers and into the presence of Parliament, wearing a scarlet cloak and hood. He stopped and looked about him, perceiving that the king was present and all the high officers of the realm. John of Gaunt was acting as high steward for the day. It was clear that Richard had called upon the royal relatives as well as the leading barons to play a part in what was to be done.

Gaunt opened the proceedings by issuing an order. "Take off his hood and girdle."

The high steward then directed that the articles against the defendant be read, adding afterward that Arundel had been imprisoned for his manifold treasons and rebellions against the king and that he was required to answer for such crimes. "You are especially charged," concluded Gaunt, "with having traitorously risen in arms with the Duke of Gloucester and the Earl of Warwick, against the king, in breach of the peace and the disquieting of the realm."

"This," declared Arundel, "was not done with any ill intent against the king's person but rather for the benefit of the king and the kingdom; if people would put a right construction on it, and look on it as it ought to be."

On further questioning, he declared that he had been pardoned. He would not recede from the favor of the king and his grace.

It was evident from the first that the bad blood between John of Gaunt and the prisoner still kept them deeply estranged. That the duke had neither forgotten the charges made against him by the earl nor forgiven them was made clear at this point.

"Thou traitor!" said the duke. "That pardon is revoked!"

Not daunted in the slightest, the earl flared back, "Thou liest! I was never a traitor!"

"Then," demanded Gaunt, "why didst thou purchase the pardon of the king, if thou wert not conscious of any guilt?"

There was no longer any pretense of decorum in the exchange between these old enemies. "I did that," declared Arundel, heatedly, "to put a stop to the malicious aspersions of those who neither loved the king nor myself but were my implacable enemies. Amongst whom," he added, turning to address the duke directly, "thou art one!" There was a moment's silence before the prisoner continued with his countercharges. "I am sure thou hast more occasion for a pardon than I."

All in the room were seated save the defendant, even the mere knights and the burghers who had been summoned from the towns to make up the House. Arundel had been led to a station in the open space before the platform on which the king and the lord steward sat. It was evident that Richard, who wore a gold circlet on his head and was wrapped in a gown trimmed with ermine, in spite of the heat, had no intention of taking an active part in the hearing. He watched and listened, well content, it seemed, to leave the Crown case in the hands of his uncle.

John Bushy, the Speaker of the House, took it on himself at this point to interject a statement. "The pardon," he declared, "is revoked by the king, the lords, and his faithful commons."

Arundel listened with characteristic scorn and then glanced about him at the assembled baronage and the men from the shires and towns. "Where are these faithful commons?" he demanded. "You are got together but not to do justice. For I see that the faithful commons of England are not here." Then he swung around again to face the Speaker. "Thou hast ever been a perfidious fellow!"

Bushy was not to be put down in this manner. "Our sovereign lord and king," he said, addressing Richard, "observe how this traitor endeavors to raise jealousies between us."

Arundel cried furiously: "You lie! I am no traitor!"

Henry of Derby, the son of John of Gaunt, and later to reign as Henry IV, was seated beside his father. He had been one of the leading appellants who had clipped the king's wings so relentlessly, one of the scornful five who had marched with linked arms into the presence of Richard to present him with their ultimatum. He had been fairer than the others, however, refusing to agree with Thomas of Woodstock and Arundel when they sought to depose the king at once, and striving later to save the life of Burley. He had since become friendly with his cousin, the king, and had not been invited to join the second conspiracy, if there had been any truth in that story. Derby was one of the handsome Plantagenets, reddish golden of hair and beard, and a bold and skillful soldier.

Derby rose to his feet at this point to address the prisoner. Of all in the room he was in a position to offer the most damaging evidence.

"Didst thou not say to me at Huntingdon," he demanded, "when we first drew together to make an insurrection"—a damaging admission but one which Derby could afford to make, being now on such warm terms with the sovereign—"that the most advisable thing of all was to seize the king's person?"

Arundel's anger rose to an even higher pitch, for the words of the young earl substantiated the charge of treasonable intent. "Thou liest in thy teeth!" he cried. "I never entertained a thought concerning my sovereign lord the king but what was just and made for his honor."

The king now spoke for the first time. He had been watching Arundel intently, thinking no doubt of the many times this stormy and obstinate peer had stood in his path. Earlier in the day Richard had been asked if he would extend mercy to Arundel and his answer had been: "Mercy? Yes, as much mercy as he allowed Burley!"

"Didst thou not say to me," he began, "in the time of *thy* parliament, in the bath behind the Whitehall, that Sir Simon Burley deserved to be put to death; and I made answer that I knew no reason why he should suffer death. And yet you and your companions traitorously took his life from him!"

It is not on record that Arundel made any answer to the king. There was nothing he could say to excuse himself for the leading part he had played in the death of the king's tutor and friend.

It may have been that Arundel had considered himself immune to any form of reprisal. There was not only the pardon which had been granted but the fact that he had won the only victory scored on the French through the last twenty years of hostilities. He counted strongly on his popularity with the people of England. Would an incompetent and far from popular king dare to punish the favorite of the populace? Moreover, Arundel had experienced something very rare indeed, a queen kneeling at his feet and begging him for the life of a friend, a request which he had brusquely refused. He and Thomas of Woodstock had held the king in leading strings for most of the years of his reign, dictating what he was to do, refusing to let him have his own way, feeling for him nothing but contempt. They had threatened him with deposition, and it had been no idle gesture. Nothing would have pleased them better than to lay the papers of abdication before him and to drive him to signing them. No bolt of royal lightning had struck them. It seems certain that he had come to regard himself as above the rules and restraints which bound other subjects. Otherwise would he have dared ignore the summons to ride in the funeral train of Queen Anne and pass without any response the invitation to dine with the king at the house of the chancellor?

His arrest must have been a shock, but his confidence in the outcome—if it came to a hearing in court—was not seriously shaken. He had been sent to the Tower before. But his arrival in the temporary structure at Westminster where Parliament was sitting had been a rude surprise. He encountered nothing but hostile looks. His enemy, John of Gaunt, was in charge of the proceedings. All about him were dukes and earls and mere lords and knights, and even the inconsequential commoners, who had to be allowed a say in the House; and he did not see a single friendly face.

Duke John's attitude had been sharp and definitely unfriendly. Every question was couched with the conviction back of it that he was guilty and must be punished. The earl's temper had flared and he had answered with equal hostility. But when Henry of Lancaster, who now held the double earldoms of Derby and Hereford, had accused him of treasonable intent on the basis of conversations between them, the outlook began to darken. The final blow had been the speech of the king.

He must have realized then that he could expect no more mercy than he had allowed Sir Simon Burley. The fierce anger of his replies ceased. He knew that he was doomed.

Sentence was pronounced by John of Gaunt.

"Richard," he declared, in solemn tones, "I, John, Steward of England, adjudge thee to be a traitor, and condemn thee to be drawn and hanged and to be beheaded and quartered, and thy lands both entailed and not entailed, from thee and the descendants of thy body, to be confiscated."

The deep silence which falls after the announcement of such a verdict was not broken for several moments. Then the duke proceeded with a statement which indicated that the verdict and the punishment had been settled before the hearing began. "The king, our sovereign lord," he declared, "of his mere mercy and favor, because thou art of his blood, and one of the peers of the realm, has remitted all of the other parts of the sentence but the last, and so thou shalt only lose thy head."

The sentence was to be carried out immediately. Six lords of the highest rank were selected to accompany the condemned man and to act as witnesses for the king. One was Thomas Mowbray, Earl of Nottingham, who was Arundel's son-in-law. Two of the others were Richard's half brothers, Thomas Holland, Earl of Kent, who was Arundel's grandson, and John Holland, Earl of Huntingdon. The six witnesses rode in considerable state with their mounted attendants. A large force of the Chester archers had been deputed to surround the condemned man on his way to Tower Hill. If there had been any hope in Arundel's mind that the citizens of London, who had always favored him and were now antagonistic to the king, would make any move to rescue him, he was soon disabused on that score. People lined the streets in thousands, silent and glum but not disposed to do anything for him. The sands were running out fast.

He had made one request of his guards. "Loosen me my hands, I pray you," he said. He was carrying some money with him and desired to distribute it among the people who would watch him pass. This request was allowed. The coins had all been tossed to the quiet Londoners before the procession reached Charing Cross.

An effort was made at Tower Hill to get from the condemned man an acknowledgment of his guilt. He refused with all the vehemence he had displayed during the questioning before the House.

"I am not a traitor," he declared. "In word or in deed!"

He felt a natural bitterness over the presence of his son-in-law and his grandson among the six official witnesses. "It would better have become you," he said, "to have absented yourselves."

It is quite possible they were present on direct order of the king and that they would have preferred not to carry out so ungrateful a task.

"The time will come soon," continued the condemned man, "when people shall be as much astonished at thy misfortune as they are now at mine."

Arundel turned then to the executioner and forgave him for what he had to do. "Torment me not long," he begged. "Strike off my head in one blow."

The executioner held out the ax and the victim felt its edge. "It is very well," he commented.

He then knelt beside the block. The executioner, who must have been a man of steady nerves and hand, did as he had been requested. He severed the head from the trunk with one blow.

### 3

With the archbishop banished from the kingdom and Arundel dead, the curtain was raised for the third act in the drama. During the first days of the session, Thomas of Woodstock's statement, which Rickhill had brought back from Calais, was presented to the House. It had been cut, and certain portions which might have seemed favorable to the duke had been eliminated entirely, including his plea for mercy.

On September 21 a writ was issued by the Commons to the governor of Calais, instructing him to produce his prisoner. Three days later a reply was received from Nottingham. He could not produce his prisoner because the duke was dead. There was no attempt at an explanation, but the intimation was that he had died a natural death. The date of the death was given as August 25.

Copies of the statement were distributed throughout all the counties of England. It was declared that Rickhill's commission had been issued on August 17, and so the inference was that the judge's interview with the duke, which resulted in the preparation of the confession, had been at some time between that date and the day of Woodstock's death.

Casting some years ahead, Rickhill was summoned to appear before Parliament on November 18, 1399, after Richard's deposition. His story was accepted as true and any suspicion which might have been held against him was dispelled. His prudence in demanding the presence of

# THE BATTLE OF
# ST. ALBANS

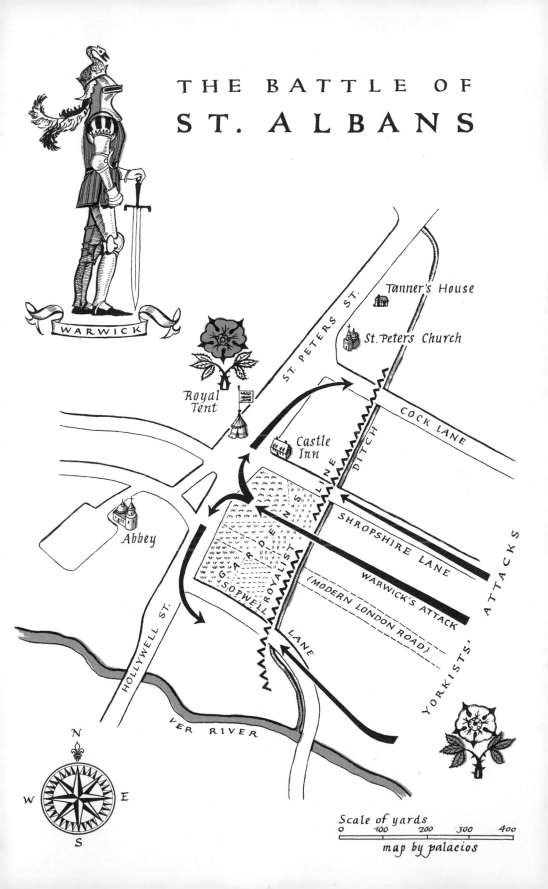

WARWICK

Royal Tent

Tanner's House

St. Peters Church

ST. PETERS ST.

COCK LANE

Castle Inn

DITCH

SY LINE

SHROPSHIRE LANE

WARWICK'S ATTACK

(MODERN LONDON ROAD)

YORKISTS, ATTACKS

GARDEN

ROYALIST

SOPWELL LANE

Abbey

HOLLYWELL ST.

VER RIVER

N
W    E
S

Scale of yards
0    100    200    300    400

map by palacios

reputable witnesses made it possible for him to present a completely believable story.

At the same time a man named John Halle, a former servant of Nottingham's, swore before the House that the duke had been smothered to death at some date in September. Halle himself had been one of the agents of death and he described the murder in detail. The duke had been removed from Calais Castle to a hostelry in the town called Prince's Inn, a much frequented haunt of rogues and beggars. Here he was lodged in a mean room. That he faced death was apparent to the prisoner and, when the door was thrown open to admit a group of men, all of whom were strangers to him, he realized that the moment had come. He was unarmed and helpless. If he attempted to cry out for assistance, the sound was cut off, probably by a muffler wrapped about his mouth. A man named William Serle, said to have been once a servant of the royal chamber, was in command of the band. Halle stood guard on the door.

The duke was forced to the ground and feather beds were piled on top of him. The assassins held him down until he had been smothered to death.

Both Halle and Serle were executed later for their part in the murder.

It seems probable that the duke was removed from Calais Castle as soon as he had written his confession. This would have given the governor, the double-dealing Nottingham, a chance to claim that he had no part in, or knowledge of, what happened. It is more than likely that the murder was carried out that night and that the duke was dead when Rickhill returned to the castle the following morning and was refused admittance.

On October 14 the king ordered Nottingham to deliver the body to a priest of the royal chapel, named Richard Maudelyn (of whom many curious things will be told later), and the latter conveyed it to the widow for burial in Westminster Abbey. In the succeeding reign it was interred in the chapel of the kings at Windsor.

## 4

The curtain had fallen on the three important figures in the drama, and what followed was anticlimactic. On September 28, Thomas de Beauchamp, Earl of Warwick, was brought from the Tower to stand trial. He lacked the courage of Arundel and broke down almost at once under questioning. He confessed his guilt and threw himself on the king's mercy. Richard apparently felt for him contempt rather than the hatred which had festered in his mind for his uncle Thomas and the Earl of Arundel. He was content to have Warwick sentenced to life imprisonment and the forfeiture of all his property.

Warwick was sent to the Isle of Man, where William le Scrope was governor. The latter spent little time on the island and the prisoner complained bitterly that he was neglected and treated harshly by the servants in whose hands Le Scrope left him.

In the succeeding reign he was released and his conduct thereafter was quite characteristic. He first attempted to deny his confession before the Commons in 1397, although no weight was attached to his explanations. Henry IV, who was present on this occasion and also when the confession had been made, brusquely demanded his silence. Later he was one of the high baronage who put pressure on Henry to have Richard killed. He himself died in 1401.

## CHAPTER XXVI

## The Absolute King

1

MUCH of the story of Richard's twenty-two-year reign is based on insufficient evidence and it has generally been told without any effort to be impartial. When a king is deposed, the story of what happened is written with an eye to the favor of the new incumbent. The boy king has been treated harshly in the chronicles of the Lancastrian period and much of what has been published since follows that lead. Perhaps he is deserving of most of this criticism, but there are certain things which must be said in his favor. He was not cast in the mold of kings and the age was one which demanded a rude and masterful hand on the helm. Richard, somewhat effeminate, a hater of war, was condemned to failure from the beginning, especially as he ascended the throne at such an early age.

Charles VI, who succeeded to the French crown at practically the same age as Richard, found himself also beset and badgered by a circle of unfriendly uncles. This may have been one of the reasons for the insanity which overtook him so quickly. Richard ruled as a minor under the powerful and sometimes menacing shadow of John of Gaunt and the incessant bullying of his uncle of Woodstock. The vindictive streak to be found in many of the Plantagenets may have been kept under cover until he felt he could strike back with impunity. It is conceivable also, though unlikely, that a second conspiracy was under way and that he acted in self-defense.

Everything good that can be advanced about Richard as King of England has now been said. Only the dark and disturbing sequel remains to be told.

When his old enemies had felt the edge of his vengeance, he seemed to change for the worse. In his thirtieth year, still handsome although growing somewhat heavy of build, he must have felt his position to be unassailable. The philosophy his father had accepted and which had been dinned into his ears as a boy now became one on which he could act. "By God's will you are king," he had been told, "and you are answerable only to Him." The opposition was broken, his uncle Thomas and the Earl of Arundel were dead, the archbishop had been banished and was languishing in Florence, Warwick had sniveled for a pardon and was in perpetual imprisonment. Who was left to stand in his way?

Before Parliament adjourned, the king took steps to strengthen his position. He scattered dukedoms about with a lavish hand. His cousin Henry of Derby became Duke of Hereford, Edward of Rutland the Duke of Aumale, his two hotheaded and obnoxious kinsmen, the Hollands, were both raised to the rank of duke, and the Earl of Nottingham, who had been the sword hand of the *revanche,* was created Duke of Norfolk. Some of the lesser figures became earls.

This largesse of honors won him the support of individuals, but did nothing to improve the king's standing with the older nobility or the common people. In the London streets they chanted songs of derision and they coined a term to describe the new favorites, the *duketti.* The citizens of London became so antagonistic, in fact, that they claimed miracles were being performed at Arundel's grave. Richard, whose sleep was said to be troubled with dreams of the dead earl and who complained that the clothes on his bed were wet with blood, went to the extreme of ordering that the tomb be paved over.

It was necessary for the king to keep his Chester troops about him to prevent the trained bands and the apprentices with their clubs and knives from venting by violent measures their disapproval of him and of the carefully hand-picked Parliament.

This question of protecting the House had been one which gave concern to many kings. In 1332, Edward III had thought it necessary to decree that "no man, upon pain of forfeiting all his substance, should presume to wear any coat of mail or other weapons in London, Westminster or the suburbs of the same." A quite different form of protection had been applied in 1205 by the infamous King John, the black sheep of the Plantagenets. This was designed to protect the king from the members! They were required to send their children as hostages for their allegiance and their obedience to the king's wishes. This method of gagging the House and preventing a free and courageous expression of opinion was, fortunately, never used again.

Undoubtedly the hostility of the Londoners influenced the king in deciding to hold the next meeting of Parliament elsewhere. It was announced that the next session would be held at Shrewsbury on January 28. This was to prove one of the shortest of all sessions, lasting for three days only. Later it was called the Suicidal Parliament because of the effect of the legislation passed on Richard's demand.

This Parliament of three days proceeded to nullify everything that had been done by the House of 1388 and restored all property rights to those who had suffered then, or to their families. It provided, moreover, for a permanent board of eighteen members to serve with the king: ten of the upper ranks of the baronage, two earls to act for the clergy, and six commoners. The men nominated to this committee were partisans of the king and could be depended on to bend to his will. The authority vested in them was such that it would not be necessary to summon a full Parliament again.

The king was granted a tenth and a fifteenth of all national revenue. The last act of this short-lived House was the almost unbelievable one of granting him a subsidy on all wool, woolfells, and leather for the term of his natural life!

In three days Richard was granted the power to rule England as an absolute king!

The Great Charter had not been revoked, but its restrictions would never be felt. The nobility were shackled to the royal chariot like conquered generals marching in chains in a Roman triumph. The House had given away its right to maintain a check on royal conduct by the withholding of financial supplies. The country was at peace and would continue to live for a full quarter century under the truce made with France. The king himself had been provided with a lifelong revenue, large enough to cover all his peace-time needs, extravagant though they might be.

Other kings had disregarded the administrative checks placed on their power. But Richard had gone much further than that. He had succeeded in having this declared as his right. He could now regard himself as answerable only to God.

2

This seems a suitable place at which to pause and introduce a character whose part in the drama of Richard's last years was veiled in mystery but who undoubtedly was to prove himself most useful to the king. There was a priest in the royal chapel named Richard Maudelyn. The first time the king set eyes on him he must have paused and wondered, for the young priest was in all respects a replica of himself. Not only did he have the same rather florid coloring and identical features but even his voice was so similar that no one could tell the difference.

Was there a blood relationship between them, one having to do with the left hand? It seemed impossible that nature could have produced so unusual a double unless there had been some crossing of bloodlines. Edward the Black Prince had brought two illegitimate sons into the world before he succumbed to the matrimonial-minded Joan of Kent. Was the existence of this handsome young priest due to another adventure on the part of that great warrior? Or could the explanation be found in the rumor widely circulated that Richard was not the son of the Black Prince? There had been, it was whispered, many handsome priests in the royal household at Bordeaux, and the Fair Joan, having lost her first son born to the prince, was determined to replace him. This far-fetched story (because Richard was born before his older brother died) was introduced later by his successor, Henry of Derby, and there were many time servers to profess a belief in it.

The only thing about which there can be no shadow of doubt is that this handsome young Maudelyn was in the service of Richard and that the king took advantage of the amazing resemblance. He was not the first king, nor the last, to use a double for his own purposes. Richard was indolent and many of the duties he was supposed to perform were irksome to him. Why not substitute Maudelyn and let him meet unimportant visitors, or attend church services while the real king lolled about at his ease?

Maudelyn was used as well for errands of much more importance—"secret and perilous missions," according to one chronicle. It is on the official records that he accompanied the king on the second, and last, journey to Ireland. Here he was given the task of repairing the buildings in the castle at Dublin. A French writer, who was in Ireland at the time and has contributed a number of intimate pictures of the king's activities, had this to say: "Many a time have I seen him [Maudelyn] riding through the country with King Richard, his master." He adds this comment: "Never for a long time did I see a fairer priest."

This fair priest will be given credit later for mysterious activities during the years immediately preceding the change of kings and for a somewhat longer period after the deposition and death of Richard.

### 3

Despotic power was too potent a brew for one with the unstable mind and temper of Richard. He began to think of himself as wise and strong and courageous, in fact as the greatest monarch in the world. He dreamed of the day when the electors would meet and cast their votes for him as Holy Roman Emperor.

But he never forgot the bitter lesson of the Merciless Parliament. Never again must he find himself in the power of forces antagonistic to him. He set his crafty mind to work on that problem or listened to someone near him who was cunning and unscrupulous. It was clear that he must get the most thickly populated and wealthy part of England under his thumb. A proclamation was issued that no longer "might he ride safely in his realm for dread of the men of London and seventeen shires lying round about." Lists were prepared of those he considered dangerous and disloyal and from each of them he demanded a "submissory letter." In these documents, which they were compelled to sign, they acknowledged themselves as "misdoers" and promised on pain of heavy fines to agree to all that the Suicidal Parliament had done. For any fines levied on this illegal basis the term *pleasaunce* was used. This far from gentle pressure helped to replenish the royal purse, but its chief value was that it gave the king a weapon to suspend over the heads of all who had signed the papers.

The Chester archers accompanied the king whenever he appeared in public. Like all hired soldiers, they began to regard themselves as privileged. They would walk into a public house, demand a flagon of mead or ale, toss it off, and leave without paying. The badge of the White Hart aroused resentment wherever it was seen. It was not surprising that the people of London and of the seventeen shires felt for this vengeful king a dislike and fear which grew finally beyond the point of endurance. All that was needed to set the trained bands to marching and the men of the shires to arming was a leader.

It is said (in the most unfavorable chronicles, it is true) that Richard's manners became unbearable. He would stroll into a meeting of his parliamentary committee like a vision from some strange world of glowing colors and nightmare designs. In a condescending tone, and with a finger pressed to his fine white brow, he would comment on a proposed amendment of laws in some such words as:

"The laws are in my mouth or in my breast. I alone can change the laws of the land."

Expressions such as this were quite as liable to cause an explosion of popular discontent as the powder with which he had experimented in the Tower when he was a boy. The crux of the matter may be found right there. Richard had not grown up.

All tyrants, no matter how powerful they conceive themselves to be, live in fear. Every man is a potential enemy; the dagger in every other belt may be the one that will be plunged between the vital ribs. This sense of menace was so deeply entrenched in Richard that he would listen to strange preachings. He was even prevailed upon to hear the words of a hermit who came like another Jeremiah with a message of divine wrath.

"Amend your ways, O King!" cried the hermit, shaking what might be called a forfending forefinger in Richard's face.

The weakness of this prophet of doom was that he believed in himself. When Richard demanded that he prove the divine source of his warning by walking on water, the hermit attempted to do so and was dragged out feet first in a half-drowned condition, to be hanged, in all probability.

The king was confirmed in this new attitude by the lack of any restraint from Rome. Pope Boniface IX, a young man of thirty, found himself so pressed for funds to hold the kings of Europe in his support against the encumbent at the magnificent court of Avignon that he descended to the most barefaced simony. It seemed possible to purchase anything. Richard even managed to get letters from Rome which threatened the punishment of the church on any who failed to accept all measures of the Great Parliament, a term selected for the sessions just concluded of what men in England were already calling the most dangerous and reactionary of all Parliaments.

## CHAPTER XXVII

## Two of the Five

1

THREE memories of the past seemed to darken Richard's mind and to fan his desire for revenge. They were the defeat of de Vere at Radcot Bridge, the unceremonious intrusion on his privacy in the Tower of London when the leaders of the opposition, with locked arms, had issued their ultimatum, and the fruitless pleading of his young queen for the life of Burley.

On a day in December 1397, two of the new dukes, the king's cousin Henry, the Duke of Hereford, although generally called Henry of Bolingbroke, and Thomas de Mowbray, Earl of Nottingham and now Duke of Norfolk, were riding together to London from Brentford. There had never been much friendly feeling between them. Henry was a Plantagenet and a very probable successor to the throne, a man of kingly presence and great courage, and a favorite of the people. Norfolk was of the upper nobility, thickset and of great strength, now holding the office of marshal of England. Henry's lack of cordiality for the other was undoubtedly due to the fact that Norfolk had acted as Richard's instrument in the purging of his confederates.

It was a cold and blustery day and so it is a matter for surprise that these two men, so different in temperament and design, would unmuffle sufficiently to indulge in extended talk as they rode fast to reach the welcome warmth of London, their horses' hoofs striking sparks on the frozen surface of the highway. The talk was of such an incendiary nature that Bolingbroke went at once to Richard and gave him his own version of it. This report Norfolk instantly and vigorously denied.

Had Norfolk been foolish enough to utter treasonable ideas to a man with whom he had never been on friendly terms? Or did the king's cousin invent the conversation for purposes of his own? The truth was never arrived at, although it seems reasonable to believe that Henry of Bolingbroke's version was close to the truth.

Norfolk, according to Bolingbroke, spoke of the day when the appellants had linked arms and marched unceremoniously into Richard's presence in the Tower. The talk seems to have developed along some such line as this:

Norfolk: "How many were there of us?"

Bolingbroke: "We were five, sir duke."

Norfolk: "Yes, my prince, we were five. The king's uncle Thomas was in the center with Arundel and Warwick on each side of him. Two of them are now dead and the other committed to life imprisonment. Who were the other two, on the ends of the line?"

Bolingbroke (turning in his saddle and looking his questioner squarely in the face): "You and I, sir duke, you and I."

Norfolk then proceeded to speak of doubts which filled his mind. Whenever he saw the king's eyes on him, there was something in them which gave him small comfort. Could it be that Richard, even after so many years, was seeing him at one end of the line, his arm linked in that of one of the other conspirators who had died? Could he and Bolingbroke place any reliance on the pardons which had been granted them?

He proceeded finally to give a positive reason for such fears. There had been a plot, he declared, to get rid of both Bolingbroke and his father, John of Gaunt. The two Holland brothers, who wanted to get all power in their hands, had been at the bottom of it. He, Norfolk, and the Duke of York had prevented the plotters from accomplishing their purpose.

It was, he had concluded, an evil world and neither of them could put any faith in the king's oaths.

Bolingbroke made no comments but as soon as he reached London he went to the king and told him what had transpired. Richard had Norfolk summoned before him. The latter denied the story. "My dear lord, I say that Henry of Lancaster is a liar!" he declared. "In what he says of me, he lies like the false traitor that he is!"

It was one man's word against the other's, both of high degree and, supposedly, of honor. Richard decided on an open hearing and fixed the day and the place: the festival of St. George sixty days thence, at Windsor Castle.

When the day arrived, a scaffold had been erected inside the castle grounds, for the seating of the king and such members of the nobility and the church as would be in attendance. It was reported to the king that both men asserted it was impossible for them to be reconciled.

Richard then ordered that both of the principals to the dispute be brought in, with heralds to present their respective cases. A knight who appeared for Bolingbroke said: "My sovereign lord, here is Henry of Lancaster, Duke of Hereford and Earl of Derby, who says, and I also for him, that Thomas Mowbray, Duke of Norfolk, is a false traitor to your royal majesty and the whole kingdom." Further it was charged against Norfolk that he had received 8000 nobles for the payment of the garrison at Calais, which sum he had kept for himself; that Norfolk had been the cause of all the treasons in the past eighteen years. Finally, it was proposed to prove this with his, Henry's, body against that of Norfolk in the lists.

Another knight then came forward and declared that everything said against Norfolk was a lie, and the duke himself stated that he had used the 8000 nobles for proper expenditures and that he beseeched the king to allow him combat against this accuser.

At this point Henry of Bolingbroke threw down his gauntlet and Norfolk picked it up. It was decided that they would be allowed to fight it out in the lists at Coventry, and September 16 was selected as the date.

## 2

It has been a custom with princes who exercise despotic sway to offer the people spectacles and entertainments as a sop for the rights which have been taken from them. The emperors of Rome kept the hungry and wretched poor from too much discontent by having gladiators fight in the arena and Christians devoured by lions before their eyes. Richard was no exception, and during the brief period of his megalomania he took every occasion to dazzle the populace with his magnificence. He decided to use the trial by arms at Coventry for this purpose.

He ordered a stately theater to be constructed on Gosford Green, with lists adjoining which would not have suffered by comparison with the famed tilting grounds at Ashby-de-la-Zouch where Ivanhoe performed so nobly. The king arrived the day before and was received as a guest in the round tower belonging to Sir William Bagot. Here he gave audiences at different times to each of the disputants. He seems to have been genuinely distressed that neither was prepared to yield an inch. They still protested that it was impossible for them to be reconciled. Somewhat reluctantly he gave instructions for the duel, which would be fought to the death, to be proceeded with in accordance with the laws of chivalry.

The hour of prime, which meant six in the morning at this season, had been set for the spectacle to begin. Henry of Bolingbroke arrived well ahead of the stipulated hour and pitched his pavilion close to the lists. He was accompanied by a lordly train of gentlemen and followers, as well as the essential squires, a surgeon, and a confessor. Norfolk had his tent placed in a thick wood which lay between the entrance to the lists and the walls of the town.

Promptly at the hour of prime, Bolingbroke came to the lists, riding a white courser with blue and white velvet trappings, on which swans and antelope were embroidered. The Duke of Aumale, who was acting as marshal for the occasion, met him at the barrier.

"Your name and station?" he demanded.

"I am Henry of Lancaster, Duke of Hereford, and I come hither to do my endeavors against Thomas Mowbray, Duke of Norfolk, so as to prove him a traitor, false to God, the king, the kingdom and myself."

He then took an oath that his cause was just and true, and was admitted. He proceeded on foot to a chair of green velvet which had been placed at one end of the lists on a cloth of blue and green.

The king arrived next with a train of great magnificence, most of the peers of the realm being with him and even that visitor on all difficult occasions, seemingly, the Count of St. Pol. The stands by this time were packed with people of substance while the high grounds adjoining were filled with spectators who had to stand. The rabble had come a-foot to revel in this exciting contest between two dukes who would break their lances in the lists and then, if necessary, belabor each other with mace and sword and dagger until one of them was dead. Standing there in sweat-stained jerkins and dusty caps, they looked avidly at the splendid raiment of those who were their betters by accident of birthing. It was a fair day, with a pleasant September sun in the sky and no threat of weather to disturb the prospects of a beautiful fight to the very death.

The only one there who looked with any disquiet on what was to follow seems to have been Richard himself. What had he to gain by letting these two young dukes fight until the weaker gave up his life on the greensward? If Bolingbroke were the victor, it must then be assumed that he had spoken the truth and that Norfolk had warned him of the vengeance of the king. It would even be established that there had been a royal plot to kill him and his father. On the other hand, if Bolingbroke died, a smirch would be left on the fair name of the Lancastrian branch of the royal family. Further, the amity that the king had been striving to restore in the royal family would be rent wide open with grief and suspicion of his purposes. It was too much to hope that both of these blustering noblemen would be killed in this hate-engendered imbroglio. That would mean there had been no truth in either of them and that the supposed plot was a mere figment of the imagination. This might have suited the king quite well, for he had been conscious of the hot breath of Bolingbroke on his shoulder and was willing to have such a dangerous contender removed from his path.

A much better solution had entered his mind as he sat there in moody magnificence on his high throne.

Norfolk appeared at the barrier and was admitted after taking the oath, a strong figure on a steed covered with crimson velvet and richly embroidered with silver lions and mulberry leaves.

"God assist the just cause!" he cried, as he crossed to his seat at the other end of the lists. Here a crimson velvet chair had been placed for him.

While Richard brooded in his eminence, the work of preparation went forward. The marshal measured the spears and found them of equal length. The chairs of the combatants were removed. The two dukes closed their beavers and were assisted into their saddles. They rode slowly to their stations at the ends of the lists. The drone of talk died down in the stands and in the spaces where the common people stood.

At this dramatic moment Richard finally made up his mind. On a signal from him, the heralds cried, "Halt! Halt!" Instructions were sent down to the marshal to see that the combatants dismounted. The steeds were led away, the chairs were brought back and placed again on their colored carpets. The spectators watched in amazement and loudly expressed their discontent as the two dukes seated themselves again. What was wrong? Why did the king interfere? Was the duel not to be held after all?

For two hours the combatants sat in their heavy armor in the full glare of the warm morning sun. The spectators, concerned with the need to preserve their positions, did not stir about, but a great hum of sound enveloped the lists. Everyone was speculating, discoursing, arguing. As the time passed slowly, the speculation mounted in intensity. The people had become angry. They did not understand what could be happening to justify such a long delay. In the meantime the king had withdrawn from the lists with members of his council. Quite clearly they were debating some form of action.

At the end of the two hours the king and his councilors returned to their seats. It became clear that a decision of some moment had been reached when Sir John Bushy, who was acting as secretary to the king, advanced to a central position in the lists, carrying a long scroll in his hands. When the heralds had succeeded in silencing the crowds he began to read from the scroll.

The king had decided that the duel was not to take place. It was his decision that both of the contestants were to leave the kingdom. Henry, Duke of Hereford, was to depart within fifteen days and not return to England for ten years. Thomas de Mowbray, Duke of Norfolk, "because he had sown sedition in the realm by his words, should likewise depart the kingdom and never return into England, nor come near the confines thereof upon pain of death, *for a hundred wynter;* and that the king should receive the income of his estate till such time as those sums of money, which he had received for the payment of the garrison of Calais, were fully repaid and satisfied."

It was a curiously unjust decision. It expressed, certainly, a belief in the guilt of Norfolk; but if he had been spreading sedition and pocketing royal funds, why was Henry of Bolingbroke, who had uncovered his perfidy, made to share the punishment? No other official act of Richard's exemplified so clearly the instability of his judgments and the unpredictable quirks of his mind. It was stated later that Bolingbroke had been banished from the realm to avoid all conflict between him and his adherents with the Norfolk men.

It seems clear enough that Richard did remember all five faces in that fateful line and that he hoped never to see any of them again.

The two combatants were stunned. The nobility and the solid citizens in the stands looked from one to another in amazement. The common men, who had tramped over many weary miles to see a fight to the death and now must walk back, were loud and scornful in their comments. As far as could be judged, the sympathy was all on the side of Bolingbroke.

The Duke of Norfolk, in great bitterness of mind and recalcitrance of spirit, went to Germany and later appeared in Venice. Here he died within a few months of the passing of the sentence.

The king had Bolingbroke come to him at Eltham to make his farewells. He tried to convince his cousin that the exile into which he was being sent was intended as a form of honorable absence until the whole truth could be ascertained. The term of exile was reduced from ten to six years, and he was granted the right to remain at Sandgate for six weeks and four weeks in Calais. The streets of London were packed with people to see him depart and to deplore the official action which sent him away.

## CHAPTER XXVIII

## The Great Mistakes

### 1

ON FEBRUARY 3, 1399, John of Gaunt died at Ely House in Holborn in his fifty-ninth year. He was buried at St. Paul's beside his first wife, and a magnificent monument was erected over them. Although he had been a failure, his passing nonetheless left a great void in England. Of the sons of Edward III, only one now survived, the innocuous Duke of York. Gaunt's oldest son was in exile. Richard, now very generally recognized as weak and dangerous, was ensconced on the throne with what seemed to be unusual security. There was peace with France but, if anything happened to disrupt it, what chance was there of a successful prosecution of war?

It has generally been felt that it was regret over the exiling of his son which brought about John of Gaunt's death, but any close scrutiny of his career must leave doubts on that score. "Great Lancaster," as he has often been called, was an intensely ambitious and selfish character. Overshadowed by the greatness of his older brother, Edward, he had most deeply desired to achieve glory himself but had been forced to observe the popularity of the Black Prince with the people and to stomach the humiliation of the burning of his palace in London. Several chances had been given him to lead armies in France, but nothing had come of these costly ventures. His scheme to secure the throne of Castile for himself had come to nought. If he resented the sentence passed on his son, he had made no open move to have it set aside. Some men who have failed are not entirely happy when a son accomplishes the desired end. He died, it may be assumed, a sorely disappointed man who, at the end, perhaps, had come to a recognition of his own limitations.

His death gave Richard a chance to make the first of two fatal mistakes. The king granted Henry of Bolingbroke the right to take possession of his vast inheritances by proxy, but soon thereafter changed his mind. On March 18 he revoked the patents by which Henry's attorneys would have assumed control of the Lancaster holdings and declared everything confiscated to the Crown. The king, in fact, came boldly out into the open for the first time by changing Henry's banishment to a life term. He even went so far as to bring charges of treason against one Henry Bowet, an attorney who appeared for Bolingbroke.

And so the vengeance of the king fell on the last of the five of the linked arms.

Reference has already been made to the vast extent of the Lancastrian holdings. It may have been that an accounting would have revealed the wealth of John of Gaunt to be greater than that of the king himself. Henry of Bolingbroke was a man of extensive property in his own right and he held also, by reason of his marriage to Mary de Bohun, a full half of the princely Bohun lands. The combined wealth of father and son would have made the ultimate holder, Henry of Bolingbroke, a figure of dangerous power. This, no doubt, was in Richard's mind but he failed to establish any legal justification for the step he took. To anyone less confident of himself, it would have been clear that an open clash could not now be avoided. Did he consider himself strong enough to stand against the popular and able Bolingbroke? He must have been quite confident that he could keep his cousin on the other side of the Channel.

The disinherited prince was in Paris at the time and in high favor at the French court. He took the news coolly and made no open boasts of reprisal. Nevertheless he lost no time in preparing under cover to fight the confiscatory measures. The first step was to receive Arundel, the ex-Archbishop of Canterbury, who was also in exile and who hurried to Paris to offer his assistance. If any rumor of his cousin's activities reached Richard's ears, which seems doubtful, he paid no attention. He believed himself seated most securely in the saddle.

Richard then proceeded to make another grave mistake. He decided to lead an army into Ireland. Conditions in that country were very bad but no worse than they had been for some time, and the reason he gave for his decision, that he sought revenge for the death of his young cousin Roger Mortimer, seemed far from adequate. It may have been that, knowing how deeply the people of England resented his failure to achieve any military victories for them, he thought that in Ireland he might win some easy glory.

**2**

The completely adult stage of Richard's life had now been reached. Gone was the boyish charm, the trace of sweetness, the willingness to listen, never very marked. He had become completely Plantagenet and, unfortunately, it was not the best side of this kingly family which he proceeded to reveal. He was now arrogant, convinced of his own greatness, sure of his unlimited prerogatives, and above all else revengeful. A strain of craftiness had taken the place of reason.

All these traits were displayed in the decision he had made to carry sword and flame into Ireland, and in the events which preceded the invasion. First he felt it necessary to cater to the populace by having a great spectacle. He arranged to hold a tournament at Windsor in which forty knights and forty squires would compete. All were to carry the colors of the queen, green with the device of a falcon in white.

The queen had grown into a quite lovely girl of eleven. She was rather tall but showed no trace of the usual awkwardness of that age. She raced to the highest turret of the King's House when the news was received that the king approached, so that she would catch the first glimpse of him riding down the road from London Town. At the tournament she distributed the prizes and behaved with such dignity and charm that she won over those who watched.

Richard found, however, that it would be necessary to make a change in the household of the young queen. The lady de Coucy, wife of the Count of St. Pol, had been taking on all the airs of a queen and was indulging in extravagances which caused the king himself, the most lavish of men, to gasp with dismay. She kept "two or three goldsmiths, two or three cutlers, and two or three furriers" continually employed. In addition, it was reported to him, she had eighteen horses always at her command, in addition to the mounted men supplied by her absent husband. Finally, she was embarking on the folly of a new chapel which was going to cost a fabulous amount.

Richard took care of this plunge into fantastic display by commanding the lady to return to France and by putting in her place the widow of his brave cousin, Roger Mortimer, now dead and buried in Ireland.

The king's final scene with his budding queen was in the chapel at Windsor. Here he heard a Mass and chanted a collect. On leaving he and his bride shared a glass of wine at the church door. He then lifted her in his arms and kissed her many times.

"Adieu, madame!" he said. "Adieu, till we meet again."

It is not recorded that anyone remonstrated with him on the folly of leaving the kingdom, with all his armed forces, at such a critical juncture. If they did, he brushed their reasoning aside. It was firmly planted in his mind that the time had come to settle the Irish problem. Equally urgent was his desire to avenge his cousin Mortimer, for whom he had entertained a great liking, knowing how honest and loyal that bewildered young man had been. If Queen Anne had been alive, it is possible she might have seen the need to maintain his defences at home and might have convinced him of it. But in the eyes of the girl queen, Richard could do no wrong. Riding away to the Irish wars, he seemed to her the perfect knight and the wisest of kings.

The final measure of his folly was the appointment of his sole surviving uncle, Edmund of York, to act as regent in his absence. Edmund was without political pretensions, but he was indolent and devoid of all qualities of leadership. A poorer watchdog could not have been found.

Richard sailed from Milford Haven late in May 1399, with an army estimated at 4000 knights and squires and 30,000 archers, although this figure undoubtedly was a great exaggeration. On July 4 of the same year Henry of Bolingbroke landed at Ravenspur on the Yorkshire coast.

### 3

Nothing was accomplished in Ireland.

Richard had decided to take along as his interpreter an Englishman named Henry Cristall, who had been captured years before by the Irish during a mounted foray. Cristall's horse had bolted and carried him into the Irish ranks where he was promptly taken prisoner. Making the best of things, he settled down among his captors and married the daughter of one of their leaders, named Bryan, who had been responsible for the mercy shown him. Cristall was released by the Earl of Desmond and returned to Bristol with his wife and one child, a daughter. There had been two daughters, but one was left with Bryan to comfort him in his loneliness.

Cristall was undoubtedly the best of interpreters. Perhaps, however, the king listened to him on military considerations and was persuaded to a prudent rather than a bold course. The French historian Froissart saw Cristall later and received from him a detailed description of the difficulties of campaigning in the green isle. "Ireland," declared Cristall, "is one of the worst countries to make war in or to conquer, for there are such impenetrable and extensive forest, lakes and bogs, there is no knowing how to pass them and carry on war to advantage—— Whenever they perceive any parties advancing in hostile array, they fly to such narrow passes, it is impossible to follow them. No men-at-arms, however well mounted, can overtake them, so light are they of foot. They have pointed knives, with broad blades, sharp on both sides like a dart-head, with which they kill their enemies; but they never consider them as dead until they have cut their throats like sheep and taken out their hearts which they carry with them; and some say that they devour them as delicious morsels."

The kind of information Richard would receive from others of Cristall's stamp may have coincided with his own ideas. The English king, as his record has demonstrated, was not of warlike spirit. In going to Ireland with such an imposing army, he had expected to frighten the natives into submission. Certainly he had no intention of leading his knights into the impenetrable forests and the impassable bogs which Cristall described.

It was clear that Richard had reservations about the outcome of his Irish campaign. In his will, made before setting out, he left a large sum to his successor, on one condition: that he preserve the conditions established by the last Parliament and if necessary fight to the death for them. In this the son of the Black Prince can be heard, for that great fighting man had placed dynastic considerations and royal prerogatives above everything.

Richard had taken the precaution to have with him young Harry of Monmouth, the eldest son of Bolingbroke, as well as Humphrey of Gloucester, the only son of the deceased Thomas of Woodstock. They were to serve as hostages for the obedience of the father, in the case of young Harry, and for the continued acquiescence of the group that Thomas had led. He sent these two youths straight to Dublin where they were comfortably lodged in the royal palace, and he seems to have been kind and considerate to them. They thus missed the one heavy brush with the Irish when the royal army became hopelessly disorganized in the thickly forested country while on the trail of that inevitable thorn in the side, Art MacMurrough. A French observer has written that "even the knights" had no food of any kind for five days.

As a result of the unsatisfactory outcome of these efforts to bring the elusive Irish to an open test, an envoy was sent to speak with the artful MacMurrough. The Irish leader was very confident and quite adamant on the terms he proposed. Richard became pale with anger when the result of these talks was conveyed to him. "By St. John the Baptist!" he cried. "I shall not leave Ireland until I have him in my power!"

But to accomplish any such result was impossible in a country which bore out in all details the description given by the prudent Henry Cristall—impossible for one as lacking in military skill as the English king. The royal army was finally extricated from the forest and bogs and marched through the relatively safe passage of the Pale to Dublin. The fighting, declared Richard, would not be resumed until the autumn. A French observer puts in his mouth the words, "When the trees shall be leafless."

The king was in Dublin, therefore, and living in comfort and luxury, when the news came of Henry of Bolingbroke's landing at Ravenspur.

### 4

The king had become fond of Harry of Monmouth in the meantime and had even knighted him, a sure evidence of preference. The latter received his first intimation of anything amiss when he observed that the king did not look at him and that a total silence fell wherever he moved. His friends in the king's train held aloof or stood in whispering groups, watching him with anxious eyes. What were they holding back, he wondered, that they had begun suddenly to treat him in this manner? The answer given him was the first intimation he had heard of his father's disobedience to Richard by returning to England. Young Harry responded with exclamations of joy. His prayers had been answered. His father had returned from exile and he would see him again soon.

But no one in the king's train was sure he would ever see his father again. Humphrey of Gloucester, who held a deep, smoldering hatred for the king, explained the situation. If the returned exile failed to establish himself firmly, he could expect nothing better than a quick death. If, on the other hand, he succeeded in setting up opposition to Richard, then he, Harry of Monmouth, might be made to pay for his father's success, such being the role of hostages.

The young son of Bolingbroke soon had good reasons to fear the worst. He heard that Richard, white-faced with rage, was declaring that his rebellious cousin would be sent to the gallows to be hanged, drawn, and quartered. His death was to be made the most cruel that could be conceived, that it would "make a noise as far as Turkey." It also came to the ears of the young hostage that the king had said "he felt sorry for Harry," an expression of sympathy that held an ominous ring.

Before Richard returned to England, he had still more reason for venting his spleen on the youth, if such had been his intention. But he refrained from the momentary satisfaction of paying off a small part of his score against Bolingbroke on the body of the latter's innocent son.

Richard's sudden furies were reserved, as any review of his conduct as king will substantiate, for those who, in his belief, had injured him. No wanton acts of cruelty can be charged against him.

The news from England became quickly more alarming. The futile king found that Bolingbroke, who had landed with a mere handful of men, had been joined by the northern barons, the Percys of Northumberland and the Nevilles of Westmorland. The returned exile had publicly declared that he had one purpose only: to regain the lands and honors which had been taken from him. Richard's brow became black and his eyes feverish with suspense when the word reached him that 20,000 men had already flocked to the Lancastrian banner. Such a demonstration meant that Bolingbroke's real purpose went much deeper than the reclaiming of mere lands.

At this point the king decided to send away his two hostages. Perhaps he did not trust his temper and wanted them out of sight and hand. At any rate he selected the great castle standing at Ath Trium, now known as Trim Castle, as the best place for them. The powerful Burghs of Ulster owned this great stronghold, as would have been apparent at moments of strain when the walls would resound with cries of *"Gall riag aboo!"* (the Cause of the Red Englishman!). The earl himself was away, but his lady received the two youths kindly and made them feel safe and welcome there. Humphrey of Gloucester was stricken by the plague and died there, although some reports have it that this happened in the course of the return voyage to England, and that the boy died on the island of Anglesey.

Harry of Monmouth remained at Trim, in the gentle care of the Countess of Ulster until the arrival of a party of armed men who had ridden fast from Tara with vital information. To the youth's infinite relief, he saw that the leader of the party was Thomas of Dorset, his uncle.

"My father?" cried the hostage, fighting his way to Dorset's side. "What of him?"

Dorset answered with smiling assurance. Harry's father was safe at Chester and he was, moreover, in the best of health. He, Dorset, had come to take the boy back to England to join his father there.

## CHAPTER XXIX

## The King Had No Horses and No Men

*1*

I T IS generally supposed that Richard delayed in Ireland and that he lost his throne as a result of his tardiness, but this is not true. Because of storms over the Irish Sea, the word of Henry's landing was late in reaching him and the same conditions continued to prevail when Richard was ready to return with his army. Although the precious days thus lost could not be charged to his account, his faulty planning played a decisive part in the victory of Bolingbroke. It was clear to some of the king's advisers that he should strike across to North Wales and land his troops at Conway. This would put him in immediate contact with the loyal Welshmen and the royal stronghold of Chester. Instead he sent the Earl of Salisbury to Conway and issued orders for his army and fleet to be assembled in order to cross with him to Milford Haven. It was believed that this could be done in six days. Sixteen days had passed before they were ready to put to sea. It was early in August when the king finally came ashore at Milford Haven and by that time two disasters had occurred. The troops that Salisbury had been able to gather had dispersed and the army of Bolingbroke had swooped down on the strategic city of Bristol.

There was a lack of enthusiasm in Richard's army which caused all but 6000 to desert the first day after they found themselves facing the Lancastrian strength around Bristol. Even Edmund of York had gone over to Henry. As would happen once again in English history, when William of Orange landed and the troops of James II melted away like April snows, a success was scored with hardly a blow struck. A rumor spread through the king's camp that Bolingbroke had laid hands on the royal treasure, a handsome sum of £700,000, and this completed the rout; for wars cannot be fought without money and soldiers like to be sure of their pay.

Richard made one mistake after another. Instead of remaining with what was left of his army and striving to instill a sense of confidence and order into his men, he left at night disguised as a friar, his purpose being to find sanctuary in the strong mountains of the north. It may have been bad judgment which prompted this move or it may have been fear for his own safety. Probably it was the latter, for Richard lacked one of the greatest Plantagenet traits, a fighting heart. He realized the full extent of his error when he reached Conway and found that all of the men who had been recruited there had scattered and returned to their homes.

It was not surprising that Richard had placed so much reliance on the people of Wales. They had always been loyal to him. They would continue active in his cause through the sporadic efforts made later to place him back on the throne. The sincerity of their devotion was reflected in one of their folk songs, "Sweet Richard," which Owen Glendower is supposed to have written. This haunting melody remained on Welsh tongues for many centuries.

But what Richard needed at this moment was more than loyalty of the spirit. He needed men of stout heart and supple arm to draw bows in his defense. Because he was sure they could be rallied again, he did not immediately lose heart. He stationed himself in Conway Castle and, in an effort to play for time, sent his half brother and nephew, those black-plumed birds of perpetual ill omen, the Hollands, to negotiate terms with Bolingbroke, believing the latter to be at Chester.

It was characteristic of Richard that, while he waited the outcome of this peace move, he composed a letter in the form of a poem to his young wife. "My mistress and my consort," he wrote, "accursed be the man who thus separates us! I am dying of grief because of it! Since I am robbed of the pleasure of beholding thee, such pain and affliction oppresseth my heart that I am near despair." Needless to state, the little Isabella never received this final husbandly epistle.

Bolingbroke had left Chester long before the Hollands arrived and was consolidating his armies in London and the western shires. The Lancastrian forces there were under the command of Earl Percy of Northumberland, who was convinced that the time for negotiation had long since passed. He put the Hollands under close confinement and proceeded to occupy the country about Conway. When he had the unfortunate king securely hemmed in, he came to the castle and demanded an audience.

Richard's moods were in a constant state of flux and it happened that he had regained his confidence when he received Earl Percy. He stormed at the latter and said that he was still king and that his people would rally around him. His faithful Welsh, he declared, would return to his standard now that he himself had returned. Pacing about in an excess of martial spirit, he predicted that he would scatter the army of Bolingbroke and put that rebellious peer to death. Parliament would be the final judge of this difference with his cousin.

Percy decided to temporize. Bolingbroke was on his way north again, being a man who moved fast, in contrast to Richard who barely moved at all. He suggested that they meet at Flint Castle and discuss terms there.

There was something about the mere mention of Flint to arouse confidence. This tall castle, overlooking the sands of Dee, had been built by Edward I and it had always been considered one of the strongest of the ring of forts raised to close in the rebellious Welshmen. Richard felt that here he could face his cousin, secure behind his own thick walls. Accordingly he made his final and most tragic mistake: he allowed himself to believe Percy's honesty of purpose—Percy, that sly and almost toothless old satyr of the north, who had turned his coat often and would continue to do so in the future. He agreed to accompany him to Flint and to grant Bolingbroke an audience there.

This rash reliance on the good faith of Percy led him into a trap. Before the turrets of Flint could be seen on the horizon, the unfortunate king became aware that the mountainous country surrounding it was filled with troops wearing the blue and silver badge.

"I am betrayed!" he cried. "There are pennons and banners in the valley!"

Percy smiled his slyest and called orders to his horsemen to draw in close about the king and the few barons who had accompanied him.

Bolingbroke, who indeed moved fast, had arrived at Flint next morning when Richard roused himself from his heavy and fitful sleep. The king saw from the top of the walls the huge army below which seemed to fill the valley with the reflections of armor and the sound of trumpets. He recognized Harry Hotspur, the impetuous and valiant son of old Earl Percy, as commander of the vanguard. Had everyone, then, turned against him?

Word was brought in from Bolingbroke that he would not enter the castle until after dinner. This meal was served before noon and a dismal group followed Richard to the donjon where a table was spread. The king looked at them with the most sorrowful expression they had ever seen on human face.

"Kind and loyal friends," he said, "since you are in like peril of death for your fidelity, sit down with me."

Accordingly they seated themselves at the table with him, all of them wearing with pride his badge of the White Hart. Few words were spoken and what little desire they might have had for food was lost by the presence in the room of Lancastrian officials who stood about and scoffed at them. "Eat well," these unfriendly witnesses said over and over again, leering and smirking at the unhappy group. "For soon your heads will be off."

When the meal was over, the king rose and made his way to the court below. There he was confronted by Bolingbroke in full armor, although his helmet had been removed. It seemed that Richard was fated to read his misfortunes in the smiles of those about him. That of his cousin was steady and triumphant, the smile of a victor who faces a vanquished foe.

"I am come before my time," said Bolingbroke.

Richard made no response. He could not fail to see now that his cause was a lost one. His armies had dissolved, the people he had ruled for over twenty years were against him. London (this he would learn later) was seething with rebellion.

"I will show you the reason," continued Henry of Bolingbroke. "Your people, my lord, complain that you have ruled them harshly. However, if it please God, I will help you to rule them better."

Richard was certain now that he should have acted on a much earlier impulse. All of the five who had forced themselves into his presence should have been put away. He had spared this one of the group of linked arms, this fair-speaking cousin, and now he was facing the consequences.

But all fight had left him. He did not look directly at his cousin. Had he done so, he would have seen that the smile had faded from the latter's face, to be replaced by an expression of iron purpose.

"Fair cousin," said Richard, finally, "since it pleases you, it pleases me well."

**2**

Henry of Bolingbroke, Duke of Hereford and now Duke of Lancaster, Earl of Derby, and the holder of many other titles, was as desirous as his father had been to wear the crown, and he had the ruthlessness of purpose which John of Gaunt had lacked. There was never a doubt in his mind as to his reason for returning to England. He had come back to oust Richard and seat himself on the throne.

But he had made no such claim openly, and he did not now when the beaten and impotent king was in his power. Instead, with a dourness of temper which had been missing in him up to this point but would come out unmistakably after he became king, he told Richard that the people of England no longer considered him their rightful king because they were convinced he was no son of Edward the Black Prince. How could he be when he lacked so completely the fine spirit of that prince and of the great King Edward before him? It was well known that his mother had seen the need to present the prince with an heir. It was also known that there had been handsome young churchmen in the vice-regal household at Bordeaux.

Richard could do nothing but listen in a suppressed fury while his cousin thus strove to weaken his spirit and to strengthen his own case for the issue which must be settled between them. This story of his illegitimacy had come to his ears before and he knew it had been in circulation throughout the country.

In Froissart's story of this meeting between them he introduces at this point a note of deep poignancy. Richard's favorite hound, Math, had been released from the stables and came bounding out into the court. Instead of rushing to greet his master, he turned instead to Henry of Bolingbroke, jumping about him with every sign of pleasure and excitement.

"What is the meaning of this?" demanded Henry.

"Cousin," responded Richard, sadly, "it means that even my dog sees which side he should be on."

There is no explanation given of how the fickle hound happened to be there. Had he followed his master when Richard donned the robe of a Franciscan and started north through Wales? Had he been allowed to come with the small group riding from Conway to Flint? It all seems most unlikely, but the anecdote is part of the saga of the unfortunate king and so is offered for what it is worth.

Horses were ordered immediately. Richard and his fellow prisoners rode in the Lancastrian train to Chester. The cavalry of Bolingbroke was received at the gates of that city with a loud blast of trumpets. Richard's hopes, if he had any left, sank to nothingness. Even Chester, which had always been so staunchly for him, had none of that loyalty left. It had been whispered to him that the great Welshman Owen Glendwyr was hanging on the flanks of the armed horsemen and waiting for a chance to rescue him, but even this failed to arouse his spirits. The Welsh leader was brave and clever beyond all mortal calculation (he was supposed to be a magician), but how could he prevail with his slender strength against the might which Bolingbroke had mustered about him?

They remained two days at Chester and during that time summonses were issued, in Richard's name, for a Parliament to meet at Westminster. The question between them, Bolingbroke informed the king, would be settled by the voice of the House. This aroused no expectations in the king's mind. The new Parliament would be hand-picked to vote as his cousin dictated. He, Richard, knew how easily this could be managed.

During the two days at Chester young Harry of Monmouth arrived from Ireland to join his father. He was amazed to find the king a prisoner and, according to some accounts, he spoke warmly of the kindness he had been shown while he served as a hostage. It is also said that, when he came to understand that his father intended to assume the throne, he was astonished and not too happy over what seemed to him the usurpation of the rights of others. This young Harry of Monmouth, as has already been explained, would one day become king and would rule with such splendor that his name would always be ranked among England's greatest men.

That young Harry came alone was due, of course, to the death of Humphrey of Gloucester from the plague. As the huge armed cavalcade made its way southward from Chester, word reached them that Humphrey's mother, the widow of Thomas of Woodstock, had died of a broken heart within an hour of receiving word of the loss of her son. The feud in the family, which had begun with the ill will between the boy king and his overbearing uncle, was still taking its toll.

### 3

The story of Richard in eclipse is so muddied by the sentimentality of the French reports that it is hard to get matters clear. The story of Math, for instance, is hard to believe, certainly, and yet has the endorsement of Froissart, who declares that all of Bolingbroke's army, which he estimated at 30,000, heard the tale. There is also the statement that Richard was compelled to ride all the way to London on a small and "wretched" steed, "a sorry hack not worth two pounds," in order to emphasize his defeat and to make him ludicrous in the eyes of the people. This cannot be true. Although his mind was firmly made up to take the throne, Bolingbroke was quite as determined to acquire it with a semblance of legality. He still addressed Richard as king and had made it clear that the latter would remain head of the realm until such time as Parliament decreed his deposition. To treat the captive monarch in the meantime like a clown in a parade of mummers was far from the victor's intent.

When they arrived in London, to be met by the lord mayor and a procession of the guilds, Bolingbroke said: "Fair sirs, here is your king. Think what you will do with him." He wanted the offer of the crown to be made him as the result of an overwhelming wave of popular acclaim. Richard was taken to the Tower and lodged in the royal apartments— but under heavy guard.

The next day he was informed that his cousin was below and desired him to go down. The king indulged in a flash of his old high temper.

"Tell Henry of Lancaster, then," he exclaimed, "if he desires speech with me, let him come to me."

There was a delay during which, no doubt, Bolingbroke was considering what course to take. Finally he came to Richard's chambers and greeted him on bended knee. The king demanded to know why he was kept thus under lock and key. Was he not King of England?

"You are my king, sir," answered Henry. "But the council of your realm thinks fit to set a guard on you until Parliament has reached a decision."

Richard was a creature of passionate moods and even in the face of complete defeat he could not keep his temper under control. He cried out that he would meet in combat any of his foes or detractors. He demanded that the queen be sent to him, to which Bolingbroke's reply was, "It is forbidden by the council." He stormed up and down the apartment, railing at his ill fortune and cursing all who had taken a hand in bringing him to this pass. Bolingbroke listened in silence and, finally, withdrew.

There was one contrast in this scene between the two chief characters in the drama. Richard had dressed himself well, although with none of the extravagances which had always been held against him. He wore no jewels of any kind (perhaps because the regal valuables had been carefully laid away by the officers of the Tower), but Bolingbroke was still in full armor. There is no way of telling if he had continued to wear his fighting gear ever since his landing on the Yorkshire coast, but on many of the occasions when he appears in the chronicles it is put on record that he was, actually, armed to the teeth. Perhaps there was a purpose in this, a desire to point up the difference between a warrior and an aimless man of peace such as Richard.

The following day the king was in a more compliant mood. Perhaps a night's reflection had convinced him that he had nothing to hope for and should accept his fate with good grace. The recollection of what had befallen Edward II was never out of his mind. Bolingbroke came to see him again, accompanied by Arundel, the deposed archbishop, and a deputation of bishops and peers. The discussion was brief and free of the passion of the previous day. In a quiet voice Richard read a statement in which he agreed to abdicate the throne, if this proved to be the wish of Parliament. He placed his signet ring on Bolingbroke's finger and expressed his preference for Henry as his successor.

On September 30, 1399, he was taken to Westminster Hall, which had been for several years in process of repair and redecoration, on his own orders, and was now thrown open for the first time. Richard entered the hall in his royal robes, with his crown on his head and the scepter in his hand. He did not, however, seat himself on the throne, but stood beside it with composed mien. He read for the second time the paper in which he agreed to abdicate.

The members of the House were not content with this. A paper of accusation, made up of thirty-three counts, had been prepared and it was demanded that this should be read. Richard was compelled to remain standing while the voice of the Speaker progressed through the long and declamatory statement. He made no attempt to answer or deny the accusations. When bidden to withdraw, he handed his crown and scepter to Bolingbroke and bowed to the members before leaving the chamber. He had conducted himself through this humiliating scene with a fine dignity.

The time had come for Bolingbroke to assert his claim. He rose from his chair and said: "In the name of Fadir, Son and Holy Ghost, I, Henry of Lancaster, challenge the realm of England, and the crown, with all the members and appurtenances; as that I am descended by the right line of blood, coming from the good lord Henry III, and through that right that God of His grace, hath sent me with the help of my kin and of my friends to recover it; the which realm was in point to be undone for default of governance and undoing of good laws."

The lords and commons were challenged for their opinions and responded with what seemed an acclamation of assent. The ex-archbishop then took Henry by the hand and conducted him to the throne.

### 4

Richard waited impatiently all through the day for word of what had happened, but no report reached him. The next morning it was raining, none of the quick passing showers of summer but a steady and monotonous downpour, the kind to further unsettle raveled nerves. The rooms in the Tower, never very bright, were gloomier than ever. The faces of the servants were a reflection of their master's mood and the food they served was plain and unappetizing.

In spite of his certainty earlier that all was lost, he may have gained some small degree of hope from the silence and delay. It had been whispered in his ear that his loyal friend, Bishop Merks of Carlisle, intended to present a defense of him in the House and to demand for him a chance to face his accusers. Had this precipitated a battle on the floor? Perhaps there were enough loyal members after all to prevent the Bolingbroke party from carrying through his dethronement with a high hand. No one told him that the stouthearted bishop had acted on his promise and had spoken strongly in the House. However, a complete silence of disagreement had followed his address and he had even failed to get a seconder. In fact, there had been some intention of bringing charges against Merks for the attitude he had taken. What had happened finally was that the bishop was sent under escort to St. Albans Abbey, there to await the will of the Commons.

Richard walked to the roof and stood somberly at the battlements, disregarding the heavy downpour. It added nothing to his gloomy forebodings that the guards, who had kept close to him all morning, were now so close on his heels that he could feel their breath on his neck. They were, it was clear, fearful of what he might attempt. On the ride to London from Chester he had thrown his guards into an uproar by almost effecting an escape at Litchfield. Knowing that the faithful Welsh were still following on the edges of the Lancastrian army, he had succeeded in letting himself down from his window with a rope but had been trapped because all exits were closed in the high stone walls of the garden in which he found himself.

The prospect from the top of the White Tower walls was disheartening for the prisoner. The townspeople, who had packed the streets below at all hours of the day and night, had finally dispersed. Had the rain driven them indoors or had they learned of a decision in Parliament and had no further need to wait for an announcement? He was certain that, if a fight still continued at Westminster, the rain would have had no effect on the curious Londoners.

Finally the word was brought to him. None of the main actors in the cast came to deliver it, and only a deputation of members from the House waited on him. They performed their task without any hint of compassion. The Speaker read the decision of deposition and then shook an admonitory forefinger at the unhappy man who had been king but was no longer.

"None of all these states or people," declared the Speaker, "from this time forward either bear you faith or do you obeisances as to their king."

The scene was closely reminiscent of the cold winter day at Kenilworth Castle nearly a century before when the word was carried to Edward II that he was no longer king. On that occasion the strong young Edward had fallen to the floor in a faint. Richard carried himself with more courage. He heard them through, realizing that this was indeed the end and that all he could hope for was to be allowed to live at peace in some obscure part of the realm. It was too much to hope that he would be allowed to leave the country, not even to find sanctuary in his first home at Bordeaux.

"I look not hereafter," he said, finally. "But I hope my cousin will be good lord to me."

## CHAPTER XXX

## The Little Queen Fights for the Throne

### 1

WHEN the news of Richard's downfall reached France, the Duke of Burgundy, one of the royal uncles, commented: "Since the English have imprisoned King Richard, they will assuredly put him to death. They always hated him because he preferred peace to war."

The duke was right for once. He had put his finger on the real reason for Richard's unpopularity. Coming after a line of warrior kings and winners of great victories, he seemed weak, effeminate, and indolent to the people. The barons, the merchants of the towns who thrived on war, and the stout yeomen who had played such a great part in the victories were ashamed to have a king who loved music, books, and paintings. This feeling had been aggravated by Richard's determination to establish an absolutism by parliamentary sanction. What did this sapling mean by declaring publicly, "I am the law?"

No, the main reason for his deposition was not to be found in the murder of Thomas of Woodstock and the execution of Arundel. In this violent age a thirst for revenge was deemed more nearly a virtue than a vice. King John killed his nephew Arthur and starved to death Maude de Braose and her son in a cell at Corfe Castle because she had alluded publicly to the deed. Edward I, a great king in most respects, was so angry over the stout opposition of William Wallace that he had that brave Scot hanged, drawn, and quartered. Edward II sent his cousin of Lancaster to the block because he had been an instrument in the death of the king's favorite, Piers Gaveston. An injury, even a mild affront, rankled in the minds of these Plantagenet kings and led to furious reprisals. Richard did no more than his forefathers would have done when he removed from his path the two chief instigators of his humiliation and the slayers of his friend, Simon Burley.

The English people hated John because he lost Normandy and dubbed him John Softsword. They despised Edward II because the decisive victories he could have won were turned into defeats. They sang parodies of "Sweet Richard." They did not want a sweet king.

**2**

The French waited impatiently for news of what was happening in England, but it was not until the Countess of St. Pol arrived home (Henry packed her off promptly with all her French ladies and servants and her lordly string of horses) that they heard the full story. There was so much concern felt then for the fate of Queen Isabella that the king suffered a particularly violent return of his mental malady.

One of the first steps taken after the crown had been placed on the head of the winner and he had assumed the title of Henry IV was to remove the little queen from Windsor and place her in the charge of the Bishop of Salisbury at his manor house on the Thames, known as Sunning-Hill. The ex-king was sent first to Leeds Castle in Kent but was then secretly conveyed to Yorkshire where he was kept successively in three of Henry's castles: Pickering, Knaresborough, and, finally, Pontefract, the scene of so many tragedies. This was done because the demand had been made in the House that he be confined in some "sure and secret place."

The next step was to punish those who had remained loyal to Richard through the brief and inglorious struggle. All who could be accused of a part in the deaths of Thomas of Woodstock and Arundel were called to account and the House was filled with one of the most violent scenes in its history. From both sides came threats and counterthreats, with bitter charges and cries of "Liar!" "Assassin!" and "Traitor!" It was said that as many as twenty gages of battle were on the floor, hurled there by angry hands, and none of them taken up. With a degree of moderation which did him credit, the new king contented himself with demoting those who had received titles from Richard in his last orgy of promotion. The two Hollands ceased to be dukes and became earls again. Edward Plantagenet, who had been made Duke of Aumale, found his honors snipped back to the mere earldom of Rutland. Dorset, the new king's brother, was deprived of his title of marquis and became again the Earl of Dorset. Scrope, who had been made Earl of Wiltshire, could not be demoted because he had no head left on which to wear laurels.

Arundel, the deposed Archbishop of Canterbury, had landed with Henry at Ravenspur and had ridden with him on his speedy campaign to raise the country against Richard. He preached from pulpits wherever they went, arrayed in the gorgeous robes of office and wearing his miter, extending in his hands so all could see what he claimed was a bull granted by the Pope offering indulgences to all who joined in the rebellion.

Arundel had announced his resumption of the office of Archbishop of Canterbury as soon as he reached England. However, it was not until Pope Boniface IX, explaining that he had been in ignorance of the full facts when he elevated Walden to the see, issued letters-patent to that effect that Arundel was free to resume his post as primate. Walden had to make a hurried exit from Canterbury, taking all his jewels with him. Arundel took no overt steps until word reached him that Walden had stripped the archiepiscopal palace of furnishings, tapestries, books, carpets, and pictures and had filled six carts with the loot. He then moved rapidly and seized all six of the carts when they reached Saltwood Castle near Hythe and had the contents taken back to Canterbury, where, moreover, the late incumbent's arms were ripped from the walls and burned. He took immediate steps to see that everything was removed from the episcopal palace at Lambeth which hinted at the existence of an intruder. Walden hurried to the new king to make his peace but he was committed for a time to the Tower of London.

There was a forgiving streak in Arundel which his brother had so sadly lacked. Five years later he used his influence to have Walden appointed Bishop of London, an honor which the latter enjoyed for no more than a year.

Almost immediately after the deposition, rumors spread through the country that Richard had escaped to Scotland where he was raising an army to invade England in the hope of regaining his throne. Another version of the story was that Maudelyn, who was now believed to be a blood connection of Richard's by the left hand, was impersonating him in the northern kingdom. There was no truth in either story. Richard was being securely guarded in his captivity and Maudelyn was engaged in a conspiracy which would cost him his life.

3

The importance of retaining good relations with France was realized by the new king and he made up his mind at once that the little queen would make the best wife for his son, Harry of Monmouth. As her marriage with Richard had never been consummated, it would not be difficult to get an annulment from the Pope, provided the French royal family were in agreement. Young Harry saw Isabella at Windsor before she was removed to Sunning-Hill and he was instantly attracted by the beauty of the twelve-year-old girl. Many years later, when he was ruling England as Henry V, he would marry her youngest sister, Katherine, a match which has been considered one of the greatest of royal romances. But the boy's infatuation for the wife of the deposed Richard was greater than the love he later displayed for the less beautiful younger sister. He was much distressed when he learned that the slender Isabella regarded him with hostility. The little queen remained strongly loyal to Richard and after his death she refused to consider the match proposed with the son of the new king.

The word was conveyed to her secretly at Sunning-Hill that a conspiracy was afoot to bring Richard back. The noblemen who had been demoted in rank were all involved in it. Their plan was to join forces and seize Windsor, where Henry (who had been weakened by an illness attributed to poison) planned to spend Christmas. Later she was told that Richard had escaped from his prison at Pontefract and would lead the army for his restoration. They talked to her in full round terms and convinced her that 100,000 men would be found under Richard's standard. Overjoyed and excited at this prospect, the girl was only too happy to promise them her support. She displayed, in fact, the firmness of character of a mature woman and even tore the Lancastrian emblems from the walls where she was confined, replacing them with the White Hart.

But Richard had not escaped and it is doubtful if any whisper of the conspiracy had reached his ears. The leaders of the plot hoped to win public support by a deception. The priest Maudelyn was to play the part of the king. He was to be dressed in royal robes in which his resemblance to the captive at Pontefract would serve to deceive the people. In all respects the plot had been as hastily conceived as might be expected of the men who were to serve as leaders.

The older of the Holland brothers, Thomas, had died two years before from natural causes, an extraordinary thing to happen to any member of this family. His son had been created Duke of Surrey by Richard, but he had been demoted to the earldom of Kent by Henry's first Parliament. This hotheaded young man seems to have been more active in the conspiracy than his uncle, John Holland, who had been Duke of Exeter before being reduced to the earldom of Huntingdon. The latter's wife was a daughter of John of Gaunt, which made him Henry's brother-in-law. John was one of the proudest of men in this arrogant age and, no doubt, he bitterly resented the loss of his higher rank. At any rate, he disregarded his family tie with Henry and threw in his lot with the conspiratorial ring. Others in the circle were the Earl of Salisbury, who had stood by Richard through thick and thin, and the Earl of Rutland. The latter was a son of Edmund of York and he was so weak and fickle that he betrayed the secret to his father. The latter went to the king and told him what was being planned. Although Henry was still in a weakened condition, he took to horse at once and rode to London to gather his forces.

The plan was doomed to failure, because of the instability of the leadership, before they approached the queen with their glittering promises. All they could count on at the time were a few hundred men of their own, instead of the 100,000 that Richard was supposed to be leading south from Yorkshire. She had no way of judging the truth of their statements and, of course, she was prepared to grasp at any means for Richard's restoration. She even permitted a proclamation to be used in her name, declaring that she did not recognize Henry of Lancaster as king.

Failing to secure the person of King Henry at Windsor, the band marched to Colnbrook where they encountered a royal force of some strength. Kent was in command and he is said to have fought for three days with courage and skill in holding the bridge at Maidenhead. When finally put to rout, the leaders realized that there was nothing more to be done. They rode off in mad haste and reached Cirencester. Here they left their men-at-arms behind and entered the town, hoping to pass unrecognized. This was a vain hope. They were seized by the towns-people. Kent, Salisbury, Despenser, and the priest Maudelyn were beheaded during the night.

Richard's half brother, John Holland, had remained near London to keep an eye on developments there. When he learned of the collapse of the plot, he tried to cross the Channel, but the ship was driven back by heavy winds and he was captured at Pleshy. Here he fell into the hands of the Countess of Hereford, the mother of the Bohun sisters and, therefore, mother-in-law of the king. This was unfortunate for John Holland because she was a woman of sternest character. Calling in the two sons of the Earl of Arundel, who had been executed on Tower Hill, to witness the deed, she had Holland beheaded without waiting to try him. His head was raised on the end of a pike over Pleshy Castle and there it remained until the king, in deference to the feelings of his sister, had it sent to her for burial with the body.

This hastily conceived and badly bungled plot cost Richard his life. There had been a strong feeling among Henry's advisers that there would never be peace in the land as long as the deposed king remained alive, one of the most vehement being the Earl of Warwick, who had been released from imprisonment and was eager to settle his personal score. Henry had resisted all such pressure. On one occasion, soon after the failure of the restoration plot, a conversation was carried on in his hearing in which the danger of letting the ex-king live was strongly stressed. Henry left in the midst of the talk, saying not a word, and went out to feed his falcons. But he had not missed a word. It is also related that once, after the manner of Henry II in crying out to be relieved of the activities of Thomas à Becket, the new king said at the dinner table to those who sat below him, "Have I no faithful friend who will deliver me of one whose life will be my death, and whose death my life?" This outburst, according to the story, led one Sir Piers Exton to recruit a party of eight who rode at once to Pontefract where Richard was being held.

Whether there is any truth in these anecdotes or not, it is on the official records that among the recommendations laid before the king's committee on February 9 was one which read: "If Richard, late king, be still living *as it is supposed he is,* order be taken that he be securely guarded." The result was the publication of an order by the council that "*if he were dead,* he should be shown openly to the people that they might know of it."

This significant statement was issued on the same day, February 9, 1400.

## CHAPTER XXXI

## The King Who Lost His Life

### 1

THE first weeks in the month of February were cold and blustery, and snow fell in all parts of Yorkshire. This was in itself a good excuse for people to remain at home of nights, but in the town of Pontefract there was another reason for keeping curfew. The eight towers of the castle looked down on the town and in one of them the king (for Richard was still spoken of as a king) was being held. Because of this, armed men kept watch about the castle when darkness fell—heavy, grumbling guards, plodding through the drifts, muffled to the ears in cloaks of wool and holding their torches low for the sake of the warmth. Any citizen who had not gone decently home to bed would be roughly treated if he fell in the way of these surly fellows.

There was enough contact in secret ways between the garrison and the town to keep the people advised of what went on above them. They knew there was no truth in the rumor that Richard had escaped to Scotland and the equally wild surmise that the prisoner in Pontefract was in reality Richard's mysterious double, the fair-faced priest, Maudelyn. No, the deposed king was somewhere in the castle, but so securely and secretly held (as the council at Westminster had ordered) that only his immediate gaolers had ever set eyes on him.

But the people of Pontefract thought they knew more about this than the guards. Peering out from behind their shutters at night, they could see a light in one of the eight towers. "That's it!" they would say. "That's where they have him, the poor, foolish king! May God and all the saints preserve him from worse."

They not only spied at night but they listened, in an almost hypnotic fear of something they might hear. All their lives there had been talk of what had happened one night nearly a century before when all about

Berkeley Castle on the Severn the air had filled suddenly with a bedlam of wild and almost inhuman sound, the cries of a strong man who was dying in torment. The villagers thereabouts had known then that Edward II, who had been held in humiliating captivity at Berkeley, was being done to death in some obscenely barbarous manner.

Everyone knew that Richard, for the sake of peace in the realm, would have to be put out of the way. Such at least was the word brought by travelers from down London way. Such also was the opinion held by the castle guards, speaking in whispers and out of the corner of the mouth. All of them, citizens as well as guards, had given their heads a shake of conviction when word came of the bungled attempt of the Hollands to pave the way to restoration. Now something would have to be done. There must be no more attempts at rebellion, no more uneasiness in low as well as high places. Would Richard's killers be as brutal as the assassins of the second Edward? This conjecture turned the nights at Pontefract into a time of dread suspense.

It is doubtful if Richard himself could have heard of the ill-timed uprising of his followers. This information would be kept from him on the strictest of orders. If so, he was saved additional fears on that account. But there are always indications of the approach of a tragic finish which a political prisoner can detect, particularly one of high degree who has known only the best of everything. The gaolers become careless and offhanded, even gruffly discourteous. The food is badly cooked and carelessly served. Complaints are brushed aside as though to say, "What boots it if your meat *is* tainted and the bread moldy when you will soon have no need for food of any kind?"

To one as sensitive and imaginative as Richard, the waiting must have been hard to endure. The hours of daylight were spent at the barred windows, if indeed the cell had anything better than an archery slit, wondering if a miracle of second thought on the part of the English people would bring an army to set him free. At night he could not fail to think of the shrieks which had escaped from the walls of Berkeley. He would have, perhaps, some brief intervals of optimistic thought when the hope of French intervention or of a Scottish attack would fill his mind; for was it not the bounden duty of kings to come to the rescue of one of their number? Certainly his father, the brave Black Prince, had believed so.

Even a former king is prevented from indulging in the niceties of toilet when political disaster has robbed him of his freedom. Richard's thick yellow hair lost its lustrous curl, his double-pointed beard became shaggy and unkempt, his cheeks showed some of the lankness of care.

He was like one of the captive lions that the kings of England had always kept in cages in the Tower of London. He had no way of filling in the dismal hours save to pace about his cell and bewail the mistakes which had brought him to this pass. Why had he been so demanding of his full prerogatives? Why had he given his thrice-damned cousin an excuse to break his exile by seizing all the Lancastrian estates? Why had he been so foolhardy as to take his army to Ireland at such a juncture?

The reason for all these errors lay in his pride. He had been determined to prove that he was not the brainless boy his heavy-fisted uncles had tried to make out. He had desired so deeply to show he had inherited the greatness of his father and grandfather, if not as a warrior, then as a man of intelligence, of superior culture, of the will power to reign strongly and well.

But all things had gone awry. He had not known how to use and display the gifts with which he had been born. It must have been that such qualities as he possessed were not suited to kingship.

On the night of February 14 the wind increased in volume and howled about the eaves of the houses and whistled through bell towers and about the stone buttresses below. If any of the townspeople, after damping out the fires, had gone to stare out through the ill-fitting shutters, they would have caught their breaths in dread. The solitary light no longer shone from that window high up in its tower.

2

The next morning the whispered word was carried down to the town that Richard Plantagenet had died the day before.

For some time thereafter there was a continual stir about the castle. Messengers arrived on smoking steeds, clearly after riding great distances. Mounted men pounded out over the drawbridge, to set off for the south with equal dispatch. Then came men whose apparel and appearance fitted such a crisis—priests, lawyers belike, surgeons, also the most dreaded of men with faces the color of the cerements they made.

On the third day a carriage with creaking wheels emerged from the castle, surrounded by a heavy guard of mounted men. No one could catch a glimpse of the interior of this vehicle as it progressed through the town, but the people knew what it contained. All that was left of a once gaudy king was being taken away for burial, almost certainly to

London where he had been received so enthusiastically as a boy king but had been so violently disliked at the finish.

The news that seeped down to the town was that Richard had died of starvation. The story was repeated many times and had something about it of a lesson carefully rehearsed. When the deposed king had learned of the bungling adventure of his foolish friends, he had declined to partake of food and drink. "He was for-hungered," said the servants from the castle. The townspeople were ready to accept this explanation, as were most of the people of England. But a more careful consideration of the circumstances would have led to doubts. In the first place there was the strong probability that the news of the rebellion had been kept from the prisoner. Still harder to explain was the time element. The Holland fiasco came to an end during the night of January 9. It would have taken some time for word of it to reach Richard, many days certainly, assuming that the story was allowed to reach him at all. Starvation is a slow process. When a victim refuses food and is so confined that his physical strength is not drawn upon, he almost certainly will live for weeks.

Further, there is no mistaking the physical emaciation and the wasted face of the victim of starvation. Was the body which was shown later in London a proof that he had died from such cause?

Another explanation is that the knight Sir Piers Exton, who as already explained had heard Henry's plea in London, came to Pontefract with eight others. A compact had been made between them to remove Richard from the new king's path. They came upon him as he sat at his dinner, all with drawn swords. They stood for a moment in a silent line, staring at him.

It was at once apparent to Richard that his time had come. He rose silently, shoving the table back to allow room to defend himself. Then he sprang at one of the intruders, wrenching his weapon from him, and began to attack them with great courage and energy. The story, as told in some detail in one of the chronicles of the day, was that Exton sprang up on the chair that Richard had vacated and struck him on the head with a poleax. This brought the uneven struggle to a rapid conclusion.

This is the explanation that defenders of Richard prefer to accept because it presents him as dying bravely, a true Plantagenet at the finish of his far from happy life. But it must be said that it seems the kind of story so often concocted when the central figure in a tragedy of history comes to a sudden death. It seems, however, more easy to believe that he died by violence than by starvation.

### 3

When word reached London that Richard was dead, a deep silence seemed to settle over the city. His removal from the high office of king had been almost universally desired and it must have been recognized that his death was an inevitable sequel to deposition. But it was still with a sense of shock that the news of his end was received. Perhaps they gave some thought to the intrepid boy king who had ridden out to face the rioting peasants at Smithfield. Perhaps also they considered the record of those years, after the uncles ceased troubling, when so much constructive legislation was put through Parliament. They might even have been inclined to think him the victim, in some degree at least, of adverse circumstances.

When it became known that the cortege was approaching the city, the apprentices put up the shutters and bolted them, the stocks were covered in the shops, the pens laid down in the countinghouses and the tools in the workrooms, and all of them—men, women, and children—dressed in their best, poured out into the streets.

The body of Richard had been placed on a litter covered with black cloth under a canopy also of black. The four horses were sable and the four knights pacing beside the bier were in black armor. Froissart reports that the cortege could proceed only at a snail's pace, so great were the crowds on the streets. When they reached the Chepe, the litter was set down and the coffin opened so the people could see the body of the deposed king. For two hours the viewers passed in silence before the bier. It was estimated that at last 20,000 people took advantage of this opportunity to look on the face of the dead king.

What they saw must have surprised and mystified them. Richard's head, sunk down on a black cushion, was uncovered. The body had been embalmed but it was soldered down in lead so that the face only was in view!

It had been the will of Parliament that the body be shown to the people, and it seems logical that, if Richard had died of starvation, that fact would have been made manifest, to prevent any belief in the possibility of violence. His wasted body would have been openly on display. It was not, therefore, to hide the ravages of want that the frame had been so completely concealed. Could it have been to hide other evidence from the eyes of the beholders, the wounds inflicted by the weapons of assassins?

The face of Richard was said to have been calm and beautiful in death.

There were rumors later that it was not the corpse of the deposed king which had been brought to London and which was buried first in the church at King's Langley. It was whispered about that Maudelyn, who had been executed at Cirencester, had not been buried with the other conspirators. Had his body been kept for this purpose, to convince the people that Richard was dead? Richard, so the story ran, had escaped to Scotland and was awaiting the opportunity to reclaim his crown.

It was established later that the Scottish rulers gave a small allowance to a man who claimed to be Richard of England and who did not die until 1419. The English government scoffed at the story, claiming the man was an impostor and that he was a certain Thomas Warde of Trumpington. There does not seem to be any good reason not to believe that the "poor, foolish king" came to some violent end at Pontefract and that it was his body which was shown to the people.

The king who had lost a shoe at his coronation seems to have been fated to suffer one deprivation after another. He lost all his friends, some of them unworthy, at the hands of the Merciless Parliament, he lost his wife, he lost the esteem and confidence of the people by his proud ways, he lost his throne, and, then, finally, his life.

PART TWO

# THE RED AND THE WHITE

## CHAPTER I

# A Sick King and a Dull Reign

## 1

HISTORY arbitrarily counts the reign of Richard II as the last in the glittering dynasty of the Plantagenets, or, as it is sometimes called, the Angevins. The reason is sound enough. Edward III left so many children that it was hard to keep the lines of descent clear and, when the two main branches became embroiled in the long continued Wars of the Roses, the need for distinctive labels became imperative. And so we have, following the unfortunate Richard II, the Lancastrian kings and the Yorkists. The blood in the veins of Henry IV, who succeeded Richard II, was pure Plantagenet, and the same can be said of Henry V and Henry VI, who continued the Lancastrian line, and of Edward IV and Richard III, who are listed as Yorkist kings. It is only when Henry VII, that highly intelligent and efficient but sly and shabby king, seized the throne that the Plantagenet line came to a definite end. The seventh Henry was the grandson of Owen Tudor, a Welsh knight with whom the French widow of Henry V fell in love after the death of her royal spouse. There is much doubt as to whether the union of the enamored pair was ever sanctified by marriage. As Henry's mother, moreover, was Margaret Beaufort, a descendant of John of Gaunt and Katharine Swynford (whose children were all born out of wedlock and were made legitimate later), the bend sinister stood out prominently on his genealogical tree and the Plantagenet tincture in his blood was small.

Richard III, who has been indelibly fixed in the memories of men by the genius of Shakespeare as the hunchback who murdered the princes in the Tower (but whose back was straight and who did *not* murder the two princes), was the last king who was completely Plantagenet.

The years from 1400 to 1485, which intervened between the deaths of Richard II and Richard III, were filled with the color and the cruelties of civil war, with stories of deep villainy and vile conspiracy and with some slight imprints of the genius of an emerging civilization. It is a period, however, which is illuminated only in small degree by authentic chronicles and so remains dark with doubts and question marks for historical controversy. There is, in consequence, a fascination about these cloudy years. Certainly no record of the virile dynasty which began with Henry II can be complete without some recounting of the savageries and mysteries of the fifteenth century. In the chapters which follow, an effort will be made to set down the sequence of events in brief form and to place on the canvas in greater length some of the more spectacular episodes and the colorful human figures of the period.

2

Although Henry IV was responsible for making the lovely *Myosotis arvensis* the symbol of loyalty to the absent under its popular name of Forget-me-not (during his years of exile he wore it in his collar with the words *souveigne-vous de moy*), it is true that to many readers of history his short reign is one of the least likely to intrigue the memory. This may be due to the ill health which settled upon him when he assumed the gold circlet and the ermine robe, but perhaps it can be traced more certainly to the fact that in many respects his few years of power seem like a continuation of the days of Richard. There was the same futility of military effort to enforce peace along the Scottish border and in Wales and a continuous planning to restore the once extensive English holdings in France without any real hope of success. Parliament continued to insist on the right to appoint the members of the royal council, and there was much criticism of extravagance in the royal household. Henry strove to repeat Richard's unconstitutional scheme to secure himself a revenue for life, which indicates that he was in desperate need of funds. He had a sharp temper and no doubt he was irked that the restrictions set up to restrict Richard's actions were being applied to him also. But having seen what his predecessor's obstinacy led to, he forced himself to give in with reasonably good grace. Parliament's negation of his gesture in the direction of a lifetime subsidy was so sharp and final that he never renewed the attempt.

In his youth Henry had been courageous and the possessor of qualities which won him popularity with the people. He had taken the risk of allying himself with the dissenters in 1388 when he believed it necessary to set new curbs on his cousin Richard, but in 1397 he stood beside

# The Battle of
# B A R N E T

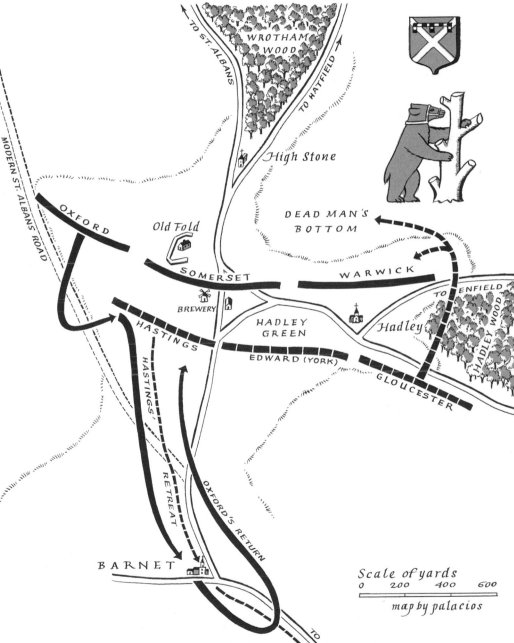

TO ST. ALBANS

WROTHAM WOOD

TO HATFIELD

High Stone

MODERN ST. ALBANS ROAD

OXFORD

Old Fold

DEAD MAN'S BOTTOM

SOMERSET

WARWICK

TO ENFIELD

BREWERY

HADLEY GREEN

Hadley

HADLEY WOOD

HASTINGS

EDWARD (YORK)

GLOUCESTER

HASTINGS

RETREAT

OXFORD'S RETURN

B A R N E T

Scale of yards

0      200      400      600

map by palacios

TO LONDON

the king in dealing with Thomas of Woodstock and the Earl of Arundel in the belief that the harsh opposition of these two malcontents had carried them into treasonable excesses. As a king he was quite a different man, beginning to realize perhaps that it is easier to criticize authority than to exercise it. He became cold-blooded, jealous, suspicious (even of his son and heir), and sometimes lacking in decision. These qualities may be charged to his ill health but they do not serve to win him any lasting degree of praise on the pages of history.

Even the campaigns he fought fail to enchain the interest, with the exception of the Battle of Shrewsbury, where he defeated the revolutionary forces of the Percys of Northumberland. The old earl had once been as regal as a king in the north country, but he is best remembered for the devious part he played in betraying Richard. His son, a hard-riding and tumultuous knight, is called in history Harry Hotspur. They felt, these haughty lords of the north, that the new king had not properly compensated them for their part in winning him the throne nor for the victory they won against the Scots at Homildon Hill. In the course of a bitter dispute with the son, the king drew a dagger and called Hotspur a traitor. The latter withdrew but cried from the threshold, "Not here, but in the field!"

The Percys expected help from Owen Glendower (as the name of their Welsh leader is spelled in modern histories) when they marched south with a hastily assembled army, but Henry expertly caught them at Shrewsbury before the Welsh could arrive. When the rebels were drawn up in battle array, the valiant Harry learned that his favorite sword had been left behind at the village of Berwick, where they had spent the previous night. It is reported that he turned pale, although this seems unlikely in such a well-tanned and vigorous, cut-and-cut-again fighting man.

"Then has my plough reached its last furrow," he said.

Henry had taken the precaution of accoutering as many as thirteen knights of his own size in armor bearing the royal quarterings. Hotspur concentrated his efforts on cutting them down, hoping to reach finally the real king. Nearly all of the royal stalking horses had fallen to his second-best sword when an arrow pierced his brain and his spurs soon cooled among the heaps of the slain. Without his tempestuous leadership the rebel forces fell into disorder and the battle was over.

In one of his abortive campaigns against the Welsh, the king had a narrow escape from death. His own lance became dislodged during the night and fell upon him. This did no harm, for Henry had sought his couch without pausing to remove his armor.

Continual trouble arose out of the rumors that Richard was alive in Scotland. The ceaseless efforts of the king's agents (the use of a secret service was not new, even then) finally resulted in locating the villain of the piece, a man named William Serle who had figured as one of the party responsible for the death of Thomas of Woodstock at Calais. In one of the truces arranged between the English and the Scots a provision was included that Serle was to be handed over to English justice. Henry, or the ministers acting for him, devised a singularly cruel method of punishment. Serle was publicly hanged at many points on the way south but always was cut down before dead. It was not until his stretched and mutilated neck could no longer withstand the further use of the rope that the rest of the sentence was carried out, with white-hot knives carving his midriff and removing his vital organs.

It was during a rebellion in the north that Henry allowed a judicial murder which did most to alienate the affections of the people. Archbishop Scrope of York, one of the leaders, was captured and immured in his own palace at Bishopsgate. The people of York begged for the life of the primate, but the king refused to listen. Archbishop Arundel of Canterbury posted north to ask that Scrope's case be settled in Parliament or by reference to the Pope. While the king and the archbishop were discussing the matter at breakfast, two of the advisers of the king, the young Earl of Arundel and Thomas Beaufort, hauled Scrope out to face an irregular court, declared him guilty, and had him executed without any delay.

The country was horrified at the deed and Henry never recovered his popularity thereafter. It was generally believed, in fact, that he was stricken with leprosy on the day of Scrope's execution.

Henry's second marriage did not please the people. His new wife, Joanna of Navarre, was disliked for many reasons, but for two in particular, both having to do with money. She brought over a large retinue of her own people who had to be fed and clothed and supported generally out of the public funds. She herself displayed a greed for annuities, manor houses, and large estates which Henry, who was soft and yielding with her and as hard as flint with everyone else, did nothing to curb. There are many items in the issue rolls for sums to be paid to her, always in the amount of one hundred pounds (a very considerable figure in those days), "in part payment of a greater sum due to the said queen upon a private agreement made between the said queen and our present lord the king."

After Henry's death, the dowager Queen Joanna continued to live in England for another quarter of a century. She was at one point confined in solitary rigor by Henry V on a trumped-up charge of witchcraft, and of planning Henry IV's death, and was relieved of much of her property before being allowed her liberty.

The story of their marriage is, however, one of the most interesting in the annals of this far from brilliant reign. While Henry was in exile, he was invited to the court of the Duke of Brittany, who is called in history John the Valiant, although at the same time it was conceded that he possessed the most vicious of tempers. In his old age the valiant John had espoused Joanna of Navarre, a daughter of another stormy petrel of history who was called Charles the Bad. Joanna, who was young enough to be his granddaughter, seemed attached to her elderly spouse, who was a handsome old tyrant and could be amusing and courtly when he so desired. They had a family of nine young children.

When Henry accepted the invitation he could not fail to be attracted by the handsome young duchess who had a brightness of good looks and a trimness of figure which verged only slightly on the voluptuous. She in turn was impressed with the manly proportions of the exile, his ruddiness of complexion, and his plume of golden hair. A spark must have passed between them which said all that they dared not put into words.

In November 1399 the violence of the old duke was quenched in death, which, coincided closely with Henry's elevation to the throne of England. The very desirable Joanna proceeded at once with a plan to win for herself the honor of being the widower king's second wife. She proceeded in the matter with the greatest circumspection. Without taking anyone into her confidence, she wrote to the Pope at Avignon, asking for a dispensation to marry again, provided the husband of her choice was not closer to her in blood than the fourth degree of consanguinity. No name was mentioned and the Pope saw no reason to put any obstacles in her way. Accordingly she received the dispensation, which had been executed on March 20, 1402. The fullest degree of punctiliousness had thus been observed and she lost no time in appointing a member of her household to go at once to England and inform Henry in great secrecy that no obstacle now remained to their union. A cool and designing lady, this comely Joanna of Navarre. She was depending on that spark which had undoubtedly passed from eye to eye as they met in the halls of the ducal palace or sat at close hand in the dining hall. Henry was still under her spell, for he proceeded at once with a marriage by proxy.

They seemed to be happy enough and certainly the new queen was a kind and faithful attendant during the years while his fatal illness fastened on the king.

The stubbornness with which she clung to her own desires and possessions was illustrated when a committee of the lords proceeded to investigate the adherents she had brought with her and who still remained in comfortable posts. She very reluctantly agreed to meet the wishes of the committee halfway. She must, she declared, keep a very few about her whose ministrations were necessary to her comfort. It was found later that the very few she had kept about her were as follows: two knights, a damsel of good birth and a chambermaid for each of her two young daughters, a cook who could prepare Breton dishes for them, two squires, two chambermaids, one mistress, one nurse, one messenger, eleven laundresses, and someone whose office was designated as a varlet launderer!

The pressure from Rome for active steps against the spread of Lollardy and unorthodox teaching generally had been getting stronger, but it is not to Henry's credit that he bowed to the clerical demands. Arundel at Canterbury was unable to stand against the pontifical voice and may have been responsible for putting on the statute books a measure which came to be called in detestation *de haeretico comburendo*. It provided for all preachers of heresy, who refused to abjure before the diocesan, to be tried before the secular courts. The punishment was designated as death by burning at the stake *for the manifest example of other Christians*.

The administration of this barbarous law in Henry's reign produced the first victims to suffer in the flames for their faith. The very first was a curate at St. Bennet Sheerhog in London named William Sawtree, who had previously been in the diocese of Norwich and had been convicted there of heresy. He had believed it right to worship Christ who died on the cross but not the cross itself. He was against pilgrimages on the ground that the money involved might be better employed in helping the poor. Finally he asserted his lack of belief in the doctrine of transubstantiation. Declared guilty of heresy, he had recanted but it was now learned that he had relapsed again. It was felt that an example had to be made and here was one with no powerful friends to fight for him. Sawtree was selected as the first to pay the penalty.

Arundel came up from Canterbury and sat on the case at St. Paul's, surrounded by a group of the bishops. The poor little curate, who seems to have desired at the last moment to escape the consequences of his outspokenness, was first degraded and deprived of all his clerical honors and defenses. He was then turned over to the secular arm and was declared guilty. The king took the advice of the lords spiritual and temporal and decreed that he was to be burned to death in accord with the new statute. Sawtree accordingly was taken out to Smithfield and there burned in chains.

It was some years later that a second victim was selected. John Badby was not a priest but a tailor in Worcestershire, a man of good understanding and rare courage. He was so firm in the assertion of his beliefs that he also was condemned to death. The Prince of Wales, who was strongly orthodox in his opinions, went out to Smithfield and endeavored to win a recantation from the brave tailor by offering him a full pardon. Badby declined and the torch was applied to the fagots heaped up about him. His agonized screams when the flames enveloped him prompted the prince to make a final effort. He had the fire extinguished and offered life, liberty, and even a pension to the man if he would give in. The blackened lips quivered but the light in the eyes made it clear that his spirit was still stronger than his tortured flesh. A shake of the head declined the offer. The prince stepped back and the fagots were relighted.

That the fires of Smithfield were set to blazing in this period adds much to the feeling of gloom and depression aroused by the general picture of the reign of the first of the Lancastrians.

Although Henry may have acquired the germ of leprosy during his crusading jaunts in the East, his symtoms seem to point rather to a heart weakness. Toward the end of his life he began to fall into trances which so closely resembled death that many times those about him were convinced he had come to his end. It was during one of these cataleptic periods that his oldest son was supposed to have picked up the crown and carried it away with him. The fact that the monarch kept all his teeth until his death and that the condition of his face, when his tomb was opened centuries later, showed no signs of the ravages of leprosy should suffice to prove that he was carried away by some other form of disease.

For one who showed so much promise in his youth, his reign seems dull and sad.

## CHAPTER II

## The Welsh Magician

1

AN OUTSTANDING figure during the reign of the gloom-laden Henry IV was a Welshman named Owen Glendower, who was generally believed to have supernatural powers. In Shakespeare's play he presents his own case in a speech which begins, ". . . At my birth the front of heaven was full of fiery shapes." Later the people of Wales declared that on the night when he was born the horses in the stables of his father, Griffith Vychan, stood in blood up to their fetlocks. It may be assumed that this great patriot was too realistic and clearheaded himself to believe he possessed magic powers, but clearly he saw the great advantage in having others believe it.

Although he has long been called by the simplified form of his name, his full title was Owain ap Griffith Vychan of Glyndyfrdwy. He was descended from the great Welsh family of Powys and this gave him a right of leadership which no one else in his day could claim. The family was wealthy, with large estates and strong castles in both North and South Wales.

That Owen Glendower was forced into assuming the leadership of the mountain people in their last concerted (and nearly successful) effort to shake off the Saxon chains does not in any degree detract from the place he still holds in Welsh memories. He was the last of the great patriots and so he is remembered above all others.

**2**

To tell his story it is first necessary to explain the conditions which existed in the Marcher country, on the edge of which he maintained his broad domain. During Norman and Plantagenet days the English kings did not have large standing armies. The country was divided into wide tracts held by the barons, who were expected to join the king with all their dependents, armed and ready, in the event of war. There would have been small advantage in having standing armies because of the bad roads and the scarcity of bridges. The Scots could come down over the border and create havoc in the north, or the Welsh could issue out from their mountains and harry the western counties, and vanish into thin air, before the king with his trained troops could get to the scene of action. It was necessary, therefore, to maintain forces in the exposed areas which would always be ready to repel attack. This was done by a system of "farming out" the defense of the north and the west to certain great families. Whole counties were turned over to them, on their guarantee to maintain the safety of the borders. In the north there were the Percy and Neville families, in the west the Greys of Ruthin, the Talbots and the Mortimers of Wigmore and Chirk. They became known as Marcher barons, and their powers verged on the absolute. In Wales the king's writ did not run beyond the Wye, and so not only the safety of the land rested on the shoulders of the Marcher families but the administration of the law as well.

To maintain themselves in security and comfort in the sparsely settled country, the barons had to create principalities of their own. They brought in tillers of the soil as well as men skilled in the use of arms. Every kind of workman had to be recruited from the outside—doctors, spinners, tailors, carpenters, masons, blacksmiths, armorers, cooks, barbers. Over the people thus assembled about them the barons ruled like absolute kings, exercising the power of life and death, and being ever ready to use it. They made their own laws. And when a man crossed over the line beyond which the king's writ did not run, he knew it was almost certain he would never return.

These principalities clustered around the strong castles erected by the barons at strategic points. The "Lordship courts" were held in the Great Halls and the justice meted out there was of the kind that might be expected from proud noblemen of no education and slight sensitivities. The common Englishman, knowing the folly of disputing those above him, had small chance of getting an honest verdict. The Welshmen, "those barefooted rascals," had no chance at all. In fact, a native who appeared there was condemned from the start because he was not allowed to speak in his own defense or to summon witnesses.

It follows that the Welsh who were unfortunate enough to live under the Marcher barons had to accept roughshod tyranny without question or protest. They labored with fortitude and resignation, although underneath there was deep hatred of the intruders and a fierceness which manifested itself, when it came to open conflict, in the mutilation of the slain. Crosses were cut on foreheads and bodies were hacked and dismembered. No mercy could be expected and so none was given.

The Welsh found their greatest relief in their love of music. In the evenings when the day's work had been done, a single voice would begin to sing and others would join in the air until the hills resounded with the chorus of the shepherds as they wended their weary way homeward. The barons, who had inherited with their Norman blood little appreciation of poetry or music, had another contemptuous term for the Welsh—"the Singers."

### 3

It is generally believed that Owen Glendower was born in 1359, which places him in his forties when the need for his leadership arose. His family was one of the wealthiest in the country and he had large estates in both North and South Wales, as well as the dower lands of his beautiful wife, Margaret Hanmer. He had a good education, including some years at Oxford and a term in the Inns of Court at London. He had then taken up the profession of arms and was in the train of Henry of Bolingbroke when the latter was first exiled to Europe. Apparently he returned before Henry and for some time thereafter was in the service of Richard. This was the natural course for a Welsh gentleman to pursue. All Wales, for reasons which have never been satisfactorily explained, remained loyal to the ineffectual son of the Black Prince through all his ups and downs and his final sad ending. It will be recalled that a small force of Welshmen under Glendower hung on the edge of the company which took Richard from Chester to London, looking for a chance to rescue him.

Owen Glendower seems to have been the personification of the Welsh race, with all their virtues and their greatnesses and also some of their faults. He was tall and compelling in looks, with vibrant dark eyes, a long nose, a forked beard, and a mouth which combined strength with a hint of urbanity. He believed above everything else in the traditions of the race and so kept about him the best of the native bards. Now minstrels constituted the most consistent of crops in Wales and this meant that Sycharth, the home which Glendower preferred, had to be both large and well provisioned to accommodate all the bards who came there with harps strapped on their shoulders and throats filled with song. One of them, Iolo Goch (the Red Bard), left a curious description of the home of the great patriot. Sycharth stood almost within sight of the frontier with a single line of hills to cut it off from the gentle lands now known as Shropshire, and so it had to be strongly entrenched. It had, says the Red Bard, a gatehouse of stone and a deep moat with the necessary drawbridge. Enclosed within the moat was a cluster of what can only be described as an odd assortment of buildings. There was "a Neapolitan building of eighteen apartments, a wooden structure raised on posts in which were eight apartments for guests, and a church in the form of a cross." The place clearly was planned to stand siege, for within the confines of the moat were establishments to provide every kind of food. There were well-stocked warehouses, a mill, a spicery, a salt house, orchards, vineyards, fish ponds, a stone pigeon house, a rabbit warren. Three separate tables could be maintained, one of them for the "encampment of bards." As for the variety of the dishes offered and the capabilities of the cooks, the Red Bard waxes ecstatic on both points. One can imagine him rubbing his well-rounded stomach and rolling his eyes as he descants on the splendor of the roasts and the piquancy of the wines. Sycharth, clearly, was the very ideal of a gentleman's house in this century which fancied itself close to perfect in everything.

But Sycharth was close to the domain of the Greys of Ruthin. At the time when Owen settled himself down with his wife and his handsome children and his warbling guests, the head of the Greys was one Reginald, who had become filled with arrogance by the exercise of his absolute power. Between Sycharth and the Red Castle of Ruthin lay a stretch of moorland which both claimed. The dispute over this land led to the wars which must now be told in brief form.

## 4

When Grey of Ruthin's craving for that piece of moorland, which was called the common of Croisau, became too urgent to repress, he simply took the property over. One day his men went in and expelled all the tenants of Sycharth who held land there. From the hills where he could see far up the banks of the Dee, Glendower watched this highhanded and wanton thievery but did not meet the move by a resort to arms. This was in Richard's time and the Welsh magnate, being still of pacific bent, carried the case to the King's Court in London. He won a verdict and the highly enraged Grey had to give up the land.

Things were different after Henry IV succeeded to the throne. Glendower had openly espoused the cause of the late king and so had no reason to expect favors at Westminster. Grey lost no time in seizing the land a second time. Still relying on the law, Glendower went to London and protested. This time his petition was dismissed without a hearing.

Bishop Trevor of St. Asaph, who knew Glendower well, was present and strove to show what consequences this rash and unfair procedure might have.

"Honorable gentlemen," he said, "you are making a mistake, a grave mistake. This man has much power. Provoke him and he will cause trouble. He can cause more serious trouble than anyone today in all these British isles."

It became apparent in time that the good bishop had been right. Owen Glendower was to cause more trouble than anyone in the British islands—England, Scotland, Ireland, Wales—with all the smaller islands thrown in for good measure, the Hebrides, the Shetlands, the Channel Islands.

Grey of Ruthin, exultant over his legal victory, consolidated his hold on the disputed land by sending in his own settlers with their flocks and herds. With watchful sagacity, Glendower took no steps to oppose him.

Grey was not yet satisfied. He was determined to complete the ruin of his neighbor. As chief Marcher lord of the north he was supposed to summon all of the king's liege men to the royal standard when Henry planned his first thrust into Scotland. He neglected to send notice to Glendower and then reported to the king that the Welshman had refused to obey the summons, labeling his neighbor both traitor and coward. Even this did not satisfy the master of the Red Castle. He asked permission, and received the royal assent, to send a force against Glendower and to seize all his possessions as confiscated to the Crown.

The move was made with more secrecy than might have been expected from one as rash and hot-tempered as Grey. With the assistance of Talbot, he marched one night to Sycharth and surrounded the castle before its owner had any inkling of an attack. The moat and the stone walls, described by Iolo Goch, were strong enough to hold out against this surprise foray long enough for Glendower to escape by a rear postern and to take refuge in the woods. The two Marcher barons sacked the house, killed many of the people, and stole everything worth carrying off. Grey then returned to Ruthin, convinced that he had suitably punished this proud neighbor for daring to oppose his lordly will.

Soon after this episode the most alarming communications began to reach the king, who was still in Scotland and also his son Prince Hal. The latter now held the title of Prince of Wales and had been left in charge of military operations there. It was proving a hollow dignity for it was impossible to collect any revenue from the Welsh people. The royal chamberlain at Carnarvon wrote that the people "were meeting in secret," that they were buying arms and horses and stealing where they could not buy. An even more disturbing evidence of racial unrest was that the Welsh students at Oxford (where they went in large numbers and figured furiously in the street riots), and even some at Cambridge, had deserted their hospitia and their books and were banding together to return to Wales, marching in secrecy by night and sleeping by day. Welsh laborers in the cities and towns were leaving their employment and crossing the border. It was very clear that an uprising was being planned, although there was nothing as yet to indicate how general it might become. Nor was there any mention of Owen Glendower.

On September 20, 1400, the annual fair at Ruthin was being held. The town was bedecked with flags, there were booths in the streets and companies of strolling players and mountebanks to amuse the people. There was even a slightly festive atmosphere to be noticed about the grimly bastioned walls of the Red Castle. In the evening there would be morris dancing and singing.

And then suddenly, swarming down out of the hills, came a large army of Welshmen, some mounted but most of them on foot. They carried their longbows over their shoulders (for the Welsh, who were great archers, had invented that tremendous weapon) and they sang as they marched. The dragon standard of Wales was carried in front and beneath it rode Owen Glendower, proclaiming himself the real Prince of Wales and heir of the last Llewelyn.

There were few armed men to defend the town, so it was swept clean of everything. Then, remembering what Grey of Ruthin had done to Sycharth, the town was burned to the ground.

The honorable gentlemen at Westminster would have been wise to listen to the Bishop of St. Asaph. Owen Glendower was slow to anger but unappeasable when once aroused. All of North Wales was up in arms.

## 5

The myth of Glendower's magic powers became generally believed after the first campaign that King Henry waged to put down the uprising. The Welsh leader had been successful in capturing some of the castles of the Marchers and even in throwing the city of Shrewsbury into a panic. Returning from Scotland, where he had accomplished nothing of note, Henry elected to redeem himself by routing the Welsh without any delay. He called up the levies of all the shires of the Midlands, as well as the border counties, and with a large and well-equipped force struck into the foothills.

Glendower showed himself at intervals with numerous and noisy followers, with flags flying and instruments blazing away and all the by-play helpful in keeping the Welsh enthusiasm at a fighting pitch. Henry struck at him savagely every time he appeared but always with the same lack of result. The cheering and the music stopped, the proud banners seemed to fade away, and the army was soon invisible. When this had gone on for a month, and the winds which swept down the peaks became cold and harsh with a threat of sleet and snow, the English king called a halt.

"There is magic in this, and the help of the devil himself," was the substance of what he said to his lieutenants. "However else, I demand ye tell me, could so many vanish so completely?"

The barons were entirely in agreement with him. The Fabian tactics of the Scots had prepared them for delaying action, but this went further than they had expected. One minute the enemy would be in full sight and the trees of the foothills would be glistening with steel and filled with bonnets, and then, almost in a trice, the Welsh would disappear and the forests into which the royal forces eagerly plunged would be empty and still.

"The secrets of Merlin have been revealed to him," was an opinion often expressed and generally believed. Merlin was associated in their minds with trees. Had he not gone to sleep in the trunk of one centuries before, and did not the Welsh expect him to emerge from it some day and lead them to victory and freedom? Perhaps the spirit of Merlin had entered the body of Owen Glendower.

The reason for the success of the Welsh in avoiding clashes with the numerically much superior English was simpler than that. They knew every foot of this wild and strange country; they knew where the deep and tortuous valleys led and where the paths penetrated the seemingly pathless forests and where the white waters of the roaring streams, pouring down from the mountains, could be crossed. It was relatively easy to disappear quickly in country such as this.

And, of course, there were caves in which scouts could lurk and rear guards take quick refuge. For centuries after these events two caves were pointed out as having been used by Glendower in his successful game of hide-and-seek with the infuriated Henry. They were each called Ogov Owain, or Owen's Cave. It must have been that he used them in his last days when he played a solitary game, for there were no caves in Wales, or elsewhere, which could conceal an army with horses and wagons and supplies.

Convinced finally that he had the Welsh leader cornered at the base of Snowdon, the great peak of North Wales which is surrounded by the most dense of forests and is accessible only to natives raised in knowledge of their complexities, Henry paraded his hungry troops through the passes and around the beautiful lakes with the greatest difficulty. They saw nothing of the enemy, and the only credit they could claim was that they crossed the water to the Isle of Angelsey and butchered some of the Franciscan friars quartered there, who were suspected of acting as spies for the Welsh patriots.

It was as late in the season as November 9 when a much disgruntled Henry returned to London and in a fit of spleen gave all of Owen's lands to the Earl of Somerset, one of his greedy and ubiquitous Beaufort half brothers. No one in England was less pleased at this than Reginald Grey, who had expected this loot would come to him. Later, Parliament passed a general pardon for all Welshmen, with the exception of Owen Glendower and his two brothers, Gwilym and Rhys. But no tendency was shown on the part of the wild hillmen to come forward and lay down their arms.

In the spring the English under Harry Hotspur (this was before the Percys turned against the king) won a battle in North Wales at Cader Idris, but Owen had no part in the defeat. He had gone south and had conducted, according to reports which reached the king, a great meeting "with the purpose of invading England and of destroying the English tongue." Henry came out like an enraged lion at this but he did not succeed in doing much in protection of the English tongue. By autumn the insurrection had spread to all parts of the country, and so again the royal forces took to horse and come galloping through the Marcher country to suppress this persistent and bold Welshman. The tireless Glendower came and went like a wraith, doing much damage to any royal corps which fell behind or became entangled in the wild forests and swirling streams.

Settling down into winter headquarters somewhere in the safety of the mysterious sentinels of Snowdon, Owen Glendower devoted himself to a full winter of planning and negotiation. He wrote letters to the kings of France and Scotland, soliciting their help, and similar letters to the kings and chiefs of Ireland. Promises came back from both France and Scotland, but nothing very definite; enough, barely, to keep his hopes high and his will strong to go on fighting. He indulged in one foray only, which took him down to the sands of Dee and a systematic harrying of the lands of Grey of Ruthin.

In the Middle Ages comets always aroused fears and strange speculations. When one appeared in the sky that spring, the Welsh people in the deep valleys, who could see little above them, climbed the rocky sides of the mountains and gazed in awe and aroused hope. The shepherds in the hills, who spent many of their nights under this new light in the sky, became filled with a rapt belief that it meant God had sent Owen Glendower to lead them.

### 6

The year 1401 saw Glendower accomplishing one success after another. He was as relentless as though fighting a civil war. The southern Welsh, who had comfortable homes and were averse to supporting this fierce leader from the north, were driven out and their homes burned. Anyone not fighting for him was an enemy and must be treated as such. Although the common people saw in his rising star the answer to centuries of prayer, the lords of the manors were not in any sense unanimous. This drove the supposed magician to bitter methods of extermination.

Grey of Ruthin had been in London when his lands were raided, but immediately on his return the Welsh bands swooped down for a second time. Grey came out to face them and fell into an ambush. Many of his men were killed and he himself was taken prisoner. He probably expected a short shrift but instead he was taken to the region at Snowdon where the rebel sanctuary was located. He may have been taken in blindfolded or it may have been that the country thereabouts was so wild that no outsider could hope to find a way through it. The master of Ruthin, at any rate, was kept in extreme anxiety and exasperation throughout the summer, and in great physical discomfort. His sorrowing family had given the captive baron up for lost, knowing that the Welsh had not been taking prisoners, and so they were astonished when word was received that he was still alive.

Glendower had a crafty twist to his mind and he understood, moreover, the character of his prisoner. He had thought of a better revenge on this personal enemy: he would hold him for ransom and fix the price of freedom at a very high figure. In one contemporary chronicle (Adam of Usk) the ransom is set at £16,000, but the best information places it at a more understandable total, 10,000 marks, of which 6000 were to be paid on Martinmas Day, November 11, on his release. His eldest son was to be turned over as a hostage for the payment of the balance.

Grey was kept in a confinement described as inhumanly harsh, perhaps in a cave but certainly not in the temporary house that Glendower had erected for his family somewhere close to the historic peak. He chafed at the conditions and grew ill with the uncertainty. Finally duly accredited messengers arrived with the first payment concealed in their saddlebags, and with his son John (a brave young fellow who later died in the great Battle of Agincourt) ready to take his place. It seemed that Parliament had met and had agreed to the negotiations. The king had made a personal contribution, but not a large one, for there was never a time during Henry's brief and unhappy reign when he was not in desperate straits for money.

The crafty Glendower had chosen the punishment hardest for his one-time neighbor to bear. Grey arrived back at Ruthin to find his lands black from burning, his stock driven off, even the Red Castle in neglected condition. Although he succeeded in raising the balance and in getting his son out of rebel hands, he never recovered from the financial difficulties into which he had been plunged. He was to live for thirty years more and to raise a second family, but always he labored unhappily under the shadow of debt.

A more agreeable prisoner in the rebel camp was Edmund Mortimer uncle to the two sons of the Earl of March, who stood closer in the lin of succession than the house of Lancaster. Mortimer had marched against the rebels with a considerable army raised in Herefordshire but, being an indifferent general, had been defeated with heavy losses. Owen took his illustrious captive back into the wilds about Snowdon and lodged him in comfort with the members of his own family.

One of the daughters of Owen, named Joan, was a handsome and agreeable girl and she made such an impression on the prisoner that he asked for her hand in marriage, an alliance which the rebel chief was only too glad to accept. From that time on, Mortimer remained an ally and was ready to do anything in his power to unseat the king, either in favor of Richard, if he were still alive, or his nephew of March. Some writers speak of Mortimer as "slow of wit, even weak of mind." It may have been that he concealed a shrewdness of wit under an outer showing of simplicity. It was he who had been heard to say, when told that Henry of Bolingbroke called himself heir to the throne, "Yea, he is so, as a pirate is heir of a merchant whom he has taken or destroyed."

He was too wary certainly to become involved in a wild plot hatched in the unsettled mind of Lady Constance of York. This daughter of Doña Isabella of Castile was the widow of the Despenser who had been executed at Cirencester. She hated Henry so much that she decided to get the two young sons of the deceased Earl of March out of his hands. They had been removed from the Tower and were being held behind the high walls of Windsor Castle.

This strange member of the royal family, who had a wildness in her hauntingly dark eyes which warned of her mental condition, located a locksmith in the town of Windsor who was able to make keys for all the doors in the castle. Armed with these, she let herself in unobserved one dark night and found her way to the Norman tower where the two boys were sleeping.

They roused uneasily when they saw this fey nocturnal visitor.

"Hear me," she whispered (or similar words which have not been recorded), "I have come to take you away. There is now a man who can perform magic and he has raised a great army with your good uncle. They will sweep this king off the throne. And you, dear Edmund," addressing the older of the pair, "will become king in his stead."

They left by the southern postern without being seen and vanished into the darkness. However, a curious-looking woman and two young boys cannot travel the countryside without attracting attention. The pursuers soon caught up with them and took them back to Windsor.

The lady Constance, under close questioning, charged so many high-placed people with being involved, including her own brother, the Duke of York, that no attention was paid to her. She was not punished.

But the poor locksmith of Windsor was not pardoned. His right arm was fastened to a block and severed with one blow of a butcher's knife. Later he was taken out and hanged.

Edmund Mortimer died some years later in the defense of Harlech Castle. His widow, with their three daughters, had been captured previously and taken to London. Here, most mysteriously, they all died. The state, however, was generous enough to pay the sum of one pound for their burial in the churchyard of St. Swithin's.

## 7

In the year 1404 it seemed that Owen Glendower had attained his great objective. Only a few of the great castles still held out for Henry. On May 10, in what he claimed to be the fourth year of his reign, Owen began to circulate letters which he signed as "Prince of Wales by the Grace of God." In one he appointed Griffith Yong as his chancellor and delegated him to go to France as joint ambassador with John Hanmer, the brother of Owen's wife. Their mission was to conclude a treaty of alliance with the French.

Philip of Orléans, acting for the still intermittently insane king, was glad to promise assistance. The ambassadors returned to Wales with a present for Owen of a jeweled helmet, habergeon, and sword, and an assurance of troops to help him in his struggle against the English.

The Welsh patriot, clearly, was in a vainglorious mood during these days of military prosperity. A seal had been struck for him, showing him seated on a throne with a scepter in his right hand and an orb in the other.

But no good ever came, during the years which preceded this or in the centuries which followed, from the importation of French auxiliaries. The army which landed at Milford Haven a year later under the Comte de la Marche proved of no assistance whatever. Their ships, left unprotected in the harbor, were pounced upon and fifteen of the largest were destroyed. The brave barons who led the land forces were appalled at the wildness of the land. They found the food unpalatable and the wines thin and sour. They faced the English once. Henry had led his forces up to Worcester and for eight days the two armies remained at bay while skirmishing parties battled in the open space between them. Finally Glendower dropped back and drew the king's army after him. It was the same old story. The English became involved in the valley of the Rhondda with a furious band of rebels who charged them from cover, shouting their battle cry of "Cadwgan, whet thy battle-axe!" At the same time the weather turned hostile (directed by Owen who was believed to control the winds and the clouds) and floods swept down the valleys, making an English advance impossible and a retreat difficult. Henry was back in Worcester by the first of October.

But this kind of victory did not suit the French. In fact, they had no stomach left for fighting of any kind, and all but a handful returned home before Christmas. How they obtained the necessary ships has never been explained. It was said later that the French were disappointed over the lack of booty. Certainly the Welsh were highly disgruntled with the futile efforts of their allies. The alliance came to an end.

The following year the Welsh armies suffered two severe defeats. The sun which had been so high in the heavens had begun to set. The military supplies, without which the most valiant armies can do nothing, were running short. The people were tiring of the continuous fighting and the hardships from which they suffered. The fiery sword of Glendower seemed to be cutting both ways.

If Owen's gift for disappearance was due to the possession of a cloak of invisibility, as the people of his day believed, he continued to possess it and to use it during the few remaining years of his life. They were not great years. From the leading of armies he found himself with nothing but small bands engaged in guerrilla operations. Then he seems to have become a fugitive, seen here and there but never visible when any effort was made to capture him. Various places are still pointed out where the once glorious leader sought sanctuary in the days of his decline: a cave at the mouth of the Dysynni and an obscure hiding place on Moel Hebog, a companion peak to Snowdon.

When Henry IV died and his gallant son, Prince Hal, succeeded him on the throne, one of the first acts of the new king was to declare a pardon for all rebels in Wales. Although he was not excluded, the stout old leader refused to benefit by it. The chivalrous young king sent special envoys to find him, including Talbot of the Marcher barons and Owen's own son, Meredith. They did not succeed in locating him.

One story has it that Owen found his way to Herefordshire disguised as a shepherd and reached the home of one of his married daughters at Monnington and remained there quietly, even secretly, until his death.

The story most often believed is that the rebel chief disappeared from the sight of all who had followed him or had known him and was never heard of again.

## CHAPTER III

## The King and Fair Kate

### 1

THE reign of Henry V was one of the shortest in English history—nine years, filled with great military achievements and both colored and dignified by a display of justice, moderation, and fairness in all respects. As a man Henry was deeply religious, chaste, and honorable, which set him apart from most kings. He was free of the besetting sin of the Plantagenets, extravagance. In fact, there was a frugality in everything he did, and it was only in the equipment and maintenance of armies in the field that he was ready to draw heavily on parliamentary support. The wildness he had exhibited as a prince, which was due in no small degree to his lack of money (Henry IV was always poor and his son was supposed to draw his income from a Wales in arms which paid not a shilling in tribute), fell from him like an outworn cloak.

As a general he must be ranked above the great Plantagenets who had preceded him: Richard of the Lion-Heart, Edward I, Edward III, and the Black Prince. There was brilliant strategy in the Agincourt campaign and in the conquest of Normandy which followed.

Everything about him seems admirable. As a negotiator he was direct and in no sense devious. He did not hide behind subterfuges or resort to vague half promises. It was said that he would listen in silence to the reasoning of those about him and finally say either, "It is impossible," or "It shall be done." When he had taken a stand, he remained firm and resolute in it.

It is unfortunate that he was so obsessed with the need to recover all the ground lost halfway in the Hundred Years War. This left him with little time to tend the legislative and administrative fields at home.

If he had given himself instead to peace-time pursuits, what straight and enduring furrows he would have plowed!

Had he lived longer he would undoubtedly have been acclaimed the greatest of English kings. Many historians so rank him. All agree that he was the best loved.

These nine brilliant, incisive years, these years so full of accomplishments and so free of chivalrous nonsense and wasteful ceremony, are chiefly remembered for two things: the remarkable victory at Agincourt which left France prostrate at Henry's feet and the king's romance with a daughter of the French king, who is called in history the Fair Kate. There is a temptation to write about Agincourt, because it was fought so boldly and aggressively and because there was better strategic planning back of it than in any of the earlier English victories. But even allowing for Henry's boldness and his cool foresight it was a case of the French losing the battle rather than the English winning it. For thirty years the single-minded nobles of France had been restrained from offering battle and it is probable that, if Henry had been disposed to load his army back on his ships and depart, they would have been ready enough to see him go. But Henry had crossed the Sleeve to fight, and so, after much marching and countermarching along the fords of the Somme, they came face to face at last on ground well suited to battle within sight of the castle walls of Agincourt.

The French had learned something from their defeats at Crécy and Poictiers, but not enough. They took up their stations along the field the night before, at least 50,000 of them as against the English 8000 to 10,000, and they were supremely confident. But they still believed in the mounted knight and there was so much cavalry around the castle that the ground was reduced to pulp by the hoofs of the horses. It is even true that many of the young knights sat all night in their saddles so their shining armor would not have a fleck of mud when the time came to ride into battle; and the next day their weary steeds floundered and went down or turned and bolted in mad panic into the thick ranks behind. In contrast Henry ordered his knights to dismount and fight on foot, a demeaning innovation in the eyes of the Gallic foe. He even arranged his thin line so his foot soldiers would provide some guard for the all-essential archers. The French still lacked archers to compete with the stout English longbow men.

The French died by the thousands, the English by the hundreds, and again it was a great English victory. But all this is familiar ground to readers of the Plantagenet story. And so—better to choose the romance of Henry of England and Katherine of France.

2

*King Henry:* Now fie upon my false French! By mine honor, in true English,
I love thee, Kate; by which honor I dare not swear thou lovest me; yet my
blood begins to flatter me that thou dost, notwithstanding the poor and
untempering effect of my visage. Now, beshrew my father's ambition! He
was thinking of civil wars when he got me; wherefore was I created with
a stubborn outside, with an aspect of iron, that when I come to woo ladies,
I fright them. But, in faith, Kate, the elder I wax the better I shall appear;
my comfort is that old age, that ill layer-up of beauty, can do no more spoil
upon my face: thou hast me, if thou hast me, at the worst; and thou shalt
wear me, if thou wear me, better and better. And therefore tell me, most fair
Katherine, will you have me? Put off your maiden blushes; avouch the
thoughts of your heart with the looks of an empress; take me by the hand
and say,—Harry of England, I am thine: which word thou shalt no sooner
bless mine ear withal but I will tell thee aloud, England is thine, Ireland is
thine, France is thine, and Henry Plantagenet is thine——Come, your answer
in broken music—for thy voice is music, thy English broken; therefore, queen
of all, Katherine, break thy mind to me in broken English—wilt thou have me?
*Katherine:* Dat is as it sall please de *roi mon pere.*

Thus, in *King Henry* V, Shakespeare describes the wooing of the Fair
Kate by the forthright English king.

But the story begins much earlier, dating back to the day when
Prince Henry first saw Isabella of France. It was soon after the deposition
and death of Richard, and the twelve-year-old girl, who had thus become
a widow before being a wife, was in the depths of despair. In spite
of her grief, it was apparent that she was becoming a slender, graceful,
and delightful-looking girl. The prince was an impressionable youth of
thirteen and he stood tongue-tied in the presence of the little queen.
Later he informed his father that he wanted to marry Isabella as soon
as they were old enough.

It happened that this was completely in accord with the ideas of the
new king, who was anxious to make a lasting peace with France. The
French government was agreeable to the union, because Charles VI was
falling with greater frequency into his spells of insanity and the country
was torn by the struggles between two political parties, the Burgundians
and the Armagnacs. But they failed to reckon with the firm spirit of the
girl widow of the dead English king. Isabella had acquired a real affection
for her handsome spouse. His defeat and death had broken her heart
(or so she believed), but without breaking her spirit. She hated the
new king who had been responsible for Richard's death and she would

have nothing to do with any member of the Lancastrian family. The roses mounted in her cheeks, her eyes flashed angrily, and she gave her answer with one word—No!

Young Henry was so obsessed with her delicate beauty that he begged his father to persist. Isabella was approached several times, but her answer never varied. No, no! Finally she was allowed to return to France, without her dowry or even her personal jewelry, and later married a prince of the Orléans line for whom she felt a deep affection. She died within a year in childbirth. It is doubtful if the prince ever outgrew his infatuation for her. It was a day of great sadness for him when he learned of her death.

But there were three younger sisters in the French royal family, Michelle, Marie, and Katherine, and he decided that one of them might fill this vacant place in his heart. Michelle, first, but she was promised to the son of the Duke of Burgundy. Marie, then; but Marie was taking the vows in a convent. Well, it must be the youngest of them, Katherine. He received reports about her and even had a portrait sent to him. She was an attractive girl, even though she seemed to him not as beautiful as his first love, Isabella; but she had charms of her own.

When he had been crowned King of England, Henry entered suit for the hand of Katherine. His demands seemed to the French wildly exorbitant. He was demanding that they give him Normandy, all the territories which Eleanor of Aquitaine brought with her when she married Henry II of England, and a dowry of 2,000,000 crowns. France wanted peace, but what grounds had this young and untried king, the son of a usurper, moreover, to make such demands? Once again Henry suffered the mortification of having his suit rejected.

### 3

It is doubtful if Henry knew of the conditions under which the three daughters were being raised. The princess who had been sent to France on approval was now serving as a queen on sufferance. As the king was in the grip of his malady most of the time, Isabeau gave full rein to her lascivious tendencies. She saw to it that the three children were raised in the Hôtel de St. Pol, where their father was kept during his mad spells. The royal finances were always low, so Queen Isabeau found it difficult to maintain herself in the full splendor she desired. Little of the royal revenue was used for the unhappy household at the St. Pol. The servants, who were not under any suitable form of super-

vision, saw to it that they themselves had plenty of food, even when
there was not enough for the children. One dress had to be used in turn
by all three, which was particularly hard for Katherine, who received it
after a second alteration. It is even said that they had no changes of
linen. The insane king was in worse stead. Kept in a dark and closely
shuttered room, he attacked with maniacal fury any servants or doctors
who attempted to enter. He was left alone and so went for months at a
time without any change of clothing or a bath. The apartments of the
royal children were some distance from this chamber of horrors but
they could hear his wailing and screaming and his bickering with the
hostile visitors he fancied about him.

On one occasion he regained his senses unexpectedly and was stricken
with horror at his own condition, and even more so when he saw the
misery of the princesses. Wine had been brought him in a gold goblet
and he ordered that it should be sold to buy suitable clothes for his
daughters.

Perhaps unaware of the true state of affairs at St. Pol, or unconcerned
about it, Queen Isabeau continued on terms of more or less open
intimacy with the Duke of Orléans, who was said to be the most handsome man in all France and the greatest philanderer. One night in Paris,
after supping with the queen, he was returning at a late hour. It was a
dark night and, as always, dangers lurked in the unlighted streets.
The duke was accompanied by two squires only and had sent a handful
of servants ahead on foot to light the way with torches. Suddenly a
party of armed men emerged from concealment behind a house
known as *Image de Notre-Dame* and surrounded him.

"Death! Death!" they cried.

"I am the Duke of Orléans!" he protested.

The servants had dropped their torches and fled for safety. In the
small light thus left, the assassins dragged the debonair duke from his
saddle and hacked him to death on the cobbled street.

Queen Isabeau fled from Paris, knowing that her affair with the duke
had been one reason for his murder. She remained at Melun four
months and then returned with an escort of 3000 men, taking up her
residence at the Louvre. The tragic consequences of her open dalliance
with Orléans had not served as a curb on her licentious conduct. She
had been scandalously open in the favors she had shown a nobleman of
Auvergne, one Louis de Bosredon. The latter had begun to swagger and
even to boast publicly. The king regained his reason quite unexpectedly
and was informed of what was going on. He acted promptly. Bosredon
was taken into custody and put to the torture. He confessed abjectly

and, on the king's orders, was sewn in a leather sack and thrown into the Seine. On the outside of the sack the words had been printed: *Let the King's justice run its course.*

Between the time that Louis de Bosredon went down with the tide in his leather sack and the momentous days when the English threat loomed upon the horizon again, Queen Isabeau experienced a change of heart. The poor mad Charles was never going to recover and the sons she had borne him had the stamp of the Valois on them—in other words, they were spindling specimens with the Valois nose jutting out from pale and hollowed faces. The two older ones had died early, and the third, now called the dauphin, was deeply immersed in the political quarrels, with a genius for getting on the wrong side. A hand was needed at the helm and she decided that her own was the only one available. It was, in fact, a beautifully white and slender hand despite the fact that the years were broadening her to an effect almost of obesity. To compensate for the passing of her period of pulchritude, the queen had actually begun to develop a sense of statecraft—to divide her interests, at least, between counterpane and chancellery. With the princess Michelle already married to the heir of Burgundy, and quite unhappy in the relationship, and with Marie taking her vows, there was only Katherine left to serve as a pawn in her mother's hands. She was whisked out of her squalid obscurity. Instead of wearing dresses cut down and stitched up by clumsy fingers, made of sleazy materials or soiled velvet, the last daughter was now attired in the silks and satins which befitted her rank.

Mother and daughter became attached to one another. There was some trace of affinity between them which both recognized. Certainly they had one objective in common. Katherine must marry Henry of England.

### 4

Even those who admire Henry most and revere his memory, and this includes all who have read much history or have seen the Shakespeare play, are compelled to concede that he had no just reason for going to war with France. He did not at first claim the French throne but limited himself to demands for the return of Normandy and the Angevin provinces in the west and south. The rejection of his offer for the hand of Katherine offered the most flimsy pretext but, in lieu of something better, he made much of it. The honesty and forthright qualities of the great warrior king were less perceptible in this phase of his career than at any other time.

His brilliant victory at Agincourt had set England aflame with enthusiasm for the continuance of the Hundred Years War. Again the ports saw the unloading of great stores of booty, and even common soldiers had come back with feather beds on their backs (the king later forbade the use of such comforts) and pockets filled with jewelry. After a brief visit home and a triumphant reception at London (where he was too modest to display the battered helmet he had worn in battle as proof of his personal part in the fighting), Parliament decreed such liberal financial support that the young king returned to France with an army estimated at 50,000 men. France was to be beaten to her knees with one more decisive blow.

The campaign which followed was a demonstration of sure strategy, and on June 19, 1419, Henry had the satisfaction of receiving the capitulation of Rouen, the capital of Normandy where William the Conqueror had ruled. Paris was now almost within sight. The poor madman was still king and the bitter strife of the factions kept France in turmoil. How could they hope to defend themselves against this conqueror?

It was not until May 28 of the following year, however, that Henry met the Fair Kate.

Charles had recovered a small shred of reason and he accompanied his queen, the Duke of Burgundy, and his last available daughter to discuss peace with the new master of Normandy. They rode regally down the Seine in a barge which blazed with color. A temporary enclosure with webbed planks had been built on the river at Pontoise, with tents on each bank. It was in this somewhat insecure structure that the great romance began.

Henry entered the enclosure after the French royal party had seated themselves. Poor Charles was not present and so Isabeau sat in the center. The English king's eyes inevitably fastened themselves on her first. Although she had become almost massive and her once wonderful complexion could no longer be simulated even with the most skillful use of cosmetics, she still commanded first attention. Her eyes were large and brilliant, her hair was lustrous, and she had an air that was not only regal but intensely feminine. It was only on a slow second glance that Henry realized there was a slender girl seated beside the dominating figure of the queen.

Katherine was still thin, but her figure promised an engaging maturity without any fear of reaching the outlines of the licentious Isabeau. Her complexion had the Bavarian freshness of snow and mountain berries.

She had her mother's eyes, quite as large and with the same brilliance. Some say they were black but a safer judgment makes them of a very dark gray with glints of a slate blue in them.

It should be explained at once that Katherine had one mark of the Valois about her. She had the Valois nose, although in modified form. It lacked the hump which some of the royal daughters had, and which seemed to qualify them for riding a broomstick through midnight clouds, but it was slender and just long enough to incline slightly over the upper lip. Such a nose might produce an effect of homeliness in middle years but, when set in a fresh beauty of coloring, it suggested that individuality and character went with the prettiness.

While the Earl of Warwick, who spoke French fluently, launched on a long speech, Henry seated himself before the princess and never allowed his eyes to wander from her face. It was clear that he was mightily pleased with her.

She was wearing a gold circlet covered with a veil like mist from a fountain. A mantle, trimmed with ermine, had been thrown over a tight-fitting gown of the richest blue velvet. She sparkled with jewels.

This first meeting was brief and there was no discussion of peace terms. When it came to an end, Henry kissed Isabeau and then drew the slender shoulders of the princess close to him and kissed her with noticeable warmth.

Later he was asked by a French spokesman if he had been pleased with the princess. Henry, honest to a fault in all matters, said, Yes, he had admired her much and wanted her for his wife. Then, it was insinuated, since he found her so desirable, he would undoubtedly be prepared to accept a smaller dower with her. Henry shook his head. No, he saw no reason for accepting a crown less.

When this was reported to the queen, the thought ran through her mind, without a doubt, This stubborn young man must be taught a lesson. When the second meeting was held, the princess was not present. Henry showed that he was disappointed. But he did not retreat from his position. He loved Katherine, but he felt his terms were just and he had no intention of moderating them.

It is highly probable that the queen and the princess were at odds on their lines of strategy. Katherine had fallen as quickly and completely in love with Henry as he had with her. The speech which Shakespeare has put into the mouth of the English king is a deft delineation of the forthrightness of Henry, except in the references to his own appearance. He had not been created with "a stubborn outside, with an aspect of iron." When he came to woo ladies, he did not "fright them." Henry had his share of the traditional good looks of the family. His face was oval in outline and his features were handsome as well as strong. His eyes were the Plantagenet blue, although his hair departed from the accepted pattern in being dark instead of flaxen. In build he was tall but rather on the slender side, which did not lessen his strength nor his skill with weapons, as he had proven at Agincourt and on countless other occasions.

He also possessed in some degree, at least, the pride (call it vanity, if that word seems more apt) which the members of the family had in their appearance. It is doubtful if he would have belittled himself to the woman he wanted to win.

After a number of conferences, none brightened by the presence of the Fair Kate, the royal family went to the extreme of not appearing at one meeting. Henry said to the Duke of Burgundy, who alone was on hand:

"Fair cousin, we wish you to know that we will have the daughter of the king or we will drive him and you out of his kingdom!"

The pride of the duke took fire at this. "Sire!" he exclaimed. "You are pleased to say so. But before you have driven my lord and me out of his kingdom, I make no doubt you will suffer much weariness and pain!"

Following this exchange of words, it was announced that a peace had been patched up between the conflicting parties in France, headed by the dauphin and the Duke of Burgundy. It looked as though the French had decided to break off all negotiations and to refuse finally Henry's suit for the hand of Katherine. The English king heard the news with a composed face.

His countermove was instantaneous and brilliant. He made a surprise attack on Pontoise and captured it without difficulty. This brought him closer to Paris than any English army of invasion had previously attained. It was reported to him that the people of Paris had not been thrown into a panic by his near approach. On the contrary they seemed ready to welcome the "Go-dams," so great was their dislike for both parties to the French political struggle. Henry, wisely, did not make any move to capture the capital city at this stage. He had proven his ability to do so and now he preferred to make his inevitable entry in the role of peacemaker.

The culminating point in this drama of tangled relationships was created by the dauphin, who had been irked by his enforced alliance with the Duke of Burgundy. The latter was invited to a conference which was to be held on the bridge at Montereau. The two leaders were to pass through wooden gates and to meet in a central compartment with exactly the same number of supporters. When Burgundy arrived there with the allotted number, the gates behind him were slammed shut and bolted. The central space was filled instantly by armed men, wearing the dauphin's colors. The duke went down under the swords of his assailants. A wave of horror swept over France and the feeble explanations that the dauphin put forth were scornfully rejected.

Philip, the new Duke of Burgundy, husband of Katherine's sister Michelle, said to his wife next day when the tragic news was received, "Your brother has murdered my father." He was gentle with her, however, in contrast to the furious haste with which he proceeded to renew his alliance with the English. He agreed to recognize Henry as heir to the French throne and to accept his other terms.

Negotiations proceeded slowly in spite of this. The English forces had moved up to take Paris in a pincer movement before Henry answered a request for a final agreement with the statement that he would treat "with none but the princess Katherine herself." Queen Isabeau, figuratively speaking, threw up her hands at this and sent the Bishop of Arras to see the English king, with authority to say that, if he would come to Troyes, Katherine would espouse him there. A letter which the bishop surreptitiously delivered to the king from Katherine was "full of sweetness" and left the ardent lover very happy.

Troyes had become the temporary capital of France in this period of incessant strife. It was a strong and high-walled city, lying a hundred miles or more southeast of Paris. However, the English forces were in possession of Melun and so lay close to the main road between Paris and Troyes. To go on to the latter city did not on that account offer too much risk. Thinking, perhaps, of the foolhardy unconcern with which the Burgundian duke had walked into the trap on the bridge at Montereau, Henry decided to go to his rendezvous in force. Early in May he assembled at Pontoise an army of 7000 men, under the command of his brothers Clarence and Gloucester. Then began a careful march to Troyes by way of the roads through Brie and Nogent. They arrived on May 20, to find the city bedecked with flags and noisy with trumpets to welcome the bridegroom.

## 5

Henry and his princess were not wedded in the cathedral of Troyes, which was large and grand and finely suited for such a ceremony. There was a reason for this which will bear explaining.

When the victorious Henry reached Troyes he was met by the Duke of Burgundy and escorted to the Hôtel de Ville where he was to stay. The next day he met the French royal family for the betrothal and had his second glimpse of Katherine, finding her more charming and desirable than before. Henry had arrayed himself with complete disregard for all the rules, coming to the ceremony in full armor and with the brush of a fox in his helmet. Another rule was broken when he placed on the finger of his prospective bride the magnificent ring which had belonged jointly to all the queens of England, being transferred from one to the other when a new consort was crowned. He had established an even more surprising precedent by announcing the appointment of Sir Lewis Robsart, one of his knights, to act as the bride's guard while she remained in France. Henry, in fact, was taking no chance of more diplomatic shilly-shallying. Katherine now belonged to him.

There was some bickering back and forth over the terms of the peace treaty and so the marriage did not take place for another week. The impatient Henry did some wandering about in the meantime and found much to please him in this medieval city over which three flags floated, the standards of England and France and the arms of Burgundy. He was pleased in particular by a church of no great size but much charm which was so closely hedged in by the massive buildings in the heart of the old town that it was not easily seen. He liked its hint of quaintness and the ivy of earlier centuries on its gray walls.

This recalls one of the most romantic of Robert Louis Stevenson's stories in which he tells of a town held jointly by the English and the Burgundians in this exact period, and of a young Englishman becoming lost at night in the maze of dark streets, leaning finally against a door which swung back and projected him into the home of a vicious uncle and his beautiful niece.

The English king paused at the church door in bright sunlight, but when he went in it was dark, still, and peaceful. The thought went through his mind, This is the place for my fair Kate and me to plight our troth, kneeling together in this friendly shadow, with no one to hear or see!

And so on June 2, Trinity Sunday, the marriage was solemnized in the church of his fancy, St. Jean, with the Archbishop of Sens officiating and the bride wearing the English royal mantle, with all its conventional tassels and jeweled embroideries, which had been brought over hurriedly. How Henry was dressed is not recorded, but, at least, he had laid aside the foxtail.

But it was not as he had pictured it, he and his Kate kneeling in the quiet of the little church, with the services chanted for their ears only. The nave was so filled with the nobility and their wives, and the high dignitaries of the church, and the townspeople who wedged themselves in somehow, that there was not an inch of standing room left anywhere.

Henry was introduced that night to a custom completely French. It was in the middle hours and, without a knock, the doors of the nuptial chamber were thrown open to admit court officials carrying tall candles in silver holders. These were followed by what seemed a long procession of royal servants. Henry struggled to a sitting position and reached for the handle of his sword, which was propped against the side of the bed.

Katherine, who had wakened at once, touched his arm and whispered: "There is no need for alarm, my dear lord and husband. It is a custom of my country."

The purpose of the intrusion was to bring wine and soup for the newly wedded pair. Henry may have fallen into accord with etiquette to the extent of drinking a goblet of wine, but one doubts if he felt disposed to try the soup. The bride, sitting up so close beside him that her arm pressed against his, may have sipped a little of it, the French being much addicted to soup. But what happened must be left to the imagination, for nothing more is set down in the records.

The next day a great state banquet was held, to which all of the English knights had been bidden. Henry here proceeded to set a precedent of his own. Hearing much talk along the tables of a tournament to celebrate the marriage, his brow clouded with disapproval. "I pray, my lord and king," he said, directing himself to the father of the bride, "to permit and I command his servants and mine to be in readiness tomorrow to go *with me* and lay siege to Sens, where are our enemies."

This was a lesson which Katherine was to learn over and over but never to accept willingly. Nothing was ever as important in Henry's eyes as the performance of his duties as a king. He felt the need of directing everything himself, even to the inspection of arrows for the archers and the contents of the barrels containing the salt fish and beef for his men. If a battle lay ahead, he must look over the ground in advance. If a conference were pending, he must study all the documents, no matter how long it took. And his wife, dearly loved though she was, must abide herself in patience until everything had been done to his satisfaction.

Henry spent the first days of his honeymoon fighting before Sens, and Katherine waited for him with her parents, and with the ubiquitous Sir Lewis Robsart lurking in the background; whether in wifely patience or the impatience that came natural to her, history does not say.

## 6

After Christmas (in the meantime Sens had fallen and Montereau as well, with great slaughter) Henry took Katherine back to England with him, anxious to show the people his radiant young bride. She was received like "an angel of God" (which indeed she was not) and her coronation took place on February 24. The banquet which followed was unique in one respect. As Lent was starting, nothing but fish could be offered. The cooks, who were artists in those days, served twenty-two kinds of fish in all manner of odd ways: bream of the sea and jelly colored with columbine, conger with cream of almonds, white leche with hawthorn leaves and red haws, perch with gudgeon, eels roasted with lampreys, roast porpoise; well, so it went.

Katherine sat in great state at one end of the table, with Archbishop Chichele, Cardinal Beaufort, and King James of Scotland grouped about her. The Earl of March (who, strictly speaking, should have been king) and Warwick squatted on their haunches on each side of the royal chair, holding her scepters, and the Countess of Kent was under the table at the queen's feet, holding a napkin. Neville was cup bearer, Stuart was sewer, Clifford pantler, and Grey of Ruthin (Owen Glendower's old enemy) was naperer. A high degree of state indeed!

The queen then went to Windsor where she expected to be joined by Henry. But at this stage she was to learn the bitter lesson over again, that she did not come first in the king's mind. He wanted heavy financial support from the House for another smashing campaign and so went off on the medieval equivalent of a "barnstorming" tour, a processional which took him to practically all towns in the kingdom. He would have taken Kate with him, because he knew the consuming curiosity there was about her, but she was with child and nothing must be done to disturb the even course of nature. Kate stood this dreary solitude at Windsor as long as she could. She had only the ladies of her household about her and their names added to the monotony of things: Joanna Belknap, Joanna Troutbeck and Joanna Coucy, all named no doubt after Henry IV's second wife. She set out to join her errant spouse, catching up with him at Leicester. They returned together in time for the meeting of Parliament in May.

As one of the king's brothers, Thomas of Clarence, had been defeated and killed at Beaugé, Henry hurried back to France, leaving Kate to have her child alone and with a stern admonition that the event must *not* take place at Windsor. But the queen felt at home in Windsor, and nowhere else in England, and so in spite of the king's instructions, she gave birth there in the Queen's House to a boy who was to be named Henry after his sire, a quiet baby with small features and very blue eyes. When Henry heard of this, he is reported to have improvised a piece of verse, with a prophetic ring about it:

> I, Henry, born at Monmouth,
>   Shall small time reign, and much get;
> But Henry of Windsor shall long reign, and lose all.
> But as God will, so be it.

Leaving the newborn heir to the throne, Katherine crossed to Honfleur in May, followed by the large army which the parliamentary grants had made possible, 20,000 men under the Duke of Bedford, the ablest of the royal brothers. She was shocked when she saw her husband, although she knew he had been through a grueling period. Henry, who had been so fleet of foot that he could catch deer in the royal enclosures without the use of dogs, now walked slowly and stumbled under the weight of his armor. The fine complexion so general in the family had deserted him and his cheeks were gray. A short time before, he had been stricken with a mysterious malady, the exact nature of which left the royal physicians at a loss. All maladies seemed to have been mysterious in this day of medical ignorance, but Henry's condition seems to have been a severe case of dysentery, from which Edward I had died.

He strove to make light of it, being certain that his strong constitution would prevail. He sent Katherine on to Vincennes to join her parents while he completed the campaign. It soon became apparent that there was no hope of recovery and he was taken in a litter to Vincennes. He died almost at once, in a penitential mood because he had accomplished so little of what he wanted to do. Jerusalem had been in his mind and he had desired to lead a final crusade for the liberation of the holy city. He had even sent a Burgundian knight named Gilbert de Lannoy to reconnoiter Palestine and had received a hopeful report.

"How long have I to live?" he asked the physicians.

They answered with great reluctance. "Sire, not more than two hours."

"Comfort my dear wife," he said to his brother John of Bedford, who stood beside the royal couch. "The most afflicted creature living."

He did not live out the time they had allowed him. Perhaps he drew on his ebbing strength to issue instructions for the government of the kingdom and for the care of his infant son. He did not name Katherine as regent nor did he commit the little king to her care, thinking probably that this would be done as a matter of course.

He died at two o'clock in the morning of August 31, 1422. It was a

night of heavy black clouds, as indeed it should have been. Black clouds
would hang over England during all the long years of the reigns which
would follow immediately after.

Katherine, who mourned her dead lord with an intensity of grief,
accompanied the body back to England. When the cortege entered
London, a large clerical body, made up of fifteen bishops and a long line
of abbots, chanted loudly as they followed the bier through the city. All
householders stood before their doors with lighted torches.

Parliament met shortly after and Katherine came from Windsor, carrying her son on her knee as they traversed the streets to Westminster.
The little king conducted himself with much gravity. It was said that
the boy developed, even in his earliest years a habit of refusing to engage
in any activities on Sundays!

### 7

With Henry dead so young and buried at Canterbury under his
emblazoned shield, his saddle, and his battered helmet, the story continues with the sorry balance of Kate's life. For three years she lived in
various of her dower homes, but mostly at Baynard's Castle in London,
and had the care of the infant king as her chief concern. She was
unhappy, as a widow who had loved her husband very much, must be.

It is said that she sought to settle a quarrel between two of Henry's
brothers, John of Bedford and Humphrey of Gloucester but nothing
could be done to create a permanent healing between two men of such
wide differences—John so able, honest, and just, Humphrey so selfish
and unprincipled. Something further should be told about her relationship with the two brothers.

Stout Bedford had been the main prop and stay of Henry, the kind of
assistant that a great chief of staff can be to a military leader of genius.
He was capable of leadership himself but willing to serve in a secondary
capacity. After Henry's death he conducted the operations in France
with vigor and skill, winning two great battles, one at Verneuil, which
is sometimes compared with Crécy and Poictiers. John of Bedford ranks
among the great men who somehow fail to come alive on the pages of
history. This may have been due in his case to a certain stolidity of
character and a degree of insensitivity which he manifested in acquiesc-
ing in the burning of Jeanne d'Arc.

There were three possible husbands for Katherine in the royal family
if the council had desired to use her in cementing the French regency.
Bedford was handsome, rather stocky in build, and Kate would perhaps

have been sensible enough to accept his hand had he offered it. But John was willing to comfort her, as Henry had desired, but not to marry this sister-in-law with her beauty and charm, her Valois nose, and her inherited tendencies, and it was almost certain that the Pope would refuse his consent. Then there was Humphrey, for whom Kate had no respect, and Edmund Beaufort, a grandson of John of Gaunt by his third wife. It is certain that Kate would have married this handsome and sophisticated young man and almost certainly the Pope would have consented. But Humphrey, the persistent troublemaker, fought the idea bitterly, knowing that Beaufort, with Kate as his wife, would be directly in line for the French regency.

Kate was not temperamentally fitted to a long widowhood and, when she found that the English council would not sanction her return to France (she was not particularly anxious to go) and was not concerning itself with finding a new husband for her, she began to notice that there was a handsome Welshman in her household, one Owen Tudor. He was serving as master of the wardrobe, which brought them in contact a great deal. He is described as having a bright eye, a well-turned pair of dancing legs, and a regard for the main chance. On one occasion some members of the household were dancing while the dowager queen sat watching with her ladies. The adroit Owen missed a step and stumbled against her, as expert a loss of balance as could conceivably be achieved.

He had to consult her about the intimate details of her wardrobe and the great lady in her mourning robes became very conscious of his presence. It was soon noticed that he was in and about her apartments oftener than duty necessitated. Despite the long and easy flowing robes that ladies wore in those days, it was impossible to conceal from the keen feminine eyes about her that she was facing the inevitable consequences of her folly.

The liaison continued for over ten years and in that time Kate brought five children into the world, three sons and two daughters. History has been at a loss on the question of the legitimacy of the Tudor children. Tudor historians, whose purpose was always to present Henry VII in the best possible light, never expressed a doubt that a marriage had taken place, although they were unable to discover when, where, or by whom the ceremony was performed. In 1428, when the scandal had become an open one, Parliament passed a law prohibiting the queen dowager from marrying anyone without the consent of the king, her son, or his council. Because of this it has been argued that she could not have been married to Tudor before that date and, in consequence, that it was later when the nuptials occurred. This supposition overlooks the likelihood that, because of the parliamentary prohibition, the marriage never took place at all.

It is significant that after his mother's death Henry VI erected an altar tomb in the Lady Chapel at Westminster in which she was inscribed the widow of Henry V and no mention made of a subsequent marriage.

There is doubt also about the antecedents of Owen Tudor. He is often described as a Welsh gentleman of minor standing and no wealth. Some historians (of the Tudor period, naturally) claim an antiquity for his family, tracing it back to Ednyfed Fychan, who had property on the Isle of Anglesey and who married a daughter of Rhys, Prince of South Wales.

The relationship between the dowager queen and the handsome adventurer, whether legal or not, was allowed to drag along until 1436 when Henry took action to end it. Tudor was arrested and placed in Newgate Prison and Kate retired or was committed to Bermondsey Abbey. The father of the children managed to escape from prison with the connivance of his servant and a priest. The boy king then made it known that he desired that "Oweyn Tidr the which dwelled wt the said quene should come to his presence." This sounded ominous to Tudor, who was living quietly at Daventry, and he demanded that he be given a written safe conduct. On reaching London he went into sanctuary at Westminster (a curious course if there were any proofs he could produce) and remained there for some time before issuing out to defend himself. He was again confined to Newgate and again made his escape.

When the king came of age he was generous enough to settle an annuity on him. Tudor repaid this generosity by fighting well on the Lancastrian side during the first stages of the Wars of the Roses. He was captured at the Battle of Mortimer's Cross and on orders from Edward of York was beheaded in the market place at Hereford. A sentimental admirer, a woman presumed in the chronicles to be mad, proceeded in a weeping condition to comb the hair and wash the face and to place around it many lighted candles.

Kate died at Bermondsey on June 3, 1437. Whether death was due to physical disabilities or grief cannot be determined; probably both figured in her early demise. She was thirty-six years of age and had survived her mother, the indestructible Isabeau of the easy morals, by one year only. And from this sordid relationship to which she had devoted all of her last years came in time the extinction of the Plantagenet line in favor of the able and arrogant Tudors. Edmund Tudor, the eldest son of the union, married Margaret, a daughter of John Beaufort, Duke of Somerset. She gave birth to a posthumous son who became Henry VII under circumstances which will be told later.

The five Tudor children were kept in a nunnery in care of the Abbess of Barking until Henry VI came of age. He then asserted himself by looking after this brood of half brothers and sisters with an affectionate care. Edmund, the first son, was made Earl of Richmond. Jasper, the second, was created Earl of Pembroke, and it was in his tall western castle that the son of the Richmond family was born. The third brother, Owen, took holy orders. Of the two sisters, Jacina married Reginald, Lord Grey of Wilton; the other became a nun. It is said that the gentle Henry VI became quite fond of his half brothers and sisters and gave them every honor, save an acknowledgment of legitimacy.

Poor Katherine's body was not to be allowed the calm of one resting place. When Henry VII became king he found it necessary to demolish her tomb because he needed the space for the elaborate new chapel he was erecting. The epitaph her son had placed above her was removed and in its place a long poem was chiseled into the stone, concluding with these lines:

> Of Owen Tudor, after this, thy next son Edmund was,
> O Katherine! a renowned prince, that did in glory pass.
> Henry VII, a Britain pearl, a gem of England's joy,
> A peerless prince was Edmund's son, a good and gracious *roy;*
> Therefore a happy wife this was, a happy mother pure,
> Thrice happy child, but grand-dame she, more than thrice happy sure!

Thrice happy wife and mother! After this absurd and inelegant epitaph, could any historian of the day do else but assert the legitimacy of the union?

The tomb over the body of the dowager queen was never raised again, but the coffin was opened and it was found that the body had become almost mummified and had remained in an unusual state of preservation. The bier was kept open for three centuries for the benefit of curious visitors. In the reign of Charles II a fee of tuppence was charged for looking at the brown and wizened countenance. Samuel Pepys paid his tuppence and that night, in excessive bad taste, wrote in his diary that he "this day kissed a queen."

## CHAPTER IV

## The Red and the White

### 1

ENGLAND was tired of boy kings. There had been Henry III who was eight years old when they placed the crown on his head and who turned out to be a devious and petty man without dignity or courage. Then there had been Richard II who had too much dignity and great courage when aroused but who, after a good start, became a bad king. And now here was Henry VI, an infant of less than a year, with England in the midst of a major war and with two factions at home fighting for control of the government.

Nothing good could be expected under the circumstances. Henry became a gentle and devotional boy, with the qualities which often go with early piety—a little smugness, some stubbornness, and a certain inflexibility. He grew into a saintly man and it was a pity he could not have gone into the church. Certainly he was ill fitted to hold the factions in control, to direct the war in France, and, in the end, to fight a cruel civil war which went on and on, through triumphs and defeats, to end in his mysterious death in the Tower.

The dissensions at home were due, as usual, to royal uncles. Bedford the reliable, in whom the late king had trusted implicitly, was in command of the armies in France. The youngest of the surviving uncles, Humphrey of Gloucester, acted as protector. Although he had won the good will of the people, Humphrey was weak, rash, and selfish. He always put his own interests first and fatally weakened the English cause by antagonizing the Burgundians. The other faction was the Beauforts, descendants of John of Gaunt by his third wife, Katharine Swynford, who took their name from Beaufort Castle in Anjou, where the children had been born. This branch of the family had never been popular although they were handsome, polished, and able. The public dislike for them was due to a feeling that they were interlopers, and in equal degree perhaps to their wealth.

The strongest member of the Beauforts was Henry, the third of the original brothers, who had taken holy orders. He had become Bishop of Winchester and had been appointed chancellor by Henry V, holding that post when the warrior king died. Beaufort had a secret desire (which everyone suspected) to become Pope. If conditions had been different he might have achieved his ambition, having charm, a subtlety of wit, and a great gift for diplomacy, in addition to being the possessor of unusual wealth. But the schism in the papacy had become three-sided and the church was degenerating into a state almost of impotence. The result was a tendency in national churches to conduct their own affairs without much control from Rome or the other centers of the papal triangle.

Beaufort appeared at the Council of Constance, which had been called to discuss unification and reform, wearing the robe of a pilgrim. He played an important part in the election of Martin V as the one Pope and was made a cardinal as a reward. Later he was selected to direct a campaign in Bohemia against the religious reformers. If he had succeeded, he would have been an overwhelming favorite to follow Martin. This left him on the wrong side of the fence in England, where the people were convinced he put Roman interests first.

To counterbalance this weakness in his position, Beaufort had one great asset: he stood strongly for peace with France. This served to open a wider breach with Humphrey, who was openly for war. Humphrey, in fact, seems to have followed closely in the footsteps of the leading malcontent in Richard's reign, Thomas of Woodstock, in his ambitions and policies and, as it developed, in his sudden end.

The boy king inclined to the Beaufort side from the beginning. He liked his uncle Henry and had small regard for Humphrey. The cardinal, moreover, was always ready to advance money when it was needed. At one time the Crown owed him close to £30,000, a sum so great that it was believed he had been helped by others in raising the money. At several stages the hostility between the cardinal and "good Duke Humphrey," as the unthinking populace called him, blazed into open conflict. Throughout it all the young king maintained his personal preference for the cardinal and gave his full support to the movement for peace.

When Bedford died in 1435 it was plain to everyone, except perhaps to Duke Humphrey, that there was no longer any hope of a successful prolongation of the war. This gave Cardinal Beaufort the upper hand.

2

King Henry had reached his twenty-fourth year. He was handsome in a quiet way, but without the spectacular good looks which had become almost a hallmark of the family. None of the designing beauties about the court had succeeded in causing the slightest flicker in the royal eye. He dressed simply and refused to bedeck himself in sparkling regalia. Extremes of fashion were not for him and he even refused to wear the fancy shoes of the period. Henry's concern was more in the educational endowments he was setting up at Cambridge and Eton than in tournaments or masques, or in fact any form of court foolery. He eschewed the swearing of oaths and spent many hours each day over his prayers. A grave, studious, and earnest young man.

The time had come for a royal match to be arranged, and one day a Frenchman named Champchevrier brought a portrait for his inspection. It showed a young girl with the bluest of eyes and with golden hair in ringlets about a heart-shaped face. Someone has described her as a *petite créature*, and so it may be assumed that she was small and with, perhaps, the first hint of plumpness. The king, studying the canvas with eager interest, decided that she looked vivacious and intelligent as well as lovely.

He was asked if he thought her attractive and replied with his only expletive.

"St. John, yes!" he said.

It was the portrait of a French princess, Margaret of Anjou, who came from one of the most unfortunate and poverty-stricken of families. Her father, René of Anjou, had been captured in a struggle for territory and was paying off his ransom slowly and painfully—painful for those who had to collect the money but not for René, who was an enthusiastic dilettante in the arts and was more interested in his painting and in twanging out new melodies on the strings of a harp. The princess, who was just fifteen years of age, resembled her father in a lively appreciation of the arts, but in no other respect. She had a tongue which delighted everyone with its wit and which could counter with the most deadly riposte. A French commentator wrote of her: "There was no princess in Christendom more accomplished than my lady Margaret." And behind this entrancing façade there was, unsuspected as yet, a will of iron and a spirit which nothing could curb or extinguish.

Although the Angevin princess would have no dower, and territorial concessions had to be made (Parliament was furious at the need to give up several provinces), the match was arranged. The young Margaret had been staying at the French court and had so entranced the royal family that the king rode some distance with her when she began her journey to England, finally turning back with tears flowing down his cheeks. By the time the party reached England it was realized that the bride-to-be had practically no wardrobe. It would be a great mistake to let the people of England see her in such modest and even shabby clothes.

It happened that Henry was also short of funds at the time and he had to raise money in a great hurry, on the security of the Crown jewels. Margaret remained at Southampton until a dressmaker named Margaret Chamberlayne could get there, in a mad clatter of horse's hoofs, to make suitable clothes for her. It took some time to complete the work but finally Margaret was ready and was escorted to London, where she met the king for the first time. He thought her more lovely than the portrait. The people of London, forgetting their disapproval, were delighted with the diminutive beauty. This was a natural reaction for, of the royal consorts who had come from France, the impoverished little Angevin was acclaimed by common consent as the fairest of all. Her emblem flower, the daisy, was in every cap in London. Henry, already deeply in love, had the daisy engraved on all the royal saltcellars.

It was soon apparent that the young queen would dominate the king. When they had any differences, which was very seldom, her will prevailed. The king was so enamored of her that he ordered a costly program of decoration in all the royal residences, which had been allowed to fall into shabbiness and disrepair. He made no protest when she displayed her resentment openly over the efforts that Duke Humphrey had made to prevent the marriage. The good duke, in fact, found himself completely out of favor and compelled to stand by glumly while the Beauforts were accorded every favor. The king himself seldom saw his uncle and never did more than toss him a few grudging remarks.

The feud came to a head two years later. Parliament was summoned to meet at Bury St. Edmunds. It was early in February and the blustering winds heaped up snow in the streets, making it necessary to close all shutters and to huddle with candles over inadequate fires. Despite the hardships of travel, the queen accompanied her royal spouse and they arrived in the town with a large armed escort. The nobility had received orders to report in force and the town resounded with the tramp of armed feet. Over all this hung an air of mystery and suspense. Did the king anticipate an attack on his person? Men with blue noses huddled on street corners and asked one another this question.

The answer was supplied on the belated arrival of Duke Humphrey. He came with nearly a hundred horsemen in response to the general order. Half a mile from Bury he was met by royal heralds with orders to go at once to his lodgings in the North Spital of St. Saviour's. That evening a party of noblemen waited on him and put him under arrest on charges of treason.

The duke was dumbfounded at this. It had never occurred to him, apparently, that the course he had followed could be open to criticism. What he wanted to do himself must always be right and proper. Was he not high in the order of succession? If he found fault with the young king, and if he ran counter to national policy, as he had done in alienating the Duke of Burgundy, how could *he* be called to account?

At the same time three of his servants were placed under arrest on charges of plotting the death of the king. Three days later twenty-eight more of his men were seized and sent to various prisons throughout the country. Later they were tried, found guilty, and sentenced to death, although the tenderhearted king did not allow the sentences to be carried out. All this was unknown to the duke, who had fallen into a coma. He had been in bad health for some time, owing to early excesses and debauchery, and the shock was too much for him. Five days later it was announced that he was dead.

Considering the slowness of all means of communication, the news of his death swept across England with great speed and, of course, caused rumors of foul play. Was this not a repetition of the death of Thomas of Woodstock? The people do not seem to have blamed the king, whose reputation for saintliness was too well founded for that. They thought of many other reasons for the supposed murder, including the inevitable supposition that the sweet voice of the beautiful French wife, who was known to have been at odds with Humphrey, had whispered in the royal ear.

All the troubled events of the next forty years stem back to this unexplained episode. Certainly it was a major issue in the civil struggle known as the Wars of the Roses.

The body of the duke was displayed in both houses of Parliament and showed no signs of violence. It seems reasonable to suppose that he died from a stroke (it was referred to as palsy in the records) to which he had succumbed quickly.

As Cardinal Beaufort died in the next month, the administration of national affairs was jointly assumed by Edmund Beaufort, now the Duke of Somerset, and the Duke of Suffolk, a grandson of that able commoner and wool merchant, William de la Pole of Hull. The people of England might have been expected to feel some pride that one of their number had thus broken through the barriers of class distinctions, especially as Suffolk did the best that mortal could do with the difficulties created by the war. Instead he was heartily disliked. The evil fortune which pursued the Poles culminated finally in his exile and murder at the hands of sailors on the ship which was taking him from England.

But that is getting ahead of the sequence of events. For a number of years Edmund Beaufort and Suffolk worked together as heads of the administration. Henry was fond of detail and liked to attend meetings of the council, where he would personally dispose of some petitions and minor appointments. It was known that both of the chief ministers took problems of greater importance to the alert and opinionated queen.

After the death of Duke Humphrey, the discontented people had to find a substitute for him and they turned instinctively to Richard of York.

Edward III left five sons: Edward (the Black Prince), Lionel of Antwerp, John of Gaunt, Edmund of York, and Thomas of Woodstock. This Richard of York was descended from Lionel through his mother and from Edmund of York through his father and so had a clearer claim to the throne than the sons of John of Gaunt. It happened that those of the line of Lionel in the previous generation had shown little ambition and little, if any, desire to push their claims. Those stemming from the house of York had been equally unobtrusive. Conspiracies had been hatched in their interests but without their consent or participation.

In his youth Richard of York had been described as having "a perturbed, unruly and audacious mind." It was clear that he was a man of stouter mettle than his immediate forebears. He was truly Plantagenet in appearance and in the thoughts and ambitions which filled his mind. In his list of titles he almost equaled the late John of Gaunt: Duke of York, Earl of March, Earl of Ulster, Lord of Wigmore, Clare, Trim and Connaught. In his youth it had been impossible to put him under restraint, as was so often done in England with those who stood too close to the throne. He could not be confined to the Tower and refused the right to marry. In fact, he made a most advantageous match, wedding Cicely Neville. His wife, who was beautiful and of an ambitious turn of mind (her envious friends called her Proud Cis), brought him great possessions, so that he had many castles and retainers by the thousands. Richard of York was, in fact, an able leader and in every respect more fitted to rule than the gentle custodian of the throne. If it became necessary to make a change, he was the inevitable choice and in his heart Richard of York wanted the chance to come. He was prepared, if it did come, to move as swiftly and as vigorously as Henry IV had done.

Nothing of these inner feelings showed as yet on the surface. He was appointed to a command in France and acquitted himself well. When the Beaufort influence led to a division of the command with Edmund of Somerset, he accepted the change unwillingly and was soon justified in his attitude by the feebleness with which Edmund conducted his part of the campaigns. Then he was appointed governor of Ireland and spent some years there, realizing that it was a form of exile but striving to rule that sadly misgoverned land as well as he could, and thereby winning the affections of the people.

### 3

While Richard of York was in Ireland, a rebellion started among the men of Kent, fomented by an old soldier from Ireland who claimed to be descended from the noble family of Mortimer. It developed that his real name was Jack Cade, or Jack the Cnape, the knave (from which comes the expression "jackanapes"). He marched with a large army to London and made a military encampment at Blackheath, guided perhaps by the memory of Wat Tyler and John Ball. Cade's experience as a soldier on the continent showed in the care he took to fortify his position with ditches and earthworks and in the stern discipline he maintained in the ranks.

The rumor spread through London, and then reached all parts of the country, that Cade was acting in the interests of Richard of York. The king marched to Blackheath at the head of an army of 10,000 men. The rebels declared they sought the removal of certain traitors from the royal council and then withdrew as far as Sevenoaks in Kent. Henry sent part of his force in pursuit under the command of Sir Humphrey Stafford and his brother William, but Cade had left an ambuscade into which the Staffords fell. The royal troops were cut to pieces and both of the Staffords were killed. Flushed with success, Cade came back to Blackheath, having arrayed himself in the "bryganders, gilt nails and all, and the salet and gilt spurs" which had belonged to the slain Humphrey Stafford.

Henry did not display in this crisis the courage that Richard, the boy king, had shown in facing the peasants under Tyler. It seemed to him and his council that the prudent course was to go to Kenilworth and he was at this safe distance when the rebels broke up and betook themselves back to their furrows and benches. Some of those who were brought to trial later declared that the Duke of York had instigated the uprising. Unquestionably this story had circulated in the ranks.

The story finally reached the ears of Richard of York in Ireland. He decided he must return and face the charges against him, but he was too shrewd to go at once to Westminster and put himself in the royal power. The king was gentle and peace-loving, but there was a complete lack of these qualities in those about him. To use a modern expression, Richard decided he must go in a conciliatory spirit but carrying a big stick. Accordingly he wrote to all his friends and liege men, advising them of his plan. As a result of this precaution, he found on landing in Wales that his friends were indeed rallying around him. As many as 4000 men had assembled to meet him, all armed for conflict and all wearing the symbol of the house of York in their bonnets.

The Yorkist leader marched with these loyal liege men at his back by the quickest roads to London. Forcing his way into the royal presence, he not only protested his innocence but vigorously assailed those he deemed responsible for pressing the accusation. One version of the scene between the two men was that the king spoke "as if inspired by the spirit of God" and succeeded in subduing the aroused temper of his Yorkist cousin. The first part may be accepted as true, for Henry had become very sure of himself and he was convinced, moreover, that he stood rather high in divine esteem. But it is almost equally certain that the conclusion drawn as to the effect on Richard was quite wrong. He listened to the fair speaking of the king, but subsequent events prove that he went away from the royal presence convinced he must take extreme steps. The only certain outcome of the meeting was an agreement that Parliament must be summoned at once to consider the situation.

Richard of York then held a consultation with his chief supporters, who included the Duke of Norfolk, the Earl of Salisbury, and other members of the powerful Neville family. Attention should be called to the presence in this group of one of Salisbury's sons, Richard Neville, who had married Anne Beauchamp, sole surviving child of the great Earl of Warwick. This young man had been created Earl of Warwick when the father of his wife died and so had become one of the largest landholders in this kingdom of immense baronial power. He was to play a remarkable part in the drama of the civil war which soon followed.

As a result of this conference, Richard of York absented himself from court and retired to Fotheringhay to await the parliamentary hearings. The story spread that in this great feudal castle the duke began to bear himself in a regal way and that his wife, Proud Cis, established a fair imitation of a throne room where she received with equal regality.

The sessions of the House, which began on November 30, were chiefly notable for a demonstration of the lack of unity among the members, particularly the nobility. The Yorkist members attended with the family symbol in their hats, the Snow Rose. Those who could not obtain flowers at this late time of the year fashioned roses from white paper which they wore boldly in their bonnets or on their sleeves. The royalist wing was quick to meet this showing of opposition solidarity. They bedecked themselves with the Red Rose, which John of Gaunt had many years before selected as his symbol. The depth of the breach was made clear when Queen Margaret, whose fiery spirit made her partisan, wore a red rose defiantly in her hair and even persuaded the king to make his appearance in the house with the Lancastrian rose on his cloak.

It was this showing of partisan temper which sowed the seeds of conflict in England. The Red and the White! For years men were to fight and die, with the fury which can be aroused most fiercely in civil war, under banners carrying the rival colors.

4

The jostling of the rival wearers of roses did not lead to hostilities at once, as Richard of York was not accused openly in Parliament of participation in the Jack Cade rebellion. Henry then proceeded to go up and down through the counties in a seemingly endless processional. This was his invariable answer to criticism and opposition. He seems to have believed that people needed nothing more than a chance to see him to bring them into line with royal policy. When the slow progress of the long trains of court attendants led to a royal residence, a stop would be made there; otherwise they sought hospitality of the nearest great holder of land. It was an honor to entertain the king but an expensive one. Cattle, sheep, and hogs had to be slaughtered every day, to say nothing of the wholesale raids made on chicken roosts and duck ponds and the mad riding of menials to bring fresh fish every day from the sea. Tuns of wine were broached almost daily and the consumption of beer was an appalling item on the statistics of such a visitation. A fortnight of this, even a week, and the much honored host found himself without a flitch of bacon left.

Then, in the spring of 1453, the word was bruited about that the queen, after nearly nine years of barrenness, would soon present her lord the king, and the nation, with an heir to the throne. Henry, alas, was in no position to rejoice over the prospect. Although he continued his dull and monotonous round of processionals, he was obviously in the worst of health. His advisers, remembering with dread the anarchy created in France by the periodical spells of insanity suffered by Charles VI, watched him with anxious eyes. Had he inherited this Valois tendency through his mother?

Henry's hopeful travels had taken him to Clarendon and there on July 6 the Valois curse descended on him. The light of reason flickered out in his mind and his body became almost completely impotent. He lay in a coma, unable to speak or hear, or even to move voluntarily a muscle of his body. The intelligence was received by the people with more grief and alarm than news of a military defeat; they had suffered through so many defeats that they were becoming inured, although not reconciled, to them. But what would happen to the nation now?

At first nothing happened. The Crown advisers continued to function under the watchful eye and the sometimes imperious guidance of the queen. The unconscious king was taken to Windsor. He did not suffer from the neglect in which the French king had existed. In fact, he was most carefully tended and fed, even though there was no sign of intelligence in his eyes. He never spoke and certainly did not indulge in the maniacal outcries of his maternal grandfather.

The royal child was born on October 13, 1453. It was a boy and the name of Edward was given him. The country, which should have rejoiced, was disturbed by rumors and baseless canards. It was said that the father of the child was Edmund Beaufort, Duke of Somerset, the minister so obnoxious to the people but so much favored by Margaret herself. Other stories followed, equally false, that the queen's child had died and that a boy of low degree had been spirited into the palace and put in the cradle of the deceased heir. It was declared that the unfortunate king, if he ever found it possible to speak again, would refuse to recognize the child as his. This wave of calumny resulted finally in a public statement by the Earl of Warwick at St. Paul's Cross that the supposed heir was the child of adultery and that the claims made for him were a fraud.

Queen Margaret, so gentle and lovely in appearance but so determined and unyielding in spirit, was furious over these vile aspersions. At first she could do nothing about them because Richard of York had not joined in the campaign of slander. But when the first hint reached her from Windsor that the king was showing some improvement under the enlightened care of Dean Kemer of Salisbury, who was accounted the wisest man of medicine in the kingdom, the queen decided to make a test. She took her infant son to Windsor, hoping that the sight of the boy would bring back the king's reason.

At the door of the sick chamber the queen confided the infant to the Earl of Buckingham and the latter carried him in. He came back shortly and shook his head. Henry was propped up in bed but had given no sign of intelligence. Queen Margaret still believed that her husband could be brought back to sanity and she carried the infant into the chamber a second time. She knelt at the side of the royal couch.

She implored the king to give his blessing to the boy. Henry's face remained without expression. He had not recognized her and nothing that was said aroused a spark of understanding in the weakened brain.

This failure was a sad blow to the royal party. Parliament convened in February of the next year, faced with the problem of naming a protector for the term of the king's mental incompetence. Richard of York presided and the tenor of the House was strongly against allowing the queen's officials to remain in power. Margaret asked to be appointed regent, but the request was set aside.

A report reached Westminster that the king was showing signs of improvement and a deputation of lords was sent down to get firsthand information. The report, however, had been premature. Henry again was sitting up in bed. He was obviously very weak although the attendants said he had partaken of a good meal. There was not a flicker of interest or recognition in his eyes. The lords addressed him earnestly and imploringly but failed to arouse the sick monarch. They returned to London, therefore, convinced that some definite decision must be reached.

On March 27 they elected Richard of York protector for the term of the heir's minority or until the king recovered his senses. The new head of state proceeded to direct things with a firm hand. The Duke of Somerset was arrested and committed to the Tower. The offices of the chancellery were cleared of all the Beaufort appointees, and Yorkist supporters put in their places. Richard's brother-in-law, the Earl of Salisbury was made chancellor. When Archbishop Kemp of Canterbury died, his successor was not William Waynflete, Bishop of Winchester and the great friend of both king and queen, but Bishop Bourchier of Ely, who traced his descent back to Thomas of Woodstock. In France the new head of state was able to check the French and to hold Calais and the island of Jersey from attack.

On Christmas Day, King Henry showed the first real signs of returning sanity. Two days later he sent substantial offerings to Canterbury and Westminster, a clear indication that the royal mind was awakening and beginning to function along normal lines. The queen waited for further confirmation and then on December 30 she took the infant Edward to Windsor. This time she did not stand on ceremony but, holding the prince in her arms, hurried to the cabinet of the king.

Henry was sitting up as usual, but this time there was a difference. There was a light in his eyes which turned quickly to recognition. The queen placed their son in his arms.

The king was still very weak and showing signs of having wakened from a long dream. But he seemed to recognize the child without difficulty.

"What name has he been given?" he asked.

"Edward," replied the queen.

The thin, grave face of the king responded with a smile. "Good," he whispered. "That is good."

Soon after, he was able to converse coherently and he told Margaret, to quote from the *Paston Letters*, that "he never knew him till this time, nor wist what was said to him, nor wist where he had been whilst sick till now."

Further evidence of the clearing of his mind was provided during the day. He asked the names of his son's godfathers and commented on the death of Cardinal Beaufort, "one of the wisest lords in this land," and he was able to sing matins and join in evensong later in the day. Several days later Bishop Waynflete came to Windsor and spoke with the reviving monarch at some length, emerging from the chamber at the finish weeping for joy.

Henry was so much better, in fact, and Margaret so impatient, that he was taken soon thereafter to London. Here he was led before the lords in session to declare the dissolution of the House. Margaret wanted to be free of parliamentary interference in the course of action she had decided to follow. The face of fortune had been turned from the royal pair for a long time, but now it turned to them with a smile. The queen acted with characteristic decision in taking advantage of the change. Her innocent blue eyes emitted sparks of triumph and determination and she did not propose to wait for parliamentary sanction. It is highly unlikely that she disturbed the still inactive mind of the king for advice before she began to wield the broom of change with vigorous hand. Richard of York was dismissed from the protectorate and was even excluded from the council. Archbishop Bourchier, who had been holding the post of chancellor, was wafted through the door of his temporal office. Every Yorkist official, major or minor, was sent away.

The Duke of Somerset was released from the Tower and put in York's place. Waynflete replaced Bourchier as chancellor. All Westminster was filled with Lancastrian supporters.

Richard was not disposed to accept these summary proceedings. He called his supporters together, particularly the members of the powerful Neville family, and it was decided to dispute the issue by force of arms. An army of 3000 men was assembled in the northern counties and along the borders of Wales, and a march on London was begun.

At Ware, a Hertfordshire town about twenty-five miles from London,

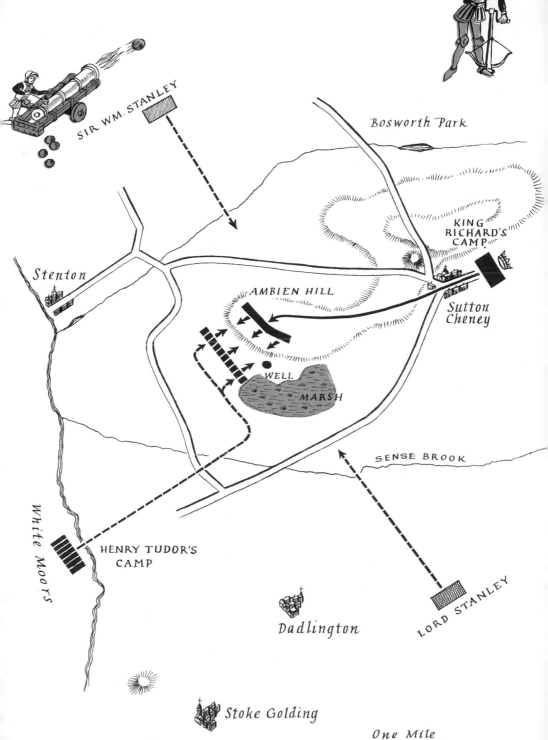

# The BATTLE of
# BOSWORTH

SIR WM. STANLEY

Bosworth Park

KING
RICHARD'S
CAMP

Stenton

AMBIEN HILL

Sutton
Cheney

WELL
MARSH

SENSE BROOK

White Moors

HENRY TUDOR'S
CAMP

Dadlington

LORD STANLEY

Stoke Golding

One Mile

map by palacios

the advancing Yorkists paused and Richard sent a letter to the king, protesting his loyalty. They were so close to the capital that there would have been small opportunity for the slowly recovering monarch to do much about this avowal. But, as it developed, Somerset intercepted the letter. The same day the royal army, consisting of 2000 men, marched out to meet the rebel forces. They came together at St. Albans, where a sharp battle was fought on May 22.

A very large broom in the hands of a very small queen had precipitated the start of the Wars of the Roses.

## 5

The first battle of the long drawn-out civil war was a rather muddled affair which showed little evidence of strategic planning on either side. The Yorkists came down the Great North Road in considerable haste, for they realized that sentiment in London favored them. The royalists, appreciating this also, wanted to meet the rebel forces as far away from the city as possible. They struck out at a tangent for Watford, intending to follow Watling Street to Leicester. This left the road to London wide open. But when they reached Royston, the Yorkists learned what King Henry had done. They decided to offer battle and swung westward through Ware and Hatfield to St. Albans, arriving there a few hours after the army of the king.

St. Albans straggled along the southern and western end of a high ridge. St. Peter's Street ran through the center of town, past Castle Inn and the abbey. Paralleling this on the east was the town ditch surmounted by a palisade, which the Lancastrians had already taken over when the Yorkists arrived. The Yorkist attack had to be launched, therefore, along the two main roads running into town from the east, Shropshire Lane and Sopwell Lane. When they came to the ditch they found the palisade swarming with the soldiers of the king. This brought them to a dead stop.

It happened, however, that the Lancastrian leaders had massed their troops behind the palisades opposite the two main roads and had left a long space between unoccupied. This mistake was responsible for the birth of a legend, the belief held thereafter and presented in many histories, that the young Earl of Warwick was a great general. He had the good fortune to be leading his column up between the two main roads and found no opposition in his path. He took advantage of this by sending his men in to cross the ditch and climb the undefended palisades. There were private gardens on the other side, through which the eager troops plunged, coming to a brick wall which they had to batter down before reaching St. Peter's Street. The young earl proudly led them out into the center of town, brandishing his sword and shouting, "A Warwick! A Warwick!"

There was no trace of the enemy in that part, so Warwick divided his forces and had them wheel right and left to catch the king's troops in the rear.

This decided the issue. The Lancastrians had been outnumbered to begin with and the Yorkists had been recruited from men with long experience in the French wars, archers for the most part. The defending army was packed so closely into two pockets that they could not do anything. Under cover of a continuous flight of arrows, Warwick's men took them in the flanks and proceeded to demolish them.

This battle demonstrated the absurd pass to which chivalry had reduced the art of war. Armor had become so cumbersome and heavy that the knights had to dismount and fight on foot. The result was a complete lack of mobility in tactical operations. The brave knights had to remain where they were and wait for the enemy to attack. If the enemy also fought by the code, it would sometimes happen that the two armies would line up face to face and proceed to fight it out with sword and mace and dagger. But if one side maneuvered about to attack from the most advantageous direction, the stationary knights were badly at a loss, being unable to change their base. When the issue had been decided, the knights on the losing side could not reach the horse lines to mount and be off. All they could do was to turn at bay and face death or capture (which was often the same thing) at the hands of the victorious foe.

The heavy losses sustained by the nobility in the battles of the Wars of the Roses were due to being thus shackled by the code. The archers and foot soldiers, wearing nothing heavier than leather jerkins, could get away from the field and scatter for safety, but the knights were anchored in muddy fields.

King Henry had been in a bellicose mood the night before the battle. "By the faith I owe St. Edward," he had cried, "I shall destroy them, every mother's son! They shall be hanged and drawn and quartered!" But when the battle began, he felt in a different mood. He was not a coward but he dreaded bloodshed and would have no part in it himself. In full armor he occupied a tent under the royal standard, which had been unfurled on St. Peter's Street. When the right half of Warwick's column came down the road, driving all opposition before it, the royal tent was surrounded after being riddled with arrows. The king was found sitting on the ground beside the Duke of Buckingham, both of them wounded. The king had been hit in the neck by an arrow, the duke in the face. The royal guards had taken to their heels.

"Forsooth and forsooth," said Henry quietly.

When Richard of York arrived, his face flushed and triumphant, the king issued a brusque order. "Stop this slaughter of my subjects!"

Henry's wound was attended to, it being slight, and he was led down St. Peter's Street to the nearest house, which belonged to a tanner. Here he remained until he could be removed safely to the abbey for the night. On the way, they saw on the steps of the Castle Inn the body of the Duke of Somerset, who had fallen early in the battle.

Henry was not treated as a prisoner. Richard of York and the Earl of Warwick knelt before him and asked to be forgiven. The king nodded gravely and said that he bore them no ill will. When sufficiently recovered from his wound, he rode to London with the victors and entered the city in great state.

Queen Margaret, who had remained behind at Coventry with the infant prince, took him with her to the royal palace at Greenwich. With indomitable will, she began to issue calls for assistance to all in England and abroad who were favorable to the cause of the Red Rose. It was at this time that her ill wishers began to call her *Captain Marguerite.*

## CHAPTER V

## *The Gentle Henry*

### 1

THE war between the Lancastrians and the Yorkists could possibly have been brought to a quick conclusion after the victory of the White Rose at St. Albans, as Henry IV had done after the capture of Richard. If Richard of York had overcome his scruples about removing his cousin and had declared his own claim to the throne, he would have found little organized resistance at this point. He held Henry as his prisoner, and there had been heavy mortality at St. Albans in the ranks of the nobility who sported the Red Rose. The determined queen, flying for safety from Coventry with her young son, was in no position to act promptly in raising more battalions. London was loud in support of Richard, and in Parliament the Lancastrian element was not in a position to fight for a captive king.

Parliament met on July 9 and, as York made no determined move, the loyalty of all the lords assembled was pledged to the king. Henry suffered another attack later and York was made protector when the House met again in November.

By this time, things had settled down. The armed contingents had been disbanded; the rival roses were no longer worn on the streets. It developed that Henry's attack was of a much less serious character. At any rate he retained sufficient sanity to be consulted on state decisions. In February of the next year, the king emerged with suddenness from his seclusion and declared himself fit to assume all his duties again. He was willing to continue Richard of York as his chief councilor, but on that point a small feminine foot came down with unmistakable vehemence. No, declared Queen Margaret, there would be no more of that. Henry was king and would rule as a king; and the Yorkist element must be removed. Henry gave in and dismissed his cousin of York from office.

And so it went. The fortunes of war swayed back and forth. Bloody battles were fought. Sometimes the White Rose was in the ascendant, more frequently at first the Red. The king continued to suffer from attacks of his mental malady and the queen remained adamant in her attitude, refusing to agree to any concessions.

The story of the long drawn-out struggle, if told at full length, would prove both repetitious and monotonous. The chief interest in the period lies in the cast of unusual characters who played the leading parts: Henry himself, a man of true devotion but limited mental capacity and with little steel in his composition, who would gladly have played a part of passive resistance in this cycle of violence, a medieval Gandhi; Richard of York, a second John of Gaunt in that his scruples sometimes outweighed his ambition, but who had courage and capacity; the Earl of Warwick, showy, brilliant, lucky (at the start), who emerged as the ablest man of the day and won in history the name of the Kingmaker, a bold, aggressive leader but lacking in many of the higher qualities; Margaret, the beautiful and brilliant queen, who had more fighting spirit in her than any of the men concerned but was utterly lacking in such qualities as fairness, moderation, and foresight; the two sons of Richard of York who were both to rule England later as Edward IV and Richard III.

Perhaps the best method to tell of this stormy period, without resorting to the tedium of chronological narration, will be to deal with these people and allow the story to emerge through the record of their activities.

2

Before going any further into the part that Henry VI played in the long years of war, a more complete picture should be given of the man.

He was a second Job, as is made evident in all the stories which have been collected about him. A prelate who acted for ten years as his confessor declared there had never been a mortal sin to be forgiven. In church he never sat at his ease or got up and paced about as royal individuals with less patience did, but knelt with bowed head throughout. He went bareheaded to chapel, even when it was necessary to go by horseback. He preferred a row of crosses on the royal crown to the customary flowers or leaves. Members of the nobility were never permitted to carry their hawks into church (a common practice, for they wanted to get out into the fields immediately), and if he saw them wearing swords or daggers, he sent orders to have the weapons removed.

His modesty and chastity were almost beyond belief in an age when all men had mistresses and sly talk of Moll Tear-sheets monopolized male conversation. Nakedness made him angry. Once at court a nobleman brought in a woman to dance in a Christmas play. Her bosom was bare and the king went at once to his chamber, muttering, "Fy, fy, for shame!"

Although it was necessary to fight for sufficient funds to maintain the army and navy at fighting strength, he never desired money for himself. When Cardinal Beaufort left him £2000 in his will, he refused at first to accept it and only relented when he realized the money could be applied to his college endowments. On one occasion a nobleman, seeking official favors, no doubt, gave him a coverlet set with gold and encrusted with precious stones. It was too grand to give away (for it would rouse sinful pride in the recipient), but he never liked it and, moreover, never slept under it.

At the table he was abstemious and frugal, being desirous that as much food as possible should be saved for the poor. He said grace standing and there was a rule in the royal household that a certain kind of food was to be served first, one that represented the five wounds of Christ. Before this dish he would pause so long in prayerful contemplation that the appetites of his guests became sharp and impatient.

In an age that ran to every kind of extreme and sinful extravagance, he dressed simply. He wore shoes, in fact, with the round toes of a farmer and, as has already been pointed out, he regarded the absurdly turned-up toes of dress shoes as abominations of the Evil One. Except on occasions when he had to wear robes of state, he dressed in long and somber gowns with rolled hoods, in which he resembled the common men of the towns. His coats fell below his knees and were almost invariably black. To offset the vanity of his kingly robes on state occasions he always wore a hair shirt next to his skin. There is nothing on record to indicate how the beautiful queen reacted to his monkish attire. Having been raised in a poverty-stricken household, she herself liked to be arrayed in luscious silks and the voluptuous softness of velvet.

Reading in the Scriptures was a daily habit with the king. "Forsooth and forsooth!" and "By St. John!" were his only expletives. He could never be roused to profanity, even by a stampede of pack horses on a night march or the blowing over of the royal tent by heavy winds.

On the grim occasion when he rode to London from the defeat at St. Albans, he stopped the cavalcade of triumphant Yorkists in which he rode to protest the sight in Cripplegate of a man's quarter displayed on the end of a pike. When told that the victim of dismemberment had been convicted as a traitor to him, he ordered the decaying flesh to be taken down at once and buried. Seemingly this was his first contact with the way in which the parts of convicted traitors were distributed

about the kingdom as a favor. It must have been that he paid no heed
to the heads which rotted over London Bridge. He said on this occasion,
"I will not have any Christian man so cruelly handled."

No attention was paid to him on such points. Heads were chopped
off and bodies were mutilated after every battle or brush of the Wars of
the Roses. He strove to assert his views at times. Once he took it on
himself to send a mounted messenger at the last moment with pardons
for four noblemen who had been condemned to barbarous death; and
there was much angry stamping of heels in the chancellery offices because of it. He even forgave a man who plunged through his guards
and wounded him in the neck. Punishment was contrary to his nature
and to the end of his days he shuddered at the deaths men died for
breaking the laws and bewailed that he was not permitted to interfere.

It will be seen from this that he was gentle almost beyond belief
and unfitted for the part in the furious struggle imposed upon him by
the accident of birth. Not that he objected to being a king (when has
any ruler honestly desired to be relieved of office?), for he often defended his right to the throne with a solemn and stilted insistence. "My
father was born a king," he would declare, "and possessed the crown
all his life. His father, my grandfather, was king before him. I, as a boy,
crowned almost in my cradle, was accepted as king by the whole realm,
and have worn the crown for nearly forty years."

No, the gentle Henry did not desire to relinquish his high office. He
clung to it through defeat and distress and even when he wandered
as a fugitive, hungry and ragged, in the woods and caves of the north.

After some years of hollow peace, Henry displayed in 1459 an unexpected burst of energy and met the Yorkist forces at Ludlow. By issuing
at once an offer of clemency to anyone in arms against him, he split
the opposing forces. Their leaders had to scatter, Richard of York going to Ireland. Warwick refused to be deprived of his governorship of
Calais and in the following year he came back with a daring which
clearly marked him as a great leader. He was greeted by eager enlistments in the south and east of England. Marching north with this
new army, he defeated the royal forces at Northampton and again captured the king in his tent. As York was still in Ireland, Warwick did not
take any decisive steps and allowed Henry to enter London in state,
he himself marching in front of the king and carrying the sword of
state.

Following in eager haste, Richard of York began his ride to London
to make his belated claim to the throne. He saw to it first that his wife was
released from the custody of her sister, the Duchess of Buckingham,
where she had been held in unsympathetic severity. Richard's horizon

had now widened and he entered the capital with 500 mounted men, riding under banners with the arms of England and trumpeters blowing loudly. He went straight to the royal palace at Westminster and broke open the door of the king's apartments. Hearing this forcible entry and the tumult in the halls behind, Henry quietly offered his chambers to his cousin and withdrew to the less imposing quarters belonging to the absent consort.

As Parliament had convened, York lost no time in facing the members. He walked to the empty throne and placed a hand on one of the arms as though to take possession. Then, in a moment fatal to himself and his claims, he paused and looked about him. The members, and in particular the lords and bishops, were watching him under dark and unfriendly brows. He failed to detect any responsive or encouraging gleam in the packed room, and so he hesitated.

Archbishop Bourchier rose from his seat. "My lord duke," he asked, "do you desire to see the king?"

Richard replied in passionate tones, "I know no one in the kingdom who ought not rather to wait on me!"

But the vital moment had passed. York did no more than state his intention of claiming the throne. On October 16 he presented his case, outlining his descent from Edward III and claiming the action of Henry IV, who had taken possession of the throne, to be illegal. There followed some days of talk, the duke's claim being presented first to the king for his comments. Finally the lords got their courage up to the point of telling the claimant that his right "could not be defeated" but that they had sworn allegiance to Henry and could not now take any action to dethrone him.

The outcome of all this convening and arguing and dodging of issues was a decision to allow Henry to retain the throne for the balance of his life. Richard of York was to be appointed protector and was to succeed to the throne on the king's death. York accepted this arrangement.

Henry agreed humbly enough, but Margaret, who was with her son in Wales, was furiously opposed to thus depriving the young prince of his rights. She cut off all communication with her husband and began with grim determination to raise another army. Undoubtedly Henry knew of her activities but he made no effort to escape from London and join her. He seems to have become fascinated by the Earl of Warwick, who was so different from himself, possessing in such superlative degree the tough will and the unshakable resolution of the born leader. The deep and compelling eyes of the young earl won the easily swayed predilections of the king. They even shared their Christmas dinner together in the bishop's palace at St. Paul's, in mutual comfort and good spirits.

But Margaret was now riding a high horse. She no longer had to defer to the sweet acquiescences of the peace-loving Henry but made her own decisions, which were inevitably selfish as well as sharp and severe. Her call for assistance had aroused the latent Lancastrian sentiment and armed forces came to her assistance from all parts of the country.

A tendency to turn coats, which would become general later and play a great part in succeeding phases of the struggle, made itself evident at this point. Richard of York sent Lord Neville, a brother of the Earl of Westmorland, to put down the levies which the queen was recruiting in Wales. The latter promptly took his forces over to the queen's banner, and the north country began to blaze with Lancastrian activities. York parted from his wife and family and rode north to face the uprising.

He discovered quickly that he had underestimated the movement which the queen had succeeded in stirring up. The Earl of Northumberland and Lord Clifford had put the Red Rose on their helmets. The young Duke of Somerset, thirsting to avenge his father's death, and the Earl of Devonshire had marched from the west to join the queen. York should have waited for reinforcements but he seems to have acquired by this time a firm belief in his star. He attacked the marching columns of the Duke of Somerset and, to his deep chagrin, was thrown off with heavy losses. As a result of this setback, he found it advisable to retire into his castle of Sandal. The Lancastrian forces closed in from all directions.

York was advised by his friends to wait until help could reach him from London, but he refused to listen. He declared that he had never been "caged like a bird." And so he led his devoted followers out to face the heavy forces arrayed against him. The struggle which ensued is called in history the Battle of Wakefield. It resulted inevitably in the defeat of the Yorkists and the deaths of the duke himself, his second son, and his great friend, the Earl of Salisbury.

The exultation of the victors was carried to the extent of cutting off the duke's head from his sadly mutilated body and raising it on the point of a pike above the gates of York, with a crown of paper on his brow.

The crowning humiliation of Henry's life followed his wife's victory in the north. Warwick, outwardly his good friend, hastily assembled his forces and marched out of London to give battle to the queen, supremely confident that he would roll up the Lancastrian lines and end the war.

Henry was taken along and was even induced to arm himself for the approaching conflict. In the second Battle of St. Albans which followed, Queen Margaret was given credit for bold and original tactics. The victory she won was complete and the Yorkists melted away before her. Henry was left, still in shining armor, to face his triumphant and contemptuous mate.

It was almost impossible to quarrel with Henry and so it may be assumed that the brilliant blue eyes of the queen finally softened at the sight of his humility. He was allowed to bless and confer knighthood on his son, a rite which he undertook with affectionate eagerness. But she could not bring herself to acknowledge the promise of immunity which Henry had given to two Yorkshire knights remaining behind to guard him, Lord Bonville and Sir Thomas Kyriel. Her temper rose at the sight of them and she took a step which revealed the real depth of her animosity. She put them on trial and appointed her son to preside. "Fair son," she asked, "what death shall these knights die?" The boy expressed his opinion that their heads should be cut off. The king, his eyes filled with tears, entreated mercy for them, but no heed was paid to him. The two men were executed.

By this time the queen seems to have become unbalanced. She was ready to agree to any terms to gain the aid of France and Scotland, even when the sacrifice of English interests was involved. Pierre de Brézé, the seneschal of Normandy, who had been sent over with troops to assist her, and who seems to have been devoted to her at first, and even personally enamored, finally became disillusioned. He wrote a letter to the King of France in which he said: "If those with her knew her intentions, and what she has done, they would join themselves with the other party and put her to death."

It is said that Margaret did not march into London after her brilliant success in the second Battle of St. Albans because her army was made up of undisciplined levies and mercenaries from the continent and she feared to turn them loose on the wealthy capital city. That was not the real reason. She knew how ill the Londoners felt about her and did not want to deepen the animosity. She contented herself, therefore, with sending demands for money and supplies for her army. She had been right about the sentiment of London. Her emissaries were not allowed inside the gates. The lord mayor, with an eye to the main chance perhaps, loaded some wagons with food and military supplies to be sent to her. The citizens promptly seized the carts and divided up the contents themselves.

## CHAPTER VI

## The Fourth Edward

1

THERE was clear evidence now that the Plantagenet stock
was changing with the passing of the years and becoming diluted
through foreign marriages. The uniformity of stature, the strength, the
startling good looks were not as apparent as before. Other strains were
showing themselves: the flaxen hair of the Netherlands, the Valois nose,
the Castilian duskiness, the black hair of the Mortimers. But at this stage
there entered on the scene a young man who was completely and
perfectly Plantagenet.

Edward, Earl of March, oldest son of Richard of York, stood six foot
three in his bare feet. He had the exact shade of blue eyes, the strong
but handsome features, the proper share of gold in his hair. The age
had many expressions of characteristic vulgarity meaning the same as
the later and more polite "squire of dames," and they fitted Edward as
closely as the hose on his splendid legs. It was said that he owed his
popularity in London to the secret passion that all housewives entertained
for him. Even when he reached middle age and became heavy, even a
little bloated as well as careless in his dress, he was still so handsome
that women could not resist him.

He had in his heart no scruples, no mercy, no fear. And of supreme
importance at this point in history, he had a fighting heart and a gift
for generalship which put him head and shoulders above the other
leaders of the day. In his mastery of strategy, he inclined to what was
sometimes called the modern school, the enlightened methods of warfare
introduced by another Englishman a century before, that superlative
leader of professional armies, John Hawkwood.

The Wars of the Roses did not end at once with Edward's appearance on the scene, but the ultimate triumph of the White Rose became inevitable.

Unaware at first of his father's defeat and death, young Edward moved out of Shrewsbury with a large army to join Richard in the north. At Gloucester he learned of the disaster at Wakefield and realized that the finger of destiny had touched his shoulder. It was now his right, or at least his opportunity, to win the throne of England. Pausing long enough to recruit his army to 30,000 men, he wheeled south and destroyed at Mortimer's Cross an army of mercenaries from France, Brittany, and Ireland under the Earl of Wiltshire and one of the king's half brothers, Jasper Tudor. It was here that a miracle of nature was observed. Before the battle began there appeared to be three suns in the sky and this, for some reason, convinced Edward that he was certain to win.

It was not the nature of this nineteen-year-old leader to delay or to temper his designs with devious reasoning. He marched straight to a junction with the defeated army of Warwick and then on to London, while Margaret withdrew into the north. A council was held at Baynard's Castle and the young victor had no difficulty in convincing the others present that he was now the rightful King of England. The next day, March 4, 1461, he walked into Westminster Hall, a resplendent vision in rich blue velvet with plumes in his cap, seated himself on the throne, and announced himself king.

Parliament was not sitting, but Edward had no intention of waiting for a new House to convene. Thrones had been lost that way. The people of London had filled the hall. Outside, the streets were black with cheering spectators. Trumpets were sounded and then a herald demanded if the people would accept this new king. A mighty shout was the answer.

"Yea! Yea!" cried the trained bands and the wealthy men of the guilds.

If the shades of John of Gaunt and his own father, Richard of York, both of whom had coveted the throne but had temporized, lacking the resolution to act in this direct way, were listening and watching, they undoubtedly said to themselves, "This is what I should have done."

2

Edward, the perfect man of action, did not sit down in London to enjoy the ease and the sweet taste of success in his mouth. He marched immediately to the north and fought a battle at Towton near Tadcaster in Yorkshire. The combined armies were over 100,000 in size, the Lancastrians having a slight advantage in numbers. It proved to be the bloodiest battle ever waged on English soil.

Fought on the converging slopes of a wide division in the hills, it was at first a contest between archers. The Yorkists had the better of it because a snowstorm came up and blew across the depression into the faces of the Lancastrians. The latter troops were under a continuously heavy barrage of arrows but were unable to reach the other line with their own. The lines then converged and for hours they fought desperately, hand to hand, foot to foot, knowing that surrender meant death. The slaughter was terrible to behold and the snow turned red as soon as it touched the ground.

The Yorkist reserves under the Duke of Norfolk arrived late in the afternoon but, as it developed, at the best moment to throw the Lancastrians into a panic. They began to show against the left flank of the Red Roses. Edward, showing rare skill, had them deploy in an ever lengthening line in order to outflank the foe. It was then that a general retreat of the Lancastrians began, in the course of which the losses were even heavier than in the fighting.

The saddened ex-king, poor, gentle Henry, had not been on the battlefield because it was fought on Palm Sunday. He went instead to York and spent the day in prayer and meditation.

### 3

Henry and his wife and son managed to retreat into Scotland, where they remained for the next four years. Margaret, who never conceded that they were beaten, spent the time in never ceasing efforts to enlist assistance from abroad. It may not have occurred to her that by allying herself with England's most active foes she was alienating all sympathy for herself and her husband in the land over which she was determined her son must reign. If it did, she brushed the consequences aside. With her it had become a fight to the death and no considerations of policy or expediency were allowed to influence her.

After an abortive effort to arouse the north of England, and another defeat, Margaret left Henry in Scotland and sailed for France. As the Scots, soon after, concluded a fifteen-year truce with Edward, now firmly ensconced on the English throne, the desolate and abandoned king had to betake himself elsewhere. For a full year he stayed in concealment in a rough stretch of hill and dale between Yorkshire and Lancashire. After that he seems to have lived in a monastery, his identity concealed from the monks although the prior without a doubt knew who he was. He probably was happy in this life, his time fully occupied by the regular devotions and periods of contemplation. For some time thereafter he maintained himself in the Furness Fells, attracted no doubt by the proximity of the great Cistercian Abbey. Much of the time he disguised himself in the brown robes of a friar, his head muffled in a cloak to conceal his lack of tonsure, a begging bowl under his arm.

Here Henry of England must be left for an interval while other aspects of this bitter and seemingly endless struggle are examined. A strange and dismal experience this, for a king, but one which the gentle Henry accepted with his usual patience.

## CHAPTER VII

# The Kingmaker

**1**

THE Wars of the Roses, seemingly, were over. The Lancastrians had been decisively beaten. Queen Margaret and her son were somewhere on the continent, begging frantically for assistance in resuming the conflict. She was willing to give back to the French every inch of their soil still held by the English, including the all-important port of Calais. She offered the English border city of Berwick to the Scots. She had no scruples whatever about the concessions she was willing to make at the expense of the English nation. Henry was known to be wandering, a sad wraith in a friar's robe, somewhere in the north of England and would inevitably be taken prisoner. Edward IV was firmly enthroned and striving to restore order with the assistance of the powerful man who had done so much to place him there.

The death of Warwick's father at Wakefield had made him the richest man in England. He inherited the earldom of Salisbury with extensive landholdings in Yorkshire and the west country; and, of course, he still held his previous honors and the quite tremendous estates which had come to him through his marriage with the Warwick heiress. His income probably exceeded that of the king. He held most of the key posts under Edward and had gradually gathered all the administrative and diplomatic reins into his extremely able hands.

Edward seems to have been willing at first to let the mighty Warwick take the burden of goverment off his own shoulders. An inconvenient attack of measles made it necessary for the siege of the northern strongholds still in Lancastrian hands, particularly Alnwick and Bamborough, to be conducted by Warwick. These massive and strategic castles passed back and forth from hand to hand but finally came into the Yorkist maw, clearing the country of all Red Rose centers, with the exception of

Harlech Castle in Wales. The Earl of Pembroke took an army up into the Welsh hills to see what could be done about Harlech. His own brother, Sir Richard Herbert, a stout Lancastrian adherent, was in command of the garrison. The younger brother scoffed at the demand for the surrender of this castle so famed in story and song. "I held a town in France till all the old women in Wales heard of it," he declared. "And now all the old women in France shall hear how I defend this castle." He held out bravely but finally all the old women in England heard that he had been compelled to capitulate.

Warwick was above everything else a diplomat. His shrewdness and his overpowering personality made him as useful as Cardinal Wolsey would later prove in Henry VIII's behalf. His chief task was to make it impossible for Margaret to arrange any alliances on the continent. To accomplish this he tried to establish a permanent peace with the French king, the shrewd and miserly Louis XI, in preference to continuing the Burgundian alliance. This was the wiser course of the two, but the people of England preferred the Burgundian bond because of trade advantages. Warwick, knowing himself right, brushed the national prejudice aside and strove with ceaseless energy to improve relations with France. He succeeded certainly in destroying the doubts of the continental neighbors and convincing them that Edward was on the throne to stay. He was soon regarded abroad as the pillar of the English throne.

Edward, now in his twentieth year, would have to marry. As he was the most prominent and eligible bachelor in Christendom, Warwick used the problem of a wife for him as his most useful diplomatic weapon. Among all the princesses available, some young, some mature, some pretty, some with large noses and bulging frames, Warwick fixed his mind on wedding the handsome young monarch to a sister-in-law of Louis XI, Bona of Savoy. This seemed such a suitable match that the resourceful commoner was on the point of going to France to see the fair Bona and to discuss terms with the devious Louis when Edward himself disrupted the plan. He chose a wife for himself and married her secretly.

2

John of Bedford, the most able and trustworthy of the brothers of Henry V, was married twice, his second wife being Jaquetta of Luxembourg. She is described in historical records as being handsome and lively, an understatement as, in reality, she was very handsome and extremely lively. When Bedford died, she was escorted to England by a guard of English knights under the command of Sir Richard Woodville. Now it happened that Woodville was considered the handsomest man in England. After an interval, the lively Jaquetta married the young knight, but the fact was concealed for five years. Parliament was very angry about it when the truth was revealed (the House seems to have been more easily stirred to indignation by such matters than by the needs of the people) and the dowry of the duchess was confiscated. Later it was restored and the duchess and her handsome spouse took up their residence at Grafton Castle. In the meantime a daughter had been born and named Elizabeth. There might be some to dispute the claims to supreme pulchritude of the parents, but there was never any shadow of doubt that the daughter grew up to be the loveliest lady in the whole land. Other children came along and they all had their share of this heritage of good looks. All of them were filled, almost from childhood, with ambition and self-will, their most amiable trait being a readiness to stand together and support one another in their avaricious designs.

Elizabeth was appointed a maid of honor to Queen Margaret and at the age of twenty-one, a dazzlingly fair creature, was married, quite happily, to John Grey, son of Earl Ferrers of Groby. John Grey took the Lancastrian side and was commander of Queen Margaret's cavalry. He died of wounds sustained in the second Battle of St. Albans, leaving his widow with two healthy young sons. When the White Rose triumphed and Edward became king, he promptly confiscated the property of Bradgate, the seat of the Grey family, leaving Elizabeth and her two boys in a condition almost of penury.

The duchess Jaquetta, who was clever and a schemer, patched up her differences with Edward, and the latter sometimes saw her while hunting in the forest of Whittlebury, a royal chase near Grafton. This enabled the new young widow to employ an old and well-tried stratagem to bring her case before the young and highly susceptible king. One day, as he was riding through the forest, he saw a lady, holding two small boys by the hand, under a stately tree which was to stand for many centuries thereafter and to be known as the Queen's Oak. He reined in his horse (perceiving how lovely she was), and the widow threw herself at his feet. She pleaded with him earnestly to take pity on the sad lot of her small sons.

To understand what followed it must be believed that, although the king was more ardent in the pursuit of fair ladies than of the deer in the royal forest, he had never seen one to compare with the slender widow kneeling beside his horse. He remained in the saddle in a state of breathless wonder.

In most descriptions her hair is called "gilt" in color, which meant undoubtedly that it had tints of copper as well as gold. Her eyes were large and blue, her features delicately molded, her figure ravishing. She proceeded to demonstrate, moreover, that she was gifted in the arts of enticement and could stir any masculine heart by the flutter of an eyelash. Certainly she played havoc with the heart beating under the velvet riding jacket of royal Edward.

His surrender to her was immediate and complete. He not only restored Bradgate to her but continued with great regularity to meet her under the same oak tree. He made every effort to convince the fair Elizabeth that she might reasonably agree to a closer relationship between them but found her adamant in her refusal.

"My liege," she is reported to have said, "full well I know I am not good enough to be your queen. But ah, dear liege lord, I am far too good to become your mistress."

That irresistible squire of dames, the king, passed through many stages of baffled feelings over this denial of his amorous plans. With great reluctance, it may be assumed, he finally offered her marriage. In the chronicle of Fabyan, the result was recorded as follows:

In most secret manner, upon the first of May, 1464, king Edward espoused Elizabeth, late being wife of Sir John Gray. Which espousailles was solemnized early in the morning at the town called Grafton near to Stoney-Stratford. At which marriage was none present but the spouse, the spousesse, the duchess of Bedford, her mother, the priest and two gentlemen and a young man who helped the priest to sing.

The next day the bride's father, who now held the title of Lord Rivers, received word from the king that he was coming to pay him a visit. Edward remained four days, and the artful Jaquetta arranged matters so skillfully that the king spent each night with Elizabeth and never a word of scandal was raised. Even the father of the bride was kept in the dark.

Finally, of course, the truth had to come out. On Michaelmas Day of that year, Edward brought together a number of the peers in the palace at Reading and acknowledged Elizabeth openly as his wife. Later in the day the new consort was publicly declared queen in the abbey and received the vows of allegiance of all the peers present, including the Earl of Warwick. The latter was seething with indignation, but apparently he concealed the fact for the time being. Clearly the Kingmaker was disturbed over the inevitable rupture in relations with the King of France because of the rejection of the match arranged with the fair Bona. Nevertheless he knelt before the lovely bride and kissed her hand with proper respect. He was even assiduous in the attentions he paid her.

Elizabeth was attired on this great occasion in gold brocade of garter blue, with robings of ermine fitted over her slender shoulders. Her golden hair had been left free and hung in shimmering ringlets to her knees. A queen in appearance, most certainly, even though commoner blood flowed in her veins.

The marriage was deeply resented by the members of the older nobility. They seem to have realized, even at this early date, that the rapacity of the Woodville family would now be openly manifested. At the brilliant tournaments and court functions which followed the announcement, the glowing queen was surrounded by her younger sisters, all nearly as lovely as she and all anxious to acquire noble and wealthy husbands. Not far in the background were her tall and handsome brothers. In October the queen's sister Margaret was married to Thomas, Lord Maltravers, the heir of the Earl of Arundel. Her sister Mary was awarded a matrimonial plum in the person of William Herbert, who later succeeded his father as Earl of Pembroke. The other sisters all married well. The greatest indignation was aroused when the thrice-married dowager Duchess of Norfolk, a skittish lady of nearly eighty, took the queen's brother John as her fourth husband. John was twenty years old, but he was agreeable to the match. Everywhere the match was derided as this "diabolical marriage," but the Woodvilles smiled and shrugged their shoulders. The raddled beldam was rich—very, very rich.

Finally Elizabeth's father, handsome sire of these handsome schemers, was promoted to the rank of earl, and at that the wrath of the baronage rose to a fever pitch.

The Kingmaker was no longer a power in the realm and, like Achilles, he sulked in his tent. Very soon thereafter, things reached a stage of tension which led to the second half of the Wars of the Roses. It seems quite possible that, except for the expert fluttering of a pair of long eyelashes one spring day in the forest of Whittlebury, the country would have remained at peace and many terrible battles would never have been fought.

### 3

For more than four years after the announcement of the king's marriage, during which the queen's family became dominant at court, Warwick withdrew largely from active co-operation with Edward. He was furious, of course, at the way his power had been taken from him and he cordially hated the Woodvilles. His character changed noticeably in this brief space of time. In place of the affability and openhandedness which had made him so popular, he became morose and critical. He even changed in appearance. His face no longer wore its customary smile and in its place was a suspicious scowl.

He still had friends in all parts of the kingdom, however, and throughout these years there were continuous irruptions in various parts of the country. They did not come to the point of open insurrection, but it was apparent that the men behind them were friends of the Kingmaker. Wherever they went they would shout, "A Warwick! A Warwick!" and they posted long statements of their grievances. In one of the engagements which resulted from these disturbances, the queen's father, Lord Rivers, was captured and beheaded. The same fate befell two descendants of the union of dowager Queen Katherine and Owen Tudor.

King Edward had good reason to believe that the hand of Warwick could be detected in these continuous breaches of the peace, but he hesitated to bring things to an open rupture. He was too conscious of the great power still wielded by his former chief minister to risk a break.

Warwick's ambitions had begun to soar. He was no longer content to stand behind a king, even though the latter might be of his own making. A revealing statement was made to an emissary of the King of France, who crossed into England to see him. This agent, whose name was Manipenny, was quite as devious as his master, but Warwick seems to have spoken quite openly to him. "It is a matter," he declared, "of being either master or varlet!" And this man of deep purpose had no intention of being a varlet. He wanted to hold the supreme power in his own hands, but he realized that he could never hope (except under extraordinary circumstances) to be crowned himself.

But there was another way. The oldest brother of the king still alive was Prince George, who had been made Duke of Clarence. That title, it may be explained, was derived from the old family name of Clare, who had had vast landholdings in Ireland and in Gloucestershire. The name George came, of course, from St. George, the patron saint of England. He seems to have been the first member of a royal line to bear the name in England. A very weak man was this George to bear so stout a name—no dragon-killer in any sense of the word. Instead he was vain, envious, and lacking in all fine qualities such as loyalty and courage. As usual with characters of this kind (the pages of history are red with their misdeeds), he believed himself capable of reigning just as well as his brother Edward, if not a little better. It irked him to stand behind the royal shoulder and to bend his knee in obedience.

Warwick had kept this weakling in his eye for a long time and considered him a perfect tool for the purpose he had in mind. If Edward were deposed, he could put George in his place, being certain that the foolish and fickle prince would be putty in his hands. It would be clear to everyone that he, Warwick, was ruler in all but name. This would suffice his proud spirit. And if George became troublesome? That would open up new vistas.

To bring the unstable Clarence over to his side, Warwick convinced him he should marry his daughter Isabel. She seems to have been too young and innocent to wed the dissolute prince and, in addition, King Edward had other plans for his brother. The purpose of Warwick became very clear when the news reached Westminster that Clarence had crossed to Calais, where Warwick was now located, and had married Isabel.

Warwick had a double purpose in mind. To throw Edward off the throne would require aid from the Lancastrian part of the population. He must, therefore, act in concert with them. Clarence was in his net but it might become necessary to cast him overboard. Henry, the deposed king, had not long to live and it might not be too inconvenient to let him sit on the throne for a few years. Warwick had complete belief in his own ability to ride the future with a firm rein, come what may. It might be possible to put a son-in-law on the throne rather than let it pass to Henry's son.

So at this stage he sought the assistance of Louis XI of France, and that most artful of monarchs was delighted to do anything in his power to renew the conflict in England. His policy had been to keep the English fighting among themselves, under their absurd rose symbols, because only in that way could they be prevented from swarming over into France to fight for the French throne. His willingness to work with Warwick had been strengthened by an announcement made in the House of Commons by Edward of his determination to regain by arms all the dominions in France formerly held by England.

The first step toward reopening the civil war was to gain the active support of Queen Margaret. That, it soon became clear, was not going to be easy.

Margaret, queen of sorrows and enmities, had been in France now for nine years, nursing her grievances and striving to secure help wherever she could. She was temperamentally incapable of forgiving an enemy; and highest of all on the list of those for whom she bore an unending grudge was the name of Warwick. It was through his energy and daring that the house of York had gained the throne. He haunted her dreams, this resourceful man against whom she had striven in vain. And, above everything else, she could not forgive him for standing up openly at St. Paul's Cross and charging her with adultery at the time of the birth of her son. Make friends with Warwick? Margaret's first reaction was an emphatic and almost hysterical negative.

But Louis had surmounted greater obstacles than the opposition of an angry woman. He made it clear to the ex-queen that this was her last chance. She could never hope to regain the ascendant with foreign levies, particularly as he had no intention of providing the funds or the men for another ill-planned foray. There was only one way left. Let Warwick, who had made Edward king, unmake him.

It was a bitter pill for the queen to swallow. "Her heart," she told the French king, "would bleed till the day of judgment with the wounds that he," meaning Warwick, "had inflicted." She had answers for every point that the wily monarch raised. "It is true there is dissension in England," she declared. "But they do not wear the red rose. They march under the bear and ragged staff of Warwick." When he proposed among the terms to be arranged that her son wed Anne Neville, a younger daughter of Warwick, she burst into a fury of dissent. "What!" she cried. "Will he indeed give his daughter to my son, whom he has so often branded as the offspring of adultery?"

Louis was a master of diplomacy and he gradually wore her down. Perhaps she had realized from the first that this was in truth the last chance and had debated the points only to give a needed vent to her pent-up emotions. In the end she gave in to this extent: she agreed to see Warwick.

There was a dip in the divisions of France between the borders of Normandy and Brittany, running south through country which in summer was rich with the yellow bloom of the *planta genesta* and ending close to the western reaches of the Loire River. Here lay the capital of the province of Maine, the romantic city of Angers, famous for its impregnable castle of eight round, grim towers. Angers had played a continuous part earlier in the English-French wars, but now it was far removed from the scene of strife. Far enough at any rate from the sharp eyes of English espionage, Angers seemed a safe place for Queen Margaret and Warwick to have their meeting. Here they could thresh out their differences and Edward in London would be none the wiser.

Margaret came to Angers in a far from receptive mood. She made one point clear to the agile Louis, who was on hand to act as entrepreneur: Warwick must come to her and beg for her pardon.

It was some time before the Kingmaker agreed to this, but finally he gave in and accompanied the French ruler into the presence of the militant queen. Margaret sat on a chair high enough to suggest a throne, her face clouded, her figure tense. She neither moved nor spoke in response to the suave speeches of Louis and the first efforts of Warwick to bridge the hatreds of the past.

Finally Warwick realized he would not be met halfway. He went down on his knees before her and, if there was nothing humble in the lines of his back, there was a hint of it in what he said. He conceded that he had wronged her in the past and for this he begged her forgiveness. He promised that what he could accomplish for her in the future would erase from her mind all animosities.

Margaret listened in an unbroken silence. Warwick, taken aback, had to bridge her silence with more assurances of what he planned to do. For fifteen minutes the resentful queen kept him on his knees before giving in to the extent of permitting him to rise. This was most humiliating for the proud baron who believed himself capable of overturning the English government and dominating any monarchial arrangements which might result. But he was a thorough diplomat and so was prepared to accept such rebuffs as the present might offer in order to gain his way in the end.

In time, with the aid of that master of guile, Louis XI, an agreement was reached. Warwick promised to land in force in England and proceed against the Yorkist king with an army which, he asserted, would not be less than 50,000 men. King Henry was to be restored to the throne, and Warwick swore on a splinter of the True Cross, called the Cross of St. Laud d'Angers, to be a true and faithful subject. The Cross of St. Laud was believed to possess the power to cause the death within a year of anyone who perjured himself thereon.

The French king then came to the fore and promised 2000 men and a subsidy of 46,000 crowns. It was due to the stand taken by Margaret's son, Edward, called the Prince of Wales in the little threadbare court they maintained, that a binding agreement was finally reached. This youth is presented in various lights by commentators of the day, some depicting him as tall and handsome and the most accomplished prince in Europe, others as the inevitable product of his mother's resentful spirit, a gloomy youth who was most concerned with the swing of the executioner's ax and the rolling of heads from the block. One point seems clear: he saw Anne Neville, who had accompanied her father to Angers, and told his mother at once that he desired to marry her. The queen's objections to the match ran very deep, but what could she do in the light of this unexpected preference? She agreed, reluctantly and bitterly.

Those two skilled manipulators, Louis and Warwick, moved at once to make the agreement binding. Clarence and his wife had been summoned to attend and arrived in time for the betrothal. It must have been apparent to the fickle Clarence that things had taken an unfavorable turn as far as his chances were concerned. What price now the promises made to him by his father-in-law? Certainly his future looked poorer than it had before he turned his coat. There is no way of knowing what things Warwick whispered in his ear, but it seems that his suspicions and fears, for the time being at least, were allayed. It may have been that Warwick hinted at dark schemes which ran counter to the oath he had sworn on the True Cross.

4

King Edward was in the north of England when Warwick and his relatively small party landed. It is hard to conceive why he allowed himself to be caught off-guard in this way. Had he disregarded the rumors which must have reached him of Warwick's activities in France? Had his low esteem of the latter as a general lulled him into a false sense of security? Or was it another proof of the young king's tendency to indolence?

Whatever the reason, Edward had gone far up into Yorkshire on the strength of a feint arranged by Warwick, who must be conceded a touch of genius in all of his early planning. A little uprising had been headed by the earl's brother-in-law, Lord Fitzhugh. This disappeared like a soap bubble or a faint puff of air as soon as the royal forces appeared, but it had served its purpose well. Warwick, accompanied by Clarence (a sorely unsettled young man by this time), the Earl of Oxford, and Jasper Tudor, landed on September 16, 1470, at Dartmoor and Plymouth. Edward was caught flat-footed. He had no army, either with him or in process of assembling. He had left London wide open to hostile entry. When he learned that Warwick was moving east on London with every semblance of furious haste and proclaiming his new adherence to the Lancastrians, he realized that his cause was lost. Nothing remained but to make his escape to the continent and wait for a favorable turn of events.

Whatever Warwick had of greatness was demonstrated in this easy victory. His daring had been shown in landing with a small force in a country where his opponent sat solidly on the throne. Few men would have made such a bold venture. Immediately following the success of his first move, the Kingmaker swung over to the other extreme and showed an excess of caution in his march on London. Flushed with the results he had achieved, and buoyed up by the way in which his army grew with each mile, the triumphant commoner still felt his way with great care.

He had the best of reasons for not rushing boldly ahead with the occupation of London Town. It was well known to him that the sentiment there favored the Yorkist cause. The young king had made himself popular with the Londoners, who admired him personally and delighted in his hail-fellow way of dealing with them. Wherever he went in the city he had been followed by admiring throngs and the loud cheers which bespoke their high regard. In addition, Edward had borrowed large sums from the Londoners. What chance would they have of getting their money back if Warwick put the glum old king, now subsisting in the Tower, back on the throne? They had no illusions about Queen Margaret. She disliked and feared London and all its ways; and they were aware that she never forgot and never changed her mind.

Warwick had learned much, moreover, about English sentiment in the course of his slowly conducted march through southern England. "A Warwick! A Warwick!" had been the cry which greeted him most often. There had been a few scattered calls of "A Henry! A Henry!" and even a very few and very faint "A Clarence! A Clarence!" He had seen little showing of the Red Rose, but had been greeted everywhere by the Bear and Ragged Staff. Did this mean that national sentiment would favor him if he reached for the highest reward?

It was not until he learned of the hasty departure of Edward for the continent that he entered London on October 6. He was not surprised to find the leading citizens cool in their reception and much too anxious to discuss the possibility of having their loans repaid under a new regime. Warwick seems to have seen from the start that he could not hope to win over these men of business, with their intent eyes and firm jaws, by any means other than a promise to pay. This posed a great difficulty, for the loans had been heavy and he could not see any way of meeting them without help from Parliament.

His path was easier as far as the "mob" was concerned, the term commonly used to describe the lesser citizens—the clerks, the artisans, and the apprentices. They had always admired the Kingmaker and they were still willing to cheer for him. They had no financial axes to grind. Warwick proceeded with undercover plans to keep their support. His agents, organized by one Sir Geoffrey Gate, circulated among them and spread promises of better days to come. They were fed on occasion and provided with free beer. The extreme step was taken of opening the prisons and granting pardons to all but the worst offenders.

Sentiment outside the city was running strongly for the Kingmaker. He had always been popular in the Cinque Ports and along the Channel coast because of his vigorous handling of naval operations (he was an able admiral, even though an indifferent general), and his new success was loudly acclaimed. Promises of armed support came in from all quarters.

Despite the reservations in the mind of Warwick on the score of his ultimate stand, the next step clearly was to proclaim Henry king. The gentle old man had been held in the Tower of London since his betrayal into Edward's hands. Little attention or kindness had been shown him, save allowing him to live, and he had by this time fallen into the seediness of neglect. When led out from his uncomfortable quarters, he found it hard to believe in this unexpected good fortune. He made no complaints of the treatment he had suffered but did not conceal his pleasure in clean linen and unpatched clothes. The food set before him was clearly a change, for he plied his knife and drained his wine cup with an artless gusto.

Clothed again in warm and rich apparel, he was taken out into the city streets with a train headed by Warwick and the Archbishop of Canterbury and lodged temporarily with the Bishop of London. If the cheers for him were neither very loud nor spontaneous, his mild eyes lighted up and he acknowledged them with a nervous fluttering of his hands. A few days later he was taken with full pomp to Westminster and lodged again in the state apartments where he had spent most of his life.

A session of Parliament was hastily arranged. The House met on November 26 and, needless to state, perhaps, it had been most carefully hand-picked. There was no delay in confirming the measures laid before it. The terms reached at Angers were approved. Warwick and Clarence were appointed joint lieutenants of the realm. This step, clearly, was a sop intended to ease the mind of Edward's turncoat brother, who had been showing open sulkiness and an unwillingness to co-operate.

## 5

Warwick was well aware that two pairs of daring and even desperate eyes were watching him from across the Channel. The closeness of the alliance between England and France, as evidenced by the *Te Deum* sung in Paris, was apparent to all Europe. Charles the Bold of Burgundy, who was aggressive and in all things decisive, began to take steps to break the tie. His plan was a sound and obvious one. Edward must be placed back on the English throne and the Lancastrian pretensions demolished for all time. Edward, living in Holland in a state of bitter regret over his own carelessness, welcomed the opportunity to co-operate with the far-seeing Burgundian. As a preliminary step the Burgundian fleet began to harry the eastern and southern coasts of England.

The Kingmaker was fully awake to the danger. He knew that the English people, and, in particular, the Londoners, had always preferred an alliance with Burgundy, which would protect and foster their profitable trade in wool with the great textile merchants of Flanders. There was as well a feeling that France was the hereditary enemy and that some day, somehow, another Henry V would arise to beat the French so decisively that he would wear permanently the fleur-de-lis crown.

Being a shrewd student of international affairs, Warwick realized that the administration he had established was purely temporary. The people would never be held in full loyalty to the daft old king, no matter how much they liked him. Henry, moreover, had not long to live. What concerned the people above everything else was their lack of security with the present arrangements. What would happen, they were asking, when the throne became vacant? Without a doubt, Warwick, in that proud, aloof mind of his, entertained the hope that the people would come to realize how great a king he could be if given the chance. He believed a sentiment was growing in his favor, that the whisper was spreading: "This man is a winner. He turns things upside down with the twirl of a finger. Why take a weakling prince because he is his father's son when we can choose for ourselves this monumental figure?"

But he saw no prospect at once of such a sudden reversal on the part of the people. The sentiment would need time to grow and plenty of skilled direction would be needed behind it. In the meantime he had to have something more satisfactory to offer than the doddering old figurehead at Westminster. He knew the questions that people were asking. Where is this Prince Edward who will succeed to the throne? Why is he dawdling at his ease in France? Is he a coward? Is he another, the saints forfend, of these princely war haters?

Being completely realistic, Warwick saw that, for a time at least, he must use Margaret and her son, and that they must be brought over at once. Irritated by their non-appearance, which ran counter to the arrangements reached at Angers, he paced about the chancellery offices in Westminster, plucking with angry fingers at his beard and striving to find the answer. He even rode down to Dover and scanned the bounding strait for a glimpse of their sails. What was the queen doing? Why this incredible, this perhaps fatal delay?

Margaret was not delaying because of any reluctance to participate in the stirring events which were shaking England. She wanted to be there and to have a voice in all decisions. She did not place full faith in Warwick. In fact she believed him as capable of turning his coat whenever necessary as that false loon Clarence. But it was taking time to organize the forces she intended to bring with her and to assemble the necessary ships. Margaret was a perfectionist, to use a modern term. She wanted to have everything done to her complete satisfaction—every last archer equipped with his well-oiled crossbow (the French could never, never see what a poor weapon this was) and every horse curried and sent aboard. But time seldom waits on perfection.

When she had all details arranged at last and was ready to start, the weather turned fiercely against her. Three efforts to set sail were balked by the winds and waves. Finally on March 24 she insisted on starting even though the portents were still unfavorable. The voyage took sixteen days (an indication of how clumsy and helpless the ships of that day really were), and it was not until April 13 that they were able to effect a landing at Weymouth, a fishing town and seaport on the Dorset coast, a full 140 miles from London.

This delay was to have fatal consequences. Edward, acting now with furious energy, had landed on the Yorkshire coast several weeks before. He had made perhaps the shortest turnabout in history. Little more than five months had elapsed since the young king had taken ship at Lynn and fled to the Netherlands; and here he was back. A large part of the country was very glad to welcome him.


6


In the last half of the Wars of the Roses a radical change in military methods was introduced with the active use of cannon. It was true that guns had been employed in a somewhat experimental way long before. The story that the English had artillery at Crécy is without foundation, although Edward III did have a primitive form of mitrailleuse called a ribaudequin in some of his French campaigns, which he employed mostly in sieges. A ballad written about the siege of Calais contains lines which indicate a lack of effectiveness in the guns of the day.

> *Thanked be God and Mary mild,*
> *They harmed neither woman nor child.*
> *To the houses though they did great harm.*

Edward IV, always alert to new ideas, was helped in winning the Battle of "Lose-coat" Field in 1461 very largely by using cannon. But, as will be told, it remained for Warwick in his last battle to use artillery as an important arm of his large forces.

Edward's flight to Holland had been so precipitous that he had landed in a state of destitution. He had not delayed, in fact, to finish his dinner when word of Warwick's success had reached him. Charles the Bold had many Lancastrians about his court and had to play a cautious hand in assisting the refugee monarch. He did send finally the sum of 50,000 florins to aid in the preparations for a return to England. He also assembled a fleet for the use of the landing party.

Edward's men came ashore at various points near the mouth of the Humber, but at first no warmth was to be detected in the reception accorded them. The country had grown tired of the incessant fighting. White or Red, what did it matter? The determined Edward might never have succeeded in landing at all in the face of Warwick's elaborate preparations to guard the coasts if it had not been for the lukewarmness of his somewhat less than valiant brother, the Marquis of Montague, who had been assigned to watch. Montague remained at Pontefract Castle and did not stir himself to drive the party back to their ships. Before anything could be done about it, therefore, the Snow Rose was beginning to sprout again in helmets and on lance tips. When Edward got as far as Nottingham he was joined by his allies in considerable strength and from that moment on his forces accelerated rapidly.

That the Kingmaker was seriously disturbed is evidenced in a letter he dispatched to Henry Vernon, the Lord of Haddon Hall, asking him to take the field.

"Henry," he wrote, "I praye you ffayle me not now, as ever I may do ffor yow."

It was soon after this that he heard of the defection of Clarence. When Edward was close to Warwick on his march south, he saw a company of horsemen advancing to meet him whose lances carried no token of allegiance to either side. Edward reined in and motioned to his brother Gloucester (afterward Richard III) to draw closer.

"Clarence?" was the question conveyed by the lift of his eyebrows.

Richard nodded in confirmation, a satisfied shake of the head. He was devoted to the handsome and masterful Edward but also loved the weak George enough to be happy to have him rejoin them after his term of apostasy with Warwick.

It took no more than a few words to reach a reconciliation. Clarence was bitter over his treatment at Warwick's hands, although he could not say in what respect the Kingmaker had broken his word. To have done so would have revealed his own treasonable designs on the throne. Perhaps Edward did not need to be told. He understood Clarence through and through and was still able to retain a spark of affection for him.

The result was that the forces under Clarence pinned the White Rose on their lances and swarmed over to join the returning monarch. The rapidly growing army headed south for London, where they were as-

sured of a warm reception. Clarence, to give him his due, strove to
effect a reconciliation between his brother and Warwick. The king agreed
to the extent of offering the Kingmaker a bare pardon. The latter, too
deeply involved, scoffed at the suggestion.

## 7

The town of Barnet lies on the north road out of London and has the
highest elevation between that city and York. It was here that the
decisive battle of the war was fought.

Although he had a larger army than Edward and more cannon,
Warwick seems to have been reluctant to come to grips with his foe.
Perhaps he held the skill of the young Yorkist in some dread, as indeed
he had every reason to do. Perhaps a premonition of disaster rode his
back and made him postpone the inevitable clash. The issue, however,
could only be settled by the sword and on Good Friday, 1471, the
Kingmaker led his troops to St. Albans, which was familiar territory.
Knowing that Edward was advancing from London to meet him, Warwick
led his divisions the following day to Hadley Green and stationed them
across the Barnet road in battle order. During the late afternoon the
Yorkist troops came within sight of the Lancastrian lines and halted,
after driving in Warwick's pickets. It was too dark to begin the action
when the king's forces had taken their positions and so the two armies
settled down to spend the night within earshot of each other.

It is estimated that the Kingmaker had in the neighborhood of 12,000
men. His position was a strong one, lying along Wrotham Park and the
ridge which intersected the main road from Barnet. Most estimates
place Edward's strength at 10,000 and it was soon made apparent that
he had fewer cannon.

The Lancastrian guns were made of cast iron and they fired rounded
stones of considerable weight. The new "corned" gunpowder was used
but it lacked the strength to project the missiles any great distance.
There was always a grave danger also of the barrels exploding, and so
the gunners went about their work warily and with an eye to suitable
cover.

Warwick seems to have believed in the power of his guns. Throughout
the night, with dark clouds cutting off the light, he kept the gunners
at work, pounding the Yorkist lines, or what he conceived to be the
position of the enemy. There had been a miscalculation of distances and
the Yorkists were much closer than Warwick supposed. As a result, the
constant bombardment netted him nothing, the stones falling well beyond

the rear of the enemy line. Edward's guns made no reply, for the best
of reasons. To have done so would make their location clear and the
Lancastrian gunners could then have corrected their sights.

Dawn came with both forces standing under arms and waiting the
dread moment when the lines would clash and the carnage begin. There
was a nightmare quality about the Battle of Barnet. It had started with
the incessant booming of the guns and continued when dawn showed
faintly through a heavy mist wrapped tightly about Wrotham and the
high points of the ridge. The damp fog drifted down over the field, so
that Rose tokens became useless and friend could not be told from foe,
and Edward in shining armor astride his white charger seemed a fantastic figure out of mythology.

The battle began with the Earl of Oxford's men, who made up the
Lancastrian right wing, charging forward through the yellowish mist and
encountering nothing but empty fields and broken hedges. Believing
that he had overlapped the Yorkist position, Oxford wheeled to his left
and fell on the rear lines of the army of the White Rose. Hastings, the
Yorkist commander on this flank, was compelled to fall back. Flushed
with what seemed an easy advantage, Oxford drove them before him all
the way to Barnet and beyond. This was exceeding instructions, for now
Oxford was completely out of touch with the rest of the Warwick forces.
When he finally brought his men to a halt, he was unable to round up
more than 800 of them. When this handful emerged through the still
obscuring mists, the impetuous commander of the Lancastrian center,
the young Duke of Somerset, mistook them for the enemy and attacked
them vigorously.

Instantly the fatal cry of "Treason!" so often heard in this bitter civil
conflict, rose all along the line. Oxford's men melted away into the murky
shadows. Somerset's men, already desperately engaged with Edward's
center, began to waver.

In the meantime the same situation had developed on the other side
of the field. Here young Richard of Gloucester, who had the makings of
a great soldier in him, led the Yorkist right wing into a similar gap.
Obeying orders, however, he did not endeavor to sweep a clean path to
the rear but brought his men around in good order to attack the exposed
flank of the Lancastrian left wing, where Warwick himself was in command. His thrust was so effective that he soon threatened the Lancastrian
position as far as Wrotham Park.

Warwick's position was now desperately serious. Having dismounted
before the fighting began, the Lancastrian leader found it hard to keep
in touch with his lieutenants. He could see that Edward was driving
hard against the faltering ranks of Somerset. As fast as the knightly

armor on his back would permit, he moved over to encourage his center.

"Stand fast!" he cried. "Withstand this charge and the day is ours!"

But the fear of treasonable desertions was still disturbing the men under Somerset. The right wing had vanished over the horizon, and on the left the hammer blows of young Richard were opening the way to a dip of land behind Warwick called Dead Man's Bottom. The voice of the Kingmaker was lost in the pandemonium of sound.

Warwick looked about him with a growing sense of despair. He could see that Edward was moving steadily forward. The glint of swords and axes could be seen through breaks in the rising mist. The occasional roar of a cannon could be heard, blasting away at nothing but creating a sulphurous streak in the fog. Mass murder, most dreadful of sights, had turned nearly a quarter mile of muddy soil into a shambles—and for nothing more important than the settlement of a dynastic dispute.

He must have realized that this was almost certainly the end of all his brilliant ambitions and high hopes, his scheming and conniving, perhaps of his own life.

Suddenly, like the breaking of a dam, the Lancastrian line gave way. The cry of "Treason!" changed to "Save!" "Save!" as the men who had sported the Red Rose threw these useless symbols away and fled in a mass panic. A single vociferous figure, confined in cumbersome iron, could do nothing to steady the lines and save the day.

Warwick tried to reach the position in the rear where his charger was being held for him, but his own men submerged him in their mad rush for safety. He staggered to a thicket but was followed and beaten to the ground. A bloodstained foot soldier broke open the visor with an ax and a companion gave a savage inward thrust with a sword.

Richard Neville, Earl of Warwick and Salisbury, holder of countless honors and the owner of hundreds of manors, had come to the end of his kingmaking.

## CHAPTER VIII

# The Queen of Sorrows and Enmities

## 1

THE day that Queen Margaret reached the abbey of Cerne to rest after the fatigues of her long sea voyage the word reached her of the defeat and death of Warwick at Barnet. She fell to the floor in a swoon. When she recovered, she loudly bewailed her misfortunes.

"I would rather die," she cried, "than live longer in this state!"

For the first time in her life of tragic conflict, the queen was willing to consider the Lancastrian cause as lost. Henry VI was still alive but a prisoner in the Tower of London. He would be allowed to live as long as possible by the Yorkists for an obvious reason: any further efforts to renew the struggle would be weakened by the necessity of placing the old man back on the throne, in the event of success. The son of the marriage, young Prince Edward, was high-spirited and brave. He would make a much stronger candidate for the throne than "Harry," whose gentleness and deeply religious turn of mind would always win him affection—as a man but not necessarily as a king. Queen Margaret was completely realistic and knew that Edward IV would react in the same way she would to certain possible developments. For instance, if young Prince Edward were killed, there would no longer be any reason to keep the poor old prisoner alive.

Because of this the bitterly depressed queen announced that she would return to the continent and that her son would accompany her. Back of the decision, undoubtedly, was the unexpressed thought that in the course of the years the opportunity might arise for him to come back to England and fight again for his rights.

If she had adhered to this decision, the lives of many thousands of men would have been saved, including the two she valued most in all the world—her husband and her son.

Margaret moved to Beaulieu Abbey in the New Forest, where she was joined by the Lancastrian leaders who had survived the battle, as well as by the widowed Countess of Warwick and her daughter Anne. They urged her not to give up. At first she refused, being still convinced of the wisdom of her decision. Then the young Duke of Somerset arrived and took matters into his hands. He had commanded the center at Barnet and had fought creditably. It perhaps should be pointed out that he was the son of the Somerset whose name had been linked with that of the queen in the question of the paternity of Edward, a completely false and absurd charge which only a political tactician as Machiavellian as Warwick would have dared to voice. Margaret's loyalties ran as deep as her enmities. She still liked and believed in the Somersets, and in fact the whole Beaufort connection. When the young duke, believing himself a great military leader, arrived at the abbey, he began a blustering argument in favor of continuing the struggle. Margaret was weak enough to listen.

It is true that Edward of York (so ran the theme of his discourse) defeated and killed Warwick. Is that any reason for fearing him, for believing him invincible? Has it been forgotten that Your Majesty also defeated Warwick at the second Battle of St. Albans?

The swords of all true Englishmen, continued the highly confident Somerset, would be drawn in her support if she animated them by her presence and her wisdom. Coming down to details, he proposed that they proceed without delay to raise an army in the west and north, where Lancastrian sentiment was strongest. Margaret, in an evil moment, allowed herself to be persuaded.

An army of probably 5000 men was raised, a small force in contrast to the unwieldy numbers who had fought to the death at the second Battle of St. Albans, at Towton, and at Barnet. Edward, now wearing his crown again, marched west to meet her with an army somewhat smaller. There were two reasons for this shrinkage in the ranks. First, men had become tired of the incessant struggle and now refused to gamble their lives and their properties any longer. Second, the losses had been great enough to diminish seriously the number of active fighting men. England, in other words, was worn out.

The two armies met at Tewkesbury, close to the junction point of the Severn and the Avon rivers, in a savage and merciless battle. Edward was again the victor.

Barnet had been the decisive battle of the war. Tewkesbury was, in a sense, therefore, an anti-climax. It is chiefly noteworthy because of the death of the young prince and the capture of Queen Margaret. Some of the chronicles of the day declared that the prince was killed in the field, crying vainly for help to his prospective brother-in-law, Clarence. It is believed by others that the youth was taken prisoner and led into the presence of the victorious Edward.

"How durst ye enter my realms with banners displayed against me?" demanded the king.

"To recover my father's crown and mine own inheritance," was the bold response.

In a rage Edward struck him in the face with his gauntleted hand. Whereupon the knightly train about the king surrounded the slender young hope of the Lancastrians and killed him with their daggers. This version is termed by one historian "a more detailed account written in the next generation." In other words, it is a story told during the reign of Henry VII when nothing was written or published that did not conform with the wishes of that strange king.

The captive queen was taken to London and placed in the Tower, in one of the smallest cells in that great stone breeding place of human grief and despair. The old king was close by in the Wakefield Tower, with his devotional books and the companionship of a melancholy canary. He died the same night that his wife was brought there, some say, of "pure displeasure and grief," and some say at the hands of assassins.

The next day the body of the dead king, poor Harry of Windsor, was exposed to public view at Black Friar's and then removed to Chertsey for burial. The Lancastrian line had come to an end in disaster and death.

**2**

The once lovely Margaret of Anjou emerged from the tower a middle-aged woman. The years and the strains of war had taken their toll. Her shoulders and neck had thickened, her hair was streaked with gray, her eyes were red from weeping. Her cheeks had enough lines to bear some resemblance to the charts of battlefields on which she had fought.

Edward considered the possibility of executing her to still forever her vitriolic tongue, but concluded that the chivalrous record of the Plantagenets must not be stained by the death of a woman. Accordingly she was sent from one dismal castle to another although the rigors of her confinement were gradually reduced through the mediation, it was said, of Queen Elizabeth. Finally she came to Wallingford, one of the large stone strongholds on the Thames, where she was in the charge of the dowager Duchess of Suffolk. The duchess was very kind to the unfortunate captive and kept her comfortably on the five marks a week allotted by the chancellery for the ex-queen's upkeep. She was still there when word came that arrangements had been made for her to be ransomed and sent back to France.

She knew it was not going to be a joyous homecoming, in fact no homecoming at all. She had lived in England so long that the memories of her girlhood had grown shadowy; and, of course, the dust of her two men would remain forever in English ground. To make matters worse, it had been necessary for her father, blithe Duke René, to diminish further his domain by selling Provence to Louis XI to raise the ransom money. That wily monarch had waited patiently for the chance, his covetous hands twitching for the satisfaction of grasping that beautiful southern land. He had bided his time with rather more than his usual patience (and of that he had more than any other man) and had not stepped in until misfortunes had begun to thicken about the aging René.

The latter took enough time from his new young wife and his endless preoccupation with his painting (he had now gone into murals) and his musical compositions to make a "deal" with the watchful Louis. He sold Provence for the sum of 50,000 crowns, which amount was to be used for the ransom of Margaret. Louis, who could act with lightning speed when his terms had been met, made an agreement immediately with Edward of England. The first installment, a fifth, was paid to Edward on November 3, 1475, and in January of the following year the disconsolate widow arrived at Dieppe. It was demanded of her that she sign away all her rights before being set free. With a resignation which showed how completely her spirit had been broken, she signed her name to a brusque document which began:

I, Margaret, formerly in England married, renounce all that I could pretend to in England by the conditions of my marriage, with all other things there to Edward now king of England.

This humiliating step having been taken, she proceeded with a train consisting of no more than three ladies and seven gentlemen to the domicile which had been selected for her, the manor of Reculée. There is nothing on record to show that she ever saw her father in the flesh. although he wrote her fond letters and tried to assure her future by grants which were summarily revoked by the French king. As a result, Margaret had to subsist on a pension which Louis granted her in return for another document in which she surrendered all her rights of succession to the lands and honors of her father and mother.

Reculée lay no more than a league away from Angers, where all her final misfortunes had begun. Did Louis cast his mind back over the time when he had exerted so much pressure to arrange the meeting with the confident Warwick in the latter city? If he did, it would be with a sense of satisfaction over the results of those protracted and difficult negotiations. Warwick was dead and England was too exhausted to cause him, Louis, a single night of sleeplessness or concern. Burgundy was being dealt with to his own advantage. And here was the firebrand queen, broken in spirit and content to live on the pittance he allowed her. The plans laid at Angers had proven most successful from his standpoint.

Margaret remained several years at Reculée, where she found it necessary to provide for the wants of a number of exiled Lancastrians. Her health was permanently impaired, and one French historian draws a most dire picture of her appearance—"eyes hollow, dim and perpetually inflamed, her skin disfigured with a dry, scaly leprosy." This was an exaggeration, but there could be no doubt that she showed signs of the approaching end.

Finally she left Reculée and took up her residence in the castle of Dampierre, which was close to the city of Saumur. This ancient town on the Loire River was famous for its churches and for the Maison de la Reine Cécile which her father had built. It is doubtful if she ever visited the town or saw the house her father had fashioned with such genuine care. Her life was spent in poverty, as the parsimonious king was apt to delay the payments due her and even, on occasions, to overlook them entirely.

Some believe she had a hand in the intrigues and preparations which led to the victory of Henry of Richmond at Bosworth and his elevation to the throne as Henry VII. This is highly improbable. She had lost her position of influence and her will lacked the iron inflexibility of her earlier years. She was not concerned over the throne of England since it could not be her son who would sit there under the Leopard banner. All interest in worldly affairs seems to have deserted her. Did she ever think of the needless prolongation of the war because of her fierce determination, of the terrible battles which were nothing less than mass murder, of the tens of thousands of widows who had been left to mourn their dead as she herself was now doing?

The household at Dampierre was a sorry one. A few exiles still remained with her, but she kept so strictly to her own rooms that they never saw her. Hopeless, dispirited, they sat about in glum groups and talked of the losses they had sustained in the Lancastrian cause. If they walked in the meager gardens, they had no eyes for the red roses growing there. These had become symbols of the blank future stretching ahead of them.

On August 2, 1482, Margaret made her will, a pitiable document in which she left what little she had to those about her and to provide for the payment of her debts. This done, she was content to take leave of life. On August 25, Margaret, "formerly in England married" and now in France a widow, with only one painting (not of her father's work) on the wall above her bed to represent the arms of England, the queen of sorrows and enmities who had shown so much of the heroic in her will to fight, passed quickly away.

## CHAPTER IX

# The Butt of Malmsey

*1*

THE reign of Edward IV was a short and not in any sense a glorious one. He seemed to have expended all his great energies in the struggle to obtain the crown and then to have settled down into indolence. He led one expedition into France, which came to nothing, largely through the apathy of his ally, the Duke of Burgundy. He then changed sides and allied himself with Louis XI of France, which proved to be a great mistake. Louis kept none of his promises except the payment of a yearly pension to Edward. The English king enlarged the chapel at Windsor by erecting an altar to the memory of a holy man from the north, one Father John Shorne, whose most spectacular exploit was immortalized by three lines printed on the wall:

> *Sir John Shorne,*
> *A gentleman born,*
> *Conjured the devil into a boot.*

The king raised funds by a system of benevolences, each person of property being asked to contribute voluntarily to the royal purse. He was so popular, particularly with the ladies, that most of the payments were made willingly enough. One rich widow, who had been asked for twenty pounds (she must have been very rich indeed), doubled the amount on being kissed by the king. This popularity involved him in a sharp exchange of views with Isabella of Castile. It had been thought he might marry the fair Isabella, and negotiations had been under way before Mistress Woodville fluttered her eyelashes to such good effect. The Spanish queen, quite obviously, was both disappointed and mortified.

She wrote a tart letter to the Spanish ambassador about Edward's preference for "a widow-woman of England."

The wives of London, to say nothing of the unattached generally,
could not resist his gift for conveying a hint of a secret liking by a mere
glint in his eye, by the casual touch of an arm or shoulder in passing,
by the intimacy with which he addressed them. Jane Shore, the wife of
a goldsmith, became his mistress quite openly, but even this evidence
of royal preference does not seem to have diminished the infatuation of
the others.

Queen Elizabeth bore the king ten children, only three of whom
appear permanently in history—a daughter Elizabeth and two handsome
sons. The royal couple seemed to be happy enough, in spite of the king's
flagrant philandering. The queen was content to live in high state and
to be more demanding of outward respect than any daughter of a
hundred kings. She dined alone in a stately chamber, with a lady of
highest rank sitting under the table at her knee, and her own mother,
the duchess Jaquetta, standing behind her to hand the fine lace serviettes.
Elizabeth's chief concern still seemed to be the advancement of her
sisters and brothers. The Woodvilles became the most cordially hated
family in the kingdom. She even strove to marry her favorite brother
to the daughter of Charles the Bold of Burgundy, who succeeded her
father. But Mary of Burgundy would not consider a match which she
considered demeaning.

The one incident of Edward's short reign which stays in the memories
of men was the execution of his brother, George of Clarence, and the
manner thereof.

2

Three sons of Richard of York had survived the wars: Edward IV,
George, Duke of Clarence, and Richard, Duke of Gloucester. The role
of George had been an inglorious one, a combination of treachery and
self-seeking. In physique and appearance he was a reduced reflection of
his massive and debonair brother, the king, not as tall, not as strong,
not as handsome. The resemblance went no further. Clarence had
none of Edward's ability. He was envious and conceited, and full of the
belief that so many younger sons in royal families have held, a firm
conviction, in fact, that he was capable of making as good a king as his
older brother. A born intriguer, he was also a man of furious temper.

Finally he was capable of the basest treachery as he had shown in several crises of the war.

Although they continued to feel some affection for this weak and unstable brother, it is certain that neither Edward nor Richard could dismiss from their minds his joining with Warwick to oust the former from his hard-earned throne. The second turning of his coat, to line up on the Yorkist side for the final stages of the war, had served as additional proof of his lack of honor and conscience. Before the last battle at Tewkesbury, there had been rumors afloat that he was ready to make a third shift and appear again with a Red Rose in his helmet. Everything he did in the last days of the fighting was under the close scrutiny of his brothers.

Even with peace established and the Lancastrian leaders dead or out of the way, Clarence continued in his favorite role of trouble-maker. He was bitterly against the queen and the Woodville family. In this he was on the right side of the fence, but his feeling against them could be attributed largely to personal interests. It irked his proud spirit to see the brothers of the queen holding national posts which he believed should belong to him. His acquisitiveness led him to quarrel bitterly with his younger brother, Richard, over the division of the War-wick lands, and this was doubly unwise, for he needed friends to stand by him and Richard had always been the stoutest in his defense.

The death of his wife Isabel, the daughter of the Kingmaker, was a blow which caused him seemingly to lose his head. He had loved her very much and was certain that she had been poisoned, an explanation continually accepted in those days when the nature of disease was so little understood. One of his wife's attendants was the widow of Roger Twynyho, whose name was Ankarette. This unfortunate woman was accused of serving her mistress a drink of ale mixed with a "venymous" poison. Clarence did not wait for any adequate investigation to be made but had her arrested without a warrant. The prisoner was taken to her native county of Warwick and put on trial. Word of the headlong course taken by the king's brother reached Westminster and a writ of certiorari was issued to stay proceedings. It did not reach Warwick in time. The woman had been convicted at one hasty sitting, with Clarence in court, and executed immediately.

One victim was not enough to satisfy the rage of the bereaved Clarence. One John Thursby was charged with poisoning the infant son of the duke. After a trial as hasty and unconstitutional as the first, he was convicted and hanged.

A wave of indignation swept over the country, for a fair trial was the one right to which Englishmen clung above all others. The duke's enemies at court were not content to let the matter rest without action. They adopted much the same method by extracting a confession by torture from a man named Stacy, who was supposed to be a dealer in black magic, that a friend of Clarence, Thomas Burdet, had been using incantations and other devices to cause the king's death. Stacy and Burdet were hanged together at Tyburn, protesting their innocence to the end.

The victims in this unsavory chapter seem to have been innocent by-standers of low degree who were unfortunate enough to stand within reach, but Edward may have believed that Clarence had set Stacy and Burdet to the task of encompassing his death. Certainly he was now convinced that his brother should no longer be allowed to display his lack of scruples and discipline. Clarence was summoned to appear before the king in London.

It has already been explained that Clarence had advanced himself as a candidate for the hand of Mary of Burgundy, although so newly a widower himself. This was going directly contrary to royal policy. Edward was now determined to maintain a firm alliance with France and he was furious when Clarence blundered into things, to afford Louis of France an excuse to delay in carrying out the obligations he was committed to by his treaty with England. It no longer needed the whispering of the Woodvilles in the royal ear to convince Edward that George of Clarence would be a troublemaker as long as he lived.

### 3

Clarence was brought to trial before the Parliament which met in January 1478, the king himself appearing in the role of accuser. A long list of offenses was produced, including a charge that he had spread a story that Edward was illegitimate and had no right, therefore, to be king. Edward summed up the evidence against his brother by declaring that he, as king, could not answer for the peace of the realm if Clarence's "loathly offences" were pardoned.

Clarence had no one to support him, to say a word in his defense. His undisciplined conduct apparently had set the whole nation against him. The members of the House listened to the witnesses in complete silence, without any effort to probe into the facts. When Clarence protested his innocence and cried out his willingness to meet anyone in mortal combat to prove it, the silence remained unbroken. Never before, perhaps, had there been more readiness in passing a bill of attainder.

The punishment was left to a court of chivalry which met promptly. Inevitably he was sentenced to death.

Edward now became the victim of doubts. Having been driven to action by his brother's treacheries, he still did not want to be responsible for his death. Their mother, the once Proud Cis of Raby, now broken by the impending tragedy, begged that clemency be shown her erring son. Richard, putting aside all his reasons for resentment, pleaded in the same cause. A week passed and the king was still unable to make up his mind.

Finally the House took the initiative by petitioning him to carry out the sentence. This display of constitutional pressure was what Edward needed. He decided that Clarence should die but declared there must not be a public execution. As a sop to his own doubts and feelings, and because of a belief that spectators must not witness the punishment of a prince, he ordered that the execution be carried out within the Tower.

By thus drawing a screen over the event, he created one of the strangest mysteries in English history. How did Clarence die?

With public curiosity at boiling point, it was impossible to conceal the fact that the sentence had been carried out on the seventeenth or eighteenth of February. But then a curious story began to circulate, to pass from mouth to mouth, to fill the minds of all people with fascinated horror, to set the customers in taverns into goggle-eyed speculation over their ale. Clarence, at his own request, had been drowned in a butt of the rare wine called malmsey; such was the story.

No other explanation has been forthcoming. Neither the officers of the Tower, nor the close-lipped custodians of policy in the halls of state, not the king himself nor his household took steps to deny the story. Either there was truth in it or they were reluctant to contradict it by telling what actually had happened. It may very well have been felt that, if no explanation were made, the rumor would be dropped in course of time by reason of its own fantastic weight.

But the story did not die. Three of the writers who were setting down the chronicles of the day, two English and one French, accepted the butt of malmsey without any qualms. And so the pens of later-day historians, which pass confidently and easily over many stories which seem to fall somewhat into the realm of fairy tales, came to a hesitation at this point. What was to be believed? And what could be written in explanation?

Some deny it as absurd. Some suggest, rather weakly, that there might have been an element of accident about it. One earnest seeker after truth went to the extent of measuring the quarters where Clarence had been kept to see where the butt could have been located. One version, in a play, suggests that the executioner, proceeding along other lines, used the butt as an easy means of completing his task.

And yet a study of the circumstances makes it possible to put some reliance in the story of the butt of malmsey.

Malmsey was a strong but sweet wine which came from the Morea in Greece. It was perhaps the most favored beverage of the day, the wine of kings and princes and people of wealth. The common man never partook of it. The cost was too high.

Clarence undoubtedly was a malmsey addict. It is clear that he had a sybaritic strain in him and so he would prefer this fine wine to any other.

A study of the character of this man makes it clear he had an acute dread of death. He was not a fatalist in any sense of the word and could not be expected to meet death with resignation. He was flighty, treacherous, impetuous, proud to a point of unreason, selfish in every thought and instinct, and he was young to die—only twenty-eight and in sound health. It goes without saying that the hours which passed after he was told he must die were filled with panic and a suffocating fear of what that meant. Although not actually a coward, every moment would pass in fear of the sharp edge of the headsman's ax. He would see it suspended over his head as he knelt at the block. He would live in dread of the moment when it would cut through his neck. Other ways of ending the privileged existence of a prince of the blood royal would seem almost as dreadful, particularly the horrible agonies of death from poisoning.

But there had always been a partial belief, or a myth, that drowning is an easy death. Perhaps Clarence thought of that and believed also that a taste of a favorite wine on his palate would lessen still further the pangs of death.

One point seems reasonably certain: if Clarence *did* make such a suggestion, Edward would have accepted it as an easy solution of a harrowing problem. George must die. Let him die, then, the way he desired.

A wine butt is a large container. In the fifteenth century it was constructed to hold 120 gallons and sometimes a little more. It might not be practical to carry one through the narrow and sharply angled passages of the prison. Certainly it would be impossible to get one through the door of a cell. The conscientious investigator who sought to ascertain where the butt stood in Clarence's cell might have saved himself his pains. The butt would not have been taken to Clarence, he would have been taken to it.

This would have been the method employed. He would have been securely trussed and then led, or carried, down into the dark, dank cellars of the Tower where the wine butts stood. And there, his knees bound close beneath his chin, the troublesome prince would have been lowered into the wine he had imbibed so appreciatively in life, and the cover closed down securely.

This is no more than a theory. The mystery which Edward IV created by his desire to get rid of Clarence as secretly as possible will always remain a mystery.

## CHAPTER X

# William Caxton

## 1

THE dynastic struggles called the Wars of the Roses were the cause of widespread suffering in England. An equally serious charge may be laid on the doorsteps of the titled contestants who split the nation apart in the latter half of the fifteenth century. While Englishmen rode or marched to battle under either one of the two symbolic roses, the Renaissance was sweeping Europe. Men were awakening to new intellectual interests, to the study of new philosophies, to the enjoyment of great advances in the arts. These significant changes, which reached a high point in the years when the English civil war attained its peak of savagery, were reflected rather dimly in the island kingdom. Chaucer had died before the fighting began, but a few other pens were still devoted to writing in the English tongue. On the whole the period was undistinguished and dreary.

It would be unfair, however, to pass by these years, after detailing the trials, the cruelties, the loves, the hates, the intrigues of an England resounding to the clash of arms and the fearsome booming of new weapons called cannon, without turning to one event which opened up great new vistas. During the reign of Edward IV a man named William Caxton set up a curious shop in London for the printing of books.

This is much more worthy of discussion than the strategy of Barnet or the folly of Tewkesbury. This eager and resourceful man, verging on old age when he began work, deserves the nod of posterity as much as the grandiose Kingmaker or the vengeful Margaret.

**2**

In October 1470, Edward of England, fleeing from the successful invasion by Warwick, came to Bruges with a party of 700 or 800 men. They were a sorry lot, a hungry and downcast collection of die-hard adherents of the Snow Rose. A throne had been lost and the coins in all of their pockets, if added together, would not have filled a wine cup. The magnificent but unready Edward had even found it necessary to strip the fur-lined coat from his back to pay the master of the ship on which he had crossed the narrow seas. The refugees threw themselves on the bounty of the few friends they had left in the Low Country.

It happened that, by virtue of an act which Edward himself had passed granting a charter to the Merchant Adventurers at home and abroad, the mercers of London had opened a hall at Bruges. Then they had established a governor there to control matters of trade between England and the Flemish merchants. The incumbent at the time was one William Caxton, once a mercer in London and a man of high courage and rare tact, and, of at least equal importance, a man with a vision. His courage he displayed by welcoming the deposed king. It required a stout heart to do this, for the Lancastrians now held London and the members of the Mercers' Guild, who had appointed him, were paying lip service, at least, to the Kingmaker. His tact entered into the arrangements he helped to make in finding temporary homes for the morose and half-stunned men who had accompanied Edward into exile. His vision would be displayed later.

The house of the Merchant Adventurers in Bruges was large but probably not imposing. It had to be of sufficient size to hold the incoming supplies of English wool and probably the goods to be exported back to England. The living quarters undoubtedly were small, for one of the rules governing the appointment of men to represent the Adventurers abroad was that they must not be married. The building probably stood tall and upright, a many-storied mart of trade, with stout timbers and a great deal of cheerful paint, these being architectural earmarks in the Flemish world. It was a busy hive with so much buying and selling to oversee.

The matrimonial prohibition of the Adventurers provides one of the few clues to the character and personality of Caxton. He was a bachelor, an aging bachelor, moreover, being around fifty years old at this stage of his life. As nothing in the way of a description of him is available, and even hearsay is silent on the subject, it is possible to use nothing more than imagination in attempting to draw a picture of him. He was undoubtedly an industrious and austere man, devoted closely to his work and the splendid ambition which filled his mind, a good foot shorter in stature than the imposing king, probably plain of face and quiet of mood. He married a little later, probably after he had given up his duties at Bruges. His wife, Maude, gave birth to one daughter named Elizabeth, who married in the course of time a merchant trader in London.

Caxton was beginning to realize that his real interest in life was shifting from merchandising problems to a curious new trade which had risen on the mighty wave of the Renaissance. Printing. The printing of books and pamphlets. The preparation of books was being removed from the skilled hands of monks who spent years on emblazoning beautiful scripts for the powerful and wealthy into the ink-stained fingers of workmen who would make books by the thousands for the reading of the many. It is certain that Edward visited the hall of the Merchant Adventurers in Bruges and that he acquired there, through contact with William Caxton, an interest in printing. With the king went his brother-in-law, Lord Rivers, who had his full share of the Woodville good looks but who possessed something the other brothers of the queen lacked—an interest in letters. Rivers and the earnest Caxton discovered an affinity at once, an admiration for the glossy and easily read volumes which were beginning to roll off presses in Italy and Germany.

Edward's stay in Bruges was a brief one, for he accomplished the quickest turnabout in history. In a space of time several months shorter than the span of Napoleon's enforced exile at Elba, the king completed arrangements for a return to England. He had been staying in the town mansion of Louis de Bruges and here his urbanity had made him very popular with the townspeople. When word reached him that a fleet of ships supplied by Louis XI of France had assembled at Damme, the port of Bruges, he left at once with a following not much larger than the party he had brought with him from England. The worthy burghers were so sorry to see him go that Edward decided not to reach the port by using a canal boat but by walking there, so that all the Brugeois would be able to see him en route. The streets were lined with people who cheered the tall monarch and shouted their good wishes. It will be abundantly clear by this time that Edward IV, with all his faults, had an instinct for popularity that has seldom been equaled and never excelled by any wearer of a crown.

Six years later Caxton had passed through some form of self-imposed apprenticeship, mostly spent at Cologne, and had mastered the mysteries of printing. He proceeded then to carry out his ambition to set up a shop in England where books could be printed in the English tongue. It now becomes apparent that Edward possessed another virtue—not found in all kings—his willingness to remember those who had helped him. Appreciating the courage which Caxton had shown when he was in exile, he now used whatever influence may have been needed to secure for the latter the use of a building at Westminster for the start of his enterprise. Two years later the king granted him the sum of twenty pounds for "certain causes and matters performed."

There has never been a time when a new trade has come into being without serious opposition. Caxton was to find that the Guild of Stationers in London was strongly against the new method of making books by machinery. What would become of the scriveners and text writers who made their living by the making of copies of books by hand? The church at first considered printing an unholy practice. It was the hand of the devil reaching out to spread wrong thinking and wrong teachings. Without the support of the Crown, Caxton might have found angry mobs gathering outside his shop, ready to destroy the ungodly instruments with which he sought to poison the minds of men. The rumor spread, of course, that he was a Lollard and a man of evil intent.

Through some influence, possibly that of the king, he was given the use of a small building called the *almonesrye* in a group of similar structures occupying an enclosure southwest of Westminster Abbey. Here he set up a *pale,* a sign painted red to denote his occupation, and began on the methods of producing books which he had learned on the continent.

No authentic description of the place has been left, but it is generally assumed that he did not live on the premises. Some of the space was devoted to the very necessary task of selling the books to the public. It was Caxton's practice to issue what were called advertisement sheets (the word "advertisement" could not have been new at the time for he uses it several times in the volumes he produced) in which he announced that certain books were available and advised customers "to come to Westminster in to the almonesrye at the *reed pale.*" People began to come in numbers which increased steadily. Caxton often had to print third and fourth editions of his books.

The work which went on inside can be explained in some detail. One biographer, H. R. Plomer, says that the center of the workshop contained "a substantial framework of timber and iron, the mechanical part being fitted with an ordinary worm-screw and iron." This was said to resemble, in fact, the old cheese presses in use up to comparatively recent times. On this mounted platform were placed the small metal frames in which the compositors (this term seems to have been a century later in achieving common usage) had set up words with small letters of lead. This appears to have been a slow process because of the necessity of carrying each line completed from the type case to the press.

Beside the press were pots filled with ink and "inking balls," which are described as much like boxing gloves tied to the end of a stick. When enough lines of type to make a page had been assembled on the press, the balls would be dipped in ink and the type thoroughly swabbed. After this a sheet of paper would be placed on the form and the pulling of a lever would press the paper against the type. This meant, of course, that only one sheet could be printed at a time. Sometimes ink stains were left on the sheet and it would then have to be discarded and another drawn. Caxton, it seems, was so determined to produce good-looking books that he would often discard many pages before securing one which suited him.

The pages would be laid in piles until all of the copy for the book had been put into print. Each pile was then sent to be bound. The trade of the bookbinder had been plied in England in the previous century. They were employed then, no doubt, in binding the illuminated sheets which came from the monasteries and the copies turned out by scriveners. It seems certain that at first Caxton did not have his own bindery.

In addition to the large room where the printing was done, there was a smaller one for the making and casting of type. Caxton seems to have designed his own type, with the exception of one "fount" which he brought with him from the continent. The type faces he designed later were much more artistic and at the same time easier to read.

Although he is supposed to have been so completely immersed in the work himself that he sometimes set type and even helped with the laborious work of printing, he depended on a foreman, a young man from Alsace who had accompanied him to England, named Jan van Wynkyn, but who is most often called Wynkyn de Worde. This ambitious young man took over the production end of the business. After Caxton's death, he acquired the plant and made a considerable success of it, issuing 110 works which are known and perhaps many more Wynkyn de Worde became so prosperous, in fact, that he moved away from the premises at the reed pale and purchased two houses on Fleet Street. One he used as his dwelling and the other became the printing plant. On the opposite side of Fleet Street stood the printing shop of one Richard Pynson who had set himself up in opposition. The proximity of these two pioneering efforts established a tradition and led to Fleet Street being the recognized site of publishing endeavors down through the centuries.

### 3

William Caxton was not content to print books; he always concerned himself with the translations and with the preparation of the copy. Before returning to England, he had made a translation of *Le Recueil des Histoires de Troye,* a romance which had been highly successful. This he produced later from his busy little plant in Westminster. The first book he printed in England, however, was a more serious venture, *The Dictes and Sayings of the Philosophers.* This had been translated from the French by Caxton's aristocratic friend, Lord Rivers, but that gentleman of varied interests realized that it required some additional attention. This he was quite willing to entrust to the busy printer, and so Caxton went to work and introduced some revisions and also wrote an additional chapter, which he believed necessary. This initial venture was so successful that the little shop at the almonesrye rang with preparations for more. One of the most commendable of his early efforts was an edition of Chaucer's *Canterbury Tales* which was much larger than any of the others. Undoubtedly it did much to acquaint the people of England with the work of their great poet. He also put out an edition of Sir Thomas Malory's *King Arthur* and a translation of Cicero's *De senectute.* That he translated the last named himself is an evidence of his scholarship.

Caxton apparently was qualified to translate from both French and Latin. His first years were frantically busy ones, for in addition to his editorial duties he always supervised the work going on in the shop under young Master Wynkyn. He did not confine himself to his more serious ventures in publishing. A continuous succession of smaller books and pamphlets poured out from the ever busy press—some devotional books, some ballads, some short romantic tales. Caxton was not only jealous of his reputation as a judge and editor of literary material, he was also a very good man of business. The smaller books, particularly the short romances, were probably the ones from which the bulk of his profits were derived. In the course of the fourteen years between the founding of the printing house and his death, he produced nearly eighty books in all classifications.

He died in harness. On his last day of life he was busily engaged on a translation of *Vitae Patrum*, which was finished after his death on instructions from Wynkyn de Worde, who later published it. No reason is supplied in the records for his death but the suddenness of it suggests that his heart failed him. There is no record of the exact day on which the busy pen fell from his hand, except that it occurred in the year 1491. He was buried in St. Margaret's Church, Westminster.

Such in brief is the story of a man who deserves to be remembered for all time. History, which seldom has endings to record because of the cycles which bring to life again and again the issues which have seemed dead and done with, is full of robust and stimulating stories of the beginnings of things. The work of this courageous and industrious pioneer lacks the excitement of political change and the fascination of the chronicles of war. But in his quiet way he provided the foundation, or at least an important part of it, from which would rise the mightiest of towers.

PART THREE

# THE GREAT MYSTERY

## CHAPTER I

## The Whipping Boy

### 1

THE whipping boy was an unfortunate youngster appointed to receive any chastisement earned by the son of a royal family, on the theory that princes were above physical punishment. Sometimes the king might take it on himself to doff his crown, roll up his ermine sleeves, and lay the erring son across his august knee, but that was outside the rule. Under no circumstances should stinging whip or menial hand be laid on the hide of an heir apparent. It was supposed that the sight of someone else suffering for his wrongdoing would create a feeling of shame in the princely breast and be fully as effective, therefore, as a good, sound, personal beating.

The custom was not universal. The whipping boy was not a fixture in all royal households as was, for instance, the court jester and the dancing master. But references creep into the pages of history often enough to indicate that it was frequently the practice. It is recorded that one Barnaby Fitzpatrick was on hand to receive the hidings which ordinarily would have been the lot of Edward VI. That delicate little fellow, who resembled his burly father, Henry VIII, in so few respects, could not have been guilty often of offenses against discipline.

There seems to have been in the main a more common-sense approach to the problem in England, a feeling that the lesson would be more effective if the beating were administered to the one who had earned it.

The classic example of vicarious punishment was placed on the scroll of time by a ceremony at Rome when permission was granted Henry of Navarre to abjure the Huguenot faith and become King of France. Pope Clement VIII had a stubborn streak in him which had to be overcome first. It may have been not too difficult for Henry to consider Paris worth a Mass, but he, Clement, was not convinced that Henry was worth receiving into the church unless he underwent a cleansing ceremony. In diplomatic circles in Rome there was a fear that the Navarene, being a prince of such high spirit, might regard this as humiliating and refuse to agree. Then someone, recalling the custom of the whipping boy, suggested that the whole matter could be carried off by proxy. It has been contended since that Henry was kept in the dark until the ceremony had been performed.

Accordingly on September 16, 1595, the two ambassadors from France, D'Ossat and Du Perron, walked on foot to a church in Rome and knelt on the worn stone steps, in recognition of their unworthiness to go inside. Here they chanted together "Have Mercy, Lord" and on the closing line of each verse a switch was laid across their bent shoulders. It is said the switch was a slender one and that orders had been given that the blows were to be light. Both of the ambassadors were later made cardinals, a more than fair exchange; a red hat for a somewhat less than pink shoulder blade.

2

Richard III, who called himself Richard Plantagenet, succeeded his brother Edward IV. He ruled briefly, for little more than two years. His accession has been judged by history to be the most glaring and inexcusable of usurpations. His motive is still believed to have been personal ambition and his methods are held up as a combination of cunning and cruelty. Edward IV had left two sons, one twelve and one nine. They were incarcerated in the Tower of London and supposedly died there at the hands of assassins employed by Richard. It was due to the wave of horror which swept across the nation, so history tells us, that Henry of Richmond was able to land in England and draw to his banner strong enough forces to defeat and kill the king at the Battle of Bosworth Field on August 22, 1485.

Shakespeare, who cannot be blamed for taking history as it came to him between staid and sacrosanct covers, has used Richard as the darkest and most devious villain in his series of historical plays. Anyone who has seen an accomplished actor play the role in *King Richard III* can never forget this evil creature hobbling about the stage and later dying on the battlefield with the cry which lingers in every memory: "A horse! A horse! My kingdom for a horse!"

This is the Richard III with whom the world has grown up. This is the version generally accepted, despite efforts which have been made, sometimes guarded but sometimes loud-spoken and decisive, to say that there is little or no truth in it.

That Richard III was the most notorious whipping boy in history is a theory which is now being widely held. Fortunately for him he did not know when he fell in battle the humiliating role he would play. It was his memory and not his body which was to bear the brunt of blame for the blackest of deeds. Richard, whose naked body had been carried off the battlefield on a donkey's back with a halter around his neck, was in his grave and there was no voice that dared speak up for him. It is perhaps not strange that all the blame has been heaped on the supposedly crooked back of the last of the Plantagenets, while Henry VII, the first of the Tudors, has emerged in the full white light of blamelessness.

And so the saga of the extraordinary Plantagenets, with their brilliant successes, their tragic reverses, their wild extravagances, does not end with the blood of Richard ebbing away on Bosworth Field. With their gift for involvement in drama of the most fantastic kind, they have left another story for history to record: a grim and terrifying story, which can without question be termed the greatest of mysteries in English history, perhaps the greatest of all time.

## CHAPTER II

## How It Began

*1*

THERE are only two sources of any value for the story which charges Richard with the murder of the two princes in the Tower of London. The first in importance, *The History of King Richard III,* is generally ascribed to Sir Thomas More. The second is *Anglica Historia* by Polydore Vergil, an Italian author who was hired by Henry VII to write a history of England. The Vergil version follows that of More in most respects but departs from it in many important omissions. The histories which were published later during the Tudor period, with few exceptions, did not deviate from what More had set down, even accepting his most absurd and inaccurate statements. A controversy has been waged ever since, with a great deal of heat on both sides. Strangely enough, most of what might be termed official history, including school-books and the reports (written long ago) in encyclopedias and dictionaries, still adheres to the More version, even quoting in full the most ludicrous of details. But modern thought seems to have moved away from complete acceptance of the thinly supported legend.

What might be termed a mystery within a mystery has developed over the authorship of the More book, which will be identified hereafter as the *History.* There were two versions, one in Latin and one in English. Some authorities declare it to have been the work of Cardinal Morton, Archbishop of Canterbury, in whose household the young More served (he was not quite eight when Richard died) throughout his youth. Twenty-two years after More's death, in 1557, a relative named Rastell found the English version among his papers and printed it. However, the Latin version had been printed in 1543 by Grafton, incorporated with more material from what was called the Great Chronicle. The Grafton edition carried the story some distance beyond the translation which

Rastell found, which might indicate that More had not completed the work he set out to do.

There is an obvious reason to support the More theory. St. Thomas More was one of the greatest and most appealing figures in English history, a man of courage, of high purpose, and of an engaging wit. As chancellor under Henry VIII he refused to support the divorce of Catherine of Aragon and the king's marriage to Anne Boleyn. For this he was sent to the Tower by Henry, who could not brook opposition, and finally he was beheaded. Coming from such a source, it is easier to believe the almost fantastic story told of Richard's wickedness and his murder of the princes. More's integrity cannot be questioned, even though acceptance of him as the author leaves doubts as to the soundness of his historical judgment.

On the other hand, Morton was the right-hand man of Henry VII and one of Richard's dangerous enemies. He is given credit for Henry's most ingenious method of extracting money from his subjects, which is called "Morton's Fork." His instructions to the collectors in the field ran to this effect: "If the persons applied to for a benevolence live frugally, tell them their parsimony must have enriched them and therefore the king may expect from them a liberal donation; if their method of living on the contrary be extravagant, tell them they can afford to give largely, since the proof of their opulence is evident from their great expenditures." Morton, conniving servant of a sly master, became so unpopular that his methods have remained an unpleasant legend in English history. Being more expert in the use of his legal fork than in the wielding of a scholarly pen, it was less likely that the story of Richard's reign would be believed if it came from him.

This, however, is a matter of relatively small importance, for it is agreed that the information on which the *History* is based was supplied by Morton.

The work in question is no more than a fragment, a matter of, roughly, 25,000 words. It is in no sense a history of the reign of Richard, paying no attention to parliamentary records and having nothing to say about the thoroughness and fairness with which the king administered the laws. In fact, it deals almost exclusively with the many charges against Richard and is the only authority for most of them, although in no case does it offer proofs. The *History*, in fact, reads like a political broadside (as many historians have pointed out), a deliberate effort to garnish the coming of the Tudors and to cast a friendly light about the new incumbent of the throne, the far-from-glamorous Henry. Never before nor since has an important stage of history depended so completely on such a brief and unsatisfactory document.

Can it have been that Sir Thomas More's failure to finish the work after keeping it for so many years was the result of doubts he began to entertain of the honesty and value of the material his erstwhile master had entrusted to him?

2

To understand this scarcity of sources, it is necessary to look at the conditions which prevailed at the time. England, with her thick green woods and lovely meadows enclosing a multiplicity of hamlets, was not a land of great distances, but it seemed to be so when all travel was by foot or horseback. The roads were always rough and sometimes swampy. The ravages of war had converted bridges into piles of rubble jutting up above the surface of the water like the last black fangs in a gaffer's jaw. Watling Street and Ermine Street, the main thoroughfares, stretched interminably north and west. The king's writ still did not run beyond the beautiful Wye as it twisted and turned and rolled down from Plinlimmon to the Estuary. England seemed far removed from the continent because the winds of the North Sea and the Channel made navigation a matter of chance and a prayer. At many momentous periods, armies and fleets were held in leash for weeks while waiting a favorable turn of weather.

It followed that news traveled slowly. The country districts were fed on rumor and surmise and hearsay, supplied by such wayfarers as chanced to come their way. Richard did his best to correct this situation by re-establishing the post which his brother Edward IV had started in 1482. This made it possible to deliver messages by fast relays for 200 miles within two days. This, of course, was an official post, and so most people, in spite of it, lived out their lives in the same ignorance of what was happening and without ever glimpsing a pen print on a letter, which disturbed them not at all because they could not read. William Caxton might be inking his plates and printing his books industriously, but rarely did the eye of even a learned prior in a monastery rest on a printed page. Newspapers would not be dreamed of for centuries to come. There was no agency at Westminster which had the responsibility of keeping a chronological record of what transpired. This had been left for centuries to the monasteries where monks had compiled chronicles of uneven value. It is unfortunate that during this particular period the page of medieval history was more blank than ever before. Perhaps the continual clamor of internal war had taken men's thoughts away from the ordinary processes of living, but it so happened that the monkish chronicles had been discontinued. Save one, the not always accurate Croyland Chronicle.

Croyland was an abbey of the Benedictine order, lying north and east of Peterborough. Despite its isolation in what was called the Fen country, with the land low and swampy about it, the abbey was the most opulent in East Anglia. The church had a nave of nine bays and the aisles were 183 feet long, which gives an indication of considerable splendor.

It is unfortunate that the only monastic record left to consult was so far removed from the necessary sources of information. A study of this chronicle leaves the impression that it also had been suspended for a time and that it was resumed later. The new incumbent was responsible for often-quoted entries bearing on rumors of the deaths of the princes as well as some of the deliberately and brutally unfair stories about the married life of Richard.

## CHAPTER III

## Throwing the Book

### 1

THERE is a much to be deplored practice in the prosecution of criminal cases in the law courts of the present day. An ambitious and unscrupulous district attorney, determined to have a long record of convictions, will ask a defendant such questions as, "Were you arrested in 1952 for criminal assault?", "Have you ever been convicted on charges of bigamy?", "Were you arrested for kidnaping last year?" There is always a brusque note about this form of interrogation. A crisp and indignant "Confine yourself to answering the question, a mere Yes or No will suffice" shuts the defendant off if he attempts to make any explanation. The innocence of the man in the dock on all these counts may be established in the course of the cross-examination; but the harm has been done, he is a suspect character in the minds of the jury and the way has been prepared for pressing the charge on which he has been brought to trial. This is called "throwing the book" at him.

It is not a new practice. Clearly it was understood by Morton, the prelate given credit for the information on which the *History* is based. He saw the value of convincing the world that Richard was a villain of the worst kind before he proceeded to lay the most heinous charge of all against him. Like an unscrupulous prosecutor, he charged the dead king with the blackest of crimes. In doing so he did not give proofs, he simply made flat statements. History followed him on all counts, citing him as authority.

Here is a list of the crimes laid at Richard's door, most of them straight from the *History* or from other books published in later generations:

He pressed for the execution of his brother, George of Clarence, who will be remembered in the matter of the butt of malmsey.

He joined in the murder of young Prince Edward, son of Henry VI, after the Battle of Tewkesbury.

He slew King Henry "Sixt" with his own hand.

He had his brother Edward IV declared illegitimate in an open announcement at St. Paul's Cross, thereby accusing his own mother of adultery.

He forced Anne Neville to become his wife, even though she hated him, and later considered having her poisoned so he could marry his own niece.

This is indeed "throwing the book" with a vengeance. The sad part of it was that the throwing was all that was necessary. The Tudor historians accepted everything that was charged. Had not Sir Thomas More said it?

Let us consider such of the charges as may be dealt with to best advantage at this stage.

**2**

The *History* has this to say about Richard's part in the death of George of Clarence: "He [Richard] lacked not in helping further his brother Clarence to his death; which he resisted openly, howbeit somewhat (as men deemed) more faintly than he was heartily minded to his wealth— he was glad of his brother's death, the duke of Clarence, whose life must needs have hindered him—— But of all this point there is no certainty."

It has already been made clear that it was Edward IV himself who forced the issue in the matter of Clarence, being ever mindful of the latter's long record of treacheries and weary of his intrigues and his assumptions of royal prerogative, his ears ringing, moreover, with the complaints of his queen and her kinsmen, all of whom hated Clarence. Edward appeared in the House to act as prosecutor against Clarence and the hearing consisted exclusively of a bitter debate between them. It was a board presided over by the Duke of Buckingham, and on which Richard did not sit, which pronounced the sentence of death.

Even the *History* is compelled to assert that Richard "resisted openly," meaning that he declared himself against the execution of his brother. By what right can the sincerity of his attitude be questioned, particularly as no act or word can be cited to prove the "faintness" of his stand?

Richard was the youngest member of the family and also the one ugly duckling, lacking the fine stature of his three brothers, Edward, Edmund, and George, and the fairness of face that all three shared with their lovely sisters. It has been conceded that the dark and poorly boy had no envy in him because of his lacks. He loved them all. His loyalty and affection for his oldest brother, great Edward, was evident at every turn. As he grew into manhood, the fine qualities of courage and judgment he developed were never employed for his personal advancement. Everything was for the mighty and sometimes indolent Edward and to keep the family in power. Never had king a brother who could be relied upon more completely.

With Clarence it was a different matter. After his open break to join Warwick and the Lancastrian cause, he always had to be watched. He was a constant thorn in the flesh. He was bitterly opposed to Richard's marrying Anne Neville because he himself was already the husband of Isabel, the older of the two Neville heiresses. Generous fellow that he was, he wanted Isabel to have everything and Anne nothing. Naturally enough, Richard disputed this but he finally agreed to an arrangement which certainly favored Clarence. It is probable there was less warmth of feeling between them after that but Richard gave no evidence of deep-seated malice. In stating that Richard was "heartily minded to his [Clarence's] wealth," the *History* overlooks the fact that the division of the estates had already been made and that he would not benefit by his brother's death.

Men may *deem* many things, and the tongue of slander may be depended upon to spread idle lies. But it is not the function of an honest historian to publish such tattle and label it fact.

### 3

The accepted story of the death of young Prince Edward is that he was killed during the retreat from the field at Tewkesbury and it was not until a generation later that the effort was made to charge Richard with his death. The *History* did not refer to the battle and it remained for Polydore Vergil, the hired historian of Henry, to assert that the prince was taken prisoner and murdered. He adds, however, that Richard was one who stood aside and played no part in the killing. The complaisant historians who followed, being tender to the nod of Tudor kings, went further and incriminated Richard in the assassination.

In consideration of the part Richard played in the battle, this seems impossible. Edward, the shrewd and aggressive commander, always the architect of victory, had a tendency to consider his part done when the enemy fled from the field. The rest would devolve on someone playing the part of a chief of staff, although that term had not come into use. It is clear from everything that can be gleaned about the last battles that it was Richard on whom these tasks fell. He had commanded the van at Tewkesbury which included the cavalry, and it was his spearheading charge against the Lancastrian center, where the Duke of Somerset and the prince were in command, that started the rout. Now Richard was not the kind of leader who led his army from behind. Instead he rode in front, his emblem of the White Boar fluttering in his helmet and on the accouterments of his horse. With the aid of a concealed body of 200 spearmen who had been craftily concealed in a clump of trees by the wily tactician Edward, he drove the Lancastrian center from its position. It was Richard who led the pursuit through the Bloody Meadow and all the way to the ford of the Avon at Abbey Mill. It was during this pursuit that the Lancastrian losses mounted up and that the young son of Henry VI was killed.

The cavalry having borne the brunt of the fighting, they had sustained most of the losses. Richard being a considerate as well as wise leader (this is attested in all records), he would have his hands full after the battle was over. A list would have to be made of the losses the army had suffered. The wounded would be brought in for proper care. Clearly he would have to see that the wounded horses (casualties were generally greater among horses than riders) were put out of their sufferings. The armor and weapons of the dead soldiers and the accouterments of the chargers would have to be retrieved, a most necessary precaution because human birds of prey appear on battlefields as quickly as buzzards from the air. This would be followed by the need to find horse replacements (because the army would move the next day), and this would not be easy in a countryside denuded of supplies by the long wars.

The great task, however, would be securing rations for the men. The previous day the army had marched thirty-one miles *without food and with little water.* Some sporadic foraging brought in a little food during the night, but most of the Yorkist soldiers had fought the battle on empty stomachs. Richard's main task, therefore, would be to get food for the hungry men.

It is not a matter of theory or guesswork that the first shafts of dawn would be appearing in the sky before the nineteen-year-old Richard would be free to throw himself down in his tent for a few minutes of rest. There would be no time for him to stand idly about in the king's tent while prisoners were disposed of, as depicted by the Tudor propagandists.

*4*

"He slew with his own hands king Henry *Sixt,* being prisoner in the Tower," declared the *History,* adding for good measure and to place the guilt more surely on one pair of shoulders, "without commandment or knowledge of the king," meaning his brother Edward IV.

Here are the facts. On May 21, 1471, the Yorkist leaders arrived in London after their victory at Tewkesbury. That night they spent in the Tower with a large company, including many of the leading citizens. Both Edward and Richard were there, and the members of the council, as well as Lord Rivers, the constable of the Tower, because matters of first importance had to be dealt with at once. The king was sorely in need of money. The funds supplied by the French king had been exhausted and Edward had organized on promises the army which won the battles of Barnet and Tewkesbury. The wealthy citizens of London held plenty of Edward's paper, dating back before his flight to the Netherlands, but it was from them that the new financing would have to come, until such time as Parliament could be summoned. One can imagine the long tussle there would be over terms, for the Londoners, although friendly to the Yorkist cause, were shrewd and demanding.

This much settled, there was a banquet. Then the council got down to the making of arrangements for summoning a new Parliament. This involved much discussion of detail, for the House had to be hand-picked. Finally there was the question of replacing all the ministers and high officials at Westminster, who were Lancastrian appointees. New men, of Yorkist selection, had to be appointed to fill the vacated places.

Undoubtedly this was one of the busiest and longest meetings the council ever held. Everything had to be done at once. The last of the Lancastrians under arms were operating in full force in Kent under the command of the Bastard of Fauconberg, after being repulsed in an attack on the Aldgate at London. No time was to be lost in meeting this final drive of the adherents of the Red Rose.

Now Edward placed the greatest reliance on the sound judgment of his young brother Richard, as he had made so evident when the Warwick rebellion began. Richard would be seated beside the king during the whole of this long and furious session on the night of their arrival. His opinion would be sought on all points.

The next morning, bright and early, Richard led the royal troops down into Kent to settle matters with Fauconberg. This he accomplished decisively, taking the leader prisoner. He was engaged for four days and is next reported at Canterbury on May 25.

While he was engaged in these operations, the death of Henry VI was announced in London and the body was placed on display at St. Paul's. The official version of his death, as told in the Fleetwood Chronicle, was that the king died of "pure displeasure and melancholy" on May 23. It seems more probable that he was killed, through Yorkist fears that the conflict would drag on as long as he was alive. But to accuse Richard of the crime is the most malicious and gratuitous of all the attacks from which he has suffered. To state that he committed the deed "without commandment or knowledge of the king," as the *History* does, is sheer invention. Richard, although still not quite twenty, was Edward IV's right-hand man, but he was not the assassin of the party. If Edward felt that the old king had to be removed from his path, he would not place the dagger in his young brother's hand.

Even the *History* concedes this much, saying "which would, undoubtedly, if he [Edward IV] had intended that thing, have appointed that butcherly office to some other than his own born brother." Determined, nevertheless, to fix the guilt on Richard, the *History* falls back on its declaration that Edward did not know what was happening; without citing a fact to back the statement, not a rumor, not a whisper; just the parson of Blokesworth (an early phase of Morton's career) at his characteristic tricks.

When Richard became king, he had the body of Henry removed from its resting place at Chertsey and buried more fittingly at Windsor with the other kings. Many years after Richard's death, those who had set themselves to detect treachery and dark design in everything he had done declared this mark of respect was in reality an act of expiation and that Richard, moreover, wanted to end the visits people were paying to the tomb of the murdered king. If he had allowed the body to remain where it was, he would have been attacked for refusing to accord Henry suitable burial. Alas, poor Richard! No matter which course he took, the whip of calumny was bound to curl about his shoulders!

## 5

It now becomes necessary to say something about Richard and the girl who became his wife.

The chief supporter of Richard of York in his bid for the throne was Richard Neville, the Earl of Warwick, called the Kingmaker. Warwick had two daughters, Isabel and Anne, the most fortunate girls in the kingdom for not only did they have a full share of the Neville beauty but they would in course of time inherit huge estates. Richard of York's wife had been a Neville and so the bond between the families became a close one.

This story begins late in 1460 when Warwick had come over from France with an army and had beaten Henry VI at Northampton, as a result of which a compromise had been reached; Henry was to remain king for the balance of his life and then the crown would pass to Richard of York. But Henry's indomitable French queen would not agree to an arrangement which barred her son from the succession. She raised an army to keep up the struggle and York lost no time in marching north to meet this new threat. He arrived at his favorite castle of Sandal in Yorkshire the day before Christmas.

Sandal does not seem to have had much to recommend it except its strength. It was a place of last resort, a great strong castle on a high mound where a determined garrison could hold out indefinitely. To achieve this height a long slope began near the Calder River and ran on a gradual rise toward the northeast. The castle occupied the highest part of the slope. A strong barbican tower guarded the entrance and, to reach the keep, it was necessary to cross two drawbridges. The keep was tall and immeasurably strong, with walls fourteen feet thick and with a ring of towers almost equally massive.

Richard of York had heard reports of Queen Margaret's unexpected strength (and later discovered this to be sadly true) and so he brought his men to Sandal to wait for his oldest son, Edward, to join him with a force he had raised in Wales, a resolution to which, unfortunately for him, he did not adhere. But that story has already been told.

There was much delight manifested when the owner rode in through the barbican and it was seen that he had brought the two Neville sisters with him. It had been decided they would be safer away from London, which was still in a turmoil and never seemed free of some taint of plague. The family of the duke consisted at this time of four sons, Edward, Edmund, George, and Richard, and three daughters. The word "glamorous" was the only one to describe these children of the White Rose. They were tall and dazzlingly fair, and endowed with charm and vivacity of manner—all save one, Richard, the youngest of the family. Richard was dark and somewhat plain, and hardly better than average in height. One of his shoulders was slightly higher than the other. A great deal has been said of this inequality, although it is not unusual by any means. He was not humpbacked and he did not have a withered arm, although later it would be asserted in histories that he had both deformities.

Little Richard, as he was called by the other members of the family, may have suffered from polio in his infancy but he was beginning to gain in health and strength at this time. He was eight years of age and there does not seem to have been any jealousy in him, certainly no tendency to repine or openly bewail his lack of the family stature. His handsome brothers and sisters returned his affection. The family had gathered in the courtyard in a group around their still beautiful mother.

Isabel Neville was nine years old and was proudly riding her own horse. Anne was just four. It is unlikely that Richard had paid any attention before to the younger of the sisters but, standing in his usual place in the rear, he watched the girl as she was helped down from her seat behind one of the Neville pursuivants, a tiny figure muffled in furs. When she ran forward to drop a deep curtsey to her aunt, she looked oddly grown-up, for her skirts were long enough to sweep the ground and her high-waisted bodice was in the latest fashion. It is probable that the heart of the plain boy with his dark and somber eyes began to beat a little faster than usual.

This was the beginning. Richard, in spite of what most historians have said, would retain his feeling for her and he could never have been satisfied with anyone else for his wife.

The head of the great Kingmaker was filled with schemes which he kept strictly to himself. Things came to a head later, as has been explained earlier, and his two delicately slender daughters were used as pawns in his ambitious plans. Isabel was married to Clarence as part of the bribe to take the latter over to the Lancastrian side. She must have been an unusually attractive girl, for Clarence, who had never before loved anyone but himself, was really attached to her. When she died, he was disconsolate, for a rather brief time. Anne, at the age of thirteen, was taken to France and was included in the strange deal which Warwick and Louis XI of France made with Queen Margaret. Warwick was to turn his coat and fight for the restoration of Henry VI to the throne. Margaret's son, Edward, was to marry Anne.

Margaret was adamant against the plan at first. She received the Warwick family with marked coldness and at first refused to speak to Warwick himself. When she found that he was making a point of the marriage between his youngest daughter and her beloved son, she flew into one of her not infrequent rages. Edward, the real heir to the throne of England, to marry a little chit like this!

Her position, however, was a weak one. This was her last chance. She must either form an alliance with Warwick or give up all thought of gaining back the throne. Both Warwick and the shrewd King of France knew she must come to their terms. And come to them she did, although she stipulated that the solemnization of the marriage must wait until Warwick had made good his promises.

Some historians say that the pair were married at once, young Edward being very much taken by the small Anne, but others contend it was never more than a betrothal. The latter explanation seems the more likely.

Warwick accomplished all that he had promised. He landed in England and took Edward IV so completely by surprise that the latter had to fly across the North Sea with a mere handful of followers. Richard was included in the party which found shelter in the Netherlands. But Margaret did not follow at once on the heels of the victorious Warwick. When she finally arrived in England with the feminine members of the Warwick family in her train (Anne still treated with particular coldness), Edward had returned with an army and had defeated and killed Warwick at the Battle of Barnet.

What had Richard's feelings been when he learned that Anne's father was marrying her to Margaret's son? There can be no doubt that he was bitterly unhappy. It was bad enough to be in exile, to be living on the cold, hard bread of charity and waiting for a miracle which might never happen. To know that the one girl he had ever wanted was to marry the Lancastrian heir made his lot seem doubly hard. All was changed, of course, when he played such a brilliant part in the final victories at Barnet and at Tewkesbury, where his rival died.

George of Clarence, being Anne's brother-in-law, took charge of her after Edward IV resumed his sway. He made it clear at once that he disapproved of Richard's open desire to marry Anne, taking this stand because he did not want the huge Warwick estates divided. Even after Edward had interposed in Richard's behalf, Clarence let it be known that if necessary he would hide the second sister from his brother. This would have been a simple matter because Clarence had castles in many parts of England and manor houses by the score. Anne, if she were willing, could have been hidden away in any of them. But, say the Tudor historians, following in line like so many sheep, "he had to conceal her by disguising her as a serving-maid and placing her in a kitchen in London." Yes, most of the books on the subject still repeat this absurd statement!

When a girl has been kept under close surveillance and disappears, to be found later disguised as a servant, it can mean only one thing. She had run away! The role of serving maid had been adopted to enable her to make her escape. The little Anne was a young lady of rare spirit. She was not running away from Richard, she was getting herself out of the clutches of her selfish brother-in-law.

The historical version goes on to say that, in spite of the ingenuity of Clarence [sic!], Richard succeeded in finding her. That again would be an unusual accomplishment. Members of the royal family were served at table by dukes and earls and members of the highest nobility, my lord This to hand the platter with the mutton, my lord That to hold the royal napkin. Richard could have dined in all the houses of London without laying an eye once on a serving maid. Is it to be assumed that he went prying into all the kitchens in London in search of his lost love or that he was casting a net over the whole countryside? Nevertheless he heard where Anne was, and the only reasonable explanation was that she herself contrived to get word to him.

Richard promptly removed her to sanctuary at St. Martin's le Grand and very soon afterward they were married. Although they were first cousins and should have had a dispensation, they did not wait to get the Pope's consent, and His Holiness was forbearing enough not to interfere.

The story is still told as proof that Richard forced Anne to marry him. It reads instead like a page from a very pleasant romance.

In the peaceful years which followed the return of Edward to the throne, Richard was employed largely in the north. He performed his duties so fairly and thoroughly that he won for himself a popularity which did not end with his death.

He resided with his bride at Middleham Castle in Wensleydale, which had belonged to the Warwick family. Here as a boy Richard had lived for some years under Warwick's guardianship and during that time his acquaintance with Anne had ripened. It was one of the most pleasant spots in all England, situated in the North Riding on the Ouse, almost within hearing distance of the bells of Jervaux Abbey and in easy walking distance of the waterfall known as the Mill Gill Force. Warwick had converted the bare walls of the castle into one of the most magnificent of family seats. The ceilings were lofty and the oak screens masterpieces of carving. The windows held the finest stained glass. Here in 1474 a son was born to the young couple and given the name of Edward. There were no signs of discord in the family.

And there they may be left for the time being.

## CHAPTER IV

# The King Is Dead, Long Live the King

## 1

To HAVE a clear understanding of what happened after the death of Edward IV, it is necessary to go rather more fully into the activities of the queen's family, the ambitious Woodvilles. In the first place it had been clear to all that the king had not long to live. Under the once fine glow of health which had added to his amazing good looks, the telltale purple of overtaxed veins was beginning to show. Edward was becoming corpulent and flabby. His breathing was short and labored, he no longer cared to ride out to hunt or, in fact, to bestir himself in any way. In the evenings he gave himself over so completely to his flagon of wine that he would fall into a state of sodden intoxication. It was generally necessary to carry him to his bed in an unconscious condition.

This last phase of his life had led to some diminution of his popularity. One of his greatest extravagances, for of course the Plantagenet blood in his veins made him lavish with his money, was the erection of an extremely costly stable. Over their wine, men would wink slyly and drink to "the princely stables and the favorite *grey* mare," a play, of course, on the queen's name in her first marriage.

With the king lapsing into habits which were certain to cut short his years, it behooved the Woodvilles to get themselves still more firmly established. The queen's father had been executed during the wars and his earldom had descended to his oldest son, Anthony, the most intelligent of the family. Anthony it was who took such an interest in Caxton and supplied him with his first book—a debonair and doughty man who shared, unfortunately, the selfish qualities of the rest. Elizabeth was not content that her oldest son, Thomas Grey, had been made Earl of Huntingdon and had secured for him the marquisate of Dorset, which set him above all the earls in the land (the backbone of the older aristocracy) and just below the dukes who had royal blood in their veins. To provide him with the wealth to live up to his title, she had married him to the richest heiress in England.

The greed of the Woodvilles made them so unpopular that even at court it was the source of sly quips. Once the court jester came into the royal presence in a costume which caused titters of amusement. His coat was so short that it did not conceal his anatomy below the waist and with this he was wearing shoes of such length that they almost made up for the deficiencies of the coat. He was carrying a marsh pike in his hand.

The king was not too far gone in his cups to fail of seeing that the jester had prepared some amusing jape for the amusement of the company. He glanced up over the brim of his flagon.

"Ha, sir fool!" he said. "Whyfor this costume?"

"Upon my word, sir king," replied the fool, "it is indeed unsafe to venture out in any other. The *rivers* are so high in your realm that I could hardly hope to get through them, save by the use of this staff."

It is reported that everyone laughed, even the king himself.

Edward's end came suddenly and it proved a disconcerting matter to the sharp-eyed Woodvilles. It had been expected that the heir to the throne would be left in his mother's care. Through her they could control the kingdom even more completely than they had done while the sodden king lived. A household for the young Prince of Wales had been set up under the control of Lord Rivers with the title of governor. A council had been appointed to assist in the boy's education and training. Richard was a member of the council, but he had found himself hemmed in by members of this ubiquitous family. Sir William Stanley was steward, Sir Richard Crofts treasurer, the two sons of the queen's first marriage were both active and voluble members. Richard, watchful and disturbed, was in such a complete minority that he carried no weight.

This household had been established in the castle of Ludlow, a long way from London and quite close to the Marcher country. The heir to the throne was here, under the watchful eye of his uncle Rivers, when fast-riding pursuivants, covered with dust and red of spur, came pounding at the gate with word that King Edward was dead. They had brought other information which was most disturbing. Edward's will appointed his brother Richard protector of the realm and made him also guardian of the heir. This disposition of power should have been expected, for the late king had always placed the greatest reliance on his younger brother. No better proof of this can be cited than Edward's action and words on the historic occasion when he learned that the Kingmaker had turned his coat. He sent a messenger in great haste to Baynard's Castle. "Bring back Gloucester," he directed. "In these difficult matters, that boy's head is better than a whole council."

The *History* states that Richard was in London when Edward died and that he persuaded the widow not to send a large escort to Ludlow Castle to bring the Prince of Wales back to the capital, thereby making it possible for him to gain possession of the prince's person. This, of course, is untrue and is only one of the glaring misstatements with which that document is crammed. It is an invention to convey the impression of plotting on Richard's part from the beginning.

Richard was in the north when his brother died. He had paid only two visits to the court from the time that he married Anne. In that period he had been successful in repelling Scottish attacks, in maintaining law and order, and in winning the respect and admiration of the people. A messenger reached him a few days after Edward had breathed his last, dispatched by Hastings, the lord chamberlain. It informed him that the late king's will appointed him protector of the realm. There was a note of urgency in the message. "Get you to London," advised the chamberlain.

Richard's motto was *Loyaulte me Lie*, Loyalty Binds Me. This applied above everything else to his feeling for his dead brother. He had loved Edward very much. In the deepest grief, he rode to York and attended a Requiem Mass, to which all the nobility of the north were summoned. After the service, they were required to take an oath of allegiance to the young prince.

Richard was anxious to have his dead brother's wishes carried out in a proper and legal way. Instead of acting on the urgent note from Hastings, he waited for formal notification from the council of his appointment. When nothing reached him, he sent a messenger to Lord Rivers at Ludlow Castle, asking what plans had been made for the departure of the prince for London. He, Richard, desired to honor the new sovereign by accompanying him. No answer was received, and still no word came from the council.

At this point a second messenger reached Richard from Hastings which explained what was going on. The Woodvilles were moving fast to get authority into their own hands. The consideration which drove them to hasty action was that a protector's authority ceased as soon as the young king had been crowned. They must, therefore, arrange to have the coronation before Richard could put in an appearance. They set the date for May 4, less than a month after the king's death. The queen's oldest son by her first marriage, the Marquis of Dorset, was constable of the Tower and so had control of the national armament and the treasure which the late king had amassed. A meeting of the royal council was held at which Dorset gained approval for a bold move. The royal fleet was needed, he reported, to repel the attacks of French freebooters along the coast. The council agreed to an order to mobilize the navy and confirmed Dorset's recommendation that the queen's brother, Sir Edward Woodville, be placed in command. Dorset then took it on himself to provide the new head of the navy with a portion of the royal treasure. Official orders were being issued in his name and that of Lord Rivers, using the terms *avuncular regis and frater regis uterinus.*

On receipt of this second message, Richard proceeded to act with the decision and vigor he had always displayed on fields of battle. With a troop of 600 men, he set out briskly for the south. The party from Ludlow was well ahead of him. But Lord Rivers had led his escort of 2000 due east until reaching Stony Stratford, intending, no doubt, to follow from there the great road called Ermine Street, which ran straight south to London; but for some reason he had indulged in a long pause before going any farther. It was when Richard was within a few miles of the earl's party that he was joined by the Duke of Buckingham with 300 more men. The latter brought information which removed from the protector's mind any doubts he may have had about the intentions of the Woodvilles. He caught up with Lord Rivers before that somewhat dilatory nobleman had stirred himself to leave Stony Stratford.

The head of the Woodville family seems to have been taken by surprise. At any rate he did not offer any resistance. Richard placed him under arrest and packed him off to Pontefract Castle, together with a number of his lieutenants, including the queen's youngest son, Richard Grey, and Lords Vaughan and Haute. He then dispersed their force and, with his own men serving as an escort for the young king, proceeded to London.

The news of what had happened reached London before he did and the queen lost no time in rushing for sanctuary at Westminster. She took with her the Duke of York (the younger of the two boys who were later reported as victims in the Tower), all of her daughters, and quite a household of ladies and gentlemen, as well as a corps of servants. Apparently she expected to stay there for some time. One report speaks of Archbishop Rotheram of York going to Westminster to speak with the queen and finding there "much rumble, haste and business; carriage and conveyance of her staff into the Sanctuary, chests, coffers, packs, fardels, trusses, all on men's backs, all in a rush, some even breaking down walls to get the possessions into the Sanctuary."

Elizabeth's son Dorset had taken even more alarm—as well he might, considering the treasonable acts in which he had indulged—and had joined her there. Becoming still more unsure of his position, he slipped out of Westminster and betook himself across the North Sea to the safety of the Low Countries. A confession of guilt can be read into the haste with which the Woodvilles abandoned the spoils and ran to cover. They had gambled and lost.

The members of the council seem to have been relieved by the arrival of Richard and they proceeded to co-operate with him in his capacity as protector. The young king was given possession of the royal apartments in the Tower and a later date, June 22, was set for the coronation.

2

It now becomes necessary to return to the wild charges, the misstatements, and the absurd details of the *History*. It is therein declared that one Dr. Shaw, brother of the lord mayor and a preacher of great eloquence, presented himself at St. Paul's Cross on June 22, the Sunday when Prince Edward was to have been crowned king, and pronounced all members of the family of Edward IV illegitimate. Taking as his text "Bastard slips shall never take deep root," he proceeded to challenge the right of the prince to succeed because the marriage of the late king to the beautiful widow, Elizabeth Grey, was not lawful. The king had brought into the world a child by another woman, one Elizabeth Lucy, who should, therefore, have been his queen.

The *History* proceeds to rule out this claim advanced by Dr. Shaw by declaring there had been no pretense of marriage in the Elizabeth Lucy affair. "She," quoting from the *History*, "confessed that they were never ensured. Howbeit, she said his grace spake so loving words unto her, that she verily hoped he would have married her; and that if it had not been for such kind words, she would never have shown such kindness to him, to let him so kindly get her with child."

It has never been explained where the *History* got this story about Elizabeth Lucy. There had been many women in Edward's promiscuous life but none bearing that name. As will be shown later, Edward was supposed to have married Lady Eleanor Talbot, years before he succumbed to the charms of Elizabeth Grey. Evidence on this entanglement was introduced into Parliament, where it was debated at length; and as a result the children of Edward IV were declared illegitimate.

It seems clear that Dr. Shaw did preach a sermon on the subject. The careless pens which concocted the *History* knew this but did not know the name of the light-of-love whose complaisance led to this problem. They must, therefore, have invented a name for the lady, which raises a question as to how much else they inserted with equal carelessness. This, as one historian says, "should put us on our guard against credulously following them in graver matters."

A much graver matter is that Dr. Shaw then proceeded, according to the _History_, to claim that Edward IV had been illegitimate himself. To back this assertion it was necessary to charge the Duchess of York, the often-mentioned and lovely Proud Cis, with adultery. Richard was asserted to be the only member of the family lawfully begotten. "Neither king Edward himself," continues the narrative, "nor the duke of Clarence, among those that were secret in the household, were reckoned very surely for the children of the noble duke [Richard of York] as those that by their favor more resembled other known men than him."

Dr. Shaw's sermon was a carefully worked out piece of stage direction, according to the _History_. When he reached the assertion that Richard was the only member of the family who resembled his father, the latter was to appear casually and pause in full sight of the audience in the expectation that the people assembled there would be struck by the truth of it and raise their voices for him as king. In other words, Richard was aware of the statements which would be made, including the infamous assertion of his own mother's infidelity.

Can such a charge be believed? At this time the dowager duchess was in London and Richard, the last remaining son of the four she had brought into the world, was living with her at Baynard's Castle until such time as his ailing wife could join him. It is said she was advising him as to the steps he should take in the difficult situation he faced. This can be believed, because Proud Cis had been a managing type of woman all her life. When her husband, Richard of York, was engaged in his cautious bid for the throne, and more inclined to spar and feint than to go right in with intent to knock his opponent out, the duchess had gone many steps ahead of him by setting up a regal household, over which she had presided with all the graces of a queen. When her eldest son, Edward, came to her to say he was going to marry Elizabeth Grey, she strove hard to make him change his mind, pointing out the unfitness of such a match. She was always against the mate her gorgeous son had chosen, partly because of the favors Elizabeth distributed among her ambitious brothers and sisters. And now, with only one son left, she was striving to set his feet securely in the direction of the throne.

It was about this time that men first began to write in the English tongue instead of in French or Latin. Unfortunately few letters of the period have been preserved. In all that come from Richard's pen, he seems normal and kind, with a pleasant if somewhat dry wit showing through, and underneath everything a hint of sadness as though he sensed what lay ahead. A year after Dr. Shaw's alleged bit of electioneering, the duchess received a letter from her son. He had become king in the meantime and was in the north in connection with disturbances there. It read:

I recommend me to you as heartily as is possible; beseeching you in my most humble and *effectuous* wise of your daily blessing to my singular comfort and hopes in my need. And, Madame, I heartily beseech you that I may hear from you to my comfort. . . . And I pray God send you the accomplishment of your noble desires.

Written at Pontefract the 11th day of Juyn, with the hand of your most humble son,

RICARDUS REX.

Not the kind of letter, certainly, that a man could write after allowing such a charge to be publicly proclaimed against his own mother; an affectionate and humble letter, rather, making it clear that the best of relations prevailed between them.

Before leaving this point, an absurd discrepancy in the *History* should be pointed out. Richard had been described on an earlier page in this wise: "In body and prowess far beneath them both [Edward and Clarence], little of stature, ill-featured of limbs, crookbacked, his left shoulder much higher than his right, hardfavored of visage."

And now let us return to the crafty stage management that was supposed to gain Richard the approval of the people of London. Richard was to stroll nonchalantly on the scene after the preacher had spoken of Richard of York as true to the Plantagenet type. "But the lord protector," the eloquent Dr. Shaw was to declaim at this point, "that very noble prince, that special pattern of knightly prowess, as well as in all princely behavior as in the lineaments and favor of his visage, representing the very face of the noble duke his father." He was then to point to Richard and declaim loudly, "This is the father's own figure, this is his own countenance, the very print of his visage, the same undoubted image, the plain express likeness of that noble duke!"

And then Richard was to step forward, bowing humbly no doubt in acknowledgment, limping, his crooked back bent, his withered arm dangling in its sleeve, his evil face contorted into some semblance of a smile. Imagine the effect of this on the people of London, who were sharp of wit and free of all subservience! This unfitting apostrophe of the learned doctor would have evoked roars of laughter and not the cries which had been expected of, "King Richard! King Richard!"

But the *History* continues by saying that Richard did not appear at the right moment. The stage directions had not been explicit enough. The good doctor had finished his panegyric and a silence had fallen on the crowded square. The preacher looked about him in alarm and appeared at a loss as to what he should do. Then he glimpsed Richard approaching in the company of his friend, the Duke of Buckingham, so he repeated it all over again, word for word, as though, says the *History,* "the holy ghost had put them in the preacher's mouth."

Which are we to believe, the picture of Richard as an ugly monster which the *History* has given to posterity or this incident where he is depicted as the image of his impressive father? We cannot believe both. If one is not to be accepted, can any reliance be placed in the other?

The failure of this piece of folly (if it ever occurred as set down) did not convey any lesson apparently to the adherents of Richard. On the Tuesday following, says the *History,* the Duke of Buckingham came unto the Guildhall which was filled with people. He proceeded to make a long speech in favor of the protector, again in anticipation of a popular demonstration. Again the audience was "hushed and muted," so the duke gave his talk a second time, speaking in a louder voice. At the finish the hoped-for clamor began, but it was no more than a sorry imitation of what had been expected. At the nether end of the hall, "a bushment of the duke's servants with some prentices and lads that thrust into the hall" began to cry "King Richard! King Richard!" and to throw up their caps in token of joy. The duke seems to have accepted this perfunctory applause as the voice of the people and to have proceeded to act upon it.

One lesson that history teaches is that thrones are not overturned by half-measures or the clamor of paid claques. The ways of successful conspiracy are swift. Certainly such weak and foolish gestures as these imputed to Richard would have no effect in the city of London where the habit of the people was to turn out in turbulent mobs. The voice of London was never hushed or muted.

Not only had Richard always been a man of action and decision, he had seen his father fail to reach the throne by compromise measures, by consultations, by listening to the protests of those who opposed him. Moreover he had seen his brother Edward step boldly in and declare himself king without waiting for action of Parliament or for the approval of the people of London.

Richard already had behind him the kind of support which counted. England was thoroughly tired of boy kings. There had been three of them—Henry III, Richard II, and Henry VI—all of them unfitted for the stern business of kingship. Trouble had developed during the term of minority in each case, which had led to strife throughout the balance of each reign. If Henry V had left a son of mature years and with some of his own magnificent competence, the Wars of the Roses would never have been fought. And now here was a fourth one to be endured, with the circumstances in the case pointing to even more serious trouble. England did not want a boy king with the hated and feared Woodvilles grouped solidly about the throne. The older aristocracy still clung to the belief that a king was no more than the representative of their class and that he must be strong enough to rule well. They wanted a man at the head of the state, a strong man. It is no idle supposition that, as he rode south to assume the post of protector, Richard had heard these feelings expressed on every hand, "Must we suffer another boy king?" and "We must get rid of these upstarts." Being an honorable man, and still fiercely loyal to his brother's memory, he would not be hasty to act in the matter of the succession. But he knew when he reached London that a large part of the people would prefer a man on the throne, and that he was the logical choice. A trying decision lay ahead of him.

The trumpery playacting which the inventor of the Fork has inserted in the *History* is doubly absurd because Richard had begun to take decisive steps to face the situation two weeks before. On June 9 he had called a meeting of the council, to which the queen was not invited. They sat in conference for four hours and emerged with grave faces. The next day he wrote to the city of York, requesting that as many armed men as could be organized be sent to London to protect him from the conspiring forces back of the queen.

It was at this meeting undoubtedly that the council had first been informed of information brought forward by Bishop Stillington of Bath and Wells. His story was that he had married Edward IV to Lady Eleanor Talbot, a daughter of the Earl of Shrewsbury, and that it had been kept secret by royal command. This had happened, of course, before Elizabeth Woodville captivated the susceptible king under the Queen's Oak. If the bishop's word were accepted (he does not seem to have produced any form of documentary proof), then the king's marriage later with Elizabeth was bigamous and her children were illegitimate. The explanation generally accepted is that there had been no more than a "troth-plight" between the lady and Edward, for otherwise the bishop would have been impelled to speak out against the marriage with Elizabeth. In theory a troth-plight was binding on both parties but in practice it seems to have been regarded as breakable. Certainly this was done frequently in the case of the matches arranged for the sons and daughters of kings.

Whether marriage or troth-plight, the story which Stillington revealed was later laid before Parliament and there accepted as proof of the illegitimacy of Edward's children.

## CHAPTER V

## Richard Takes the Throne

*1*

IT BECOMES necessary to quote again from the *History* at this point to make clear what happened on June 13. Many lords had assembled in the Tower and the protector joined them in a mood of great amiability. First he said to the Bishop of Ely (Morton himself), "My lord, you have very good strawberries at your garden in Holborn. I request you let me have a mess of them."

"Gladly, my lord." And in all haste the bishop sent his servant for a mess of the strawberries.

The protector in the meantime had retired from the meeting, not to return for more than an hour. When seen again, he had "a wonderful sour, angry countenance, knitting the brows, frowning and frotting, and gnawing at his lips." Finally he broke into words, accusing two women, "that sorceress" the queen and "that other witch of her counsel, Shore's wife" of wasting his body by witchcraft. As Richard talked, he plucked up the sleeve of his doublet on the left arm and showed them "a weerish, withered arm, and small, as it was never other." All in attendance knew, declares the *History*, that his arm had been withered from his birth, but they agreed that the two women were worthy of "heinous punishment." At this, Richard rapped loudly on the board and immediately men in harness came rushing in, crying, "Treason!", so many of them that the chamber was filled. There was scuffling and brandishing of arms. Lord Stanley, who was among those present, received a wound on the head. Richard said to the chamberlain, Hastings, to the astonishment of all, "I arrest thee, traitor!" Several of the others, including Morton himself, were also named as guilty and were quickly bestowed in divers chambers. Hastings was taken from the chamber without trial and beheaded on a long log of timber. Richard then proclaimed that the lord chamberlain had been in a plot to do away with him. His next step was to send Jane Shore to prison and later have her walk across London in bare feet with a taper in her hand, as a sign of penitence. It is stated that he pursued this alleged sorceress with great malignancy.

There are two points of truth only in all of this. A meeting *was* held that morning in the Tower and Lord Stanley did acquire a broken head in the fracas. Or, perhaps, the strawberries should be exempt. All historians have used this bit with glee, as a shining example of reality in historical narrative. Shakespeare has used it: so let it be.

Everything else can be thrown aside as glaring mistakes, inventions, embroideries, or plain downright falsehoods, whichever one desires to call them. Let us take them up in order.

Richard did not have a withered arm, and perhaps this is a good place to deal once and for all with the question of his physical make-up and appearance. He was not a hunchback, but one shoulder was higher than the other. If a poll could be taken of all the tailors of all time, summoning them from the shades with their cushions in hand and pins in their lapels, it would be found that a man with shoulders of perfect evenness is rather rare indeed. The difference in Richard's shoulders was noticeable and, being sensitive, as the youngest and least attractive in a family of eleven, he sought to cover up by having his clothes padded and by draping cloaks over the lower shoulder.

As for his arm, could a man with a withered arm fight so manfully in many battles, particularly at Bosworth where he went down to his death so bravely?

All the evidence needed with reference to his face can be found in the portraits still in existence. He lacked the remarkable good looks of his brothers but his features were strong, if not beguiling. It seems a tragic face, with a saddened expression which might come from ill health in youth or the lessons he learned in a tragic life. It was a face, moreover, which one commentator asserts might be found on the judge's bench but never in the prisoner's dock.

A final and decisive piece of evidence comes to light from an unexpected quarter. In his *Historical Memorials of Westminster*, Dean A. P. Stanley tells of Richard's brilliant coronation and refers to "the strange appearance of king and queen as they sate stripped from the waist up to be anointed." This was a French custom and it was being employed at Westminster for the first time. Is it conceivable that Richard would have agreed to an innovation which made it necessary for him to appear with bare torso in the full sight of his most powerful subjects if he had a great hump on his back and a withered arm? No, he would have insisted on following the old ritual which would spare him this humiliation.

References such as this often lead to the truth more surely than any amount of argument and surmise. And so from this moment in the most important day of Richard's life comes the truth about his physical condition and out goes the story of his deformities through the stained glass of the Abbey windows!

The story of his deformities, in fact, is a part of the concerted campaign to make him out a man of despicable parts, a campaign begun in the reign of Henry VII and continued ever since, perhaps through an unwillingness to discard a theory so long accepted and so unrelentingly taught in history book and classroom.

And now for the charge of sorcery against the two women, the queen and Jane Shore.

Jane Shore was a beautiful young woman who had been married at an early age to one William Shore, a prosperous goldsmith in London. She was petite, trim, vivacious. The *History* describes her at great length: "Proper she was and fair; nothing in her body that you would have changed—a proper wit had she—merry in company, ready and quick of answer, neither mute nor full of babble—in whom the king took therefore the greatest pleasure—for many he had but her he loved." Her beauty made such an impression on the prowling king that he proceeded to make her his mistress. The relationship between them continued until Edward's death.

She seemed to captivate all men. Thomas of Dorset, the queen's oldest son, who became in the last years Edward's boon companion in revelry and also in lechery, had a warm eye for her and was quick to take her as soon as the king died. Standing off to the side was Hastings, who, it was said, "doted" on her and to whose arms she went when Dorset had to rush to the continent with smoking coattails after the Woodville plot miscarried. Richard would hear of her, of course, but it is not certain that he ever saw her, for it must be remembered that he paid only two visits to London during the last eight years of Edward's reign. To him she would be only one of the many mistresses that the king took and he would have no reason to single her out for enmity.

It is not known what arrangements the philandering Edward made when he stole the affections of the goldsmith's wife. She was seen a great deal at court and made many friends there, but had no place in the household. Nor did she remain with her husband, for one sentence creeps into the records about him—and a sad one it is—"he went away, or died." Poor Will Shore had been made very unhappy. Queen Elizabeth did not object to her royal spouse's errant ways but it is reasonable to assume that she conceived no liking for this gay little interloper with her pleasing manners. A definite antagonism must have developed between the two

women when the queen's son became Jane's protector. To believe they
formed an alliance at this stage and began to employ witchcraft to such
good effect that Richard's arm withered is to run counter to all the laws
which govern feminine behavior. Neither of them, from what is known
of their characters, would turn to the ugliness of sorcery, the punishment
for which was burning at the stake. Certainly they would not assume this
grisly risk together! To believe in addition that Richard, who was proceeding to his ultimate decision with deep thought and care and whose
judgment had earned his late brother's strongest praise, would blurt
out in public such an astonishing charge is fully as absurd. Moreover he
did not have a withered arm to display.

That Jane Shore was compelled to do penance for her loose morals
may have been due to clerical influence. At any rate, when Richard
decided to pardon her, he addressed himself to the Bishop of London.
His letter is worth quoting, for it provides an intimate glimpse of the
inner man, of his dry humor and real kindliness.

It seems that Richard's solicitor, one Thomas Lynom, had been sent
to see the lady when she was in prison and had fallen head over heels in
love with her. So badly was he smitten that he proposed marriage. The
king's letter to the bishop reads as follows:

"Signifying unto you," wrote Richard in his own hand, "that our servant and
solicitor, Thomas Lynom, marvellously blinded and abused with the late wife
of Wm. Shore, now being in Ludgate by our commandment, hath made contract of matrimony with her, as it is said, and intendeth to our full great
marvel to proceed to effect the same. We, for many causes, would be very
sorry that he should be so disposed; and pray you therefore to send for him,
in that ye may exhort and stir him to the contrary. And if ye find him utter
set for to marry her, and none otherwise would be content, then, if it may
stand with the law of the church, we be content (the time of marriage being
deferred to our coming next year to London) that, upon sufficient surety being found of her good a-bearing, ye do send for her keeper, and discharge
him of our commandment by warrant of these; committing her to the rule and
guidance of her father or any other, by your discretion."

There is no evidence here of any feeling about Dame Shore other
than disapproval of her immorality, no hint of an intention to charge her
with witchcraft, of punishing her to the extreme. Her pardon is arranged, with certain sensible restrictions, and that is that; an amiable
decision in an almost routine case. The silly fellow Lynom was brought to
his senses, apparently, for he did not marry the pretty lady of light heart
and light morals.

Unfortunately it must be told that she came upon evil days finally;
but that was long after Richard's death.

Finally there is the matter of the execution of Hastings. He was not dragged out that morning to the Tower court and beheaded on a log which was found there. He was tried, convicted, and executed five days later in the manner prescribed by law.

In the earlier passages of the *History,* Bishop Morton speaks, or writes, from hearsay and so falls into many serious errors. But he was a participant in the scene which is dealt with above. He was detained in custody and even stood in danger of losing his head for his part in the Hastings conspiracy. Every bit of action, every word spoken, would be indelibly etched on his memory. The version he gives, therefore, cannot be brushed aside lightly. He has been guilty of a series of deliberate falsehoods.

2

What motives were behind Richard's assumption of power? Was it personal ambition as practically all historians have said? This is a point which must be considered before approaching the main point of the enquiry which is, of course, the death of the two princes.

Edward IV had made one effort to resume the wars with France. On June 22, 1475, he landed at Calais with a well-equipped army of 16,000 men but found the French king more disposed to negotiate than fight. Expecting help from his Burgundian allies, the English king had waited for nearly two months at Peronne. During this long inactivity, Louis XI sent to Edward 300 wagons loaded with the best wines. Finally an agreement was made between the two monarchs. Edward was to withdraw his army to England on receipt of 75,000 crowns and an annual pension of 50,000 crowns. The truce was to be for seven years and the eldest son of Louis was to marry Edward's daughter Elizabeth as soon as the children reached marriageable age. To expedite the proceedings, Louis offered large sums to the men about Edward. The pensions and bribes paid to the English nobles are listed in the French Chamber of Accounts, still in existence. Most of these fine noblemen accepted their shares openly and gladly. However, Lord Hastings refused to sign a receipt for the 2000 crowns which constituted his share. He said, rather glumly, "This gift comes not at my request. If you would have me take it, slip it here inside my sleeve."

The younger brother of the English king, Richard, was the only one who refused to accept a share. He even absented himself from the meeting at Picquigny where the two monarchs met on a bridge and signed the treaty. What, he asked, would the world think of the wisdom and courage of England after this? For the first time in his life he openly disagreed with his brother.

It has always been acknowledged that Richard behaved like an honorable man. Even Lord Bacon, who was ready to accept all the ugly stories about Richard a century later, because of his reliance on the statements in the *History,* had this to say about the young brother who stood so manfully aloof: "As upon all other occasions, Richard, the duke of Gloucester, stood upon the side of honor."

The story of Picquigny is told here because it establishes one fact about Richard, that he was honorable. It makes it equally clear that he had deep patriotic instincts. His desire to act in the best interests of the English people was to be demonstrated in the brief span of his reign. In the one Parliament he summoned, he had provisions put into the statutes which proved his desire to rule with fairness and justice.

What would an honorable and patriotic man do when he stood in Richard's shoes?

It was clear to him that the length of time in which he could make his authority felt as protector was a short one at best. As soon as his term ceased, the Woodvilles would close in again about the throne. The young prince had already shown a definite disposition in favor of his mother and his handsome and debonair uncles. The inevitable result would be another civil war, because most of the nobility were determined to prevent the "upstarts" from acquiring more wealth and from taking over the highest offices in the kingdom.

There were many precedents for Richard to follow. In English history, Henry I stepped in to displace his older brother Robert; Stephen had brushed Matilda aside; John became king instead of Arthur, the rightful heir, and then saw to it that the boy was murdered; Edward II was deposed and killed; the same fate was meted out to Richard II, when Henry IV seized the royal power.

Richard may well have felt that the unpleasant duty of setting aside the sons of his beloved brother was imposed upon him by patriotic necessity. This viewpoint is one which can be accepted even while believing that Richard was actuated by ambitious designs as well. Jealousy has always been the most apparent trait in the brothers of kings. While Edward lived, Richard felt none of the green-eyed desires which ate so deeply into the bowels of the other brother, Clarence. But with Edward in his new-made grave, the situation was different. Richard, the youngest, the one drab-feathered member in a family of brilliant plumage, was finding himself now in a position of power In addition, because of his very great success in the northern counties, he knew himself capable of ruling well.

It would be natural for him to desire the best of everything for his not overly strong son at Middleham. He had been watching the growth of the one child with an anxiety fully shared by the boy's mother. Anne had lost her sister, Isabel, to a disease which is supposed to have been consumption, and her own cheeks had turned to an almost transparent and waxlike whiteness with occasionally a telltale flush. Richard undoubtedly hoped that his son would outgrow his frailty as he himself had done. But with Anne the case was different. He must have seen that she had not long to live. It would be gratifying for her to wear the golden circlet if for only a few brief months and to see him, the once little-considered younger son, the ruler of England. It may be more in keeping with the facts to say outright that Richard shared the ambitions of all the determined Yorkists. Should he be blamed for that more than the other members of his family, or their dynastic opponents who were equally possessed of the urge for power?

Without attempting to deny, therefore, that he felt such ambitious impulses, and with no will to absolve him from blame on that score, it still remains easy to believe his impelling motive was a conviction that he was needed at the head of the state.

Richard took a long time to make up his mind. This was to be expected. A man of honor, and one who had loved his tall and masterful brother, he could not take the step with an easy mind. One can imagine him standing on the walls of Baynard's Castle and looking with knitted brows in the direction of Westminster. Why, he must have asked himself many times, could not Edward have lived long enough for his son to come to man's estate? For then this responsibility, and this temptation, would not have been thrust upon him.

Definite conclusions are out of the question. But to anyone who has studied the character of Richard Plantagenet, and such facts as there are, without accepting the *History* blindly, as the Tudor historians and Shakespeare did, the conviction seems reasonable that he was actuated first of all by the dictates of patriotism.

Richard decided finally to place the crown on his own head. When Parliament accepted Bishop Stillington's story and proclaimed the children of Edward illegitimate, a statute was issued declaring Richard king. This was called *Titulus Regius*.

It is probable that Richard grasped at the bishop's belated exposure as a means of easing his conscience. If this were so, his usual sound judgment was at fault. He did not need to mask his intentions under so frail an excuse. The reasons Henry IV had given when he made himself king were still good enough. He was the best man to rule at a time when a strong hand was needed at the helm.

## CHAPTER VI

# A Short and Unhappy Reign

## 1

ALTHOUGH most men saw good reason for the change in kings, many still held reservations. They did not want another boy king, especially one backed and influenced by the dowager queen's greedy relatives, but they looked askance at what seemed the injustice of it. In their eyes the son of Edward was "the Lord's anointed." A discordant note was heard on men's tongues. What would happen to the two boys now? No one had forgotten how Edward II was barbarously murdered after his deposition and they recalled how Richard II had been cut down by the swords of assassins as he sat at supper in the castle of Pontefract. Would the princes suffer the same fate?

The relationship between Richard and his most powerful and active supporter, Buckingham, began to show signs of fraying. It has never been made clear how the seeds of discord began to grow. Was Buckingham dissatisfied with the rewards he had received? Did he nourish a secret feeling that he would make a better king himself, as some historians have suggested? Under the circumstances, it was a great mistake for the new king to release Morton into Buckingham's custody at his castle in Breconshire. Morton lost no time in spreading his nets before the feet of the already disgruntled duke.

"The bishop," says the *History*, in the preparation of which the honest bishop had at the least a collaborating hand, "was a man of great natural wit, very well learned, and honorable in behaviour, lacking in no wise ways to win favor." After this gentle bit of self-laudation, the report of what happened in the grim castle in the foothills goes on to tell how Morton proceeded to ply the overly proud and not too scrupulous duke "with fair words and many pleasant praises," finally coming to this: "As for the late protector, sith he is now king in possession, I purpose not to dispute his title. But for the weal of this realm—it might yet have pleased God, for the better store, to have given him some of such other excellent virtues, meet for the rule of a realm, as our Lord hath planted in the person of your grace."

The Duke of Buckingham had become the second man in the kingdom. At Richard's coronation, he bore the king's train and almost eclipsed the royal magnificence, his badge of the flaming wheel being flaunted everywhere. He was appointed the high constable of England and given wide powers in Wales and in the western counties. But he listened to the whispered words of the bishop and decided his power was great enough to oust the new occupant of the throne and to place in his stead Henry of Richmond, now the leading claimant on the Lancastrian side. Having laid the train, Morton made his way in disguise to the Fen country, where he remained in concealment until a ship could be found to take him to the continent. There he joined Henry of Richmond at the French court and between them they spun a clever web.

In the meantime the sadly misguided duke raised a force in Wales and proclaimed Henry the rightful king. He seems to have expected that the whole country would rise to support him.

Other men talked but Richard acted. He sent troops to guard the fords on the flood-swollen rivers in the Marcher country and so made it impossible for Buckingham to get his small army across. After waiting for over a week, the Welsh levies lost heart and began to disperse. The duke, knowing his cause lost, fled in disguise into Shropshire where he was finally found in the hut of a shepherd. A court at Salisbury condemned him to death and he was beheaded in the market place.

## 2

The conspiracy which resulted in Richard's defeat and death was hatched in his own household. At the coronation, Queen Anne's train had been carried by a tall and very slender lady with long thin features and the profile of a finely cut cameo. This was Margaret Beaufort, Countess of Richmond and Derby, daughter of John Beaufort, Duke of Somerset; in direct descent, therefore, from John of Gaunt and the family born to him out of wedlock by Katharine Swynford. Despite the austerity of her rather lovely face, she had lived an adventurous and dangerous life and had been married three times. Her first husband was Edmund Tudor, a son born to Owen Tudor, the dancing wardrobe man, and the widow of Henry V, the Fair Kate of legend and story.

Margaret had presented him with one son, born posthumously, who was named Henry and was later to reign over England as Henry VII. Her second husband was Henry Stafford of the Buckinghams, and her third was the Lord Stanley whose head was damaged during the scene in the Tower when Hastings was charged with treason.

Margaret Beaufort was the possessor of great wealth and was most fortunately of a deeply religious spirit. She spent much of her income in the support of religious institutions and at her death left her considerable estates to an educational foundation at Cambridge. She had outlived her son, so Henry VIII, her grandson, did his best to break the will in his own favor but failed in the face of a papal bull, prohibiting it.

It was strange that this remarkable woman, so very generous and philanthropic, should have married Thomas Stanley, who was often referred to as the Wily Fox. In the course of long internal wars, such as the country had suffered, there are always certain men who prefer to follow a devious course and not stake their lives and prosperity on allegiance to one side. Of these the most conspicuous was Stanley, who had immense wealth himself in West Derby and the Isle of Man. It had been necessary for him to bring forces into the field, wearing the Red Rose, but somehow he had always contrived to get off to one side of the contesting armies and not become involved in the actual fighting. If he had lived in a later century, he would not have believed that sound strategic rule laid down by Napoleon: "Always march to the sound of the guns."

Henry VI's militant queen thought of having him impeached as a traitor for keeping his force of 2000 men out of the Battle of Blore Heath. When Edward IV took the throne, the Wily Fox lined up with the winning side and was made a chief justice. Then the Kingmaker chased Edward from the country and Stanley did not delay one moment in changing back from the White to the Red Rose. When the Kingmaker was killed, one of the first to greet the home-coming Edward was the smiling and wholehearted Stanley, the master of gyrations, the baronial Vicar of Bray.

On taking the throne, Richard made Stanley steward of the royal household and afterward constable of England, being convinced, say some commentators, that the whirling dervish would never turn against him unless he could do so with absolute safety, and thinking perhaps that he wanted him where he could be watched.

The only clue in history to the appearance of the brave Stanley is a portrait which shows him with a long, thin face and a full beard. Did he possess the physical portliness and the outward geniality so often found in political opportunists? A strange mate, certainly, for Margaret

Beaufort, with her fine spirit and her face of a dedicated martyr. But marry him she did, one of those curious matrimonial alliances which are hard to understand or explain.

Margaret's son Henry, in spite of the two-edged illegitimacy which clouded his bloodlines, became the leading claimant for the Lancastrians. She was fanatically devoted to his cause and became so deeply involved in the Buckingham uprising that she might have shared his fate. On Richard's request, Parliament did no more than confiscate her estates and titles. In an excess of leniency, the king then transferred the estates into the keeping of Stanley on his agreement to keep her "in some secret place or home, without any servants or company, so she might not communicate with her son."

These precautions were of little avail. The undaunted Margaret began to attack her husband's neutrality. She had been responsible for not too secret negotiations during the Buckingham upsurge by which a match had been arranged between her son and Princess Elizabeth, the eldest daughter of Edward IV. With that as an objective, Stanley became convinced that his position would be sounder with a son-in-law on the throne. Still continuing to serve Richard as his confidential minister, he began to take a hand in the intrigue.

With the Wily Fox to spin the web at the English end, and Morton at young Henry's shoulder to manipulate things abroad, it was not surprising that very soon the country began to hear rumors of an impending invasion.

### 3

The first stage of the conspiracy took the form of propaganda. The story was spread that the two princes in the Tower had been murdered. All of England, it was asserted, was filled with indignation and horror. The only contemporary mention of these rumors is found in the Croyland Chronicle. And it may be pointed out that Morton, in the course of his hurried exit, had paused for several days in the Fen country. He may have risked a visit to Croyland in order to drop some hints in the ear of Peter Blois, the newly appointed chronicler. In the paragraphs that the latter wrote, there is a charge that, "Also he had poisoned the queen his wife." This reference is to happenings in the first half of the year 1484. Queen Anne did not die until March 16, 1485.

That Morton ("honorable in behaviour, lacking in no wise ways to win favor") was responsible for prompting the stories in the Croyland Chronicle is, of course, pure speculation. It acquires some merit, however, from the fact that soon after Morton arrived at the French court, having made good his escape from England, the French chancellor referred to the death of the princes in a speech to the States-General at Tours. Morton was a persistent propagandist and did his best to spread tainted tidings wherever he went.

There was continuous speculation in the country about the relationship between Richard and the queen mother. The latter remained in sanctuary for ten months. Finally she left Westminster and took the quarters assigned her in the palace, after exacting an oath from Richard for the safety of her children. The princesses were then received at court with every evidence of friendliness and favor. The queen mother followed her surrender by writing to her son, the Marquis of Dorset, advising him to return to England. The tone of her letter was such that Dorset became convinced it would be safe for him to come back and had ridden as far as one of the French ports before an envoy of Henry of Richmond overtook him and persuaded him to remain.

This happened after the people of England, as it is claimed, had accepted as fact that the two boys in the Tower were dead. Is it conceivable that any mother would consent to resume normal relationships with the man guilty of the murder of her two sons? Would she have done so before visual proof that the boys were alive? Tudor historians rush into the breach by asserting that Elizabeth acted under duress, that Richard held threats of reprisal over her. As it happened, Henry VII himself showed this explanation to be fallacious, as will be explained later.

It seems certain that the queen mother's action is an indication that she had no reason to believe at the time that her sons had been put to death. No other explanation of her conduct is even faintly believable.

In connection with charges of murder, the motive for the crime is always of major importance. If Richard had the princes killed, it was because they had better claims to the throne than he had. But there seem to have been eleven other people alive at the time who had better claims under the law of primogeniture than Richard. Edward IV left five daughters as well as the two boys. Clarence left a son and a daughter. There were three of Richard's older sisters still living and one of them had a son, John de la Pole, Earl of Lincoln. If he wanted to clear his path to the throne, it would have been necessary to make a clean sweep, to remove all his sisters and nephews and nieces. Instead of this, he seems to have treated them with much kindness. After the death of his own son, for whom he grieved deeply, he first named Edward of Warwick, Clarence's son, as his successor. Later he changed his mind and put forward John de la Pole, Earl of Lincoln, the son of his sister Elizabeth.

The reason for this was a certain cloudiness of mind in Edward of Warwick which unfitted him for the office.

This may be the place to draw a parallel. One of the first things Henry VII did on finding the crown of gold pressed down firmly on his brow was to send for Edward of Warwick and lock him up in the Tower. Here the unfortunate youth remained for the balance of his life, there being no charge against him save that of being the son of George of Clarence. He was finally declared to have taken part in a conspiracy against Henry and was beheaded, on the sorriest of evidence. The daughter of Clarence, Princess Margaret, married the Earl of Salisbury and survived into the reign of Henry VIII. Bluff King Hal had her beheaded, in one of the most revolting of judicial murders. Richard had an illegitimate son named John, a harmless and likable lad from all reports. Henry VII had him put out of the way on a trumped-up charge of having plotted to run away from the kingdom. The writer of a comparatively modern textbook, who had no qualms at all about affirming Richard's guilt, nevertheless began his story of the reign of Henry VII with these words, "It was the settled and considered policy of the Tudors to rid themselves of all rivals to the throne."

In the spring of 1484, Richard made a processional through the eastern counties, accompanied by his queen. Anne had become very thin and more wan of cheek than before. She liked to go with him wherever he went, which does not seem to point to a dislike for him on her part. When they arrived at Nottingham, the word reached them that their young son had died. They hurried to Middleham with a double sense of grief, because the ailing boy had died with neither of them beside him. Anne was so prostrated that it did not seem likely she would survive her son for any great length of time.

Nevertheless the royal couple made a brave effort to share in the Christmas festivities at Westminster. It was during the Yuletide season that another charge was conjured up to hurl at the saddened young king. The princess Elizabeth, the oldest and fairest daughter of Edward IV, was at court and appeared at a dance in a costume exactly similar to that worn by the queen. The anti-Richard elements tried to read into this something strange and sinister. Was it not clear, they asked, that the king was setting up the gay young princess as a rival for his own consort? Did he intend to make her his second wife after Anne died, in order to prevent Henry of Richmond from claiming her?

It seems highly improbable that the king, who was hard pressed for time to perform all the duties of his office during the brief span of his reign, would pay any attention to such purely feminine detail as what the ladies of his court were going to wear. More likely it was a sign of affection planned by the gentle queen to show her pleasure that the princesses had come out of retirement to grace the court proceedings with their beauty and gaiety. But this quite reasonable explanation was brushed aside by Richard's critics. It was a scheme hatched in his dark and wicked mind.

The queen died on March 16 when the sun was in eclipse. To Richard it must have seemed that nature was displaying some sympathy for his grief, which was heartfelt and excessive, but commentators see in it a proof that he had poisoned her. Immediately, the clamor of propaganda was raised against him more fiercely than ever. Had he poisoned his wife in order to get her out of the way so he could marry his young niece Elizabeth? It had been apparent to all for some time that the queen was dying from the disease which had cut down her sister, so who could think seriously that poison would be used to hasten her end?

Immediately after the funeral, Richard summoned his council for the purpose of denying the malicious story that he thought of the princess as Anne's successor. Later he appeared before the prominent citizens of London at St. John's Priory, Clerkenwell, and repeated his disavowal of such a purpose, protesting his innocence of "having contemplated a marriage so repugnant to the habits and ways of the English nation."

Of all the charges made against him, this was the only one he faced in his lifetime and so had the opportunity of denying. What could he do to clear his name? He sent Princess Elizabeth to the castle of Sheriff-Hutton, in order to still the ugly assertions. If the bereaved king had been put on the stand to defend himself, one can easily believe his innocence would have been asserted in some such words as these, "My lords and honest citizens, I loved the lady, Queen Anne, every day of my life."

Now that she was dead, he made no plans to put anyone in her place. No furtive visits were paid to Sheriff-Hutton. He did not call in the ambassadors of other countries to discuss possible matrimonial alliances. He went before the House and nominated John de la Pole as his successor. It was clear he had given up all thoughts of having a son to take his place.

It is doubtful, in fact, if these unfair charges were heard much outside the inner circle of the court, where there are always whispered undercurrents of malice and much ill-natured tattle. If the country at large had known what was being said, Richard's conduct after Queen Anne passed away must have been completely reassuring. But in the pages of history in later centuries the charges were brought up again and again, refurbished and bolstered with labored reasoning and addled surmises.

## CHAPTER VII

## On Bosworth Field

### 1

IT IS time that the second figure in this drama, who has been kept standing in the wings, should be called out to the center of the stage.

The word "Norman" had long since dropped from use but it seems necessary to revive it in dealing with Henry of Richmond. He was twenty-eight years of age, tall and slender like his mother. There was a hint of the Norman strain in his cold gray eyes and in the lightness of his hair which fell lankly about his brow. His nose was Norman also, unless it may have achieved its length from the Valois blood in his veins. One thing is certain: he was not a Plantagenet.

Henry saw to it that England remained at peace during his reign and so brought back prosperity to the land on a sound basis. He was a good administrator and a close student of detail. His term on the throne was not marked by constitutional advances or any effort to improve the lot of the common man. But he faced certain problems with a clearness which no other king before him had displayed. There was, for instance, the absurdity of the coinage situation. The country was submerged with small money, such as pennies and farthings, and for purposes of calculation coins of account were used. Men talked of pounds and shillings but no such coins had ever been in existence. Henry saw the folly of people accumulating huge supplies of pence and he had the courage to begin the minting of actual pounds and shillings, making the Trial of the Pyx (the weighing of new money at the mint) an important function instead of a bit of ritual.

It was because of such forward steps as these that history began to speak of him as an enlightened monarch. Some waxed enthusiastic enough to call him the Solomon of England. At the same time it can be said that no King of England acquired unpopularity with the people as quickly as he did. He was disliked personally. The common people saw early that he was devious and acquisitive to an almost unbelievable degree. If only one thing remained in the public mind about the reign of the first Tudor, it would be, of course, the story of Morton's Fork. The second choice for this honor might be his habit of repaying expensive receptions in his honor with heavy fines, based on some never used statute or an old sumptuary law. Then there was his caution in organizing the first permanent king's guard (how the expense of it must have irked him!) and in having a secret room constructed near his bedchamber at Windsor Castle, the knowledge of which was shared only with his valet and the builder. Finally there was the story of John Cabot.

When that bold seaman returned from his discovery of the North American continent, an achievement second only to that of Christopher Columbus, Henry (who had not risked one of his newly minted shillings in the venture) did not receive him with open arms and shower him with honors and rewards. He did not even fill Cabot's flat mariner's cap with gold pieces. No, this outgiving prince presented the commander with the handsome sum of ten pounds, an amount often paid to old royal servants or to the faithful nurses of illegitimate children.

Midas had the touch which turned everything to gold, but Henry had a different gift. He could make gold disappear at a touch—right into the royal pocket. The robust patrons of inns and taverns, who were benefiting by the rising prosperity to the extent of being able to afford fennel in their ale, spoke openly of Henry, nevertheless, as a nip-cheese and a begrudgemuch. Well, there is no doubt that he was niggardly, sly, and shabby.

Henry had an ingenious mind. He could think of curious ways of achieving his ends. Some said of him that he reasoned like a corkscrew, allowing his mind to go around and around and never being direct and understandable. He had, in fact, a passion for secrecy.

In this respect he resembled Louis XI of France, who preferred to twist and turn and burrow rather than proceed along straight lines of thought and action. Henry even resembled Louis in his choice of hats, a flat affair with a peak in front. A more important parallel was discovered after he died and left an estate of £1,800,000, the equivalent of a monstrous fortune today. And how quickly his boisterous, spendthrift son, Henry VIII, succeeded in throwing that inheritance away!

**2**

Henry displayed his courage by landing at Milford Haven in August 1485, with no more than 3000 French mercenaries. He was relying on two things: the loyalty of the Welsh people for one of Welsh blood and, something of more value than any number of the knaves and rapscallions he had recruited from the gaols and stews of the continent, the promises of support won by his lady mother. He chose to land at Milford Haven for the first reason, dropping on one knee when he landed to kiss the soil of Wales.

The Welsh people did respond in some degree and by the time the forces of invasion swarmed over into the Midlands, Henry had a much more considerable following. He had received in addition the promises of support from many quarters. Richard's system of postal intelligence seems to have broken down and it was several days before he learned of the landing. At first he was not unduly alarmed, openly deriding his antagonist as a milksop. Nor had he any inkling yet of the web which had been spun with such secrecy.

He sent out commands to his barons to arm their retainers and join him in the defense of the realm. Although weary of the incessant uproar and bloodshed (it was estimated that 105,000 men had been killed in the Wars of the Roses), many responded at once. A much larger army than Henry could count upon followed the king when he rode on a white charger into the city of Leicester on August 20. But Richard was not easy in his mind, for from the first there was a scent of treachery in the air. He issued an urgent summons to Stanley, who had betaken himself to Lancashire earlier but who returned an excuse that he was suffering from the sweating sickness. The oldest son of Stanley had been left with Richard and had tried to make his escape. On being caught, he confessed that he and his uncle, Sir William Stanley, had been in touch with the invaders. There was also a certain aloofness about some of the lords of the north. These great barons, who lived in semi-regal style, were easily offended and not always happy to bend the knee. It will be recalled that Henry IV had found himself under the necessity of fighting Harry Hotspur, the heir of the Percies.

No eyewitness has left an account of the Battle of Bosworth and the record of events preceding the clash are scanty, so what is told about it consists largely of conclusions drawn from such few facts as are available. It is said that Richard rose early on the morning of the battle, having spent a disturbed night, beset in his dreams by visions of all his victims (Shakespeare can be blamed for this) and seriously concerned because

Stanley, who had raised an army of 5000 men in Derby and Chester, was hovering about and refusing to join him. The atmosphere in the royal camp was one of suspicion and suspense, even of dismay. It was believed that the Stanleys would go over to Henry. The Northumberland levies stood about with grounded arms and seemed reluctant to have any part in the battle. A rumor ran through the ranks that a paper had been discovered that morning attached to the flap of the Duke of Norfolk's tent. On it were written these lines:

> *Jockey of Norfolk, be not too bold,*
> *For Dickon, thy master, is bought and sold.*

The information thus conveyed was authentic enough. Richard Plantagenet had been bought and sold. Under cover of darkness the night before, Henry had held a meeting with the Stanleys and a course of action had been decided upon.

Richard studied the enemy lines across the plain known as Redmoors, beyond which he could see the green and white tents of the invaders and Henry's banner with its fiery red dragon. This, he knew, would be the last battle of the long wars, whether he won or lost. A fatalistic mood seemed to have settled upon him. The loss of his wife and son still weighed heavily on his mind and he could not read in the future much promise or hope. He was willing and eager to put the issue to a sharp test, to destroy his enemy or to go down himself on the field of battle.

The Lancastrians had the sun on their backs and seemed to have the better of the first clash. This was what Stanley had been waiting for. The Wily Fox, changing his coat for the final time, advanced with his troops and joined Henry's right wing. It was a critical moment and Richard realized his one chance now was to strike at the enemy ranks behind which the inexperienced Henry was watching the struggle. His scouts had brought him word of Henry's position.

"A battle-ax!" demanded the king.

Followed by a small mounted group of his most faithful men, the young king (he was only thirty-two years old) charged headlong into the enemy lines. Swinging his ax, he bore down and killed Brandon, Henry's standard-bearer. Before him now loomed the gigantic figure of Sir John Cheney. A single blow unhorsed that powerful knight. Richard's right arm seemed strong enough to cut his way clear through to where his opponent stood. On his left arm, his "weerish, withered arm," he bore his heavy shield and with it also he controlled the wild course of his maddened steed.

It was a magnificient effort and almost brought the two leaders face to face. But the king's handful had thinned behind him. He stood alone at the last and fought singlehanded against the Lancastrians who now swarmed about him. His armor broken, his ax limp with his weariness, he went down under the blows of his enemies.

Nothing in history excells this mad exploit for sheer daring, although it brings to mind another piece of spectacular bravery. A century before, the Black Douglas threw the casket containing the heart of Robert the Bruce into the ranks of the Moors and then cut his way singlehanded into their ranks, to fall at last under the blows of their infidel swords.

Richard's crown, retrieved from a clump of bushes, it is said, was placed on Henry's head before he rode out across Redmoors to direct the pursuit of the royal army.

The Wars of the Roses had come to an end and a new family of kings and queens would succeed the Plantagenets.

## CHAPTER VIII

## Some Curious Measures and Omissions

1

THE princess Elizabeth was nearly twenty years old and, as might have been expected in the child of such surpassingly handsome parents, she was a great beauty. It is clear from her portraits that she was rather tall but that her figure was mature and pleasing. She had her mother's golden hair and large blue eyes. Her cheeks had the slightest tendency to plumpness and showed the pink of perfect health.

Ever since reaching an age of understanding, she had known of the ambitious plans being made for her future. No matrimonial alliance was too good for her. She would sit on a throne beside a king and wear a golden circlet on her lovely hair. Because of breaches in international relations, it had finally narrowed down; her one chance to become a queen was to be Queen of England, and so she must marry Henry of Richmond. She heard reports of his manly attractions and of the shining light of his intelligence, and her maidenly fancy had been caught. Watching developments closely, it seemed to her that Richard's death at Bosworth made it certain that the desired match would now be brought about. She was, therefore, relieved and pleased when Henry summoned her at once to London from Sheriff-Hutton. Her young cousin, the youthful Earl of Warwick, had been living there and was to travel with her.

Henry surprised the nation by riding to London from Bosworth in a covered chariot, a type of vehicle which has crept into the records in connection with the travels of great ladies. If an evidence of modesty, this was not wise, for the people of England wanted to see the man who had made himself their king. If due to a sense of the need for protection, it may have been sensible, for feelings still ran high. At any rate he had a safe, if slow, journey but arrived in London before the princess, going into residence at first in the palace of the Bishop of London and transacting his affairs at the Tower. When Elizabeth and the cloudy-witted earl arrived, she was sent to Westminster where her mother was in residence. The unfortunate youth vanished into the closed and mysterious life of the grim Tower, to emerge therefrom only once in the balance of his sad life, when he was taken out and paraded on horseback through the streets of London to prove that Lambert Simnel, who claimed to be the real earl, was an impostor.

If Henry met the fair Elizabeth at this time, there is no report of it. Perhaps this would be due to the prevalence in London of the sweating sickness, which had been brought into England by his French mercenaries. Perhaps he was in the throes of ceaseless activities. One of his first acts was to organize a personal bodyguard. Then he had many vexed matters of business to transact with Parliament.

These were anxious moments for Elizabeth, who did not want to see another crown whisked out of the reach of her willing hands. She and her mother heard he was to be crowned on October 30 and their faces clouded with bewilderment and anxiety when there was no hint of a marriage. Their worry deepened when he had Elizabeth declared the Duchess of York and claimed the throne in his own right "to be, rest, and abide in his own person." To make matters worse, there were rumors in London which came quickly and unerringly to their disturbed ears. Henry, it was said, was considering other possible matches. A princess of Brittany was mentioned and also Lady Katherine Herbert. Henry knew each of these ladies and had been favorably impressed.

The situation finally took a more favorable turn in the second week of December. Information reached the queen mother which sent her with much hurried rustling of her rich violet and fur-trimmed skirts along the drafty halls from her apartments in the palace to the handsome corner suite, hanging with tapestries and the costliest of furnishings, where the princess (the position of mother and daughter having been reversed) abided in considerable state. In happy whispers she told her daughter that Parliament in full meeting the next day would petition Henry to observe his promise and take her as his wife and consort. The queen mother knew how potent the voice of the House could be. Henry's purse was as flat as his hat and he was desperately in need of the financial supplies which only Parliament could supply. Would he dare disregard such a demand from the members? The queen mother thought not.

The approaching Yuletide season, which had promised so little, assumed a brighter tinge for Elizabeth. The crown seemed within her reach after all. She probably gave no thought to the brave gaiety at Christmas the year before when she had been happy enough and rather excited to dance in the gown which was identical with that of the queen— gentle Queen Anne who had died a few months after.

### 2

Henry may have carried in his mind certain reservations when he faced Parliament the following day, December 10. But he was shrewd to a degree and he understood one thing very clearly. The wishes of the House were conveyed to him in the form of a petition, but there was a latent suggestion of an exchange. "Fulfill your promise to unite the two great warring families by marrying Elizabeth of York and so ensure the peace of the realm," was the implication, "and we will grant you the tunnage and poundage for life which you ask of us." When they rose and faced him, he bowed his head.

"I am willing so to do," he said.

Parliament was prorogued until January 27, and on January 18 in Westminster the new king took the heiress of York as his wife. The people celebrated the event with "dancing, songs and banquets throughout all London."

As the king had already been crowned, it was neccessary for the queen to have a coronation separately. It seems to have been her first public appearance, and the streets were thick with cheering people. Elizabeth was dressed in a kirtle of white cloth of gold and a mantle edged with ermine and fastened with a cordon of lace and rich tassels of gold. Above the "caul of pipes" that she wore on her hair was the circlet of gold which attested to her new rank. It was to be expected that she would be beautiful in a truly resplendent way. Did she not unite in her person the two most resplendent of family lines, the Plantagenets and the Woodvilles?

It does not seem to have been in any sense a love match, but there is no proof of the assertion often made that Henry was cold to his wife and the direct opposite of a uxorious husband. Henry was cold to everyone. His was a withdrawn nature, secretive in all things. And his lovely young queen was a real Plantagenet in two respects. She was wildly extravagant and generous to a fault. To borrow a modern phrase, she made the money fly! Most of it was expended on others, particularly her younger sisters. Henry was continuously under the necessity of straightening out her finances and paying off her debts. And this irked him in every atom of his parsimonious self.

Henry did not confide in those about him. "His mother," wrote Francis Bacon a century later, "he reverenced much but listened to little." The queen, according to the same source, could do nothing with him. He never rushed into a decision but always thought things out in a silence which none dared invade. Being a believer in system, he kept a notebook with him and entered everything in it: what he had spent, what he had decided, who was to be punished and who rewarded, his private opinions of people and events. This was well known and all the officials of the state and all the nobles and servants at court walked in fear of what the well-thumbed book contained. One day, through some unusual lapse, he left the book carelessly about and someone saw that it fell into the hands of the pet household monkey. The result was that the pages were torn to pieces and scattered about the royal domain, which added less than nothing to the feeling of affection for the little pet.

Mention of the mischievous monkey suggests that the way he treated the animals in the royal menagerie was an indication of the strangeness of this man's inner thoughts. One day four English mastiffs were pitted against a lion for the entertainment of the court. They fought so grandly that they got the better of the lion, who was in the king's mind a symbol of royal authority. He had the four hanged as traitors! This, of course, was one of his methods of letting everyone know his feelings about any infringement of his rights, any doubt of his omnipotence.

This story must be authentic because it has been cited by a number of writers who incline to the fulsome in praise of him.

Elizabeth had been radiant in her health as well as in appearance, but she died early of the trouble which sent most women of the Middle Ages to their graves, excessive childbearing. She brought seven children into the world, two sons and five daughters. When she died in 1503, in her thirty-seventh year, she was survived by one son and two daughters. Her first-born, Prince Arthur, who married Catherine of Aragon, died in his youth, leaving the healthy, burly son Henry to succeed to the throne. The surviving daughters were Margaret, who married the King of Scotland and lived a tumultuous life, and pretty dark-eyed Mary, who married Louis XII of France in his last and senile year. Mary is one of the best remembered of English princesses.

Henry was properly grieved at the early demise of his fair consort, so it may have been that they were not seriously incompatible.

In the early months of his reign Henry passed through Parliament some unusual measures. First he demanded the repeal of *Titulus Regius*, stipulating that it was not to be read before the House and that all copies in existence were to be destroyed! This may have been due to a deep repugnance for the act and a desire to expunge it from the memories of men. But everyone in England knew what it contained, and a monarch's personal feelings should not be allowed to create a gap in national records. The repeal may have been an indication that he knew the princes were dead and that now they could safely be declared legitimate, as his wife was the third in line.

The next measure which provides a glimpse into the unusual work-ings of his mind was a bill of attainder against the dead Richard and all men who had fought for him at Bosworth. This would make it legal for him to confiscate their properties and scoop everything into his own empty pockets. The weak point in the scheme was that these men had fought for the crowned king of the realm and so were not guilty of treason. Henry saw a way around that difficulty. He dated his reign from the day before the battle!

It happened that some sharp parliamentary eye detected the error while the attainder was under discussion in the House. The date was corrected and the copy was sent to the king with the change made. Henry undoubtedly lapsed into one of his deep silences, his pale eyes blazing with inner fire as he realized that he could not now confiscate to his own use any of these fat and profitable acres and the honors that went with them.

This act was to prove one of Henry's major mistakes in the matter of the charge of murder against Richard. For the second time the book was being thrown at the dead king. There was a long list of generaliza-tions. He was charged with "unnatural, mischievous and great perjuries, treasons, homicides and murders, in shedding of infant blood, with many other wrongs, odious offences and abominations against God and men and in special our said sovereign lord——" No specific misdeeds were enumerated and *no direct reference was made to the murder of the princes.* Now Henry's claim to the throne was so extremely weak that he had to depend on proving the unfitness of the dead king. Why then this most inexplicable omission? The death of the princes was the trump of trumps, the thunderbolt of retribution, the voice in the clouds cry-ing vengeance. Only because of it could Henry claim justification for overthrowing Richard and retrieving the crown from among the bramble bushes to set it upon his own brow.

Only two possible reasons can be found for the lack of use in evidence of this black deed. First, the princes may still have been alive. Second, Henry had been in possession of the Tower for months and *may have had reasons for not wanting an investigation.*

A complete silence fell over the fate of the two unfortunate youths and this continued for a long time. Was it any wonder that people began to have doubts of Richard's guilt and that some of them were led to believe in the impostures of Lambert Simnel and Perkin Warbeck?

There was one precedent for this curious silence, the fact that the truth about Richard II's death was never allowed to come out. But there was a difference in the two cases. Henry IV, who succeeded Richard II, had been directly or indirectly responsible for the murder of his cousin and so had every reason to spread the pall of official silence over the grave of his predecessor. On the other hand the murder of the princes was charged against the dead Richard and there were good reasons for spreading the story over all of Christendom. Why then should the newly seated Henry refuse to fulfill his duty as monarch to bring out the facts and punish the guilty aides in the dark crime?

It would have been an easy matter to get at the truth. A double murder could not be committed in the Tower without some officials knowing of it, and without whispers spreading in the dark corridors which the guards patrolled. If the officers of the Tower had been questioned, the truth would soon have been arrived at.

Moreover it is not in the nature of criminals to keep still tongues. The hand of justice has always depended on the indiscretions of the guilty. One of the fine fellows who participated would have dropped a casual word somewhere, to a wife, to a walking mort (a woman of the streets), to a gossip in a tavern.

But Henry did nothing about it.

## CHAPTER IX

## The Murder of the Princes

*1*

SIR James Tyrell came of a family with strong Yorkist sympathies and he had been knighted after the victory at Tewkesbury. When Henry VII succeeded to the throne, however, the perhaps nimble-witted Tyrell managed to insinuate himself into his favor. He was given some properties and posts of importance. His most notable post was that of lieutenant of the castle of Guisnes in France and there he remained for the largest part of Henry's reign, which may indicate a desire on the king's part to keep him employed outside the kingdom. Tyrell had been born at Gipping in Suffolk and seems to have entertained a liking and respect for Edmund de la Pole, the Earl of Suffolk. At least, when the latter fled from England he was received by Tyrell, and still later Tyrell was induced by a trick to surrender the castle to Suffolk. This was too much for the king to swallow and so Tyrell was made the victim of another trick which took him aboard a ship in Calais harbor. The captain upped sails at once and in the briefest possible time Tyrell found himself a prisoner in the Tower, charged with treason.

He was found guilty and was led out to Tower Hill. There he saw before him the most terrifying of sights—a black block so small that it seemed impossible for anyone to lay his neck upon it, and a masked executioner standing beside it and holding a curved ax on which the warm May sunshine glinted brightly.

At practically the same moment a priest named Dighton, who had been examined during the hearing, was released through the main gate and made off so promptly that he never again came into notice.

There was intense excitement in London when criers proclaimed the execution of Tyrell and declared him to have confessed the killing of the two princes under orders from Richard. As this was happening in the year of our Lord, 1502, there was nation-wide speculation on many points. How had the deed been committed? Why had the punishment of the murderer been delayed for nineteen years? The answers were to be found in the confession which Tyrell had made and in which his confederate Dighton had shared. But that most important paper, strange to relate, was never produced. Some historians say it was not preserved but others are convinced that it never existed, that Tyrell was convicted on the treason charge and made no confession at all.

2

The story of the murders which came to be accepted as more or less official did not come out until much later. In 1534 Polydore Vergil's *Anglica Historia* was published in Italy and contained some details. The Latin version of the *History*, generally credited to Archbishop Morton, had appeared earlier but it was not until 1557 that a relation of the then deceased Sir Thomas More discovered the unfinished English translation in his handwriting and had it published. It is the version of the murders as given in the Morton-More book that has been accepted and has been followed by most historians.

Let us pause here to give consideration to a fantastic point in this connection. Tyrell's confession was given before his death in 1502. Whether Morton or More wrote the Latin version of the *History*, it has been universally conceded that Morton supplied all the material, More having been a boy of seven when the Battle of Bosworth was fought. But Morton died in 1500! How could he have had all the intimate details which are contained in the *History*?

"I shall rehearse you the dolorous end of these babes," begins the narrative which Morton was in some miraculous way able to recite. It occurred, it seems, soon after Richard's coronation. "Whereupon he sent one John Green, whom he specially trusted, unto Sir Robert Brakenbury, constable of the Tower, with a letter and credence also, that the same Sir Robert should in any wise put the two children to death."

At the outset, therefore, we are offered something which cannot be believed. Richard was shrewd and intelligent. Would he be indiscreet enough to commit his guilty purpose to writing and then entrust the delivery of the incriminating document to a servant as obscure as "one John Green?"

The man Green rejoined his master at Warwick with the report that the constable had refused to act as instructed.

"Whereupon he took such displeasure and thought, that the same night," continues the *History*, "he said unto a secret page of his, 'Ah, whom shall a man trust? Those that I have brought up myself, those that I had went would most surely serve me, even those fail me, and at my commandment will do nothing for me.' 'Sir,' quod his page, 'there lieth one on your pallet without, that I dare well say, to do your grace pleasure, the thing were right hard that he would refuse'; meaning by this Sir James Tyrell, which was a man of right goodly personage, and for nature's gifts worthy to have served a much better prince. . . . The man had a high heart, and sore longed upward, not rising yet so fast as he had hoped, being hindered and kept under by the means of Sir Richard Ratcliffe and Sir William Catesby . . . Which thing this page well had marked and known."

This secret page seems to have been one of the furtive and unscrupulous underlings who are found at all courts, who poke long noses into things and gather up whispers and lies to be used to base purposes. Would Richard have been so absurdly unwise as to confide in an instrument of this slimy type and to put into the fellow's knowledge a secret which might rock his throne? Ah, well, let us on with the story.

"For upon this page's words King Richard arose (for this communication had he, sitting at the *draught*,* a convenient carpet for such a counsel)"—really, Sir Thomas!—"and came out into the pallet chamber, on which he found in bed Sir James and Sir Thomas Tyrell . . . Then said the king merrily to them, 'What! sirs, be ye in bed so soon?' And calling up Sir James, brake to him secretly his mind in this mischievous matter. In which he found him nothing strange."

Does it seem that the *History* shows moderation here in not going further, perhaps in having Richard discuss the matter with the court jester or comment *merrily* to his barber on the sharpness of his blade and the use it could be put to in cutting youthful throats?

Richard, therefore, sent Sir James Tyrell, with a signed warrant—another damning piece of evidence casually supplied—to Brackenbury to deliver up the prison to him for one night. This was done and Tyrell's groom named Dighton (but who, as we know, was not a groom but a priest) was admitted to the chamber where the two boys slept. The princes were in the charge of a man named Will Slaughter (how felicitous that might have seemed to the wicked uncle), who was called Black Will. It is not clear whether Black Will was in the chamber

* A medieval term for the privy.

at the time but another man was with Dighton, one Miles Forrest, "a fellow flesh-bred in murder beforetime." Dighton and Forrest then smothered the sleeping princes under pillows. Tyrell inspected the bodies and ordered them buried at the foot of the staircase.

"Then rode Sir James in great haste to king Richard, and showed him all the manner of the murther, who gave him great thanks. . . . But he allowed not, as I have heard, the burying in so vile a corner, saying that he would have them buried in a better place, because they were a king's sons." It seems then that Brackenbury had a priest "who took the bodies and secretly interred them in such a place as, by the occasion of his death, who only knew it, the very place could never yet be very well known."

A word of comment seems needed here. Murders can be committed successfully sometimes, but the disposal of the body is always a difficult matter. It can be taken out and buried in a back yard or it can be carried away in a wagon and thrown into a body of water, although both methods lead almost inevitably to detection. It can be disposed of by fire although some of the bones will remain in the ashes. One killer in a well-known piece of fiction got rid of the body of his victim by cooking it and eating it!

But now we have a priest with not one body but two to be disposed of, in a closely guarded prison, swarming at all times with armed men as well as gaolers. With no one to assist him, he dug up the bodies from their first burial place and then transferred them, still by his own un-aided efforts, to a more fitting grave. No one saw him, not a whisper about him began to circulate in that warren of halls. He told no one where the bodies had been buried. And then, most conveniently, he died. The term convenient is used because the writers of the *History* needed a reason for the spot to remain a complete mystery. And so to the dramatis personae add the Unnamed Priest, who is projected into the story with the same high disdain for probabilities and the sense of things which mark all the other inventions. There has never been a figure in the annals of crime to equal this priest. Move over, Father Brown.*

To sum it up, this is the testimony which history has used to fix the black mark of guilt on Richard Plantagenet. This was the manner in which the murders were conceived, this the way in which they were carried out by the tools of the king. Look back over the list of those who played parts in this *secret* job of conspiracy and murder: the man

* Father Brown is the priest with the parasol who finds the solution in all the mystery stories of G. K. Chesterton.

Green, Sir Robert Brackenbury, the secret page, Sir James Tyrell, the man Dighton, Black Will Slaughter, Miles Forrest, the Unnamed Priest. Eight, exactly the number of the villagers who rode on one horse to Widdicombe Fair, *Uncle Tom Cobley and All*. The list of the guilty could be sung to the same air, even if it does make a much less credible tale.

What kind of naïve simpleton did they think this Richard Plantagenet to be? It is hard to believe that this shoddy evidence is still found in many histories, almost word for word.

### 3

The Wars of the Roses could be called the Wars of No Quarter. There is always a special ferocity in civil conflict, but the wearers of the Red and the Snow Roses were particularly revengeful. Margaret of Anjou is given credit for introducing much of the acrimony, but Edward IV, that handsome gladiatorial figure, carried it on by wholesale decapitations after the battles he won. Richard was as ambitious as any member of his family and did not scruple to use the sharp medicine of the headsman's ax in disposing of those who leagued against him. But a similar course, which won admiration for Edward because he succeeded with it, was condemned in the case of the younger and less spectacular brother because he failed. Enmity was built up against him.

It is unfortunate that no other way to fight out the indictment of Richard has been found save in the Court of the Printed Word, with historians, writers, and editors to act in all capacities, as witnesses, as counsel, as pleaders, and, finally, as judges. What would the outcome be if the case could be introduced into court today with the modern conception of evidence to be applied? One thing can be set down as certain, that the prosecuting attorney would spend horrified hours over the *History* and in the end would almost certainly decide not to put it in as evidence, knowing only too well how the defense attorneys would tear it to rags and tatters.

What a day it would be in court if the central figures in this bizarre case could be summoned from the shades to take their turns on the stand and face a grueling examination and cross-examination: Richard himself, and Queen Anne and her mother, who elected voluntarily to live with them through the last years of her own life, Edward IV, Clarence, Henry VII, Tyrell, Jane Shore, Brackenbury, the secret page who whispered his suggestions in the royal privy, the unnamed priest who delved like a mole in the darkness of the Tower to raise unaided the bodies of the two princes and bury them in a more fitting part of that great prison, Black Will Slaughter, and, of course, the star witness, Morton of the Fork, who died two years before the arrest of Tyrell "broke" the case but whose prophetic sense enabled him to put down in black and white before his death the whole story to which Tyrell is said to have confessed before he was rushed to the block. From such a hearing would emerge, surely, inevitably, the whole truth.

## CHAPTER X

## The Great Impersonations

*1*

THE princes were murdered, either by Richard or by some agency after his death. They could not have died natural deaths because that would have been recorded and there would never have been any mystery about it.

The question of Richard's possible participation has now been rather thoroughly discussed. But what of Henry and the chance that he ordered the killings?

What was he doing during the ninety-eight days which elapsed between his arrival in London after Bosworth and the meeting in the House when he promised the members to marry the princess Elizabeth? He seems to have found it hard to make up his mind. Could it have been that he realized the need to remove the stain of illegitimacy from his bride's name but feared to take a step which would clear the two princes of the same stigma? If they were still alive, this would be a hard decision for the careful Henry to make. *The two boys would then have become a greater danger to him than they could ever have been to Richard.* And this must be kept in mind: that during those ninety-eight days the Tower was filled with the officers and guards of Henry's choosing.

This is not intended as a charge against Henry and is put forward as no more than a possibility. The air has been filled with the possibilities brewed up against Richard, so why not let Henry taste some of the same medicine?

No clear and convincing solution can now be reached as to how, when, and where the princes died. But there came about a rather curious series of events which seem to tie together, to hint at a determined and cunning mind at work and a subtle hand moving under the surface.

Henry married the princess Elizabeth on January 18, 1486. On June 16 of that year Sir James Tyrell was granted what was called "a general pardon." There was nothing unusual about this. It seems to have been the rule for men to seek such a clearance on leaving office. But one month later, on July 16, this was repeated. What need was there for a repetition within such a brief period? Had something occurred between the two dates which made it necessary for Tyrell's record to receive a second official scrubbing?

The following year Henry paid a visit one day to the administrative offices at Westminster. The officials had learned already to study his moods and to act in accordance. If money had to be spent, the king would be silent and unapproachable. But on the occasion in question, Henry was smiling. There was a trace of warmth in his pale eyes and certainly there was eagerness in the way he settled down before his writing table. He proceeded then to sign papers which granted to his beautiful young wife, Elizabeth, the lordships and manors of Waltham Magna, Badewe, Mashbury, Dunmow, Lighe, and Farnham. Being the kind of man he was, this amounted to taking these extensive landholdings into his own possession.

The important point about the transaction, however, was that all these properties belonged to Elizabeth's mother, the dowager queen. It was clear that she had fallen into the bad graces of the king. Had something happened to open a breach between them? Had she shown, for instance, an undue inquisitiveness in any matters? The way he treated her for the rest of her life seems to indicate that he felt the need to keep her in seclusion.

The dowager queen was no longer young. Eight years older than the king she had married, she was now launched into the span of years which women of that day seldom achieved, the fifties. Her personal maids were clever and had managed to retain some of the gilt in her hair. Her eyes were clear and expressive. Her figure was good and she was still a handsome woman. She had been suggested as a wife for the young widower King of Scotland but the plan had not matured.

This once influential figure was greatly distressed when Henry ordered her to withdraw into the abbey of Bermondsey. She did not want to retire from active life. Twice before she had spent lengthy terms in sanctuary and she did not want to experience more of it. But Henry was adamant. After taking over all of her dower properties, he gave her a pension of 400 marks a year, and into Bermondsey she went. There were handsome apartments in the abbey for her use, but the rules laid down for her amounted almost to imprisonment. She spent the rest of her remaining years in what one historian calls "a wretched and miserable life," dying after five years of it. Her will expressed a plaintive regret that she had nothing to leave to her daughters. The body was taken to Windsor without any ringing of bells to bid her farewell and there she was buried quietly.

Henry gave a reason to the royal council for treating her in this summary way which provides one of the strongest reasons for believing Richard innocent. The queen mother, he declared, had broken a promise she had made to him in writing when he was an exile in France. The promise was that she would never allow her daughters to suffer the contaminations of Richard's court. But the only excuse which had been found by Tudor apologists for her willingness to reopen normal relations with the supposed murderer of her young sons was that Richard had forced her to leave sanctuary by threats. Openly stating thus his conviction that the queen mother acted of her own free will and should be punished, Henry makes it clear there was every reason to believe the princes were still alive at the time!

Thus does cupidity in its blindness sometimes clear the way for truth.

2

Starting probably in 1485, the story was circulated widely that the princes had died at the hands of their wicked uncle, but as the new king did nothing to bring the guilty to punishment, a tinge of doubt was soon noticeable in the reactions of the public. It was this uncertainty which led to the Great Impersonations. The reign of Henry VII is chiefly remembered by those who enjoy the color and excitements of history because of two youths who came forward at different times with claims to the throne.

The first was Lambert Simnel, whose father is said to have been a pastry cook in Oxford. This boy was handsome, bright, and very likable, a perfect tool for the purpose. A young priest at the university, named Richard Symonds, saw the boy and a daring plan took possession of his mind. If the youth were trained with sufficient care, he could be passed off as a member of the Plantagenet family. He had the fair hair, the vibrant blue eye, the fine features. Accordingly, young Lambert was taken away from his father's shop and kept in seclusion while the diligent and astute priest taught him to read and write, to become learned in the arts, and to deport himself with the graces of royalty. Young Lambert was a quick study and soon he carried himself with many of the outward marks of good birth.

While his tuition was being carried on, Symonds sent word to the dowager Duchess Margaret of Burgundy, one of the daughters of Richard of York. She was an ardent Yorkist still and had been deeply attached to the late King Richard. Her detestation of Henry was so great that she displayed a quick interest in the priest's story. The boy in his charge, wrote the wily priest, was the real Earl of Warwick, son of George of Clarence, and the youth being held in the Tower as Warwick was a "double" of obscure birth and weak intellect. The dowager duchess accepted the story and promised to lend her support.

The boy was taken to Ireland where he was received literally with open arms. Some of this was due, no doubt, to the continuous desire of the Irish leaders to make trouble for the kings of England. But the boy's manners were so gracious and his appearance so winning that the support given him was practically unanimous. He was crowned king as Edward VI in the cathedral of Christchurch in Dublin. The duchess Margaret sent funds and promises of armed support. She was as good as her word, for a contingent of German mercenaries arrived in due course. It was a small force of 2000 men but this was sufficient to touch off Irish enthusiasm, which manifested itself in enlistments. A landing was made in Lancashire, but the expected reinforcements from English sympathizers did not materialize to any extent. Henry marched north with a much larger force and a battle was fought at Stoke-on-Trent. The German mercenaries behaved bravely but the royal army had little difficulty in winning the decision. Both Simnel and the priest Symonds were taken prisoner.

The priest was condemned to life imprisonment and the boy was pardoned because of his tender years. He was taken into the king's service as a scullion. This act was held up as an example of the king's leniency, and perhaps rightly. Henry was a great believer in household system and did not hesitate to make tours of inspection himself. There may have been satisfaction for him in seeing this young impostor, who had caused him so much trouble and expense, scaling fish in a greasy jerkin and scouring dirty kettles.

### 3

He was less lenient in the case of the second impostor. This was a boy named Perkin Warbeck, who was born in the Flemish city of Tournay. Again this lad of humble birth had all the external attributes of aristocracy, seeming to all who saw him to be cast in the Plantagenet mold. By accident he found employment with English families and began to speak the English tongue. Whether he conceived the idea himself or had it implanted in his mind by his English employers, he began to fancy himself capable of playing the part of one of the missing princes. People began to say, "This is a strange youth. He is much above the station in which he lives. He is indeed a very prince." Word of him was carried to Ireland and the Earls of Desmond and Kildare became interested in him. Finally, the ever receptive Margaret of Burgundy had him sent to her. Perhaps she was willing to make use of any tool to disturb the hated Henry; perhaps she was genuinely convinced by the boy's intelligence and his graceful deportment. At any rate she professed to believe him to be her nephew Richard. Charles VIII of France was won over, as were the youthful Duke of Burgundy and James IV of Scotland. Maximilian, King of the Romans, became interested in the boy and was the chief contributor to an expedition which was fitted out for the invasion of England.

The English people might be entertaining doubts, but few of them were willing to fight for another boy king, no matter how good his claim might be. A landing was attempted along the Kentish coast but without success. The masquerader and his supporters were hasty in getting aboard again and setting sail for Ireland. But the Irish people had learned their lesson from the failure of their efforts for Lambert Simnel. They turned out in cheering mobs to see this handsome young man but they showed no desire to fight for him. Perkin, therefore, left the country and sailed to Scotland.

The Scottish king was sufficiently impressed with his princely visitor to believe his story. He arranged a marriage for him with Lady Catherine Gordon, daughter of the Earl of Huntley. It developed into a love match and, by the time the king arranged to lead an army into England, the fair Catherine had borne Warbeck two children.

The invasion was a failure. Later a few ships were provided for him and, being a youth of stout heart, he made a landing near Whitesand Bay near Land's End, late in the autumn of 1497. This time he took heart from the warmth of the reception he received. Henry had been taxing the people beyond the point of endurance.

A little army gathered to support the pretender but they were unable to make a stand against the royal troops. Perkin Warbeck and his faithful wife were taken prisoner. This time the law moved with severity and dispatch. Warbeck was hanged in the Tower. But not before he had been allowed to see the young Earl of Warwick and to discuss with him the possibility of a joint escape. That unfortunate youth was misled into making some form of confession. He was taken out at once and beheaded.

It was at this time that the Spanish ambassador in England wrote to his master, "Not a doubtful drop of royal blood remains in the kingdom."

But he was not accurate in that statement. There was the youthful Edmund de la Pole, a nephew of the dead Richard. He had escaped to the continent and did not return until the reign of Henry VIII, who promptly sent him to the block.

## CHAPTER XI

## *The Hired Historian*

*1*

THERE came to England in 1501 an Italian priest and writer named Polydore Vergil. He was a nephew of Adrian de Castello, who held the post of collector of Peter's pence in England. This was one of the plums that Vatican appointees scrambled for, because they could stay in Rome and live on the stipend while a deputy in England did all the work, on very meager pay. It was to serve as his uncle's deputy that Polydore Vergil had been sent. On first thought it is surprising that he was willing to accept such a subordinate post. He had been publishing books with great success. Two years before he had put out at Venice his *De rerum inventoribus* and it had been so eagerly sought after that in a course of years 102 editions came off the presses.

But further consideration makes it clear that the lot of an author was not a happy one from a financial standpoint. It was about this time that a ruling was made in Paris, allowing booksellers to keep for themselves no more than two per cent of the price of a book. (Yes, gentle reader, the percentage *is* higher today.) The author's share, no doubt, was small also; even, dread thought, he and the bookseller had to share! Clearly it was the need for a regular income, no matter how small, which induced the talented Vergil to undertake the prosaic task of gathering in the pennies which each family had to provide for the Holy Father at Rome. At first he could not have enjoyed it very much. His uncle in Rome, waxing fat and wheezy, without a doubt, did not allow him more than a bare subsistence. And nothing was done immediately to get him a church appointment in England. It took some little time for pressure from Rome to obtain for him the living of Church Langton in Leicestershire.

In 1505 there was a turn in his fortunes. The king sent for him and made the suggestion that he write a history of England. The financial support which went with the offer must have been large enough to free him of all worries. Henry, in fact, must have wanted him quite badly, for it is clear that Master Vergil was well looked after, so well that he was able to devote himself from that time forward to the preparation of the history. The responsibility of collecting Peter's pence still rested on his shoulders but it is likely he found someone, an Englishman, to perform the duties. The deputy of a deputy for a Roman absentee beneficiary! Could anything be less lucrative?

Vergil ceased to be a starveling churchman whose gift for putting words down on paper had paid him so badly. It is on record that he presented hangings for the choir of Wells Cathedral with his own arms stamped on them, a laurel tree supported by two crocodiles. He had become a man of property.

Historians have never made the mistake of underestimating Henry VII, not even those who like him little. He was above everything a long-distance planner. Nothing is more indicative of this than the steps he took to be sure of the verdict of time and of favorable notice on the pages of history. He knew what Morton had written in his book, or the nature of the notes he had supplied to More, whichever explanation of the much discussed *History* is accepted. No doubt they had gone over the story piecemeal. They had discussed all the ingenious inventions which were sprinkled through Morton's version: the secret page, the dark happenings when the assassins invaded the Tower in such numbers, the unnamed priest who hid the bodies and died so conveniently soon after. But this was not enough. Corroborative evidence was required to have the story accepted in history, to assure a continuance of public belief. Another version, clearly, was needed, one which would follow much the same line of narrative. And who could do it better than this young Italian whose romanticized writings were proving so agreeable to readers?

Polydore Vergil's part in shaping the records of English history has always been under suspicion. It has seemed that he allowed a lively gift for invention to color the events of which he told. He is often mentioned among those who have sponsored certain of the best anecdotes, sometimes as the sole authority. Take as an example that recherché story of the naming of the Order of the Garter: how the beautiful Countess of Salisbury lost her garter at a royal ball and how Edward III, who was said to be an ardent admirer of hers, picked it up and said, "*Honi soit qui mal y pense*" (Evil to him who evil thinks). Certainly the words were adopted by the Order, which ties the anecdote into a neat bundle and makes it one of the little gems that even the most sober historian feels called upon to relate, though with due warning of its apocryphal character. Of this story it is said, "First published by Polydore Vergil, a stranger to the affairs of England."

A disturbing thought arises out of these considerations. Could it be that other anecdotes, for which he is given at least partial credit, are equally suspect? Has some of the liveliest color in English history been applied by the pen of this not too scrupulous Italian romancer?

One thing seems clear enough: he did not have to invent the legend of Richard Plantagenet and the princes. Morton had already supplied whatever inventiveness went into it. The latter, being much less subtle and much more willing to make use of any hasty bit of improvisation, had not been as expert as Master Vergil would have proven himself. But Morton was first in the field and what was required of Vergil was to strengthen the story with the power of repetition and by following the heavy-footed prints already provided by the churchman. His selection for the task was a late development, coming at a time when Henry was carrying the wrinkles of a deep worry on his face and was becoming concerned with what the future might say of him. It would take years for Vergil to complete his commission, but Henry had always kept an eye on the future. He would be content to have placed on his grave the tributes of Vergil's pen. Which is what happened; for Henry died in 1509 and the first volumes of the history were not printed until 1534. They were published in Basel and were dedicated, ironically as it seems, to Henry VIII!

What rewards did Vergil reap? It is recorded that on one occasion he offered financial assistance to Erasmus. But the real test of his prosperity was supplied when he made one of his last trips back to Rome. He traveled "with six horses and six servants!" The servants, no doubt, were in livery of his favorite color of green with the slavering crocodiles stitched on their sleeves. Quite, in fact, like a fat rich abbot returning home from town.

The most serious charge alleged against Vergil is that he destroyed documents before returning permanently to Rome. According to one writer, Caius, "Vergil committed to the flames as many of our ancient manuscript volumes as would have filled a waggon, that the faults of his own work might pass undiscovered." A French authority, La Poplinière, declares that Vergil caused all histories to be burned which by the king's authority and the assistance of his friends he could possibly come by." A third, Gale, says he shipped manuscripts to Rome and that the vessel on which they went sailed from Rochester Bridge. If all this is true, there might be another explanation for the destruction of the source material, that Vergil burned some of it so a lack of sources for his stories could be explained.

It is further alleged that Vergil borrowed manuscripts from Oxford and did not send them back. The university authorities were properly indignant and refused to send him more. He, accordingly, secured a mandate from the king for the use of anything else he needed. Presumably, the university had to give in. It is stated also that he borrowed from other libraries and was equally remiss about returning the material.

None of these charges can be either proven or dismissed at this late date. But one fact seems to be established: that Vergil fell under the suspicions of his contemporaries.

## CHAPTER XII

## The Bones in the Tower

*1*

IN THE month of July in the year 1674, when Charles II was King of England, some workmen were engaged in rebuilding the stone stairs which led from the royal chapel of St. John in the White Tower. This was one of the most beautiful of the chapels built by the Normans, but the walls were thirteen feet thick and the steps which led down to the river front had been planned to resist the endless passage of time. In consequence the workmen had to apply their tools with right good will. When they finally broke through at a point where the stairs led to the royal apartments, they found some bones under the masonry. The workmen, having small concern with history, threw them out carelessly on a pile of rubbish. The news spread rapidly, however, and it was believed that the bones must be those of the two princes. They were gathered up, together with much other material, including the remains of chickens, rabbits, sheep, and pigs, some rusty nails, and a few pieces of sandstone. By order of the king, they were sealed in an urn designed by Sir Christopher Wren in the Henry VII Chapel in Westminster.

More than 200 years elapsed before interest in the case of Historical Opinion versus Richard III developed to such a high pitch that it was believed the urn should be opened. This was done on July 6, 1933, and the bones were turned over to Professor William Wright, dean of London Hospital. The latter began an examination with the co-operation of Dr. George Northcroft, ex-president of the British Dental Association. They completed their work in five days and the bones were then gathered together again, wrapped in fine lawn, and replaced in the urn. The urn carries an inscription in Latin which translates as follows:

Here lie the relics of Edward Fifth, King of England and Richard, Duke of York, who, being confined in the Tower, and then stifled with pillows, were privately and meanly buried, by order of their perfidious uncle, Richard, the usurper. Their bones, long inquired after and wished for, after laying 191 years in the rubbish of the stairs (i.e. those lately leading to the Chapel of the white Tower), were, on the 17th of July, 1674, by undoubted proofs, discovered, being buried deep in that place. Charles II, pitying their unhappy fate, ordered these unfortunate Princes to be laid among the relics of their predecessors, in the year 1678, and the thirtieth of his reign.

On November 30, 1933, a report was read before the Society of Antiquaries, containing an historical review of the case prepared by Mr. Lawrence E. Tanner and the findings of Professor Wright. The latter expressed his belief that they were the bones of the two princes and that they had been killed at some time previous to the Battle of Bosworth. The case, it seemed, was closed. Richard was guilty.

There was quite a little excitement in the daily press and rather considerable satisfaction was manifested by historians and scholars who had supported the traditional view.

The satisfaction was not general, however. None of those who believed in Richard's innocence, nor any of the larger body of scholars and readers who considered the case could not be solved, were convinced the last word had been said.

2

Without any thought of suggesting a lack of knowledge or care on the part of Professor Wright, there was a widespread feeling that it would have been more satisfactory if a board of authorities had been appointed to examine the bones. This, after all, was a matter of the utmost historical importance. And should not a longer period than five days have been devoted to the work? The bones had been buried under the masonry for many centuries: was there any pressing need to conclude the examination so quickly? In his report Professor Wright said of the photographs, "These were taken under great difficulties since it was not possible to remove the bones from the chapel." No reason for the prohibition on moving was stated. The objection was raised at once that no regulations should have been allowed to stand in the way of getting the most complete information.

The conclusion might be reached from studying the report that the determination of age from a set of bones was a relatively simple matter, but many authorities do not agree with this. Dr. Thomas Dwight says in his *The Range and Significance of Variation in the Human Skeleton,*

"No part of medical literature is so perfunctory, artificial and altogether unsatisfactory as medico-legal anatomy." Dr. R. B. H. Gradwohl in his *Legal Medicine* says, "The whole subject of the delicate balance between bone formation and destruction is almost still as much of a puzzle as it was two centuries ago." In *Personal Identification*, Bert Wentworth and R. H. Wilder say, "One must bear in mind, however, in all data resting upon development, whether of bone or teeth, that the dates for the events show some individual variation, in certain cases a considerable one, so that an age thus determined can be only approximate."

Professor Wright bases his conclusions on three points. The first is a general survey of the teeth which, he states, "permit of Edward's age being determined as somewhere between twelve and thirteen years." There was, however, every indication of advanced osteitis, particularly in the skull of the older boy, and this would suggest an older age than that set by the examiners. Osteitis will retard the growth of the teeth from six months to a year.

The second point on which the case against Richard is built is that the axis cervical vertebra was without the apical part of its odontoid process. The third was based on a first sacral vertebra which showed the laminae still half an inch or so apart. In this connection Wentworth and Wilder say that "when the cartilage between two growing centres is entirely replaced and the pieces are in contact, a long time may elapse before they entirely fuse with each other." The conclusions reached in the report do not make any allowance for the possibility of a long time lapse of this nature.

Nor is there any reference to the making of longitudinal sections with a saw on any of the long bones, a method which Thomas Gonzales in his *Legal Medicines, Pathology and Toxicology* speaks of as a desirable method of reaching conclusions as to age. This applies particularly to long bones, several of which were found complete.

In a survey conducted some years ago in the United States, a complete six-monthly radiographic record of the bone formations of several thousand healthy children resulted in some curious evidence. There was, for instance, the matter of the knees of three children which were so closely similar in point of development that they suggested the same age for each. One knee belonged to a mature six-year-old, one an average eight-year-old, and one a retarded ten-year-old! A general conclusion was reached from the survey that an average scale of maturation in the bones can be accepted but that *it is impossible to tell the ages of children from bone formation without allowing a four-year variable* (i.e., two years each way).

An outstanding American authority, Professor T. Wright Todd of California, was convinced that glandular conditions determined the

maturing of children and that certain diseases will retard bone development from two to four years. He introduced a point of supreme importance in his *Study of Skeleton Maturity* by asserting that in ascertain-
ing skeleton age hand and foot studies are *indispensable*.

In his report Professor Wright makes no mention of hands and feet.

It is unfortunate that any room for doubt was left. Those who take
the traditional view are convinced, of course, that the results clear up
the case. But it seems to an equally large body that the clouds of
uncertainty have not been dispersed.

There is one factor which seems to weigh rather heavily in lay
minds, although it is not referred to in the report. The bones indicate
that both boys were very tall for the ages which Professor Wright
assigns to them. The height of the older, Edward, is fixed at 57.50 inches
and that of the younger at 54.50. In a *Housebook of Hygiene*, published
in England in 1913, the average heights for both country and town boys
were given as follows:

| | |
|---|---|
| 12 years | 54.97 |
| 13 years | 56.91 |
| 14 years | 59.33 |
| 15 years | 62.24 |

How many men of the present day could squeeze themselves into
the suits of armor worn by the brave knights of old? Could many
fifteenth-century men, even measuring from the tips of the "steeple"
hats of Yorkist days, equal in height the normal man of today? Comparatively few, for the human race has increased very considerably in
stature in the centuries which have intervened. It follows that the sons
of these stocky men, the boys who wore the bright-colored gallygaskins
of the fifteenth century, who swaggered with bows over their shoulders
and attached polished bones to their shoes to make skates when there
was ice on the ponds, were shorter than the boys of today, very much
shorter. But the figures given above would indicate that Prince Edward
was close to the average height of boys of fourteen, based on the 1913
scale. Allowing for the greater stature of present-day youth, it seems
reasonable to place him at an age of at least fifteen years, which would
mean that he could have lived into the first years of the reign of Henry
VII.

There is always, of course, the possibility of individual variations
from every rule and every scale, but to assume that both boys were so
far in excess of the normal for their day would be to fly in the face of
the law of averages.

## CHAPTER XIII

## The Evidence of an Eyewitness

### 1

THE amazing thing is that this mystery should have remained unsolved when it could have been cleared up with such apparent ease. If Richard were guilty, Henry VII could have moved to punish the men employed for the black deed immediately after the Battle of Bosworth. He did nothing. The man Green did not die until the following year. It is on record that sums of money were paid to Black Will for two more years. The chief accomplices, Sir James Tyrell and Dighton, were both alive and were received into Henry's open favor. Tyrell was given many honors and appointments, and Dighton was presented with the living of Fullbright.

If Richard were not guilty, it is easy to understand why nothing was done and why no official announcement was made until all of the conspirators had been done away with, excepting Dighton who, according to the *History*, "indeed yet walketh on alive, in good possibility to be hanged ere he die."

If the testimony of even one of these men had been made public, the mystery would not have continued until a solution of it was sought in an examination of the teeth and bones found in the Tower; at a time when all of the alleged tools of the wicked uncle had been moldering in their graves for centuries and could not be summoned from the shades for questioning.

There is one piece of vital evidence supplied by a man who can be classified as an eyewitness, the only man, in fact, who was in a position to know the truth. He did not leave his testimony in writing nor did he give any verbal statement. But he performed an act which truly spoke as loud as any words.

It has seemed fitting to leave the story of what he did until the end.

To provide this incident with a proper background, it will be necessary to retell in part the story of the killing of the two princes as it appears in the *History*.

"Whereupon," says the *History*, "he [Richard] sent one John Green, whom he especially trusted, unto Sir Robert Brackenbury, constable of the Tower, with a letter and credence also, that the same Sir Robert should in any wise put the two children to death. This John Green did his errand unto Brackenbury, kneeling before Our Lady in the Tower, who plainly answered he would never put them to death, to die therefore." The meaning of which is that the constable would die himself rather than commit such a crime. Then the story proceeds with the sending of Tyrell to the Tower later. "Wherefore, on the morrow, he sent him to Brackenbury with a letter, by which he was commanded to deliver Sir James all the keys of the Tower for one night, to the end he might then accomplish the king's pleasure." There is a final reference to the constable in the report. "Whereupon they say that a priest of Sir Robert Brackenbury took up the bodies again, and secretly interred them."

Sir Robert was the one man, therefore, who knew if the princes were murdered on Richard's orders. On the other hand, if they were alive and still in the Tower when Richard's reign reached its early ending, he was in a position to know that also.

Now Sir Robert Brackenbury was an honorable man. Nothing has been said or written against him, not a hint of criticism is found in the records of the day, not a jot of malice, nor a tittle of complaint. It has been made clear that even the *History* absolved him of all blame.

When the word reached London that the crucial battle was impending between the army of the king and the invading forces of Henry of Richmond, Sir Robert Brackenbury gathered a few horsemen about him and set out for the scene of action. It was a long and hard ride from London to the bogs on the borders of Leicestershire and Warwickshire where the battle would be fought, more than one hundred miles as the crow flies. It is difficult to estimate what the actual distance was over the twisting, shifting, treacherous, unpaved roads of that day. Sir Robert and his men had to "flog their horses all the way from London" to cover the ground in time. The impatience of this brave knight can be understood, hasting to strike a blow against the infamous uncle who had commanded the murder of his nephews, riding madly through the Midlands, galloping through gaping lanes of watchers in the towns, forgetting the need for sleep and food!

But hold! When Sir Robert reached Sutton Cheney, he turned off the road to Dickon's Nook where King Richard was said to be. When he saw the royal standard flapping in a light breeze above the tents, he pulled up. With a sigh of relief, he slipped out of his saddle. He was in time, after all!

Sir Robert had made that furious ride in order to lend his sword to the cause of the king and not to Henry of Richmond. What is more, he fought the next day both boldly and well and gave up his life in the final stages, a short few moments before Richard made his magnificent last effort by charging almost singlehanded into the ranks of the Lancastrians.

It was a sad thing, for Sir Robert was a brave and honorable knight and he deserved to live longer. And it was an unfortunate thing for history that his tongue and hand were stilled.

But can more than one meaning be read into what he did? The princes had not been killed when he led his horsemen out through the Ald Gate and turned in the direction of the Great North Road.

# A Personal Postscript

FOR reasons which will soon be apparent it is necessary at this point to adopt a personal approach.

The time to begin the reading of history is when you are young. I do not mean by this the hasty study of textbooks and the memorizing of a few dates. I mean the reading of history for pleasure as well as information. To begin in later years is to lose much of the eager delight, the tendency to become emotionally involved, a tendency which is increased because so much history is written in two colors, black and white.

As I was born in Canada, my early and insatiable appetite for the subject was fed, first, on the colorful sequence which stretched from Jacques Cartier to Wolfe and Montcalm on the Plains of Abraham. Then I took up English and I found myself emotionally involved from first to last. I remember distinctly that there were tears in my eyes when I came to the last sentence of Charles Dickens' description of the Battle of Hastings. "—And the Warrior, worked in gold thread and precious stones, lay low, all torn and soiled with blood—and the three Norman Lions kept watch over the field." How much I had wanted Harold the Saxon to win!

It is on the question of battles that the feelings of readers can become most deeply engaged. I indulged in long periods of speculation as to what would have happened to England if the Saxons had won at Hastings. I was so eager a partisan of the Scots during the wars in the reign of Edward I that I was quite broken up when my hero, William Wallace, was beaten at Falkirk. If only the haughty (it seemed that the word haughty was used more often in those days than any other adjective) members of the Scottish aristocracy had not been too proud to serve under the great but relatively lowborn Wallace!

When I came to the Battle of Bosworth Field, that was a different matter. Here the hunchbacked monster of a wicked uncle, who had ordered the murder of his nephews, was punished with defeat and death, seemingly by the direct intervention of God. It never occurred to me then to ponder what might have happened if Richard had won. It was not until I heard of Horace Walpole and his *Historic Doubts* that I began to follow along the trail which led back to Bosworth. It seemed possible then that a great injustice had been done; and I began to feel the first faint quiver of the old emotional absorption.

It was at an early stage of my interest in matters historical that I fell under the spell of the Plantagenets. It began with the story of the Fair Rosamond in the maze at Woodstock and grew into a passion with the mighty deeds of Richard of the Lion-Heart. Even after I realized that the wicked Queen Eleanor was actually a very wise and discerning woman and that Rosamond Clifford died in a convent of natural causes, even after I discovered to my horror that the great Richard had heels of clay, even then my interest in these fascinating people continued unabated. As I read deeper into the sources, I saw how many of the Plantagenets had been great kings—Henry II, Edward I, Edward III, Henry V, and, finally, what a fine king-in-the-making Richard III had been. The weaknesses they displayed were of a kind to add to their fascination. They were story-book kings, with their yellow hair and blazing blue eyes; and the wives they brought over to England were fairy-story queens, beautiful always and often wicked, sometimes very wicked. And back of these spectacular qualities, they relied on Parliament and, with some exceptions, they showed a proper regard for constitutional forms. In which latter respect they were far better kings than those who followed after them.

But to get back to the last of the Richards. In reading history it should be borne in mind that, in spite of the general belief to the contrary human nature does change with the years. The stouthearted Englishmen who loved and hated, who quarreled and laughed and sang, and who lived and died through the Hundred Years War and the Wars of the Roses were actuated by instincts and habits which we do not share today, save, perhaps, in a latent form. We cannot judge the leading figures of centuries ago by our own modern standards. Even if Richard had ordered the deaths of the two princes (which so many fanatically disbelieve), it has to be considered that such things had been going on almost from the beginning of time. Although not a parallel in any sense, the Black Prince, considered the greatest of the knights of chivalry, slaughtered all of the innocent inhabitants of Limoges, and thousands of boys and girls died in the course of a few hours. Is this terrible day remembered still?

From the welter of contrived history, of book throwing, of efforts to explain away discrepancies of fact by theorizing, there still emerges from the gloom of this particular span of years the figure of a Man. The more I found to read about Richard, the last of the Plantagenets, the harder it became for me to think of him as the murderer of his nephews. I found so many glimpses of him as a warm and understandable human being. There was the delicate boy, thin and quiet but not allowing himself to be warped by jealousy because all his brothers and sisters were tall and fair; the youth who took over in his late teens the command of the Yorkist horse and led the thundering cavalry charges which helped so much to win the decisive battles; the honorable younger

brother who scorned the French king's bribes and refused to set foot on
the covered wooden bridge at Picquigny; the shrewd adviser on whom
the lordly and successful Edward depended so much; the administrator
of firm hand who ruled the turbulent north; the king who applied
himself so earnestly to the ruling of England and to introducing common
sense into some of the legal statutes; the saddened man who lost his
son and his wife within a few months; the king, betrayed on the field
of battle, who charged almost singlehanded against the enemy, slashing,
cutting, shouting his scorn and defiance before going down.

The outcome of the Battle of Bosworth became, therefore, the one
issue in English history in which my feelings were most deeply engaged.
In addition to the sidelights which I found in the course of my reading,
I studied the measured reasoning of Horace Walpole and the ardent
advocacy of those who followed him, ending with the original and
convincing approach employed by Josephine Tey in her *Daughter of
Time*. And so it has been impossible for me to agree with what seems to
have been a somewhat hasty verdict in the matter of the bones. There is
too much proof on the other side.

Is it necessary to recapitulate all the evidence in Richard's favor in
order to believe that the verdict of history should be changed, to the
extent at least of admitting that the mystery of the princes has not
been solved? Is it not time to concede that there are many good reasons
for believing Richard innocent?

Unfortunately it now seems impossible to reach any definite verdict.
But if Richard cannot be declared innocent, should it not be made
clear that he cannot in all honesty be accounted guilty? Should not
the history taught in schools be changed to an impartial basis in accordance with what is now known? Must schoolrooms and reference
books go on indefinitely with the old version, stubbornly grinding the
Tudor ax? It once had a very sharp edge, but that is of no consequence
now.

Ah, if Richard had conducted the battle with more strategic caution
and perhaps with less pride! By living, he might have allowed himself
a long span of years in which to employ his great administrative gifts
as king and to put into the form of laws the changes he had in his
mind.

This might have made possible a more satisfying end to the chronicles
of a great dynasty. It could then perhaps have been possible to
present Richard, not as the last and the blackest of that fantastic family
whose achievements and adventures have engaged our attention through
these long volumes. It might even have been possible to show him as
one of the most constructive, perhaps as one of the greatest, of the
kingly Plantagenets.

# Index